*Research Guide to the
Russian and Soviet Censuses*

Studies in Soviet History and Society

edited by Joseph S. Berliner, Seweryn Bialer,
and Sheila Fitzpatrick

Research Guide to the Russian and Soviet Censuses
edited by Ralph S. Clem
Revolution on the Volga: 1917 in Saratov
by Donald J. Raleigh

Research Guide to the Russian and Soviet Censuses

EDITED BY

RALPH S. CLEM

Cornell University Press

ITHACA AND LONDON

Copyright © 1986 by Cornell University

All rights reserved. Except for brief quotations in a review, this book, or parts thereof, must not be reproduced in any form without permission in writing from the publisher. For information, address Cornell University Press, 124 Roberts Place, Ithaca, New York 14850.

First published 1986 by Cornell University Press.

ISBN: 978-1-5017-0715-5

Library of Congress Catalog Card Number 86-47638
Printed in the United States of America.
Librarians: Library of Congress cataloging information appears on the last page of the book.

The paper in this book is acid-free and meets the guidelines for permanence and durability of the Committee on Production Guidelines for Book Longevity of the Council on Library Resources.

This book is dedicated to
A. J. Jaffe

CONTENTS

Preface	9
Contributors	11
How to Use This Guide	13

PART ONE: GENERAL AND TOPICAL ESSAYS

1. On the Use of Russian and Soviet Censuses for Research 17
   Ralph S. Clem

2. Data Comparability Problems in the Study of the Soviet Population 36
   Robert A. Lewis

3. A History of Russian and Soviet Censuses 48
   Lee Schwartz

4. The Ethnic and Language Dimensions in Russian and Soviet Censuses 70
   Brian D. Silver

5. Occupation and Work Force Data in Russian and Soviet Censuses 98
   Michael Paul Sacks

6. Urbanization and Migration Data in Russian and Soviet Censuses 113
   Richard H. Rowland

7. Marriage, Family, and Fertility Data in Russian and Soviet Censuses 131
   Barbara A. Anderson

8. Education and Literacy Data in Russian and Soviet Censuses   155
   Ronald D. Liebowitz

PART TWO: INDEX AND GUIDE TO THE RUSSIAN
AND SOVIET CENSUSES, 1897 TO 1979
Peter R. Craumer

Contents	173
Introduction	177
List of Census Tables	187
Keyword Cross-Index	269
Geographic Units of the Russian and Soviet Censuses	304

PREFACE

Those engaged in social science research on the USSR have evinced a steadily increasing interest in Russian and Soviet census data. Along with this interest, however, has come the realization that using this vast reservoir of information on Russian and Soviet society entails many practical problems. Although often innovative and far-reaching, attempts to deal with these difficulties have usually taken place in isolation, as individual specialists pursue their own research agendas.

It was in this context that the idea of synthesizing available knowledge of census-based research on Russia and the USSR suggested itself as a valuable contribution to the study of that country. Further, the need was clear for an inventory and index of the various published censuses. Accordingly, a project was proposed to provide researchers with both an overview of the Russian and Soviet censuses, including discussions of specific topics for which census data are particularly relevant, and a complete description of the contents of the census volumes.

After these goals had been established, scholars with recognized expertise on given subjects were asked to contribute essays detailing the state of the art in their respective areas, the problems associated with the use of census data for those subjects, and the potential for further research. Second, a comprehensive index, incorporating a description of census tables, a keyword index, and a listing of political-administrative units for the different enumerations, was compiled.

This volume represents the completion of a project to develop a general reference work on the Russian and Soviet censuses which meets the above criteria. Initially, the Research and Development Committee of the American Association for the Advancement of Slavic Studies provided funds for planning a project proposal. Most of the project itself was funded by a grant from the National Council for Soviet and East European Research. In May 1983, project participants and other interested researchers convened for a conference on Russian and Soviet censuses funded by the National Council and hosted by the Kennan Institute for Advanced Russian Studies in Washington, D.C.

The editor/project director acknowledges important contributions by several persons in the preparation of the final report. Elizabeth Lyn and Karen Pennington typed the original manuscript. Roberta McLaughlin, Judy Sheffield, Karen Hill, and Patty Clifford were responsible for word processing. Zweneslava Clem was a meticulous proofreader, and Carmen Wampole provided administrative support. Finally, John Ackerman and Linda Wentworth of Cornell University Press were of invaluable assistance in the editorial process.

RALPH S. CLEM

Miami, Florida

CONTRIBUTORS

RALPH S. CLEM (Ph.D., Columbia University) is Professor of International Relations at Florida International University, Miami. He is coauthor of *Nationality and Population Change in Russia and the USSR* (1976, with Robert A. Lewis and Richard H. Rowland) and author of several chapters and articles on ethnicity and demography in the USSR.

BARBARA A. ANDERSON (Ph.D., Princeton University) is Professor of Sociology and Research Scientist at the Population Studies Center, University of Michigan. She is the author of *Internal Migration during the Modernization of Russia in the Late Nineteenth Century* (1980) and coauthor of *Human Fertility in Russia since the Nineteenth Century* (1979, with Ansley J. Coale and Erna Härm). She has also written many articles on Soviet population and society.

PETER R. CRAUMER (Ph.D. candidate, Columbia University) is a geographer specializing principally in the study of Soviet agriculture. He is currently conducting research on the Virgin and Idle Lands program in Kazakhstan.

ROBERT A. LEWIS (Ph.D., University of Washington) is Professor of Geography at Columbia University. He is the coauthor of *Population Redistribution in the USSR* (1979, with Richard H. Rowland) and has written many articles on population, urbanization, and migration in Russia and the Soviet Union.

RONALD D. LIEBOWITZ (Ph.D., Columbia University) is Assistant Professor of Geography at Middlebury College. He works mainly on Soviet regional economic development and has published articles on political geography.

RICHARD H. ROWLAND (Ph.D., Columbia University) is Professor of Geography at California State University–San Bernardino. He is the coauthor of *Population Redistribution in the USSR* (1979, with Robert A. Lewis) and several articles on urbanization and migration in Russia and the Soviet Union.

MICHAEL PAUL SACKS (Ph.D., University of Michigan) is Associate Professor of Sociology at Trinity College. He wrote *Women's Work in Soviet Russia* (1976) and *Work and Equality in Soviet Society* (1982) and edited *Contemporary Soviet Society* (1980, with Jerry G. Pankhurst).

LEE SCHWARTZ (Ph.D., Columbia University) is Assistant Professor of Geography in the School of International Service of The American University. His current research interest is Soviet political geography and ethnicity.

BRIAN D. SILVER (Ph.D., University of Wisconsin) is Professor of Political Science at Michigan State University and Research Affiliate at the Population Studies Center, University of Michigan. He has published many articles in professional journals and monographs on Soviet ethnic, demographic, and political processes.

HOW TO USE THIS GUIDE

This book is divided into two parts. *Part One* consists of three chapters on general subjects dealing with the published censuses of Russia and the USSR, followed by five chapters on ten specific topics, the study of which requires the use of census figures. Thus, a researcher investigating ethnicity and language use in the Soviet Union should read the first three chapters for background and then the topical chapter dealing with that particular subject (in this case, the chapter by Brian D. Silver).

Part Two is an index to and list of every published table in the six major censuses taken in Russia (1897) and the USSR (1926, 1939, 1959, 1970, and 1979). Cross-tabulations (i.e., combinations of topics, such as "Educational Attainment by Age") are provided in great detail. Because the organization of such a complex set of information is itself complicated, the user is urged to read carefully the Introduction to the Index by Peter R. Craumer.

Part One

GENERAL AND TOPICAL ESSAYS

Chapter 1

On the Use of Russian and Soviet Censuses for Research

RALPH S. CLEM

The quest for more data and better data is a perennial one in demography, as in all science. The improvement in demographic and related data will undoubtedly, however, continue to be limited by the changing conceptual framework and research interests of the demographer; the techniques available for obtaining the information with desired reliability, validity, and precision; and the values of differing cultures which dictate what information may be politic or impolitic to obtain. (Hauser and Duncan, 1959b: 55)

Seeking better to understand human societies, social scientists constantly confront the question of how to investigate socioeconomic and political issues. If these issues suggest themselves and are properly framed, the main problem then becomes the manner in which evidence can be marshaled, evaluated, and used analytically.

Although there are several generic types of social science data (e.g., surveys, opinion polls, registration systems), in practice the primary source of empirical information on a society is almost always the national census of population. The United Nations defines a census of population as "the total process of collecting, compiling and publishing demographic, economic and social data pertaining, at a specified time or times, to all persons in a country or delimited territory" (1958: 3). In fact, the attributes that define a census, universality, simultaneity, enumeration and compilation of individual characteristics, and specified territory, are collectively the reason why census data are so useful.

As Kingsley Davis (1966) put it, the census typically "reveals not only the basic demographic trends, such as population growth, internal population redistribution, urbanization and alterations in the age and sex structure, but also contributes indispensably to a knowledge of changes in the nation's occupational and industrial composition, in its level of living, education and employment." To this list of census topics one might add ethnic and racial composition, marriage and family structure, religion, and language use. It should be evident from the range of subjects covered in censuses that the information in them is of use not only in the study of demography (narrowly or broadly defined) but also in the study of anthropology, economics, education, ethnic studies, geography, history, political science, sociology—indeed any discipline concerned with the numbers and characteristics of a society or socioeconomic group (Hauser and Duncan, 1959a: 37–43).

As the social sciences have matured in the era after World War II, the demand for more and better data referred to by Hauser and Duncan has grown commensurately. In addition, bureaucrats and politicians have increasingly realized that knowledge, if not a complete understanding, of socioeconomic conditions and trends as manifested in census data is a useful tool for policymakers. In the postwar period there has accordingly been a rapid expansion and technical upgrading of census taking worldwide, an activity promoted and aided by the UN through its various agencies (UN, 1958; 1967; 1977). Consequently, the volume of census information available to the researcher has grown tremendously over the last twenty years (University of Texas, 1965; Goyer and Domschke, 1983). Likewise, greater interest has focused on censuses taken before World War II, as more and more researchers have come to appreciate the value of such enumerations for period or longitudinal studies. In both the historical and contemporary contexts, the acquisition, cataloging, and preservation of national censuses, such as the program at the University of Texas Population Research Center and the Census Library Project of the Library of Congress and Bureau of the Census, have been invaluable (Goyer, 1980; Dubester, 1969).

The use of census data is not without problems, however; in many respects, just the opposite is true. Despite the potential implied by the growing quantity of empirical information in the censuses of various countries, the researcher must take a wide array of troublesome difficulties into account when using census figures. Hauser and Duncan (1959b) characterize these difficulties as threefold: coverage, comparability, and quality. In the first instance, they refer to "the completeness with which the target population or class of events is enumerated or registered and the range of information about the unit [ordinarily, the individual] of observation" (Hauser and Duncan, 1959b: 65). Thus, one might be concerned about the accuracy of the count in terms of individual enumeration and also about the coverage across the range of subject matter.

Problems of comparability among censuses and between censuses and other sources of data are often so extensive as to render impossible meaningful direct comparisons over time and space. Unfortunately, such pitfalls as different definitions for categories and units are not always recognized, and unwarranted conclusions based on an imperfect understanding of the data are not unknown. At the very least, considerable work is often required to establish some useful standard of data comparability.

Finally, the issue of data quality—the extent to which the data contain errors of coverage, response, recording, and processing—forces the user to evaluate the figures given and assess their accuracy (if only generally) before drawing judgments from them. Recognizing the immensity of effort involved in conducting a national enumeration, the difficulties in making such concepts as "migration" operational in census questionnaires, and the possibilities for misunderstanding questions or misstating answers, one should approach even the most technically sophisticated census with skepticism.

Over the years demographers and other social scientists have developed many methods for recognizing and, in some cases, overcoming census-data problems. The variety and complexity of these methods are far too vast to be recounted here; instead, the reader is referred to several of the standard works on the subject (Jaffe, 1951; Barclay, 1958; Shryock and Siegel, 1980; Coale and Demeny, 1966).

Census Data in Russian and Soviet Studies

As in most countries, the published censuses of Russia (1897) and the USSR (1926, 1959, 1970, and 1979) constitute by far the largest and potentially the most useful collection of data on that society.[1] Modern Russian and Soviet enumerations since 1897 cover about one-sixth of the world's land area and provide considerable information on many aspects of the country's population, including age and sex composition, ethnic and language identification, marriage and family structure, migration patterns, urban and rural residence, educational attainment and literacy levels, and occupations. There are, of course, other important sources of quantitative data in Russian and Soviet studies, many of which relate to and are used in conjunction with census data; these sources will be described below.

Given the wealth of information in these volumes, it may at first seem surprising that the Russian and Soviet censuses have been substantially underutilized by researchers, both in works that focus exclusively on Russia or the Soviet Union and in comparative studies. This situation is in part attributable to the fact that in the West the field of Russian and

---

1. There are many valuable sources of quantitative data on Russia before the census of 1897, including a few population counts that do not qualify as complete censuses.

Soviet studies is overwhelmingly nonempirical in its topical foci and research methodology; the field is dominated by nonquantitative history, literature, politics, and language studies. A review of American and Canadian doctoral dissertations for the 1970s revealed that only about 10 percent dealt with subjects even remotely quantitative in nature; in fact, almost five times as many dissertations were written in literature as in economics, geography, and sociology combined (Dossick, 1971–80).[2] Thus, a relatively small number of researchers are trained in the empirical social sciences in Russian and Soviet area studies. This pronounced nonquantitative bias reduces the demand for and utilization of census data (or other types of socioeconomic data). Moreover, this topical tendency is inertial, for each new generation of scholars finds coursework and mentors concentrated in the dominant nonquantitative disciplines.

One can surmise that language barriers, the added work involved, and a general unfamiliarity with sources have contributed to the dearth of comparative or conceptual studies—the most likely types to require the use of census data—that treat Russia and/or the USSR. Beyond these practical concerns, however, is the important, yet subtle influence of ideology and politics on the objective analysis of Soviet society. As Lewis, Rowland, and Clem (1976: v) explained, "when one specializes in a region or country in any of the social sciences, there seems to be a natural inclination to treat that region as if it were a special or unique case in terms of societal processes, and this inclination is particularly strong if that region has a totalitarian government." With the nonquantitative orientation of Russian and Soviet studies and the unwillingness of most scholars to engage in comparative studies across cultural, national, and ideological boundaries, it is perhaps not surprising that few have chosen to delve into the Russian and Soviet census volumes.

Using Russian and Soviet Census Data: General Problems

Although the Russian and Soviet censuses hold great promise for research into historical and contemporary socioeconomic issues, major problems are connected with the use of these data. Of course, these problems may have discouraged potential users and contributed to the chronic underutilization of the censuses. Nevertheless, the use of census data in any context involves difficulties, and those confronting the researcher in Russian and Soviet studies are generally not insurmountable.

Of the census problems included in Hauser and Duncan's typology, by far the most serious involving the Russian and Soviet enumerations are

---

2. This review, of necessity, involved making some determinations as to subject matter and methodology from dissertation titles and therefore should be considered approximate.

those of *comparability.* As Robert Lewis discusses at length in Chapter 2, problems of temporal, definitional, and geographic comparability must be dealt with before one can use the Russian and Soviet data meaningfully. Temporal comparability is vexatious owing to the irregular intercensal periods in Russia and the USSR, which are an impediment especially to cohort analysis. Definitional comparability problems arise when questions and categories of responses fail to translate reality into operational terms. The investigator must then find some way to reorder the data into comparable (or at least similar) definitions or commit the sin of comparing "apples and oranges." For example, in their study of historical and geographic trends in urbanization in Russia and the USSR, Lewis and Rowland (1969) found it necessary to reorder all data on urban places into a standard operational definition of "urban" to take into account major differences in usage from census to census. To be sure, in some cases such a reordering is simply not possible, and the data must be used with appropriate caveats for changing definitions and an assessment of the extent to which these differences influence the analysis.

Finally, changes in the national territory and the internal political-administrative unit structure of Russia and the USSR have created significant problems of geographic comparability in the use of census data. As detailed by Lewis, such difficulties can be overcome only through determined efforts. In several studies researchers have compiled data based on a consistent unit structure to facilitate historical and longitudinal analysis of demographic and socioeconomic characteristics and trends. Lorimer (1946: 241–49) reordered data from the 1897 and 1926 censuses into a set of "study areas" based on 1939 political-administrative units. With these figures, he analyzed regional population changes (including both the urban and rural components) for the periods 1897–1926 and 1926–39 (Lorimer, 1946: 150–72). However, because the territory of the USSR was appreciably smaller in 1939 than it was in the census years of 1897, 1959, 1970, and 1979, Lorimer's units and figures cannot be used for comparisons among all censuses; nevertheless, they are of great value as a check on the validity of other methods.

In the most extensive undertaking of its kind, Leasure and Lewis (1966) derived population estimates for nineteen geographically comparable regions (the major economic regions of 1961) for the censuses of 1897, 1926, and 1959; with a few modifications, data from the 1970 and 1979 censuses can be retrofitted into these units. In addition to the total population, the Leasure and Lewis project also generated estimates for the urban population (based on a standard definition), for the rural population, and for a variety of socioeconomic characteristics. These data were utilized in the study of migration (Leasure and Lewis, 1967; 1968), urbanization (Lewis and Rowland, 1969), ethnicity (Lewis,

Rowland, and Clem, 1976), and population redistribution (Lewis and Rowland, 1979). Using essentially the same method, Clem (1977) developed a set of population estimates for 1926, 1959, and 1970 which had the 142 oblast and equivalent level units of 1959 as the standard geographic framework. These units can be aggregated into the larger economic regions employed in the Leasure and Lewis study.

In another major study, conducted at the Office of Population Research at Princeton University, Coale, Anderson, and Härm (1979) reconstructed the population in 1926 within both 1897 and 1959/70 unit boundaries. Their work, which centered on fertility and its correlates, included variables for nationality composition, literacy, marital status, and age and sex composition for urban and rural components. Because the pivotal 1926 data were fitted backward and forward, a direct comparison in consistent units among all censuses was not presented. A detailed list of data from this study available to researchers has also been published ("Available Data...," 1979).

The principal Soviet work on this subject consists of estimates for the total, urban, and rural populations for 1926, 1939, 1959, and 1970 (and also an estimate for 1974) at the oblast level for units as of the 1970 census (USSR, 1975: 14–25). No figures are given for areas outside the USSR in 1926 (western Ukraine, the Baltic republics, Kaliningrad oblast, western Belorussia, and Moldavia), although Sakhalin is included. Unfortunately, no information is provided regarding the methodology employed to derive these estimates; presumably the team of researchers from the Central Statistical Administration who worked on the project had access to data unavailable in the West, making some insight into their procedures most welcome. Another Soviet source provides some population figures for 1926 and 1939 in comparable units; these data are of limited interest because of the brief period covered and units used but may be of some value for comparison with other estimates (Konstantinov, 1943).

For coverage and quality of data, we can assume that the later Soviet censuses are more complete and less error prone than those of Russia in 1897 or the USSR in 1926. This assumption, however, is based largely on common sense and not on a rigorous comparative study. It seems reasonable to suppose that the introduction of more sophisticated techniques in the most recent enumerations has reduced errors of tabulation and presentation of data. As Lee Schwartz explains in detail in Chapter 3, quality-control procedures (such as test censuses, postenumeration checks, tighter administrative supervision, training for enumerators, and the introduction of sampling techniques) and the accumulation of census-taking experience would be expected to improve the accuracy of the count. In this respect, Soviet census procedures are in accord with UN recommendations (UN, 1967).

Details of census procedures and facsimiles of the census schedules (questionnaires) for the 1926, 1939, 1959, 1970, and 1979 enumerations are in publications of the Central Statistical Administration; these are very important sources and should be consulted by the researcher as appropriate (USSR, 1926; 1958a; 1969a; 1978; Pod"yachikh, 1957a; 1957b). Likewise, reports of census-planning conferences, meetings of statisticians, and other works that include discussions of key points involving census questionnaire design are valuable for the insights they provide into methodological issues (Isupov and Borisov, 1978; Maksimov, 1976; Ter-Izrael'yan, 1979; USSR, 1958b; 1969b).

Availability of Data

Regardless of the accuracy of the count and tabulations, census data are of little value to the researcher if they are not published or otherwise made available in a form suitable for scientific analysis. Serious discussion in the West about the reliability and availability of Soviet statistics dates back at least to the extended debate on the subject in *The Review of Economics and Statistics* in the late 1940s and early 1950s (Dobb, 1948; Gerschenkron, 1950; Jasny, 1950; Marx, 1950; Rice, 1952; Schwartz, 1948; Turgeon, 1952). Although most of these—and later—treatments dealt mainly with economic statistics, demographic data (from either the censuses or the registration system) are certainly subject to the same vagaries.

The essence of these examinations of Soviet data problems is that whereas outright falsification of the figures is unknown, Soviet statistics of all types have always been published selectively and often in a format that is not entirely straightforward. It appears, moreover, that through the 1970s data publication was curtailed in a variety of statistical sources. For example, one study disclosed that the amount of economic and other data published in the annual *Narodnoye khozyaystvo* volumes declined between 15 and 20 percent over the period 1974–79 (Crosnier and Tiraspolsky, 1980).

This severe retrenchment in the publication of data by the Soviet government is especially ironic in light of the rapidly expanding economic and demographic data base for most of the world, including many developing countries. Thus, it is striking to note that the published volumes for the 1970 Soviet census (242 million people, 8.6 million square miles) contain less data than the 1973 census of Colombia (23 million people, 440,000 square miles). It is interesting to note that this paucity of published data has been criticized by Soviet scholars as well:

> The published results of the censuses and the delays in their release by no means encourage the utilization of the data. The materials of the population census for 1926 came to 56 ponderous volumes; for 1959, to only 16 volumes, most of which were slender little notebooks in size. But size is not the chief thing. The scientific value of the published 1959 census data is incomparably less than that of the 1926 census. Little scientific meaning can be squeezed out of the data. (Perevedentsev, 1967)

This is not to say, of course, that extensive data from the 1959 and later censuses do not exist. Indeed, probably the most frustrating aspect of research on Soviet society occurs when one encounters unpublished census data in work by Soviet scholars. For instance, in an important article on the social structure of ethnic groups of the USSR, the Soviet sociologist Yu. V. Arutyunyan referred to the 1959 census as the source of data on labor-force participation by nationality; in fact, the data do not appear in the printed volumes (Arutyunyan, 1972: 3–20). In another case, a study of the socioeconomic development of the Yakut ASSR includes figures on the ethnic composition of that unit from the 1939 census; no ethnic data for subnational units from the 1939 census have ever been released as census publications (Gogolev, 1972: 247). Examples of this phenomenon are common in the Soviet literature.

It is difficult to understand why the supply of Soviet census data was so limited to begin with and even more difficult to comprehend why the published results are being further curtailed. One reason for this hesitancy to publish figures might be that the Soviet government views some social and economic trends as unfavorable or as reflecting badly on conditions in the USSR. This desire to avoid embarrassment by concealing socioeconomic or demographic trends not in strict accord with official portrayals of life in the USSR has in a number of cases served to make research on Soviet society difficult.

The principal methods employed in this often subtle form of censorship are the withholding of entire categories of information and—a tactic that has a major impact on published census materials—the changing of format in which data are given in order to disguise unbecoming details. Sacks (1979) found that in cases where female workers were underrepresented in certain occupations or in the higher ranks within an occupation, categories were often combined or full particulars withheld altogether to obscure the actual situation. As he noted, "it is enlightening not only to study this material for what it reveals directly about Soviet society, but also for what it systematically concealed or distorted and how this changes over time" (Sacks, 1979: 1).

If, as seems apparent, the Soviet government seeks to manipulate data for the purpose of obfuscation, its attempts are frequently clumsy and often produce the opposite result. The much-publicized cutoff in the publication of infant mortality data for the USSR after 1974 illustrates this point (Davis and Feshbach, 1980). For three consecutive years, figures were released showing a rise in infant mortality, after which time publication of the data ceased. It hardly appears clever to provide evidence of an unfavorable trend and then to compound negative publicity by withholding amplifying or mitigating information; as a result Western scholars have taken much adverse notice of the situation in the belief that the Soviet government is hiding something. Likewise, in the case of the missing female occupational data, the fact that more detailed information had been given earlier made it possible to uncover later omissions and to infer from the pattern of format changes which trends were contrary to the official view.

In any event, social scientists in the West have long had to use various statistical methods and considerable ingenuity to overcome problems of missing data or deficiencies in the published figures. It may be that the tenacity and inventiveness of these efforts have proven nettlesome to those in the USSR who seek to veil the country's socioeconomic conditions. If the Soviet government decides to withhold additional census information, researchers requiring Soviet data may need to be even more resourceful in their attempts to obtain maximum benefit therefrom.

Census and Noncensus Data

In addition to the analytic uses to which census data may be put directly, there are any number of research topics that require the use of figures from the censuses together with quantitative information from other sources. A thorough review of noncensus socioeconomic data is beyond the scope of this work; what follows is meant to be illustrative and not exhaustive. Anderson (1977) is an excellent reference to a number of noncensus-data sources (as well as census subjects). Essays in this volume on particular topics include discussions of noncensus sources and the relationship of these data to census figures.

Ordinarily, noncensus socioeconomic data on the USSR originate from various branches of the registration system in that country and therefore pose certain problems in terms of both their completeness and their definitional consistency with census information. These two problems emerge mainly because the registration system is incomplete and inconsistent in its coverage and often employs definitions of socioeconomic characteristics different from those used in census enumeration. The degree to which inconsistencies among different sources of data measuring the same or essentially the same thing exist was demonstrated convincingly by Anderson and Silver (1985). Employing survival techniques based on various mortality assumptions, they used school enrollment data to assess the completeness of birth registration and the accuracy of the enumeration of children in the 1959 and 1970 Soviet censuses. The three sources produced figures that were often markedly different.

One usually finds census data used as a base population to calculate rates in conjunction with noncensus figures. Thus, the publication of books in the languages of certain peoples of the USSR (noncensus data) can be compared with the population of different ethnic groups (census data). In another case, data on marriages according to ethnic identification (noncensus data) can be combined with the population of ethnic groups (census data) to develop an index of endogamy (Chuiko, 1975).

Census and noncensus information can also be used jointly to estimate population change. Grandstaff's study of interregional migration in the USSR (1980) employed a residual method using census populations and reported vital statistics, a census survival method based on census age distributions, and migration data from the 1970 Soviet census.

Noncensus Sources of Socioeconomic Data

Again, the range of noncensus sources of information on the USSR is wide; here we will only refer to those commonly used for the study of Soviet society.

In 1956, the Soviet government began publication of the *Narodnoye khozyaystvo* series, a yearly compendium of social and economic statistics. Typically, an annual volume contains information on territory, population, and the economy for the country and for subnational units. Demographic characteristics might include nationality groups; educational attainment; population estimates (in some cases actual census figures) for various units and cities; and rates of marriage, divorce, birth, death, and natural increase. Data on the labor force, on the education and health care systems, and on different indicators of the quality of life are also present. In addition, most subnational units of the USSR have published similar statistical handbooks, albeit irregularly; in many cases these regional editions contain data not found in the national volume. The Center for International Research of the U.S. Bureau of the Census has published a bibliography of regional statistical handbooks as a research aid (Heinemeier, 1984).

At least two volumes with the title *Narodnoye obrazovaniye, nauka i kultura v SSSR* have been published (USSR, 1971; 1977). They contain considerable information on education, science, culture, literature, and the arts for different years for the country as a whole and for subnational units.

Vestnik statistiki is the monthly journal of the Central Statistical Administration. In addition to articles, reviews, and notices, the journal contains statistics on a variety of socioeconomic subjects (many are series published annually).

Other Sources of Population Data

The Foreign Demographic Analysis Division (FDAD) of the U.S. Bureau of the Census has long been deeply involved in the study of the demography of the USSR and as part of that effort has produced several sets of population estimates and projections which may be of value to other researchers. Specifically, Brackett (1964) gave detailed age and sex estimates and projections for the period 1959–85 based on the 1959 census and other sources. Baldwin (1979) presented population projections by age and sex for the USSR, the fifteen union republics, and nineteen major economic regions for 1970 to 2000 (see also Baldwin, 1973; 1975). In addition to the estimates and projections, these reports contain information on methodology and on population trends in the USSR. Further, FDAD has conducted studies of the labor force and employment in the USSR which incorporate census and noncensus data for estimates and projections (Depauw, 1968; Rapawy, 1976; Reed, 1967). Independently, Biraben (1976) derived single-year age distributions from different censuses.

Finally, the researcher may find it useful to consult compendiums of Soviet statistics published in the West; not only are various socioeconomic and other data series presented but some useful discussions of sources and methodology are included as well. Ordinarily, such volumes give figures only at the national level and, unfortunately, some are out of date. In particular, the *Handbook of Soviet Social Science Data* (Mickiewicz, 1973) and *The East European and Soviet Data Handbook* (Shoup, 1981) are good examples of this genre.

Age Data in Russian and Soviet Censuses

The Importance of Age Data

Census data on the age composition of the population deserve special attention for three reasons: they reflect and influence basic demographic trends and indices thereof, they can be used to evaluate the accuracy and completeness of enumerations, and—most important—age relates directly to virtually all other socioeconomic characteristics (Shryock and Siegel, 1980: 201). Accordingly, age data in the Russian and Soviet censuses are treated in this introductory essay by way of a general overview and are also discussed in the individual topical chapters that follow (where appropriate as age is cross-tabulated with other subjects).

In the first regard, the age structure of a population is determined by levels of fertility and mortality (and, in some cases, migration), as new increments are added (through fertility and migration) and subtracted (through mortality and migration) over time. Thus, the distribution of the population by age will reflect past demographic conditions, with certain patterns recognized as consistent with different combinations of fertility, mortality, and migration. In its turn, the age structure will influence future demographic trends, as cohorts tend to "echo" through the population; for example, a "baby boom" resulting in a larger than normal number of births will likely produce more children in absolute terms when that large birth cohort passes through the marriage and childbearing ages. Because age is such an important determinant of demographic events (i.e., most demographic events are age specific), it is essential to have the aggregate population decomposed by age as the basis for analyzing and projecting population trends. In studying fertility, for example, it is vital to know the "at risk" component of the total population, in this case the number of women ages 15–44 (sometimes 15–49 is used). The fact that the percentage of the total constituting that component group varies considerably from place to place or from time to time makes age standardization a requirement for rigorous analysis.

Second, age data are valuable to the demographer and social scientist because tabulations by age provide insights into the accuracy of the enumeration; as was suggested earlier, at least some attempt should be made to assess the quality of census data before using them as the principal basis for research. In the case of age data, deviations from established, or expected, regularities in the composition of the population by age (and sex) probably indicate qualitative shortcomings in the enumeration in general. The UN, for example, regularly evaluates the accuracy of national population censuses by means of Whipple's Index, a measure that gives an indication of errors in age reporting (UN, 1974; 1980a). Other than the obvious problem of underenumeration, the most common deficiency in census age data involves the misreporting of age, especially the tendency to prefer or avoid certain ages or digits (which produces "age heaping"). Age heaping is most common in censuses taken in less-developed societies, but the phenomenon manifests itself to some degree even in modern, industrialized countries. Several methods exist whereby the reasonableness of a census age distribution can be judged, and techniques for correcting major discrepancies (which cannot be accounted for by other evidence) or estimating a more likely distribution are well established (Shryock and Siegel, 1980: 204-29).

Finally, most socioeconomic characteristics of a population vary considerably by age to the extent that it is necessary in most instances to take age structure into account in the analysis of such phenomena. For example, researchers must consider the importance of age structure when estimating the school-age population for a study of education, the number of adults for a determination of labor-force participation, and the percentage of the population over 65 for purposes of investigating the situation of older persons. Because the distribution of a population by age is likely to change (sometimes dramatically) over time or vary among groups within a society, failure to control for these variations can bias comparisons significantly. For example, Jones and Grupp (1982) demonstrated how numerous studies of the ethnic situation in the USSR were seriously in error because no account was taken of major differences in age composition among Soviet nationalities—differences that had an especially important influence on the measurement of political participation, educational attainment, and specialized occupations.

Several relatively simple age structural indices are widely employed in the social sciences to give an indication of longitudinal or cross-sectional variation in age composition; the ratio of children and older persons to the working population (the dependency ratio), which is often used to illustrate the economic and social implications of rapid population growth, is such an index (Shryock and Siegel, 1980: 235).

Russian and Soviet Census Age Date: Inventory and Assessment

Each of the Russian and Soviet censuses contains considerable age data and cross-tabulations of socioeconomic characteristics with age. Ironically, the earlier censuses (1897 and 1926) not only include more detailed age data and cross-tabulations but also provide figures for lower-level political-administrative units than do the later enumerations (1959 and 1970). The 1979 census presents the most serious problem in terms of age-data availability, since *no* figures by age are contained in the single volume published to date (USSR, 1984). The extent to which the earlier censuses are more richly endowed with age data can be appreciated by looking at the entries for the major category "AGE" in the keyword index section of this volume.

Specifically, the 1897 and 1926 censuses contain data for single years of age, for age in months for children under one, and by ten-year groups in units down to the uezd level and for many individual towns and cities. Additionally, as the keyword index shows, there is a wide range of cross-tabulations by age group with other characteristics of the population. The 1959 and 1970 censuses abandoned the practice of publishing single-year-of-age data; the 1939 census figures, published in the 1959 tables, are likewise grouped by age. Furthermore, the number of cross-tabulations published has been curtailed, as has the availability of figures for tert.ary level political-administrative units (i.e., oblasts, ASSRs, and krays). In certain categories, different age groups are utilized, thereby increasing the difficulty of constructing other cross-tabulations; although this can often be accomplished by combining smaller into larger groups, the detail inherent in the original smaller groups will be lost. Finally, as was mentioned earlier, the different lengths of intercensus periods create difficulties in using the 1959 and 1970 census age data because the eleven-year span does not allow for direct matching of the published five-year age groups. Thus, to evaluate preliminary age and sex data from the 1970 Soviet census, Lewis and Clem (1971) had to disaggregate the reported 1970 figures into single years using Sprague's constant multipliers and recombine the results to fit the eleven-year period. If age data from the 1979 census are eventually forthcoming in detail, the same problem will arise in comparisons with 1970 owing to a nine-year period and five- and ten-year age groups. The researcher will find the age estimates made by the Foreign Demographic Analysis Division (Brackett, 1964; Baldwin, 1973; 1975; 1979) and Biraben (1976) to be useful supplements to the published figures.

The accuracy of Russian and Soviet census data almost certainly improves over time. The 1897 census especially suffers from age heaping; thus, researchers would be prudent to combine the single-year figures into age groups. Unfortunately, Soviet age data are not evaluated by the UN because the USSR does not report the single-year-of-age figures needed to derive Whipple's Index of digit preference. This index, which ranges from 100 (no preference) to 500 (maximum preference for the digits "0" and "5"), is normally calculated for the ages 23 to 62, with greater digit preference indicating lesser accuracy in the data (Shryock and Siegel, 1980: 205–26). However, one Soviet study of age-data accuracy, presumably based on unpublished single-year figures, gave values for Whipple's Index for the Russian and Soviet censuses as: 1897–175, 1926–159, 1939–113, 1959–109, and 1970–101, values that lend credence to qualitative improvements over time (Kolosova, 1976: 167).

However, evidence suggests that—as is true for any census—inaccuracies continue to be a problem, even in the most recent enumerations. In an analysis of age data from the 1959 Soviet census, Myers (1964) concluded that there was reason to suspect age reporting, particularly among older persons. Similarly, the Soviet demographer M. S. Bednyy (1972) criticized age data in the censuses as likely to be in error. Lewis and

Clem (1971) found serious inconsistencies in a comparison of reported age groups for the 1959 and 1970 censuses. In one case, for example, a cohort increased in numbers from the earlier to the later enumeration (an impossibility in a society closed to large-scale immigration), indicating a likely underenumeration or significant age misreporting (or both) in the 1959 count. Bennett and Garson (1983) conducted an extensive study of age and mortality patterns in the USSR using 1959 and 1970 Soviet census data, Soviet life tables, and a method for deriving estimates of life expectancy. They determined that official data were characterized by pronounced age overstatement, calling into question the much-publicized overrepresentation of centenarians in the Soviet population. Finally, by comparing census age distributions with school enrollment figures, Anderson and Silver (1985) noted apparent underenumeration of preschool children and adolescents older than mandatory school age in both the 1959 and 1970 censuses. They attributed this phenomenon to an incomplete housing registration system (on which the census count is conducted) and to the universal problem of the enumeration of highly geographically mobile young persons.

At least some of these inaccuracies derive from the manner in which people are asked about their age in Soviet censuses. The UN recommends that individuals be asked their date of birth, from which the census agency can figure the person's age in its data tabulation process. Until the 1970 census, the USSR employed a less desirable (but common) method whereby people were asked to provide the enumerator with their age in completed years. This method has been shown to increase the ambiguity in responses (UN, 1980b: 74–76). Beginning with the 1970 enumeration, the Soviet census included both the question requesting date of birth and the one requesting age in completed years, allowing an individual to respond to either. Finally, the Soviet census does not allocate persons who report age unknown, but the number of such cases is usually quite small.

References

Anderson, Barbara A. 1977. "Data Sources in Russian and Soviet Demography." In *Demographic Developments in Eastern Europe*, ed. Leszek A. Kosinski, 23–63. New York: Praeger.

Anderson, Barbara A., and Brian D. Silver. 1985. "Estimating Census Undercount from School Enrollment Data: An Application to the Soviet Censuses of 1959 and 1970." *Demography* 22: 289–308.

Arutyunyan, Yu. V. 1972. "Izmeneniye sotsial'noy struktury Sovetskikh natsii." *Istoriya SSSR*, no. 4: 3–20.

"Available Data from Research on the Decline of Fertility in Russia." 1979. *Population Index* 45, no. 2: 196–201.

Baldwin, Godfrey. 1973. *Estimates and Projections of the Population of the U.S.S.R., by Age and Sex: 1950 to 2000.* U.S., Bureau of the Census, International Population Reports, Series P–91, no. 23. Washington, D.C.

———. 1975. *Projections of the Population of the U.S.S.R. and Eight Subdivisions, by Age and Sex: 1973 to 2000.* U.S., Bureau of the Census, International Population Reports, Series P–91, no. 24. Washington, D.C.

———. 1979. *Population Projections by Age and Sex for the Republics and Major Economic Regions of the U.S.S.R., 1970 to 2000.* U.S., Bureau of the Census, International Population Reports, Series P–91, no. 26. Washington, D.C.

Barclay, George W. 1958. *Techniques of Population Analysis.* New York: Wiley.

Bednyy, M. S. 1972. *Demograficheskiye protsessy i prognozy zdorovya naseleniya.* Moscow: Statistika.

Bennett, Neil G., and Lea Keil Garson. 1983. "The Centenarian Question and Old-Age Mortality in the Soviet Union, 1959–1970." *Demography* 20: 587–606.

Biraben, Jean-Noel. 1976. "Naissances et répartition par age dans l'Empire russe et en Union Soviétique." *Population* 31: 441–78.

Brackett, James W. 1964. *Projections of the Population of the U.S.S.R., by Age and Sex: 1964–1985.* U.S., Bureau of the Census, International Population Reports, Series P–91, no. 13. Washington, D.C.

Chuiko, L. V. 1975. *Braky i razvody.* Moscow: Statistika.

Clem, R. S. 1977. "Estimating Regional Populations for the 1926 Soviet Census." *Soviet Studies* 29: 599–602.

Coale, Ansley J., and Paul Demeny. 1966. *Regional Model Life Tables and Stable Populations.* Princeton: Princeton University Press.

Coale, Ansley J., Barbara Anderson, and Erna Härm. 1979. *Human Fertility in Russia since the Nineteenth Century.* Princeton: Princeton University Press.

Crosnier, Marie-Agnes, and Anita Tiraspolsky. 1980. "The Decline of Economic Information in the USSR: An Attempt at Explanation." *Le Courrier des pays de L'Est,* no. 245: 3–30. Translated in Foreign Broadcast Information Service, JPRS, USSR Report, 1/10001, 22 September 1981.

Davis, Christopher, and Murray Feshbach. 1980. "Rising Infant Mortality in the U.S.S.R. in the 1970's." U.S., Bureau of the Census, International Population Reports, Series P–95, no. 74. Washington, D.C.

Davis, Kingsley. 1966. *Encyclopaedia Britannica,* s.v. "census."

DePauw, John W. 1968. *Measures of Agricultural Employment in the U.S.S.R.: 1950–66.* U.S., Bureau of the Census, International Population Reports, Series P–95, no. 65. Washington, D.C.

Dobb, Maurice. 1948. "Further Appraisals of Russian Economic Statistics." *Review of Economics and Statistics* 30, no. 1: 34–38.

Dossick, Jesse J. 1971–1980. "Doctoral Dissertations on Russia, the Soviet Union, and Eastern Europe." *Slavic Review* 30, no. 4: 927–41; 31, no. 4: 951–66; 32, no. 4: 866–81; 33, no. 4: 848–62; 34, no. 4: 882–96; 35, no. 4: 786–801; 36, no. 4: 734–47; 37, no. 4: 733–48; 38, no. 4: 727–37; 39, no. 4: 728–41.

Dubester, Henry J. 1969. *National Censuses and Vital Statistics in Europe, 1918–1939:*

An Annotated Bibliography. Reprinted from 1948 edition. New York: Burt Franklin.
Gerschenkron, Alexander. 1950. "Comments on Naum Jasny's 'Soviet Statistics.'" *Review of Economics and Statistics* 32, no. 3: 250–51.
Gogolev, Z. V. 1972. *Sotsial'no-ekonomicheskoye razvitiye Yakutii*. Novosibirsk: Nauka, Sibirskoye Otdeleniye.
Goyer, Doreen S. 1980. *The International Population Census Bibliography: Revision and Update, 1945–1977*. New York: Academic Press.
Goyer, Doreen S., and Eliane Domschke. 1983. *The Handbook of National Population Censuses*. Westport, Conn.: Greenwood Press.
Grandstaff, Peter J. 1980. *Interregional Migration in the U.S.S.R.: Economic Aspects, 1959–1970*. Durham: Duke University Press.
Hauser, Philip M., and Otis Dudley Duncan. 1959a. "The Nature of Demography." In *The Study of Population*, ed. Hauser and Duncan, 29–44. Chicago: University of Chicago Press.
———. 1959b. "The Data and Methods." In *The Study of Population*, 45–75. See Hauser and Duncan, 1959a.
Heinemeier, Meredith M. 1984. *Bibliography of Regional Statistical Handbooks in the U.S.S.R.* 3d ed. U.S., Bureau of the Census, Center for International Research, Washington, D.C.
Isupov, A. A., and V. A. Borisov. 1978. *Vsesoyuznaya perepis' naseleniya 1979 goda*. Moscow: Znaniye.
Jaffe, A. J. 1951. *Handbook of Statistical Methods for Demographers*. U.S., Bureau of the Census, Washington, D.C.
Jasny, Naum. 1950. "Soviet Statistics." *Review of Economics and Statistics* 32, no. 1: 92–99.
Jones, Ellen, and Fred W. Grupp. 1982. "Measuring Nationality Trends in the Soviet Union: A Research Note." *Soviet Studies* 41: 112–22.
Kolosova, G. I. 1976. "Pol, vozrast i sostoyaniye v brake naseleniya SSSR." In *Vsesoyuznaya perepis' naseleniya 1970 goda: Sbornik statey*, ed. G. M. Maksimov, 165–80. Moscow: Statistika.
Konstantinov, O. A. 1943. "Geograficheskiye razlichiya v dinamike gorodskogo naseleniya SSSR." *Izvestiya Vsesoyuznogo Geograficheskogo Obshchestva* 76, no. 6: 11–25.
Leasure, J. William, and Robert A. Lewis. 1966. *Population Changes in Russia and the USSR: A Set of Comparable Territorial Units*. San Diego: San Diego State College Press.
———. 1967. "Internal Migration in the USSR: 1897–1926." *Demography* 4, no. 2: 479–96.
———. 1968. "Internal Migration in Russia in the late Nineteenth Century." *Slavic Review* 27: 375–94.
Lewis, R. A., and R. S. Clem. 1971. "An Evaluation of Preliminary Age and Sex Data from the 1970 Soviet Census." Paper presented at the Joint Annual Meeting of New England and Middle Atlantic States Divisions, Association of American Geographers, New York.
Lewis, Robert A., and Richard H. Rowland. 1969. "Urbanization in Russia and the

USSR: 1897–1966." *Annals of the Association of American Geographers* 59: 776–96.

———. 1979. *Population Redistribution in the USSR.* New York: Praeger.

Lewis, Robert A., Richard H. Rowland, and Ralph S. Clem. 1976. *Nationality and Population Change in Russia and the USSR.* New York: Praeger.

Lorimer, Frank. 1946. *The Population of the Soviet Union: History and Prospects.* Geneva: League of Nations.

Maksimov, G. M. 1976. *Vsesoyuznaya perepis' naseleniya 1970 goda: Sbornik statey.* Moscow: Statistika.

Marx, Daniel, Jr. 1950. "Comments on Naum Jasny's 'Soviet Statistics.'" *Review of Economics and Statistics* 32, no. 3: 251–52.

Mickiewicz, Ellen, ed. 1973. *Handbook of Soviet Social Science Data.* New York: Free Press.

Myers, Robert J. 1964. "Analysis of Mortality in the Soviet Union according to 1958–59 Life Tables." *Transactions of the Society of Actuaries* 16: 309–17.

Perevedentsev, V. 1967. "Controversy about the Census." *Current Digest of the Soviet Press* 19, no. 2: 15–16. Original in *Literaturnaya Gazeta*, 11 January 1967, 13.

Pod"yachikh, P. G. 1957a. *Vsesoyuznaya perepis' naseleniya 1939g.* Moscow: Gosstatizdat.

———. 1957b. "O proyekta programmy predstoyashchey v yanvare 1959 g. Vsesoyuznoy perepsisi naseleniya i osnovnykh polozheniyakh organizatsionnogo plana ee provedeniya." *Vestnik statisiki*, no. 4: 49–76.

Rapawy, Stephen. 1976. *Estimates and Projections of the Labor Force and Civilian Employment in the U.S.S.R.: 1950 to 1990.* U.S., Bureau of Economic Analysis, Foreign Economic Report, no. 10. Washington, D.C.

Reed, Ritchie H. 1967. *Estimates and Projections of the Labor Force and Civilian Employment in the U.S.S.R.: 1950–1975.* U.S., Bureau of the Census, International Population Reports, Series P–91, no. 15. Washington, D.C.

Rice, Stuart A. 1952. "Statistical Conceptions in the Soviet Union Examined from Generally Accepted Scientific Viewpoints." *Review of Economics and Statistics* 34, no. 1: 82–86.

Sacks, Michael Paul. 1979. "Missing Female Occupational Categories in the Soviet Censuses." Paper presented at the Annual Convention of the American Association for the Advancement of Slavic Studies, New Haven, Conn.

Schwartz, Harry. 1948. "A Critique of 'Appraisals of Russian Economic Statistics.'" *Review of Economics and Statistics* 30, no. 1: 38–41.

Shoup, Paul S. 1981. *The East European and Soviet Data Handbook: Political, Social, and Developmental Indicators, 1945–1975.* New York: Columbia University Press.

Shryock, Henry S., and Jacob S. Siegel. 1980. *The Methods and Materials of Demography.* 2 vols. Washington, D.C.: Bureau of the Census.

Ter-Izrael'yan, T. G., ed. 1979. *Sovershenstvovaniye gosudarstvennoy statistiki na sovremennom etape (Materialy Vsesoyuznogo soveshchaniya statistikov).* Moscow: Statistika.

Turgeon, Lynn. 1952. "On the Reliability of Soviet Statistics." *Review of Economics and Statistics* 34, no. 1: 75–76.

United Nations. Department of Economic and Social Affairs. 1967. *Principles and Recommendations for the 1970 Population Censuses.* Statistical Papers, Series M, no. 44. New York.

———. 1974. *Demographic Yearbook, 1973.* New York.

United Nations. Department of International Economic and Social Affairs. 1980a. *Demographic Yearbook, 1979,* 12–14. New York.

———. 1980b. *Principles and Recommendations for Population and Housing Censuses.* Statistical Papers, Series M, no. 67. New York.

United Nations. Fund for Population Activities. 1977. *National Censuses and the United Nations.* Population Profiles, no. 3. New York.

United Nations. Statistical Office. 1958. *Principles and Recommendations for National Population Censuses.* Statistical Papers, Series M, no. 27. New York.

University of Texas. Population Research Center. 1965. *International Population Census Bibliography.* Volumes 1–6 and Supplement. Austin, Tex.

USSR. Tsentral'noye Statisticheskoye Upravleniye. 1926. *Sbornik proektov programm Vsesoyuznoy perepisi 1926 g.* Moscow: Ts.S.U. Soyuza SSR.

———. 1958a. *Vsesoyuznaya perepis' naseleniya 1959 goda.* Moscow: Gosudarstvennoye Izdatel'stvo Politicheskoy Literatury.

———. 1958b. *Vsesoyuznoye soveshchaniye statistikov 4–8 yunya 1958 g.: doklady, vystupleniya v preniyakh i resheniya.* Moscow: Gosudarstvennoye Statisticheskoye Izdatel'stvo.

———. 1969a. *Vsesoyuznaya perepis' naseleniya—vsenarodnoye delo.* Moscow: Statistika.

———. 1969b. *Vsesoyuznoye soveshchaniye statistikov 22–26 aprelya 1968 g.: stenograficheskiy otchet.* Moscow: Statistika.

———. 1971. *Narodnoye obrazovaniye, nauka i kultura v SSSR.* Moscow: Statistika.

———. 1975. *Naseleniye SSSR 1973.* Moscow: Statistika.

———. 1977. *Narodnoye obrazovaniye, nauka i kultura v SSSR.* Moscow: Statistika.

———. 1978. *Vsesoyuznaya perepis' naseleniya—Vsenarodnoye delo.* Moscow: Statistika.

———. 1984. *Chislennost' i sostav naseleniya SSSR: Po dannym Vsesoyuznoy perepisi naseleniya 1979 goda.* Moscow: Finansy i Statistika.

Chapter 2

Data Comparability Problems in the Study of the Soviet Population

ROBERT A. LEWIS

Problems in the comparability of census data—that is, the extent to which definitions and geographic units vary over time—constitute a major obstacle to research in the social sciences. The purpose of this chapter is to discuss the problems of data comparability in the Russian and Soviet censuses with respect to territory, the definition of various categories, and the periods between censuses. Also, details of a major effort to overcome many of these technical difficulties will be provided as an illustration both of the magnitude of the data comparability problems inherent in the Russian and Soviet censuses and of the procedures by which these problems can be mitigated.

The Significance of the Study of Population Processes

To emphasize the importance of census data and their use in social science research, I will preface my remarks on problems of data comparability with some thoughts on the significance of the study of population in the broader socioeconomic context. Simply put, if relevance or significance in the social sciences is defined in terms of increasing our understanding of ourselves and the society and world around us, then a knowledge of basic demographic processes is essential because these processes involve fundamental aspects of human experience and constitute a major force shaping any society. We are born, we age, we go to school, we work, we move, we reproduce, and we die. Censuses are our chief sources of data for the study of these demographic processes and their determinants and the manner in which the size and structure of a population interrelates with the socioeconomic and natural environments.

The most momentous and pivotal events in human history have been the dramatic declines in mortality and fertility and the rapid urbanization of society which have occurred in the West in the past century or so. These profound changes have resulted in other pervasive societal trends, affecting virtually all aspects of society. It is probably fair to say that these events have not been adequately reflected in historical writings.

In addition to economic, political, geographic, and social factors, demographic forces shape a society and must be studied if we are to understand a society and make guarded forecasts as to future trends. With respect to forecasts, more can be said about demographic processes than can about other social or economic trends because the workers and parents for the next twenty years have already been born. The principal reason why a knowledge of demographic processes is essential to understanding social change—aside from the obvious fact that they are interrelated—is that so many crucial events affecting society are age specific, including birth, death, marriage, migration, work-force participation, educational attainment, crime, consumption, voting, retirement, and generational differences in life-styles. Consequently, major shifts in age distribution resulting from demographic trends can have desirable or undesirable effects on a society. For example, the impact of the rise in fertility which resulted in the "baby boom" generation in the United States on nurseries, schools, colleges, the work force, the housing market, and eventually the retired population and the social security system is well known. To cite another case, the decline in death rates in developing countries brought about rapid population growth and a younger population, which in turn resulted in a less favorable ratio of productive to nonproductive individuals. Under certain conditions, this demographic situation affected savings and investment and hindered social and economic development; these and other problems that rapid population growth has caused in the developing world are well documented.

Changing age composition can also have beneficial effects on a society. Thus, a decline in fertility—which occurred in most developed countries—results in a declining rate of growth of new entrants to the work force, a development that over time should alleviate unemployment problems (if work-force participation rates and economic conditions remain constant). Fertility decline also results in an increasing share of the population in the working ages and thus a decreasing dependency burden. Other alterations in the structure of a population, such as the sex ratio or ethnic composition, can also affect a society.

Suffice it to say, then, that virtually every social or economic problem facing a country has a demographic dimension. However, one must avoid what might be termed "demographic determinism" in appraising the effects of population change on a society because demographic processes interrelate with a variety of other forces; after all, the "sins" of environmental and economic determinism resulted from exaggerating the influence of one factor in the human milieu. One illustration of single-factor determinism in the Soviet context is the purported psychological and political impact of the decline in the Russian ethnic group's share of the Soviet population. Clearly, dominance in a multiethnic state does not relate solely to brute numbers but to political, historical, economic, cultural, and ideological factors as well. Moreover, there is no indication that the dominance of the Russians has varied relative to their share of the population. In the Russian Empire in 1897, the Russians comprised 44 percent of the population, a figure that rose to 53 percent in 1926—primarily because of the loss of territory inhabited by non-Russians—and to 58 percent in 1939. Largely owing to the territorial acquisitions during World War II, the percentage of Russians in the Soviet population declined to 55 percent in 1959 and, because of declining natural increase compared to other Soviet ethnic groups, to 53 percent in 1970 and 52 percent in 1979. There is no reason to believe that political or psychological trauma or a diminution in the dominance of the Russians will ensue when their share slowly drops below 50 percent. Likewise, the changing ethnic composition of draftees into the Soviet armed forces or the decline in the growth of the work force does not necessarily herald demographic crises. The essential point is that population changes, important as they may be, are not the only factors to be considered and that the effects of demographic trends on the Soviet society and polity should not be overstated if we are to assess conditions in that country.

The Importance of Data in Social Science Research

Data, theory, and method are the essential elements of research. Scholarly research requires a rough balance in these elements in order to avoid the common academic inclination toward excessive and tedious description, method for its own sake, and theory unconfirmed and unrelated to reality. Whereas theory and method are the subject of considerable academic attention and admiration, data considerations are generally neglected and considered mundane. Even in demography, a heavily empirical discipline, little has been written on data problems relative to work on theory and method. Most failures in research, however, can be attributed to lack of data. If theories are lacking, new hypotheses can usually be formulated, and if new methods are required, they can ordinarily be devised, but as a rule appropriate data cannot be generated.

Thus, the first concern in applied social science research is acquiring the requisite data; the application of method and theory is normally of secondary importance. Because data are not collected specifically for one's own research and are frequently lacking, in most instances it is necessary to use surrogates or to employ a complex methodology to deal with less than satisfactory data. On the other hand, if data are adequate, elaborate methods are often not required. The above, of course, is not to deny an appropriate respect for theory and method.

In the social sciences, data skepticism is of the utmost importance and is the mark of scholarly maturity. The mindless acceptance of published data as accurate or representative of the phenomena under investigation often results in erroneous interpretation and bad scholarship. Kingsley Davis has rightly deplored the tendency in demographic research to apply sophisticated methods to unevaluated and often unreliable data without a conceptual framework and then uncritically accept the results (Davis, 1965: 147). If the essence of good scholarship is asking the right questions, then the questions that are asked should be appropriate to the accuracy of the data at hand. Thus, investigating operational definitions and evaluating data are crucial steps in research. Some questions can be answered with relatively bad data, but others cannot. Instead of asking if the data are accurate, the researcher should consider how accurate they are and if they are sufficiently representative of the subject under investigation.

But above all, with respect to data skepticism, the researcher should realize that virtually all population data contain errors resulting from deficiencies in collection and tabulation and from inconsistencies in response to questions. These types of errors occur in censuses, even though census data are usually collected more systematically and result from more straightforward questions than most other kinds of socioeconomic data. Census questionnaires, instructions to census takers, and census sample surveys are of great importance when evaluating the accuracy of the data. Errors in the registration of vital statistics are even more common because of the difficulty in defining some demographic events (such as what constitutes a birth), regional variations in the use of medical facilities, and other factors that affect reporting.

In addition to its crucial importance in analysis, the disaggregation of data is very useful in evaluating accuracy because there are frequently geographic differences in the quality of enumeration. This is especially true of the USSR. Thus, if unexpected variations in data are discovered, the first step should be to question the accuracy of the figures themselves.

Data considerations are particularly important in the study of population because the essential elements of demographic research are (1) the ordering of the data into consistent definitional and territorial categories;

(2) the evaluation of the data; (3) the calculation of standardized measures; and (4) the application of demographic and statistical methods and theory to the data for estimation and analysis. Thus, data comparability and data considerations are central in demographic research.

The Problem of Data Comparability

The basis of the general problem of data comparability is that most data are artifacts, and thus there are few uniquely correct definitions, territorial units, or temporal periods for which data can be collected. This is so because most statistical data are continuous, and their demarcation into categories is, in most instances, arbitrary (Jaffe, 1982: 5–8). In practice, one encounters three types of comparability problems: definitional, territorial, and temporal. In the first instance, if there were uniquely correct, universal, and constant definitions for demographic phenomena, there would be no problems of definitional comparability. Instead, of course, operational definitions of seemingly unambiguous events differ markedly from country to country and over time because changing conditions require changing definitions.

Likewise, the territorial units in which data are collected and published are also artifacts and can bias data. Regionalization is merely the spatial aspect of the classification problem; just as there is no all-purpose statistical or taxonomic interval or class, there is no perfect set of regions for any country. A different set of regions might be required for each aspect of population that is to be studied. In this regard, regions should be homogeneous in terms of the problem under consideration and based on one factor or a combination of factors. Also, spatial units of analysis should be delimited on a consistent basis in a way that maximizes external and minimizes internal variation. Unfortunately, population and other data are not collected at the required scale in the USSR (or most other countries) to permit the construction of an ideal set of regions for every analytic purpose. Furthermore, when comparisons are made over a long period of time, the problem of establishing a set of homogeneous regions becomes virtually insoluble if significant economic and social change has occurred. Consequently, researchers are usually forced by circumstances to use some set of existing units, but in all cases they should be aware of the set's limitations.

A related problem to that of territorial comparability is that of scale, which is in itself extremely important in spatial analysis because results often differ depending on the scale of the units used. For example, data by union republic in the USSR are not suitable for use in most research projects owing to the differences in size as well as in population and socioeconomic diversity among them; the RSFSR is almost twice the size of the United States, whereas Armenia is only about the size of Belgium, and the population of the RSFSR is about ninety-two times that of Estonia. A major data problem in the study of the USSR is that for most subjects more data are available by republic than by the more useful lower-order units.

Finally, for most research problems the time intervals between censuses should be constant. Ideally, censuses should be taken every five or ten years, so that trends and projections can be more easily measured by aging or tracking five-year age cohorts from one census to another. In many instances, however, this does not occur, and difficulties of temporal comparability arise. The steps necessary to overcome these inconsistencies and the biases that are introduced are often formidable.

The Problem of Data Comparability in the Study of the USSR

Data comparability—definitional, territorial, and temporal—is the central statistical problem in using the censuses in the study of the population and society of the USSR. Owing to severe comparability problems, trends over time which are crucial to demographic analysis cannot be established among censuses unless data are in some way rendered comparable. Largely because of these statistical obstacles, researchers have used the censuses relatively little in the study of Russian and Soviet society. These problems may be compounded because at this writing it appears that only very limited results, and virtually none of the vital age data, will be published from the 1979 census. This dramatic curtailment of census publishing in the USSR will limit the number of variables for which comparable data in all censuses can be derived. At a time when major international efforts are being made to provide basic demographic data for the world, it is indeed unfortunate that only such a limited coverage of the largest and one of the most important countries will be available.

Because the national territory of the USSR has changed several times over the last century, its present-day borders differ from those of 1897, 1926, and 1939. Consequently, to provide even comparable aggregate data based on the territory of the USSR today, researchers must gather data from East European and other censuses for the border areas formerly outside, but currently within, the USSR. However, aggregate data for a country as large and diverse as the USSR are not especially meaningful, and therefore some subnational regionalization is necessary to analyze population and socioeconomic trends. Unfortunately, frequent and drastic changes in the internal political-administrative divisions into which census data and other data are ordered make it very difficult to compare regional, demographic, and socioeconomic characteristics over time. For example, the number of major enumeration units in 1897 was 89; in 1926, 189; and in 1959, 1970, and 1979, about 140. Furthermore, no enumeration unit in any census had the same boundaries in all census years. Thus, the major tasks with respect to territorial comparability of Soviet census data are to gather data for border areas from the censuses of neighboring countries and to reorder the Russian and Soviet data into a consistent set of territorial units.

Problems of definitional comparability—most of which are discussed in detail by others in this volume—are especially nettlesome in demographic research on Russia and the USSR. First, and most obviously, many important categories are defined differently from census to census, including such key socioeconomic indicators as urban residence, educational attainment, ethnicity, and occupation. In fact, sex and age were the only two characteristics for which the definitions were directly comparable in all censuses, although the categories in which age data were given changed from census to census. A second and more subtle problem is that little systematic attention is given to operational definitions, and consequently changes in categories are often difficult to determine. Thus, one finds confusion over apparently straightforward details, such as the number of persons enumerated at the national or subnational level; there are significant differences between the de facto (*nalichnoye*) and de jure (*postoyannoye*) populations in the Soviet censuses (Anderson and Silver, 1985).

Still another problem is that of temporal comparability, a difficulty that arises because of the irregular intervals over which censuses have been taken in Russia and the USSR. That the censuses were not conducted every five or ten years greatly complicates research on the population of the USSR. Therefore, when measuring change among the various censuses, researchers must use average annual rates of change to standardize for the different intercensal periods. They should also avoid assuming that change between two censuses was linear. In the two intercensal periods that included wars, for example, most demographic trends were not linear but fluctuated considerably. Even between 1926 and 1939, when there was no war, it is not reasonable to assume that change in such variables as mortality and fertility was linear because famine, drastic economic reorganization, and variations in socioeconomic conditions clearly had a specific temporal impact.

The 1897 census was conducted on February 9 (January 28 according to the Julian calendar), the 1926 census on December 17, the 1939 census on January 17, the 1959 and 1970 censuses on January 15, and the 1979 census on January 17. In the computation of average annual rates, a period of 19.9 years is used for the 1897–1926 period, 12.1 years for 1926–39, 20.0 for 1939–59, 11.0 for 1959–70, 9.0 for 1970–79, and 82.0 years for 1897–1979.

A Method to Overcome Data Comparability Problems

For the past two decades, my colleagues and I have done considerable research on problems of territorial and definitional comparability related to the Russian and Soviet censuses. As a result of these efforts, we have generated a wide array of variables that are comparable in terms of both territory and definition. In this section I will describe in brief the procedures that we derived in an attempt to solve the many comparability problems associated with the original census data (Lewis, Rowland, and Clem, 1976: 29–60; Leasure and Lewis, 1966: v–41).

As was previously mentioned, there is no ideal set of regions for the study of demographic change. Nevertheless, a careful selection of regions into which population data will be ordered is important to avoid biasing the data excessively. For our study, the nineteen major (*krupnyye*) Soviet economic regions of 1961 were selected as the consistent territorial units into which the original data would be ordered. We chose these regions because their scale was appropriate for regional analysis, because it was easier to order data into these regions than the more numerous lower-order political-administrative units, and because these regions were largely congruent with the ethnically based federal structure of the USSR. Moreover, the 1959, 1970, and 1979 political-administrative and census units conformed to these regions without major adjustments, and other data pertinent to demographic analysis had been presented in these regions.

In order to allocate original data into the comparable territorial units (i.e., the nineteen economic regions), we assumed that the rural population was evenly distributed within each administrative unit. Thus, a variation in area would result in a proportionate variation in rural population. For our purposes, we defined the rural population as the population not living in centers of 15,000 and over; because the definitions of "urban" varied considerably from census to census, we chose the size criterion of 15,000 (the smallest urban center for which data were available in all censuses). The procedures for allocating the rural population were simple and straightforward. The first major step was to superimpose a map of the economic regions over a map of the political units for each census year and then to measure with a polar planimeter the percentage of the area of a given political unit that fell into a given region, a percentage that we termed the "area allocation." We used equal area maps of relatively small scale and where possible checked the results with maps of larger scale. In practice, many political units fell totally within the larger economic regions, obviating the need for allocation. Thus, the rural populations of the units that constituted an economic region were multiplied by their area allocation and summed to obtain the estimate for the rural population of that region.

The allocation of the urban population required fewer calculations because the urban population is spatially concentrated and its location known. Thus, urban centers could be allocated directly into the appropriate economic region. Accordingly, the summation of the population in centers of 15,000 or more from the given political units allocated to a given economic region yielded the urban population estimate for that region. An estimate was made of the urban and rural populations and of the total (i.e., urban plus rural) population of a given political unit which were allocated to a given region. The percentage that this allocated population represented of the total population of the original unit was termed the "population allocation." Once the total, urban, and rural populations of each unit had been apportioned to the appropriate regions, it was possible to estimate these populations for each economic region simply by a summation of all constituent allocations. These procedures—with adjustments for census dates—were also applied to border areas currently within the USSR which were outside the boundaries of the Russian Empire in 1897 or the USSR in 1926 and thus not included in the Russian and Soviet censuses.

To estimate demographic variables for the total population of each region in 1897 and 1926, we multiplied the number of persons in a given unit with certain characteristics by the population allocation. For the few border areas for which data were not available, we assumed that the characteristics of the population for which we had data could be applied to the entire population of the region or we made independent estimates, as was frequently necessary. The allocation of the demographic characteristics of the urban population was somewhat more complicated. The most logical procedure was to allocate the urban (census definition) characteristics on the basis of the urban (census definition) population, which is the percentage of the urban (census definition) population of a unit which was fitted into an economic region. The summation of the allocated figures for each region resulted in an estimate of the characteristics of the urban (census definition) population of each region. To derive an estimate of the characteristics of the urban (15,000 and over) population—our comparable urban definition—we adjusted these data by assuming that the characteristics of the urban (census definition) population could be applied in the same proportion to the urban (15,000 and over) population. This assumption was not unwarranted because in fact the vast majority of the urban (census definition) population is in centers of 15,000 or more. For example, if 20 percent of the urban (census definition) population were in the 0–9 age group in a given economic region, this same percentage would be applied to the urban (15,000 and over) population to derive an estimate of this age group according to our comparable definition of urban. After the demographic characteristics of the total and urban (15,000 and over) populations of each region were derived, the characteristics of the rural population could be easily figured by subtracting the number involved in the urban (15,000 and over) population from that of the total population.

Available tests indicate that the error involved in these procedures was small. One check on the accuracy of the method is a comparison of the official area of the 1961 economic regions with the sum of the estimated area of the component units of these regions for 1897 and 1926. In most instances, this comparison yielded an error of less than 2 percent, and only once did it exceed 4 percent. These results are reassuring when we consider that in this period some parts of the country were not accurately mapped and it was necessary to transfer projections to obtain an equal area map for 1897.

Another check is a comparison of our figures with the few available Soviet estimates. For example, our estimate of the total population in 1897 within present-day borders was only about 400,000 above the official Soviet figure. Differing estimates of the population of Khiva and Bukhara probably account for most of this discrepancy, although no indication has been given as to how the Soviet figure was derived. Official Soviet estimates for the population of the Transcaucasus, Central Asia, and Kazakhstan in 1926 have also been published. Because the external boundaries of the Transcaucasus and Central Asia have changed only slightly, that our estimate and the Soviet figure are very close does not constitute a good check. However, a comparison with the Kazakh Republic (which is also an economic region) would be an excellent validation because a more complicated division of units and an uneven population distribution (related to the diversity of the natural environment) increase the chance for error in this case. Nevertheless, the difference between our estimate of the population of the Kazakh Republic in 1926 and the Soviet estimate was only about 2 percent.

Recently, the Soviet government published population estimates for the 1926 population in 1970 units at the oblast scale; typically, no indication was given as to how these figures were derived (USSR, 1975: 14–25). However, no data were provided for areas that were outside the USSR in 1926, so the western border regions and the Far East cannot be compared with our estimates (which do include these areas). Aggregating the Soviet data into the 1961 economic regions reveals a very close correspondence with our figures; in most cases they were within 1 percent of each other and never above 5 percent.

Moreover, Ralph S. Clem independently developed estimates of the 1926 population in 1959 lower-order units (oblast scale) by using the allocation procedure described above; his figures can be aggregated into the 1961 economic regions and compared with our estimate (Clem, 1977: 599–602). These two sets of estimates were also very close, almost always falling within 2 percent and in most cases within 0.5 percent of each other. All told, therefore, we have considerable confidence in the estimates that we have derived.

Summary

The most basic aspect of demographic research is the determination of trends over time, which in turn are essential in the analysis of the determinants of population change and demographic comparisons over time and space. As we have seen, population trends cannot be derived from the Russian and Soviet censuses unless major problems in territorial and definitional comparability are solved. The procedures that we derived make it possible for the first time to establish these trends longitudinally for the present-day territory of the USSR for a wide variety of census variables, such as ethnicity, urbanization, labor force, sex, age, fertility, and literacy, for the total, urban, and rural populations.

Aside from making possible the measurement of trends over time, solving problems of data comparability by these or other methods presents other advantages. Data can be put into comparable categories that permit the application of estimation procedures or that can be used to adjust other data. For example, after comparable data by five-year cohorts have been ordered into territorially consistent regions for the various census years, stable population procedures, life tables procedures, and indirect standardization can be used to estimate fertility, mortality, and natural increase. Five-year age groups can also be used for direct standardization of other variables (fertility, mortality, marriage, etc.) to take into account the effects of changing age distribution. These data can also be aggregated to make comparisons over time in age groups related to the life cycle: working-age, dependent, and retired populations.

Moreover, comparable data can facilitate comparative research, although problems of data comparability at the international scale are staggering. Comparative research can provide insights into how universal the processes under investigation are and—if they are universal—provide cautious predictions as to future trends. Also, the comparative method can enable researchers to hold constant the effects of a given political or economic system. Clearly, the demographic or social processes in the USSR cannot be understood solely by studying that country, for a broader understanding of these processes is required. Therefore, whenever possible researchers should attempt to order their comparable data into categories that permit international comparisons.

The development of procedures to solve the many problems of comparability is particularly important in the Soviet context because the available population censuses constitute a major source of socioeconomic data for the study of Soviet society. Moreover, because demographic processes are an important force shaping Soviet society—or any society— and are interrelated with many other socioeconomic phenomena, a contribution to our knowledge of the population of the USSR should greatly increase our understanding of that country and facilitate our making some guarded and objective forecasts as to the course of events in the near future.

References

Anderson, Barbara A., and Brian D. Silver. 1985. " 'Permanent' and 'Present' Populations in Soviet Statistics." *Soviet Studies* 37: 386–402.

Clem, R. S. 1977. "Estimating Regional Populations for the 1926 Soviet Census." *Soviet Studies* 29: 599–602.

Davis, Kingsley. 1965. *Problems and Solutions in International Comparison for Social Science Purposes*. Population Studies Series, no. 192. Berkeley: University of California, Institute of International Studies.

Jaffe, A. J. 1982. "Some Observations of the Nature of Basic Quantitative Data." *New York Statistician* 33: 5–8.

Leasure, J. William, and Robert A. Lewis. 1966. *Population Changes in Russia and the USSR: A Set of Comparable Territorial Units*. San Diego: San Diego State College Press.

Lewis, Robert A., and Richard H. Rowland. 1979. *Population Redistribution in the USSR*. New York: Praeger.

Lewis, Robert A., Richard H. Rowland, and Ralph S. Clem. 1976. *Nationality and Population Change in Russia and the USSR*. New York: Praeger.

USSR. Tsentral'noye Statisticheskoye Upravleniye. 1975. *Naseleniye SSSR 1973*. Moscow: Statistika.

Chapter 3

A History of Russian and Soviet Censuses

LEE SCHWARTZ

Many of the problems associated with the use of Russian and Soviet census data, as described in later chapters in this volume, derive from the historical and political context in which the different enumerations were conducted and the state of the art of census-taking at those times. Although the earlier enumerations were less technically sophisticated and less accurate than more recent ones, the availability of published figures has been increasingly curtailed in those censuses taken just before and after World War II. The following chronological review of census-taking procedures in Russia and the USSR addresses issues such as the organization of the census-taking apparatus; the conducting of individual censuses; the completeness of the count; and some of the methodological, statistical, and political difficulties involved in presenting the results. Analysis of results, instructions to census takers, definitional issues, and questionnaire comparisons will be dealt with here in an overall sense; the individual chapters that follow discuss these topics in more detail as they relate to the utilization of various categories of census data. In addition to works cited in this chapter, the reader may want to consult the excellent bibliographies in Lorimer (1946) and Dubester (1969).

Prerevolutionary Population Counts

Historical Background

The earliest censuses, in Russia and throughout Europe, were conducted by feudal principalities primarily to determine the population eligible for taxation or military service and, therefore, typically left out women and children. Population counts were taken for taxation purposes in the lands of Novgorod and Kievan Rus as far back as the eighth century. Later, various Russian principalities enumerated their populations in order to determine measures of tribute and duty demanded by the Mongol-Tatar overlords. Such counts were taken in Kiev (1245), Ryazan (1257), and Novgorod (1273) (Bruk and Kozlov, 1977: 174).

After the overthrow of the Tatar yoke, the gradual elimination of feudal remnants, and the formation of a central Russian state, counts of the population began to take a new direction. By the fifteenth and sixteenth centuries, landholdings came to be considered taxable units, leading to the development of land-tax censuses upon which the population was estimated. These so-called *pistsoviye knigi* (cadastres) registered characteristics of the population as well as descriptions of cities, villages, estates, churches, and monasteries, and records of prison debts (Kolpakov, 1969: 9). These counts were at best incomplete, and many have not been preserved, succumbing to various historical circumstances (e.g., the 1626 Moscow fire).[1]

In the seventeenth century, as the result of the development of trade and handicrafts, "courts" (or household economies) gained consideration as units of taxation, and Russian censuses were transformed from land- to household-based counts. The censuses of 1646 and 1678 were the first to count households, based on men of estate class, at least throughout the territory of the principality of Moscow. The 1710 household census encompassed the entire territory of the Russian state and was the first to include females. The detail provided by these counts (age, occupation, social class) far exceeded many censuses of western Europe at the time.

An edict of Peter I in 1718 changed the counting of the Russian population from a household to a person-by-person census. Such a compilation first took place in 1720–21 and was subject to subsequent verification—or *reviziya*. Ten *revizii* were conducted over the next 140 years, the last from 1857 to 1860. These limited their enumeration to the male population in the taxable gentry classes. Apart from soldiers, eighteen nontaxable privileged classes were exempt from the *reviziya* counts, including the palace retinue, titled citizens, state civil servants *(chinovniki)*, and the nobility. Outlying areas of the state were often omitted, and landowners (*pomeshchiki*) tended to understate the number of persons on their estate subject to taxation. Despite these deficiencies and limitations, the *revizii* provided, in addition to a count of taxpayers, useful data regarding the population composition by sex, nationality, social position, and family status (Feshbach, 1981: 3).

After the abolition of serfdom (1861), the need developed for a more

---

1. For a detailed survey of early counts of the prerevolutionary Russian population, see V. Plandovskiy, *Narodnaya Perepis'* (St. Petersburg: 1898).

detailed count of the population. Yet, nearly forty years passed before the tsarist government prepared a comprehensive census. In the meantime (between 1860 and 1889), seventy-nine local and city censuses were independently conducted throughout the Russian Empire, mostly in Moscow, St. Petersburg, Kiev, Pskov, and the Baltic provinces (USSR, 1978: 17).

The Russian Census of 1897

The first and only "All-General (Universal) Census of Population" of tsarist Russia was conducted on February 9, 1897 (January 28, according to the old calendar). Encompassing the entire Russian Empire with the exception of Finland, this census was the culmination of years of labor (Russian Empire, 1905). Given the size and diversity of Russia's territory, only a massive effort could have achieved the comprehensive and relatively unified census program that resulted. The undertaking was an intellectual exercise as well, incorporating members of the Russian intelligentsia into the preparation and conducting of the census. Lenin and Kalinin wrote of the importance of the census, as did Mendeleyev, Tolstoy, and Chekhov. The latter two directly participated in the census taking as enumerator and controller respectively; very few segments of Russian society remained untouched by the census effort.

The well-known Russian geographer P. P. Semenov-Tyan-Shanskyy played an especially significant role in the organization and coordination of the 1897 census. As director of the Central Statistical Committee (1864–75), he helped prepare a proposal for just such an endeavor, only to have the Statistical Council limit the count to a census of men in Russia subject to the new universal military service statutes, which had become effective in 1874 (Lincoln, 1980: 60). After a prolonged period, a revised plan was approved in 1895, calling for an empirewide census based on scientific statistical principles similar to those used in conducting western European censuses.

The organization and conducting of the census was entrusted to civil servants of the Ministry of Internal Affairs and its regional offices. They administered and trained over 100,000 enumerators to count the 127 million Russian subjects living in village dwellings as well as urban apartments. Along with the population present at the time of the census survey, temporary and permanent populations were also calculated at each place of enumeration. Census forms with a single set of questions and instructions were filled out individually for each person. The census form was distributed according to three main categories: Form A was for peasant households on agricultural land, Form B was for landed estates, and Form C was for urban populations. The basic form consisted of fourteen questions that determined relationship to head of household, age, family composition, social class, place of birth, place of permanent dwelling, status of transients, religion, native language, literacy, and main and secondary occupations. Only a limited number and range of answers to these questions were provided, although columns were available in which to write further necessary or explanatory details.

It is interesting to note that the information collected for the 1897 census was compiled and calculated with the aid of the same tabulating machines that were developed in the United States by Herman Hollerith for automating the work of the 1890 U.S. census. These machines recorded data via a system of holes punched into special cards (Russian Empire, 1905: ii–iii). A card was punched for every person, and each person was given a number corresponding to the number on the census form in case a check was necessary. For the compilation of tables, each category required a separate run of the appropriate cards.

Despite these automated statistical manipulations, which provided for the cross-tabulation of massive amounts of information, and the direct participation by many of the country's leading figures, the census program and its methodology still had deficiencies. There was, for example, a shortage of trained personnel who fully understood the meaning and methods of statistical analysis. Furthermore, because many of the categories provided a limited set of possible answers, it was impossible to differentiate fully occupations, educational levels, or class stratification among peasants (kulaks, middle, and poor peasants were all listed together under one census heading). In addition, there was no question about nationality (only native language and religion). Finally, although the census reached most regions of the vast Russian Empire, it by no means reached them all. Many communities continued to shun the census because of its tax purposes; according to some estimates, the population in parts of Siberia was miscalculated by as much as 30 percent and Finland was excluded altogether.

In early 1902, the Central Statistical Committee published results of the 1897 census in one volume for eighteen gubernii and in two volumes for another six. The published categories, however, were considered to be inappropriately designated and a special conference was called to rework the results based on the de facto and de jure population figures. (Robert Lewis discusses in his chapter the importance of checking whether figures from the Russian and Soviet censuses are for the de facto [*nalichnoye*] or de jure [*postoyannoye*] population and how de jure is defined operationally in a given enumeration. As Anderson and Silver (1985) noted, there may be a significant difference between the two categories.) The final census was fully published by 1905, eight years after its inception. Results were presented in twenty-five main tables for each of the eighty-nine gubernii, a summary volume for the empire, supplements listing urban settlements greater than 2,000 people and places with more than 500 inhabitants, and volumes on several specialized topics.[2]

The question about the necessity for a new Russian census was raised several times in the early years of the twentieth century. The Central Statistical Committee planned to hold a second census in 1910, later postponed to 1915 because of bureaucratic delays. With the outbreak of World War I in 1914, this census never took place.

The Soviet Censuses

When planning is paramount, as it is in socialist economies, the government must be able to take stock of the country's labor resources and materials so that a record of past production can be related to future goals. It is somewhat ironic, therefore, that the officially recognized censuses of the Soviet Union (1920, 1926, 1939, 1959, 1970, and 1979) fell at such irregular intervals. Ideally, according to the International Statistical Congress organized by Semenov-Tyan-Shanskyy in St. Petersburg in 1872, a census count of the population was to be taken every ten years, beginning in 1900. Unfortunately, the USSR periodically encountered difficulties or adversity (revolution, civil and world war, famine, and economic reorganization) severe enough to prevent such a regular count.

The Early Post-Revolutionary Period

The first Soviet census of population was conducted in April 1920, according to a resolution by the Seventh All-Russian Congress of Soviets. A demographic-professional census and a brief calculation of industrial enterprises were planned to coincide with a scheduled agricultural census in one statistical operation (Drobizhev, 1977: 69). Data were collected according to occupation, native language and nationality (*natsional'nost'*), and literacy; in addition, maps of urban apartments and lists of rural homesteads were compiled.

The 1920 census took place under the grave conditions of foreign and civil war and economic devastation. Both paper and literate cadres were in short supply, and several enumerators were reported to have been murdered by the people they were attempting to count. Owing to war-related events, the census could not be conducted in Belorussia, the Crimea, the Transcaucasus, the Far East, Turkestan, Khiva, Bukhara,

---

2. Russian Empire, Tsentral'nyy Statisticheskiy Komitet, *Pervaya vseobshchaya perepis' naseleniya Rossiyskoy Imperii 1897 goda*, 89 vols. (1899–1905).

and various regions of the Ukraine, the Volga, the North Caucasus, and Siberia; altogether about 28 percent of the population was not contained in this count. Including those areas not counted, the Soviet population in 1920 has been estimated at 136.8 million (Kolpakov, 1969: 20–21).

Although not regarded as accurate and published only in part, the 1920 census did make some significant contributions. Unlike the 1897 count, it included a question about nationality (*natsional'nost'*) as well as a question about native language. A question about general and special education was asked along with the question about literacy. According to a suggestion by Lenin, however, no question was asked about religion.

The experience of the first Soviet census of 1920 was useful in its application toward subsequent census counts. A 1923 urban census was conducted according to the same principles as the 1920 census but applied only to cities; settlements connected with factories, plants, and railroad stations; resorts of 500 people and more; and rural population points of less than 2,000 inhabitants where the dominant means of employment was provided by a local industry or trade (Kolpakov, 1969: 17). This urban census was conducted concurrently with a census of industrial enterprises and trade institutions (Zhak, 1958: 20).

The Census of 1926

The next Soviet census was taken on December 15, 1926, after peace had arrived and economic recovery was under way. For the first time during Soviet rule, the census included the entire territory of the country and provided a barometer by which to measure the success or failure of economic rehabilitation. For example, of the population of 147 million, the census found that only 18 percent (26.3 million) was urban in 1926; this rather low urban share indicated that the country remained primarily agrarian despite significant industrial strides.

The 1926 census had as its goal the collection of data about the population necessary for the compilation of the first Five-Year Plan. Indeed, this census remains the most comprehensive yet compiled by either Russia or the Soviet Union; its volumes provided a wealth of statistical information used by the government in planning the economy right up until World War II. In addition, complete life tables of the population were generated from the collected age data from the Ukraine, Belorussia, and the European part of the RSFSR.

The conducting of the census proceeded according to a detailed program. Prior to the census, community Committees of Cooperation circulated propaganda materials in order to inform the populace of the importance of census accuracy. Local census bureaus conducted surveys for the mapping of census regions and city plans, and much time and effort was spent training enumerators to fill out forms properly. To insure an accurate return, special directives were issued by the Council of People's Commissars which promised to treat all information as confidential, although the regional executive committees were known to threaten reprisals to those who gave false information (Petersen, 1975: 669).

The questionnaire itself was also more comprehensive than those of the previous censuses. Questions were arranged in a series of six census forms, the first of which was a personal survey providing the standard census information. While the 1926 census was essentially a demographic one, the additional forms requested data by family lists, ownership charts for urban dwellers, and homeowner details for rural locales. These data provided statistics on housing resources, taxes, construction, and accommodations by urban and rural area.

As with the 1897 census, the cross-tabulation of the collected data for 1926 required a tremendous effort, most of which was done by hand. Nonetheless, the analysis proceeded rapidly, and the census was ready for publication by the end of 1929 (USSR, 1929). Results were issued in fifty-six volumes of seven major categories and in nineteen short summary volumes. These results were published based on twenty-four census regions which had been established for planning and administration to coincide with the economic and political divisions at the time; there were nearly twice as many political units in 1926 as there were in 1897.

The 1926 census, as indicated previously, marked a vast improvement in the general knowledge of the population within the borders of the Soviet state. This was especially evident in the increased number of categories designating the various ethnic groups (*narodnosti*), about whom the authorities now had a more comprehensive knowledge. In addition, questions were added about unemployment, physical handicaps, and mental illness.

However, the 1926 census had several deficiencies. Perhaps most glaring was the fact that the permanent population in the 1926 census, that population living permanently at the place of enumeration and born within the 1926 borders of the USSR, was not the de jure population because temporary residents were not allocated back to their places of permanent residence as temporarily absent (Lewis and Rowland, 1979: 87).

There were also discrepancies in the levels of training and education of the census takers. An effort was made to recruit more enumerators with higher or secondary education or where possible to encourage university students, teachers, and employees of statistical organizations to participate in the census-taking effort. Still, in 1926 only 10.5 percent of the instructors had any higher education, while 18.3 percent had no education at all. Regional variations were significant. Thus, where in the RSFSR nearly 65 percent of the enumerators were school employees, student volunteers, or members of statistical organizations, only 35 percent of the Central Asian enumerators fell into these categories (Vorob'yev, 1957: 43–48). Similar urban-rural differentials existed. Although there were 163,132 enumerators for a population of 147 million, it was necessary to call in the army to take stock of the population in certain regions of the country.

The Censuses of 1937 and 1939

The next full-scale census conducted in the Soviet Union took place in 1937, following the postponement of censuses scheduled in 1930 and 1935. Although the results were apparently circulated in government agencies, the 1937 census figures never appeared in print. The results were evidently seen as unsatisfactory and declared statistically invalid; blame was placed upon alleged violations of the basic principles of science and statistics. The statistician Kvitkin, who had protested the withholding of results, was removed as head of the census department (Galin, 1951: 2).

The specific statistical principle that was criticized was one that provided a check of households to prevent a double counting of temporarily absent persons. As a result of such an innovation, the 1937 census total was reported at 158 million, several million (about 10 percent) less than had been expected. If accurate, this figure would have indicated the substantial impact that collectivization, famine, and the purges of the early Stalin years had on the Soviet population. It has also been claimed that confusion among local officials and enumerators and the lack of cooperation by respondents led to an inaccurate count (Somerville, 1940: 52–55).

On January 17, 1939, two years after the 1937 count, an all-Union census was again taken. The census form contained sixteen questions, three of which were geared towards the calculation of the de facto and de jure inhabitants for each population point of the entire country. The questionnaire was printed in twenty-two languages. For the first and only time, a system was developed for counting both convicted criminals and political detainees. This was important at the time because it has been estimated that as many as 15 million people were either incarcerated for criminal activity or interned in prisons and camps for political reasons (Galin, 1951: 2). The census provided instructions for conducting counts of prisoners, although details of the system were kept strictly secret. In terms of the work-force data, political detainees were entered according to their occupations before internment; convicted criminals, however, were listed based on the jobs they performed at the camp or prison. Convicted criminals, but not political prisoners, were enumerated in later censuses.

Several new procedures were developed in the method of tabulation. For the first time a complete control round was instituted, whereby all residences were submitted to a follow-up check the week after the completion of the regular census (however, forms were not issued to keep track of double counting). The totals were once again tabulated by electric machines utilizing hole-punched cards. Three regional administrative centers were established at Moscow, Leningrad, and Kharkov.

Within four months, preliminary results were issued. For reasons that remain unclear, however, only partial data were ever released, in less than ten pages of tables. A tabulation for the entire population was never published, although complete totals were announced (Kulischer and Roof, 1956: 280–90). Because of its lack of detail, the 1939 census has not been particularly useful for population analysis. Nevertheless, the totals released, while considered questionable, do provide some measures for comparison with the data from 1926.[3]

In twelve years the urban population more than doubled, reaching 56.1 million (33 percent of the total population) by 1939, a rate of urbanization historically without precedent. In terms of the economic structure of the working class, the share of workers and employees (along with their family members) reached half of the total population by 1939, up from roughly one-sixth in 1926.[4] The virtually complete collectivization of farming was also indicated by census figures.

While the 1939 Soviet census has not been widely utilized, it nevertheless provided a framework of organizational experience and added to a popular understanding of statistical methods. These developments helped especially in conducting the numerous emergency survey counts that were necessary during World War II.

The 1959 Soviet Census: The Organization of the Census-Taking Apparatus

Twenty years passed before another comprehensive census took place on Soviet soil, on January 15, 1959. The date chosen at least allowed for comparisons by twenty-year intervals, and the published tables often included previously unreleased 1939 totals as well. However, the large

---

3. For the published 1939 results, see *Izvestiya*, 2 June 1939, 1; and *Izvestiya*, 29 April 1940, 1. Results also appear in U.S., Bureau of Foreign and Domestic Commerce, *Russian Economic Notes* 2 (1 July 1940): 7–10; and *American Quarterly on the Soviet Union* 3 (February/March 1940): 97–100.

4. Part of the increase was due to a change in the definitions of social classes.

territorial gains following World War II and the devastating effect that war losses had on the age and sex structure of the population made comparisons between census years quite difficult. Furthermore, unlike the Soviet censuses of 1920 and 1926, the 1959 questionnaire did not request information on place of birth, making difficult even a crude estimate of migration.

The organization and administration of the population count in 1959 marked a standardization in Soviet census-taking procedures; most of the methods instituted in 1959 remained virtually unchanged for the succeeding Soviet censuses of 1970 and 1979. Before 1959, census questionnaires and instructions were distributed by the bureau undertaking the census (1897—Central Statistical Committee; 1926—Central Statistical Administration; 1939—Central Administration of National Economic Accounting of GOSPLAN, the State Planning Committee). The forms were sent to the statistical boards of the union republics, which sent them on to regional and local organizations where they were distributed to the district inspectors of the census. In previous census years a temporary Bureau of the Census was established in each union and autonomous republic, in each kray and oblast, and in major cities (Somerville, 1940: 54). These bureaus were disbanded after totals were tabulated at the local levels and summarized versions were mailed in to the union republic statistical boards.

By 1959, the system for sending in census results was centralized. All enterprises, regional boards, and district inspectors sent their totals directly to the Central Statistical Administration of each republic, where results were totaled without intervening stages. Census materials were also sent by telegraph rather than post. These changes hastened the processing and analysis of census data; 1959 preliminary results were published less than four months after the census taking was completed.

In 1957 the Council of Ministers established a Department for the Supervision of the National Population Census, which was administered by the Central Statistical Administration. In one form or another, this commission, entrusted with the preparation and conducting of the census, would remain the permanent census bureau of the USSR. Attached to it were various other standing councils of the Central Statistical Administration organized to help deal with problems involved with the conducting of the censuses (Yezhov, 1967: 123). The procedural organization of census taking instituted in 1959 can be applied to the conducting of the 1970 and 1979 censuses with very few changes. While many of the procedures described below were applied in 1939, they were not established as official policy until the 1959 census.

A great deal of preparatory work goes into an event as encompassing as a national census of population. Accordingly, in June 1957 a national conference of statisticians and representatives from various scientific, industrial, and planning institutions was held to formulate the general program and discuss some of the methodological problems associated with the census (Yezhov, 1967: 123). Preliminary work also included drawing up a list of units to be investigated, supplying the materials needed for the census, and briefing census personnel. The effectiveness of a census depends in large measure on the reliability of the data entered into the questionnaires. A great deal of effort, therefore, went into the training of personnel. An increasing number of enumerators were people with higher education and those familiar with statistical techniques, especially in the outlying republics. All organs of statistical information associated with the census at all levels were prepared, mobilized, and practiced.

The Central Statistical Administration initiated a substantial propaganda effort prior to the actual census taking. Lectures, exhibits, and discussions were conducted by inspectors and controllers of the local census department at industrial enterprises, institutions, state farms, and schools. The media actively participated as well; television, radio, newspapers, and journals carried frequent news of the impending census, and large numbers of special brochures were issued (USSR, 1958a: 26).

On August 1, 1957, a trial census counted approximately a million people in seven geographically diverse regions of the country. The experience aided in questionnaire design and set the numbers of enumerators for urban and rural locales. Regional census divisions were established by GOSPLAN for the compilation and collection of data, and set figures were decided upon for wages and time off from work for those involved in the census.[5] Finally, the Council of Ministers chose a census date based on the assumption that a midweek day in January would find a large portion of the population in their homes, including schoolchildren on vacation. For the 1959 census this date was January 15, a Thursday. Procedures were established for conducting the census early in the Far North and remote mountain areas.

A few days before the census (January 11–14) a preliminary round was conducted, during which the enumerators made themselves familiar with their territory. They visited all of the households in each district, informing the inhabitants of the census procedures and asking what the best time would be for enumerators to come by for the actual survey. The census itself lasted eight days, from January 15 to January 22. All people, including temporary residents, were listed at the place where they were counted as the de facto population as of midnight, January 14–15. Permanent residents who were temporarily absent were noted as

---

5. For further details on census-taking procedures, see A. Yezhov, *Organization of Statistics in the USSR* (Moscow: Progress Publishers, 1967), 121–28.

well. To avoid the danger of double counting, enumerators issued to all those who were listed as temporary residents a special certificate (*spravka*) indicating they had already been counted. This was especially important for those on long-distance transport at the time of the census count.

Details were provided for the counting of those in hospitals, sanitariums, and vacation homes; they were to be listed as temporary residents if their length of stay was less than six months. University students were considered permanent residents at their place of study, even if they resided there less than six months out of each year. People who had moved their residences for work, study, or training more than six months before the census were counted at their new location as permanent residents, even when they had kept material connections with their family at a previous location. Members of the armed services were enumerated at their place of duty but were counted as permanent residents at the location where they were employed before entering military duty (USSR, 1958a: 24). (Users of Soviet census data are advised to check carefully the definition of the population employed in any given table as to whether the figures are for the de facto [*nalichnoye*] or de jure [*postoyannoye*] population. In the 1979 census volume, for instance, tables 1–4 are de facto population, but the remainder are de jure (USSR, 1984: 6, n. 1). Anderson and Silver (1985) is a good guide to the nuances and possible problems connected with this usage.)

For ten days following the census (January 23–February 1) the census takers made another complete check of all dwellings in a given district in order to insure that no one was omitted or double counted and to verify the registered number of temporarily absent and temporarily present dwellers. During this round, enumerators filled out special control sheets for those people whose whereabouts were not definitely known at the time of the census count. All those who had required control sheets were issued *spravki*, which they were to maintain in their possession until February 10. Control sheets were also filled out when persons knew they might have been included in the census count at another location (USSR, 1958a: 23). The control sheets, which requested registration of the exact address at which the subject should have been counted as well as responses to the same questions as the regular questionnaire, revealed another 1,074,000 people who were missed the first time around or 0.51 percent of the total population (Yezhov, 1967: 126).

In addition to the questionnaire form, the Central Statistical Administration provided a list of detailed instructions in order to clarify certain ambiguities. The enumerator was instructed to fill out the census form in the words of the respondent; the contents of the answers were to be kept confidential, and no one was required to show any of their documents. The census was to be conducted by place of dwelling, not place of work;

dormitories at schools and factories were considered permanent places of dwelling. The enumerators counted people at work during the time of the census as part of the de facto population at their place of residence and *not* as temporarily absent. The same held true for those on suburban trains and local buses, those at children's homes and night sanitariums, and those spending the night with friends or relatives living in the same census district (USSR, 1958b: 23). Temporary workers and those counted on long-distance trains, buses, and ships or at stations, ports, and airports were to be listed as temporary residents and included in the de facto population at the place they were counted.

The 1959 census achieved a relative degree of sophistication by raising the level of training of the enumerators, improving the application of statistical techniques, and consolidating specialists from various disciplines. As was mentioned previously, many of the preparations and operational methods introduced for the 1959 count remained similar or identical in the succeeding census programs.

Censuses of 1970 and 1979: The Use of Sampling

Perhaps the most significant innovation in conducting the censuses of the 1970s was the acceptance of sampling as a legitimate statistical tool for compiling population data. Sampling was first instituted into the census program at the urging of the All-Union Congress of Statisticians in April 1968. A sample format was developed on the basis of results from a trial census conducted in nine regions during March 1967 (USSR, 1978: 26).

The Congress also provided a forum for a long-standing debate between demographers and statisticians in the Soviet Union (Perevedentsev, 1967: 13). Demographers called for a reworking of the questionnaire in order to collect more detailed information for the analysis of the population, while statisticians held fast for the standardization of the basic questionnaire and the increased use of sampling and data-processing techniques. Such a debate has been repeated at various times prior to both the 1970 and 1979 censuses (Isupov, 1975: 5), but the questionnaire has remained relatively unchanged over the years. Instead, the Central Statistical Administration issued more detailed instructions in an attempt to increase the accuracy of the responses to the 1970 census questionnaire. Enumerators were instructed to explain thoroughly that the census was not in any way connected with such matters as tax ratings, the use of living space, or visa registration. The collected data were to be used by the central authorities exclusively for analysis and for the compilation of summary indexes by which to categorize the population. Census workers were not to reveal any of the responses, which were to be used only by organs of the state and economic administrations, planning organizations, and scientific institutions (USSR, 1969a: 29).

The 1970 census, originally scheduled for 1969, was postponed until January 15, 1970, most likely because of technical difficulties encountered during the course of a trial census conducted in 1967 (Voronitsyn, 1978: 1). While the reason for the delay is unclear, the new date has been cited as marking the one-hundredth anniversary of Lenin's birth. The basic questionnaire consisted of eleven questions asked of the entire population; a second form, distributed to every fourth household, contained eighteen questions, including the same eleven answered by everyone. Thus, the 1970 census used a 25-percent sample to collect information for questions 12–18, which concerned work-force and migration data. This was the first time sampling had been accepted in a Soviet census count, ostensibly to decrease the expense and accelerate the analysis of the material. Two additional questionnaire forms were also issued in 1970. Form 3 requested information on persons of able-bodied working age occupied in household and private subsidiary agriculture; Form 4 served to collect information about commuting (Pod"yachikh, 1976: 31) Sampling also came into use during the control round, which was held for six days, from January 24 to January 29. For urban areas, the control round was conducted in all districts for 50 percent of the dwellings; in rural areas, enumerators checked all of the dwellings for 50 percent of the districts (USSR, 1969a: 33).

The basic questionnaire (first eleven questions) in 1970 was similar in form and content to that of 1959, but some slight changes merit mentioning. The question about age was expanded to determine not only the number of years lived, as in all previous censuses, but also the year and month of birth. This allowed for a reduction in the distortion in data about age composition which occurs because of the tendency of many to round their ages to the -0 and -5 groups. The Central Statistical Administration modified other questions to gather more detailed information about second languages spoken and reasons for temporary absences. In addition, the 25-percent sample survey obtained data about the previous occupations of pensioners, the duration of work in the previous year, and migration trends.

The intercensal period between 1959 and 1970, although a rather unwieldy eleven years, revealed some interesting facts. With the war long over, the male-female gap had begun to return to normal. The urban population reached 136 million, surpassing 50 percent of the total for the first time (from 48 percent in 1959 to 56 percent in 1970). The growth of large cities was especially rapid; in 1959 there were three cities with over a million people, while by 1970 there were ten.

The actual conducting of the 1970 census required nearly 662,000 participants, including 534,000 enumerators and 97,000 supervisors (USSR, 1978: 26). With the help of calculators, information was compiled and processed into summary tables, and results were analyzed and ready in time for the implementation of the Ninth Five-Year Plan. The 1970 census was more comprehensive and slightly larger than that of 1959 (3,238 pages to 2,830 pages). It was fully published in seven topical volumes beginning in 1972.[6]

The program of the January 1979 census was based on results from the 1970 experience. Slight modifications were made in the questionnaire, which totaled sixteen questions, eleven of which were to be answered by the entire population.[7] The last five questions were again issued to only 25 percent of the population (i.e., to every fourth dwelling). As in previous years, the census effort included a trial census (for nine regions in May 1977) and the convening of an All-Union Conference of Statisticians for a discussion of the methodological and organizational questions connected with the 1979 census program. The government conducted an early survey for outlying mountainous and northern regions, and the importance of the preliminary and control rounds was stressed in order to insure completeness in the count (Ivanova, 1976: 49). The control round was based on a 25-percent sample (as opposed to 50 percent in 1970), underscoring an increased confidence in sampling.

During the preparation of the 1979 census program, several points of controversy arose which had to be clarified before the new questionnaire could be formulated. It was proposed, for instance, that the term "native" (*rodnoy*) language be replaced with "conversational" (*razgovornyy*) language and also that the qualification "fluently" (*svobodnyy*) be omitted from the question on second language (Voronitsyn, 1978: 2). A change never ensued, partly because of the need for consistency and partly because native language was felt to connote a social function in terms of relations between people (Voronitsyn, 1978: 2). A decision was made by the Central Statistical Administration to register members of the armed forces where they were stationed and not at their former places of residence; the same applied to persons in confinement (Voronitsyn, 1979: 2).

The first eleven questions in the 1979 census were nearly identical to

---

6. USSR, Tsentral'noye Statisticheskoye Upravleniye, *Itogi Vsesoyuznoy perepisi naseleniya 1970 goda*, 7 vols. (1972), Vol. 1: *Number of people;* Vol. 2: *Sex, age, and marital status;* Vol. 3: *Level of education;* Vol. 4: *Nationality composition;* Vol. 5: *Distribution according to social group;* Vol. 6: *Distribution according to occupation;* Vol. 7: *Migration*.

7. In ASSRs, autonomous oblasts, and autonomous okrugs with less than 500,000 inhabitants, the entire population was required to answer all sixteen questions (USSR, 1978: 27).

those asked in 1970. The new forms, however, no longer requested the reason for or length of absence for temporary residents and absentees. For the first time since 1926 the questionnaire provided marital status by type (widowed, divorced, or never married). Meanwhile, the education question (number nine) has, with each succeeding census year, required less and less information about literacy. This development has most likely come about because nearly the entire population, with the exception of the elderly and the very young, has become literate. In fact, the 1979 form had no separate list for those who were illiterate. If the enumerator came across a person who was illiterate, he was instructed to note the fact on the census blank and to indicate the reason for illiteracy.

The All-Union Conference of Statisticians suggested several changes in the program of the sample survey (questions 12–16). A reworking of the 1970 migration questions in order to account for those who had moved more than once was considered and abandoned (Isupov, 1975: 5). Instead, a question was inserted requesting the number of children ever born to all women aged 16 and over. Furthermore, the supplementary form on commuting was dropped from the 1979 program. Data gathered from commuters in 1970 had most likely already been utilized (although not published) to help determine an estimate for the number of people on local transport at the time of the census count. Finally, a poll was conducted simultaneously with the census which sought information on the work force engaged in housework or in private agriculture. This form requested details on the number of dependent children, the composition of the working-age population, and the source of livelihood, as well as willingness to accept employment and the reason not employed (i.e., not "occupied in the social production") at the time of the census.

The 1979 census, while involving over 700,000 workers (enumerators, controllers, and supervisors), was the first Soviet census to make wide use of a sophisticated network of computers. The census questionnaires, although not filled out directly by the respondent, were mark-sensing forms that were machine readable and could be transmitted onto magnetic tape for direct input into a computer. The census-processing operation utilized a unified system of twenty-nine regional computer centers connected with a main terminal in Moscow (Feshbach, 1981: 6).

Because the census day needed to fall in the middle of the week, the date was changed from January 15 (a Monday) to January 17 (a Wednesday). The Council of Ministers also decided to conduct the census only nine years after the previous one. This decision resulted in irregular intervals between census years but brought a return to the pattern established with the 1939 and 1959 counts (the 1970 census, it should be recalled, was originally slated for 1969). Furthermore, the earlier date meant that the results would be available in time for the compilation of the Eleventh Five-Year Plan (Voronitsyn, 1981: 1).

Notwithstanding the technical advances connected with the 1979 census, the publication—or lack thereof—of results from the enumeration is quite limited for a country with resources and vast data-gathering apparatus such as the USSR possesses. Although preliminary total results, by political-administrative unit, were released in April 1979, additional information appeared only sporadically and in highly incomplete form in issues of the journal *Vestnik statistiki*. These figures were subsequently compiled and republished (with some minor additions) in a single volume in 1984, more than five years after the census was taken (USSR, 1984); by contrast, the initial volume of the 1959 census was published in 1962 and that of the 1970 census in 1972.

Of much greater concern than timeliness, however, is the lack of detail provided in the *Vestnik statistiki* tables or the 1984 compendium. Despite the deliberations about the age question and the decision to improve the quality of responses by asking for month and year of birth, no age data have yet been published from the 1979 count. The absence of such figures to date significantly reduces the utility of the census for many important analytic purposes. The Soviet Union can now be regarded as ranking behind most developing countries in terms of the volume of available published census figures.

The Russian and Soviet Censuses: A General Assessment

Although the censuses constitute by far the largest body of empirical information on the socioeconomic situation in Russia and the USSR, there are important shortcomings in the data as collected, tabulated, and published; specific definitional, operational, and availability problems are discussed at length in the topical chapters that follow. It is clear, however, that census data from *any* country present the researcher with a variety of difficulties. Thus, it might be useful to make some general comparisons between the Russian and Soviet censuses and international standards as a means by which these problems can be placed in a relevant context.

Compared to the most advanced countries, the USSR has lagged behind in the introduction of some technical advances in the enumeration process. For example, whereas sampling was first used in the U.S. census of 1940, the USSR adopted this technique for the 1970 census. A question on month and year of birth (a better means of obtaining age data), included in the 1970 Soviet census, had been incorporated earlier in European and U.S. censuses. Mark-sensing forms and readers were first introduced in the U.S. census in 1960 but in the Soviet census only in 1979. Certainly, the USSR has been slow to utilize computers fully in the census operation, although this tendency is characteristic of the Soviet bureaucracy, economy, and society in general.

Beginning in the 1950s, the Statistical Office of the United Nations (now a branch of the Department of International Economic and Social Affairs) initiated a series of publications containing guidance for countries in planning and carrying out national population censuses; this office also sponsored numerous technical manuals dealing with different operational aspects of census taking (United Nations, 1958; 1967; 1974; 1980). These important documents, which reflect the growing international concern for obtaining more and better information on socioeconomic conditions in the world's countries, incorporate lessons learned in previous censuses, the results of conferences and expert consultations, and recommendations submitted by international, regional, and national statistical bodies.

In the most recent of these publications, the UN (1980: 2–3) considers that four "essential features" are desirable in any population census: individual enumeration, universality, simultaneity, and defined periodicity. With reference to the Soviet censuses, including the latest ones, the first three of these features are adhered to; the last is violated by the troublesome irregularity of intercensal periods. At one point, the UN recommended that countries take censuses in years ending in zero to facilitate international comparisons, but that suggestion has been downplayed of late (UN, 1980: 3).

Beyond these very general "essential features," the UN provides more specific guidelines for the planning, organization, and administration of censuses (UN, 1980: 12–37). First, extensive *preparatory work* is necessary for any national census, including establishing a legal basis for the enumeration, securing funding, agreeing on a census calendar, setting up administrative bodies, publicizing the census, mapping census units, preparing the questionnaire, and recruiting and training staff. Although not privy to all internal workings of the Soviet census apparatus, we do know that considerable effort goes into the preparatory work of the census. For example, planning conferences involving demographers, ethnographers, statisticians, and other social scientists, and representatives of the Central Statistical Administration are convened well in advance of the projected census date to review procedures and discuss changes in technical or operational aspects of the enumeration; lengthy reports on the issues discussed, as well as copies of the household list and questionnaire forms, are published regularly (USSR, 1958a; 1958b; 1969a; 1969b; 1978). Of particular interest in these publications are descriptions of test census results, which in some cases prompt refinements in the full census. In this connection, the fact that the USSR has had a permanent census bureau since 1957 provides for continuity in matters relating to census methodology.

Second, according to the UN, *operational aspects* of the census process must receive attention. Decisions must be made regarding the manner in which the population will be counted (enumerator or householder methods), the timing and length of the enumeration period, and the use of sampling. The Soviet census has always employed enumerators rather than relying on self-enumeration. As was discussed earlier in this chapter, serious consideration is given to fixing the date of the Soviet census in an attempt to minimize undercounting or double counting due to travel, work, and schooling. During the census period, control slips (*spravki*) are used to keep track of persons already counted. Remote areas are usually enumerated early to avoid delaying the process. Finally, sampling is now an important feature of the Soviet censuses.

Third, *data processing* and, fourth, *evaluation of results* must proceed once the census is completed. Computers and their applications have become more common in data processing in the USSR, and this trend will no doubt continue. However, although initial results of the Soviet census are released reasonably early, the tabulation process is slower than in the U.S. census. The evaluation of results through internal checks and postenumeration surveys is standard practice in Soviet census taking.

Finally, the UN considers the *dissemination of results* to be the last stage in the census process and a vital one for the obvious reason that even the most accurate and extensively tabulated data are of limited utility unless they are made available to researchers (UN, 1980: 36–37). In this chapter and throughout this volume it is made abundantly clear that the major failure of census taking in the USSR is in the area of dissemination of results.

The UN series on population censuses also contains recommendations for topics to be investigated and tabulations to be made therefrom (UN, 1967: 40–41; 1958: 18–19). In terms of topics covered by the census, the USSR has a good and improving record (UN, 1974: 9). For example, of fifteen high priority topics recommended by the UN, the 1959 Soviet census covered twelve (missing only place of birth, children ever born, and children living); children ever born was added in the 1979 census. By comparison, the 1960 U.S. census also included twelve of fifteen high priority topics (missing de facto residence, children living, and literacy). The tabulation of results varies from census to census, but—with the obvious exception of the 1979 count—the USSR satisfies the vast majority of recommended direct or derived tabulations (UN, 1967: 40–41).

In conclusion, by accepted international standards the censuses of the USSR conform to most recommendations regarding the preparation and conducting of the enumeration but fall far short in rendering available results of the count and tabulations. As was mentioned in the earlier chapter by Ralph Clem, the accuracy of Soviet census data has improved over the years, an improvement that makes it especially ironic that the publication of the figures has been so severely reduced.

References

Anderson, Barbara A., and Brian D. Silver. 1985. "'Permanent' and 'Present' Populations in Soviet Statistics." *Soviet Studies* 37: 386–402.

Bruk, S. I., and V. I. Kozlov. 1977. "K istorii ucheta etnicheskogo sostava v perepisyakh naseleniya." In *Problemy istoricheskoy demografii SSSR*, ed. R. N. Pullat, 173–85. Tallin: Akademiya Nauk Estonskoy SSR.

Drobizhev, V. Z. 1977. "Nekotoriya voprosy istochnikovedeniya istoriko-demograficheskikh issledovanii Sovetskogo obshchestva." In *Problemy istoricheskoy demografii SSSR*, 67–72. See Bruk and Kozlov, 1977.

Dubester, Henry J. 1969. *National Censuses and Vital Statistics in Europe, 1918–1939: An Annotated Bibliography.* Reprinted from 1948 ed. New York: Burt Franklin.

Feshbach, Murray. 1981. "Development of the Soviet Census." In *Soviet Population Policy: Conflicts and Constraints*, ed. Helen Desfosses, 3–15. New York: Pergamon Press.

Galin, M. 1951. *Kak proizvodilis' perepis' naseleniya v SSSR.* Munich: Institut po izuchenii istorii i kul'tury SSSR.

Isupov, A. 1975. "O predstoyashchey Vsesoyuznoy perepsisi naseleniya." *Vestnik statistiki*, no. 9: 3–9.

Ivanova, V. 1976. "O podgotovke k Vsesoyuznoy perepisi naseleniya 1979 g." *Vestnik statistiki*, no. 7: 49–52.

Kolpakov, B. T. 1969. *Vsesoyuznaya perepis' naseleniya 1970 goda.* Moscow: Sovetskaya Rossiya.

Kulischer, Eugene M., and M. K. Roof. 1956. "A New Look at the Soviet Population Structure of 1939." *American Sociological Review* 21: 280–90.

Lewis, Robert A., and Richard H. Rowland. 1979. *Population Redistribution in the USSR: Its Impact on Society, 1897–1977.* New York: Praeger.

Lincoln, W. B. 1980. *Petr Petrovich Semenov-Tian Shanskii. The Life of a Russian Geographer.* Newtonville, Mass.: Oriental Research Partners.

Lorimer, Frank. 1946. *The Population of the Soviet Union: History and Prospects.* Geneva: League of Nations.

Perevedentsev, V. 1967. "Spor o perepisi." *Literaturnaya gazeta* 2 (11 January): 13.

Petersen, William. 1975. *Population*, 2d ed. New York: Macmillan.
Pivovar, E. I. 1985. "Perepis sluzhashchikh Sovetskikh uchrezhdeniy Moskvy 1918 goda kak istochnik po istorii intelligentsii." *Istoriya SSSR* 1 (January/February): 146–57.
Pod"yachikh, P. G. 1966. "O predstoyashchey Vsesoyuznoy perepisi naseleniya 1969 g." *Vestnik statistiki*, no. 8: 38–48.
———. 1976. "Programma i osnovnye voprosy metodologii Vsesoyuznoy perepisi naseleniya 1970 g." In *Vsesoyuznaya perepis' naseleniya 1970 goda: Sbornik statey*, ed. G. M. Maksimov, 9–48. Moscow: Statistika.
Russian Empire. Tsentral'nyy Statisticheskiy Komitet. 1905. *Pervaya vseobshchaya perepis' naseleniya Rossiyskoy Imperii, 1897 g.* 89 vols. St. Petersburg.
Sautin, I. 1938. *Vsesoyuznaya perepis' naseleniya 1939 goda*. Moscow: Gosudarstvennoye Izdatel'stvo Politicheskoy Literatury.
Somerville, Rose M. 1940. "Counting Noses in the Soviet Union: The 1939 Census." *American Quarterly on the Soviet Union* 3 (February/March): 51–73.
United Nations. Department of Economic and Social Affairs. 1967. *Principles and Recommendations for the 1970 Population Censuses*. Statistical Papers, Series M, no. 44. New York.
———. 1974. *Handbook of Population and Housing Census Methods*. Studies in Methods, Series F, no. 16. New York.
United Nations. Department of International Economic and Social Affairs. 1980. *Principles and Recommendations for Population and Housing Censuses*. Statistical Papers, Series M, no. 67. New York.
United Nations. Statistical Office. 1958. *Principles and Recommendations for National Population Censuses*. Statistical Papers, Series M, no. 27. New York.
USSR. Tsentral'noye Statisticheskoye Upravleniye SSSR. 1929. *Vsesoyuznaya perepis' naseleniya 1926 goda*. 66 vols. Moscow.
———. 1958a. *Materiali po Vsesoyuznoy perepisi naseleniya 1959 goda*. Moscow: Gosudarstvennoye Statisticheskoye Izdatel'stvo.
———. 1958b. *Vsesoyuznaya perepis' naseleniya 1959 goda*. Moscow: Gosudarstvennoye Izdatel'stvo Politicheskoy Literatury.
———. 1969a. *Vsesoyuznaya perepis' naseleniya—vsenarodnoye delo*. Moscow: Statistika.
———. 1969b. *Vsesoyuznoye soveshchaniye statistikov 22–26 aprelya 1968 g.: Stenograficheskiy otchet*. Moscow: Statistika.
———. 1978. *Vsesoyuznaya perepis' naseleniya—vsenarodnoye delo*. Moscow: Statistika.
———. 1984. *Chislennost' i sostav naseleniya SSSR (Po dannym Vsesoyuznoy perepisi naseleniya 1979 goda)*. Moscow: Finansy i Statistika.
Volkov, A. 1967. "Voprosy migratsii v programme perepisi naseleniya." *Vestnik statistiki*, no. 2: 34–38.
Vorob'yev, N. Y. 1957. *Vsesoyuznaya perepis' naseleniya 1926 goda*. Moscow: Gosudarstvennoye Statisticheskoye Izdatel'stvo.
Voronitsyn, S. 1978. "On the Eve of the All-Union Census." *Radio Liberty Research* 230/78: 1–5.
———. 1979. "The All-Union Census Starts." *Radio Liberty Research* 16/79: 1–5.

Yezhov, A. 1967. *Organization of Statistics in the USSR*. Moscow: Progress Publishers.
Zhak, D. K. 1958. *Mekhanizirovannaya razrabotka materialov perepisey naseleniya SSSR*. Moscow: Gosudarstvennoye Statisticheskoye Izdatel'stvo.

Chapter 4

The Ethnic and Language Dimensions in Russian and Soviet Censuses

Brian D. Silver

The Soviet government emphasizes its leading role in the social and economic transformation of society. Information gathered from censuses is important for the periodic assessment of state policies. Therefore, census data on nationality and native language of the population serve as a way both to determine the ethnic composition of Soviet society and, in conjunction with other data, to assess and compare the progress of policies designed to promote the economic and social development of the nationalities of the USSR. Censuses, moreover, are the only source of systematic information on change in the ethnic composition and language preferences of the population as a whole.

Russian and Soviet census planners have always included questions about nationality and language in the census forms (see Table 4.1). The First General Census of Population in 1897 contained questions about native language (*rodnoy yazyk*) and religion of the imperial population. The five general censuses reported since the 1917 Revolution (1926, 1939, 1959, 1970, and 1979) asked questions about native language and nationality of the Soviet population. In addition to the questions about native language, the 1970 and 1979 censuses included a question about second language or, more precisely, "another language of the peoples of the USSR" that an individual could "freely command."

The utility of the information on nationality, language, and religion depends both on the exact formulation of census questions and on the

Acknowledgements: Initial work on this chapter was completed while I was a Mellon Fellow and Visiting Scholar at the Russian Research Center of Harvard University. Work on the chapter was supported by NICHD Grant Nos. HD–18027 and HD–19915. Murray Feshbach, Lubomyr Hajda, and Stephen Rapawy kindly made available copies of certain source materials. I am grateful to them, as well as to Barbara Anderson, Paul Goble, Fred Grupp, Ellen Jones, and Robert Lewis, who made constructive comments on the manuscript.

Table 4.1. Availability of nationality, language, and religion data in Russian and Soviet census reports, 1897–1979

	1897	1926	1939	1959	1970	1979
Native language	x	x	x	x	x	x
Second language					x	x
Religion	x					
Nationality/*Narodnost'*		x	x	x	x	x

form in which the results are reported, in particular, whether the data on ethnicity are cross-tabulated in the census reports with information on age, sex, education, marital status, occupation, migration history, and other variables. A summary of the extent to which each indicator has been cross-tabulated with other census variables is presented in the Index (see also Anderson, 1977; Arutyunyan et al., 1984: 42–43) but will not be discussed in the text. The main issues treated here will be (1) the formulation of questions on nationality, religion, and language; (2) the meaning of the responses; and (3) the use of Soviet census data on nationality and language in conjunction with other sources of information on the ethnic composition and linguistic practices of the Soviet population.

In treating the formulation and meaning of the census questions on nationality, religion, and language, I focus on the questions' validity—the correspondence between the census measures and the concepts for which the measures are the operational indicators. There are two main sources of invalidity of the census measures: (1) vagueness or uncertainty in the definition of the concept that the census question is intended to measure operationally; and (2) imprecision or bias in the measurement of the concept—in the wording of the census question, the method of asking the question (including the instructions to the census enumerators), and the method of tabulating the results. A focus on the validity of the census measures is appropriate because no single publication has compiled information on the formulation and interpretation of the measures and because several important features of these measures have not been examined carefully by users of the census data.

For example, although nationality, language, and religion may each be regarded as self-standing dimensions of the ethnic or cultural composition of a population, and although for the most part the three dimensions have been treated as independent questions during the gathering of Russian and Soviet census data, the independence of these indicators has often been compromised during the processing of the data for publication. Certain operational rules have been employed that lessen the independence of the indicators. The significance of these rules has not been widely recognized.

The 1897 Census

The history of the confounding of the different ethnic dimensions can be dated from the interpretation of "native language" in the 1897 census (Russian Empire, 1905a; 1905b; 1905c). In the six general population censuses for which results have been published, only the 1897 census asked about religion; the unpublished 1937 census also included a question on religion (Gozulov, 1936: 131–32; Pustokhod and Voblyy, 1936: 202–5). Because the 1897 census is also the only one that did not include a question about nationality, one might initially suppose that the census designers intended to treat religion as a surrogate for nationality. In fact, however, they intended to treat native language as a surrogate for nationality, while religion was a self-standing question included for other purposes (Russian Empire, 1905b).

Because of a series of problems caused by the reliance on the native-language question, the ethnic composition of the Russian Empire in 1897 cannot readily be determined from the census. Most of these problems were openly acknowledged in the introductory remarks to the general summary volume of the census report (Russian Empire, 1905b: II, ii). As was noted in the report itself, native language "far from always gives a correct idea of the nationality of one or another group of the population." Confusion occurs because persons of one nationality often declare the language of another nationality as native language. In particular, the 1897 census data on native language underrepresented the size of the populations of nationalities and ethnic groups that were experiencing linguistic russification (adoption of Russian as native language), such as the Votyaks (Udmurts), Mordvinians, and Zyryans (Komi). At the same time, the data overrepresented the number of Russians in the population—perhaps intentionally, as has been suggested by Soviet population specialists (e.g., Gozulov, 1936: 201–2).

To improve the reliability of native language as an indicator of nationality, certain "corrections" were introduced. For example, the information gathered on the estates (*sosloviya*) and on religion often contained information on nationality, information that was then used to derive better estimates of the ethnic makeup of the population of certain regions. As a result of these corrections, reported native language is not derived solely from the direct census responses to the question on native language.

An even more serious problem with the native-language data, which was also acknowledged in the introduction to the summary volume, is that inadequate anticipation of the kinds of responses that would be generated led to post hoc reclassification of the responses during the preparation of the data for publication. In Dagestan, for example, many people reported as their native language the language of their village or town, making it difficult to allocate the population according to standard linguistic categories. In addition, the widespread use of such terms as "Tatar" and "Tyurk" by many different Turkic-speaking groups and the use of the term "Cherkess" as the language of many different groups in the North Caucasus confounded the problem of deriving information on ethnic groups from the native-language information. At the same time, potentially valuable information on native language was lost because the information gathered on the many different Caucasian languages or dialects was aggregated into a general category termed "Georgian."

The 1897 census report devotes much attention to religious affiliation (*religioznaya prinadlezhnost'*) or religion (*veroispovedaniye*) and presents many detailed cross-tabulations with other variables such as native language, literacy, sex, urban-rural residence, and region of the country. Every person was placed into one or another religious category, with no allowance for nonbelievers or indication of the intensity of religious belief. Furthermore, there is reason to believe that the census was constructed to maximize the estimated number of people who adhered to the Russian Orthodox religion (Gozulov, 1936: 202–3). Nonetheless, precisely because of the omission of a direct question on nationality in the 1897 census, the substantial detail in the reporting of religion in combination with native language and with numerous demographic characteristics makes the data an indispensable source of information on the ethnic composition of late-nineteenth-century Russia. However, in recent efforts to determine the ethnic composition of the Russian Empire, Soviet scholars have avoided using the 1897 census results (e.g., Bruk and Kabuzan, 1980a, 1980b; Polyakov and Kisilev, 1980).

The Soviet Censuses

Table 4.2 summarizes the formulations of the census questions on nationality and language used in the Russian and Soviet censuses. Although I follow the practice of Soviet census administrators of referring to the items on the census form as questions, the questions on nationality and native language are each simply terms on the census form, with blank spaces or boxes for the census taker to fill in. Proposals by Soviet ethnographers to have the questions on nationality and language expressed on the census protocol in sentence form have not been adopted (e.g., Bruk and Kozlov, 1968: 34; USSR, 1969c: 227).

Table 4.2. Wording of questions on nationality and language in the Russian and Soviet censuses, 1897–1979

Census year	Formulation of question	General instructions to census taker*	Answers for children
		Nationality	
1897	——	——	——
1926	*Narodnost'* (People) For foreigners: of which state are they a citizen?	To what *narodnost'* does the respondent consider himself to belong? If the respondent has difficulty answering the question, preference is given to the nationality of the mother. Since the census has the aim of defining the tribal (ethnographic) composition of the population, it is not appropriate to replace *narodnost'* by religion, citizenship-country of origin or an indicator of residing in the territory of some republic. It is possible for the answer to the question on *narodnost'* not to correspond with the answer on native language. Supplemental Instruction: Although the term *narodnost'* was adopted with the aim of emphasizing the tribal (ethnographic) composition of the population, nonetheless the definition of *narodnost'* is left to the respondent himself, and in writing the answer down it is improper to alter the respondent's answer. Persons who have lost their link with the *narodnost'* of their ancestors can indicate a *narodnost'* to which they regard themselves as belonging now.	In Urban Areas: if the *narodnost'* of children is missing and the parents belong to one *narodnost'*, children should be assigned the same *narodnost'*. If the parents belong to different *narodnosti* and an answer is missing on the *narodnost'* of a child, then preference should be given to the *narodnost'* of the mother. In Rural Areas: If the *narodnost'* of a child is missing from the form, the blank spot can be filled in only if all members of the family are of the same nationality.
1939	*Natsional'nost'* (Nationality) Citizen of which state?	Write the nationality to which the respondent considers himself to belong.	For children under 16, if their nationality is not listed on the census form, then the child is attributed the nationality of the parents if the parents both belong to the same nationality.

Ethnic and Language Dimensions

Census year	Formulation of question	General instructions to census taker*	Answers for children
		Nationality	
1959	*Natsional'nost'* (Nationality) Citizen of which state?	Write the nationality that the respondent himself indicates. For citizens of the USSR, write "USSR," but for foreigners the name of the state of which the respondent is a citizen. For persons who have no citizenship, write "without citizenship."	Nationality of children is determined by parents. In families where the father and mother belong to different nationalities, and the parents themselves have difficulty defining the nationality of the children, preference is given to the nationality of the mother.
1970	*Natsional'nost'* (Nationality) For foreigners indicate also citizenship	Write the nationality that the respondent himself indicates. For foreign citizens, after the inscription of nationality, write the name of the state of which the respondent is a citizen.	Nationality of children is determined by parents. Only in families where the father and mother belong to different nationalities and the parents have difficulty themselves in determining the nationality of children, should preference be given to the nationality of the mother.
1979	*Natsional'nost'* (Nationality) For foreigners indicate also citizenship	Write the nationality that the respondent himself indicates. For foreign citizens, after the inscription of nationality, write the name of the state of which the respondent is a citizen.	Nationality of children is determined by parents. Only in families where the father and mother belong to different nationalities and the parents have difficulty themselves in determining the nationality of children, should preference be given to the nationality of the mother.

Census year	Formulation of question	General instuctions to census taker*	Answers for children
		Native Language	
1897	*Rodnoy yazyk* (native language)	Here is written the language each person considers native for himself.	—
1926	*Rodnoy yazyk* (Native language)	The language the respondent knows best of all or that he usually speaks is identified as his native language.	If an answer to the question on native language is missing for a child age 1 or less, fill in the blank on the basis of the mother's native language.

Census year	Formulation of question	General instructions to census taker*	Answers for children
		Native Language	
		Supplemental Instruction: The native language of deaf people is considered the language that they use for communication with their associates.	Supplemental Instruction: The native language of children not knowing how to talk is considered the language of the mother.
1939	*Rodnoy yazyk* (Native language)	That language the respondent himself considers to be his native language.	For children under 16, if their native language is not listed on the census form, then the language of their nationality is to be used.
1959	*Rodnoy yazyk* (Native language)	Write the name of the language that the respondent himself considers his native language. If the respondent has difficulty naming some language as native language, then write down the language that the respondent commands best of all or that is usually used in the family. The native language of deaf people is considered the language that they read and write or that is used by their family or by a person with whom they primarily communicate. It is possible for native language not to coincide with nationality.	As the native language of children not yet able to talk, write the language usually used for conversation in the family.
1970	*Rodnoy yazyk* (Native language)	Write the name of the language that the respondent himself considers his native language. If the respondent has difficulty naming some language as native language, then write down the name of the language that he commands best of all or that is usually used in the family. The native language of deaf people is considered the language that they read and write or that is used by their family or by a person with whom they primarily communicate.	As the native language of children still not able to talk, write the language usually used for conversation in the family.

Ethnic and Language Dimensions

Census year	Formulation of question	General instructions to census taker*	Answers for children
		Native Language	
		It is possible for native language not to coincide with nationality.	
1979	*Rodnoy yazyk* (Native language)	To the question on native language write down the name of the language that the respondent himself considers his native language. It is possible for native language not to coincide with nationality. If the respondent has difficulty naming some language as native language, write down the language that he commands best of all or that is usually used in the family. The native language of deaf people is considered to be the language that they read and write or the language used by their family or those with whom they primarily communicate.	The native language of children still not able to talk, and of other young children is defined by their parents. If the parents have difficulty defining the native language of a child, write down the language usually used in conversation in the family.

Census year	Formulation of question	General instructions to census taker*	Answers for children
		Second Language	
1970	Indicate also another language of the peoples of the USSR that he freely commands.	After writing down the native language, for people freely commanding another language of the people of the USSR (i.e., able to speak freely in that language), write down which one (for example, Russian, Ukrainian). If the respondent, in addition to the native language, freely commands two or more languages of the peoples of the USSR, write down only the one of those that he commands best.	———

Census year	Formulation of question	General instructions to census taker*	Answers for children
		Second Language	
		For people who do not freely command another languge, and also for children not yet able to talk, after writing down the native language draw a line.	
1979	Indicate also another language of the peoples of the USSR that he freely commands.	After writing down the native language, for people freely commanding another language of the peoples of the USSR or knowing only how to converse freely in the given language, write down the name of the language (Russian, Ukrainian, Kazakh, Latvian, etc.).	———
		If the respondent, in addition to the native language, freely commands two or more languages of the peoples of the USSR, write down only the one of those that he knows best.	
		For persons not freely commanding another language of the peoples of the USSR, after writing the native language write "No."	

*The instructions listed in the table are general instructions that have been published by the Central Statistical Board or reported in other sources given in the References. Certain specific instructions dealing with special problems and circumstances were also issued. In the case of the 1926 census, each volume of the census report summarizes some of the special instructions that applied in particular regions.

For example, in Volume XIII it was reported that "to clarify the written answers for persons calling themselves 'Russian,' it is necessary to determine in precisely which—Russian, Ukrainian, or Belorussian—the individual places himself. 'Great Russian' (*Velikoross*) is considered the same as 'Russian' and is recorded as 'Russian' in the individual census lists."

"To clarify the written answers on language of persons answering 'Russian' language, it is necessary for the respondent to specify precisely which language—Russian, Ukrainian, or Belorussian—he has in view. If someone calls his language 'Great Russian,' then write 'Russian' in the individual census lists."

As additional examples, in the volumes reporting data for Uzbekistan and Turkmenistan, the census takers were told that "in no circumstance" were they to write Moslem, Christian, Orthodox, and so on, as an answer to the question on *narodnost'*. In Uzbekistan, census takers were instructed to interpret "Sart" as "Uzbek (Sart)." In Turkmenistan, census takers were instructed to write down not only *narodnost'* but also tribe and clan (*rod*). They were told not to confuse "Tyurki" with "Farsi" and that Persians often called themselves Tyurki-Azerbaidzhantsy or Tyurki-Persidskiy.

While there has been a reliance on self-enumeration in the U.S. Census since 1960, in the Soviet Union census takers visit each residence. Census takers are supposed to follow certain instructions in eliciting information from the respondents. Table 4.2 lists the general instructions for the questions on nationality and language in each Soviet census. Although the instructions may clarify the intended meanings of certain terms for the census takers, the instructions are not necessarily read to the respondents. Hence, the respondents are less likely than the census takers to be informed of the intended interpretations.

Subjective measures. The census questions are designed to elicit the subjective nationality and the subjective native language of the respondent. "Nationality" is a completely open-ended question, with the response to be written verbatim on the census blank. Similarly, "native language" is supposed to be inscribed verbatim and is whatever the respondent declares it to be. The census takers are instructed not to check any documents during the census; they are to accept an answer to the question on nationality that is inconsistent with the answer to the question on native language. The classification of the population by nationality and by native language is exhaustive, and everyone has a nationality and a native language. There are no reported "don't knows" or missing data on these questions.

Because of the subjectivity of the census measures of nationality and native language, neither characteristic of an individual is necessarily permanent or "official." Although it has been suggested that the use of nationality labels on individual internal passports, personnel records, and other official documents may "fix" the subjective nationality of people in the USSR, especially after adolescence (Kozlov, 1969: 298; 1975: 230–31), strong empirical evidence exists that self-identified nationality often changes between censuses even among people who are beyond their adolescent years (Anderson and Silver, 1983).

There is no inconsistency between international practice and the Soviet census's treatment of nationality and native language as subjective indicators because there is no uniform international standard. A large variety of classifications by race, language, nativity, citizenship, and ethnic group are used in the censuses of other countries. There is no standard classification of ethnic groups or languages comparable to the International Standard Classification of Occupations. U.S. censuses have used a variety of classifications by race and "nativity"; measures of country of birth of the respondents or of their parents have often served as imperfect surrogates for measures of "ethnic group" or "nationality" (Shryock and Siegel, 1976: 145–46).

A positive feature of the Soviet census's approach to measuring nationality is its consistency with the notion of ethnicity preferred by many contemporary scholars as essentially a notion based on self-definition (e.g., Barth, 1969; Kozlov, 1969; Armstrong, 1982). By not linking census nationality by definition to official nationality, Soviet census planners have made it easier for census respondents to define their own nationality and to change their ethnic self-designation between censuses. The same emphasis on measuring change applies to the self-designation of native language.

For this reason, inconsistency of individual responses from one census to the next is not necessarily indicative of measurement error in the censuses. Measurement of nationality and language in successive censuses is not designed as, and should not be regarded as, a test-retest reliability check. In contrast, inconsistency between successive measures of characteristics such as race or country of birth used in the censuses of other countries would be a sign of unreliability. Instead, the Soviet measures are designed to register intercensal change—although on the aggregate, rather than the individual, level.

Instructions to census takers. When questioning adults in a household, the census taker has essentially only (according to the typical instruction—see Table 4.2) to "write down the nationality (native language) that the respondent himself indicates." The census takers receive written instructions about what to do if the respondents have difficulty answering the questions. What is not known is how well the formal instructions are followed in practice; there are no published studies by Soviet scholars of the extent to which census enumerators comply with the instructions, although some errors by census takers have been mentioned.

During both the 1959 and 1970 censuses, for example, many census takers mistakenly inscribed the word for a female Even (*evenka*) when they should have used the term for a female Evenk (*evenkiyka*), and this mistake led to a serious undercount of female Evenks and an overestimate of the number of female Evens (Ter-Izrael'yan, 1979: 192). A more consequential error may have occurred involving Ukrainians living in the Kuban' region of the RSFSR. A. S. Bezhkovich (1967) has speculated that in the 1959 census, census takers frequently confused the response "*rus'kiy*," a term used as a self-identification by some Ukrainians, with its near homonym "*russkiy*," which means Russian. Although official census documents for the 1959 and 1970 censuses (USSR, 1959; 1969a), to which Bezhkovich does not refer, clearly state that people who claim *rus'kiy* as their nationality were supposed to be classified as Ukrainian, he suggests that the response "*rus'kiy*" was mistakenly interpreted as "*russkiy*." This practice (in addition to assimilation, the agricultural collectivization and the 1932–3 famine, and emigration from the region) could partly account for the sharp decline in the number of reported Ukrainians in the Kuban' between 1926 and 1959.

We would like to know who in the household generally answers census questions and how accurately and consistently the recorded responses to the questions on nationality and native language represent the direct oral responses of each member of the household. Either the general instructions to the census takers or the specific instructions for the questions on nationality and native language deal with the situation of children, of deaf people, and of people who are temporarily absent from their permanent place of residence. The information on the nationality and native language of children is especially important because it can be used to measure intergenerational change, but the instructions themselves are not complete (see Table 4.2). For example, the instructions do not state clearly under which circumstances the answers for children are to be given by parents (Kuvshinova, 1984: 27). Although in the last three censuses the nationality of children was supposed to be reported by parents, the instructions do not define what age these "children" were supposed to be. For the questions on native language, census takers were instructed in most censuses to follow one rule or another to determine the native language of children who were not yet able to talk, but how the native language of children who *were* able to talk was supposed to be determined or was in fact determined is not clear.

The instructions for the 1979 census stated that the native language of all "young children" (age not defined) was to be determined by the parents (see Table 4.2). This seems to imply that the native language of "old" children was to be determined by some other means, perhaps by the children themselves. The instructions for earlier Soviet censuses, however, did not tell how to determine the native language of either young or old children who were able to talk. Thus, although in principle all census responses to the questions on nationality and native language are to reflect the subjective judgment of Soviet citizens, the nationality of children (age not specified) is defined by the parents, and the native language of children not yet able to talk is also determined by the parents, but the native language of other children (except for "young" children) is presumably not determined by parents.

Nationality in the Soviet Censuses

Terminology. A special Soviet terminology classifies ethnic units or communities according to their stage of historical development as clan/tribes, peoples, and nations. However, leading Soviet ethnographers have recently supported use of a general term "ethnic community" (*etnicheskaya obshchnost'*) or "ethnos" (*etnos*) that incorporates or subsumes the different types of ethnic community (e.g., Kozlov, 1969: 15-26; Bromley, 1981: 10-45). In addition, the term "ethnic group" (*etnicheskaya gruppa*) is commonly reserved for references to small ethnic communities or to clusters of people belonging to larger nationalities but residing as minorities away from the primary area of geographic concentration of their nationality.

In administrative practice and in census usage, however, the Russian concept of *natsional'nost'* (nationality) is the common generic term used to refer to the ethnic affiliation of Soviet citizens (Kozlov, 1977: 32). The Russian meaning of *natsional'nost'* is essentially equivalent to the Western notions of both ethnic affiliation and ethnic group (Clem, 1980: 12). Therefore, despite the special Soviet usage of the term "ethnic group," the term "nationality" is used here interchangeably with the terms "ethnic group" and "ethnic affiliation."

Except for the 1926 census, which used the term *narodnost'* (people), the general population censuses of the Soviet Union have consistently employed a single Russian concept to express the basic ethnic or nationality affiliation of the population: *natsional'nost'* (nationality). The 1926 census employed the concept *narodnost'* rather than *natsional'nost'* even though the latter term had been used in the censuses of 1920 and 1923. During the planning for the 1926 census, a controversy arose between those who wanted to obtain a picture of the ethnographic composition of the population and those who wanted to depict the nationality composition of the population in the form that it was taking as a result of the post-revolutionary self-determination of nationalities (Vorob'ev, 1957: 27). The proponents of the first opinion won out, and the term *narodnost'* was chosen because this term was thought to reflect better the notion of ethnic origins. It was believed that people would more readily claim affiliation with a *narodnost'* or ethnic group of the population than with a *natsional'nost'*—a concept closely linked to that of *natsiya* (nation).

The 1939, 1959, 1970, and 1979 census forms included a question on *natsional'nost'* (nationality) in place of the question on *narodnost'*. The concept of nationality as employed in the censuses has been criticized by Soviet ethnographers (e.g., Bruk and Kozlov, 1967: 5) who argue that it is not well understood by the broad masses of the population, but its repeated use over time—with no change in the wording and little change in the instructions to the census takers—has the virtue of permitting longitudinal comparison of the distribution of the Soviet population by ethnic group. In addition, the use of the term "nationality" in Soviet

Ethnic and Language Dimensions 83

administrative practice and in official documents and statistics is by now so well established that few people are likely to have any difficulty identifying themselves as belonging to a nationality.

The number of distinct nationalities. One important problem in the study of ethnicity in the USSR is that of labeling and counting distinct ethnic groups. Determining how many nationalities existed in the USSR at each census date is not simple. The number of the nationalities actually listed in tables of the census reports always falls short of the number mentioned in Soviet literature about the census. Even within a given census report, some nationalities are listed only in footnotes, are included in some summary tables but not others, are collapsed together with other nationalities for some purposes, or are lumped into an "other" category. For example, one secondary source (Isupov, 1964: 12) refers to an official list of 126 ethnic groups used for tabulating the 1959 census results, but the summary volume of the 1959 census report (USSR, 1963) lists only 109 nationalities in the main tables and roughly another half dozen in footnotes.

Nevertheless, Soviet scholars generally acknowledge that the number of nationalities enumerated in the censuses has diminished substantially over time. Furthermore, the reduction in the number of distinct ethnic or nationality groups is often said to result not only from ethnic assimilation but also from a change in the main concept employed in the census question from *narodnost'* in 1926 to *natsional'nost'* in later census years. As evidence supporting such a conclusion, it is noted that the 1926 census report listed 194 distinct ethnic titles (160 titles of nationalities that are treated as indigenous to the USSR), while the 1939 census listed only 97 such titles (62 indigenous to the USSR) (e.g., Isupov, 1964: 12). One difficulty with this argument is that about 20 of the 194 *narodnosti* listed in the 1926 census report either had no recorded population, had populations so small that the groups were subsumed under other ethnic labels in the published reports (USSR, 1928; 1929), or were combined with other groups in some tables (e.g., Czechs and Slovaks). Bruk and Kozlov (1967: 6) note that separate population figures were provided in the 1926 census report for only 178 *narodnosti*.

A second difficulty with this argument is that in tabulating census results from 1959 and later census years approximately 125 different ethnic titles were employed—that is, an increase since 1939, even though the term *natsional'nost'* was used both in 1939 and in all subsequent censuses. The major reason for the pattern of change over time is that the number of officially recognized nationalities in the 1939 census was, in the words of Bruk and Kozlov (1967: 6), "artificially contracted." A. A. Isupov, the director of the 1979 Soviet census, in 1964 attributed the small size of the list of nationalities in 1939 to the "influence of the [Stalin] personality cult" (Isupov, 1964: 12).

A third difficulty with the argument that use of the term *natsional'nost'* in place of *narodnost'* led to a reduction in the number of distinct ethnic entities is that it assumes that the set of nationalities or peoples listed in the census reports is determined empirically by the number of ethnonyms that people offer in their verbatim responses to the census question on nationality. It is not widely recognized among Western scholars who use Soviet census data that the "nationalities" included in the census reports are partly synthetic. The way in which native-language responses in the 1897 census were handled was not repeated in later censuses; instead, much planning preceded the tabulation of the questions on nationality and language. This planning was not only technical but also involved policy decisions on whether or not to treat some groups as distinct nationalities.

For the 1926 census, for example, the compilation of the data by *narodnost'* was based on a "List of Peoples of the USSR" (*Perechen' narodnostey SSSR*) prepared by the Commission of the Academy of Sciences on the Study of the Ethnic (*plemennogo*) Composition of the Population of the USSR (USSR, 1928; Vorob'ev, 1957: 55; Bruk and Kozlov, 1967: 12–13). As is stated in the 1926 census report, the "List of Peoples of the USSR" was supplemented by a "Glossary of Peoples of the USSR" (*Slovar' narodnostey SSSR*) to be used by local statistical administrations to place the numerous concrete names of *narodnosti* within the categories of the official "List." The 194 *narodnosti* listed in the 1926 census report amounted to only one quarter to one third of the actual number of ethnic subdivisions in the Soviet population (Kozlov, 1982: 7).

Both a glossary of nationalities and a glossary of languages were employed in the 1939 census (Pustokhod and Voblyy, 1940: 155; Pod"yachikh, 1957b: 32) Work by Soviet ethnographers and linguists also contributed to the tabulation of the data on nationality and language from the 1959 and 1970 censuses. The 126 ethnic titles (92 of which were for "indigenous" nationalities) used for tabulating the 1959 census results were reduced from 733 distinct ethnic titles included in a "Glossary of Nationalities and Languages" prepared before the census was fielded (USSR, 1959; Isupov, 1964: 12). The 117 main languages identified in the census report were condensed from a total of more than 320 "names of languages and dialects" in the glossary (Bruk and Kozlov, 1967: 13; USSR, 1959). A slightly modified "Glossary of Nationalities and Languages" (USSR, 1969a) was used in tabulating the results of the questions on nationality and language in the 1970 census, and a similar glossary was employed in the 1979 census (Zinchenko, 1984: 151).

Unfortunately, no figures on the distribution of the Soviet population among the over 700 ethnic self-designations or the over 300 language-dialects listed in the glossaries in 1959 and 1970 have been published. The published census volumes report the ethnic and linguistic composition of the population only within the larger synthetic groupings. However, when one considers the need for such large lists of ethnonyms and languages to complete the census tabulation, it seems reasonable to conclude that the shift from the concept of *narodnost'* to the concept of *natsional'nost'* is much less important than other factors in determining how many separate ethnic groups are listed in the census reports.

Even if we do not have tabulations of the Soviet population using the detailed ethnographic and linguistic groups identified in the glossaries, the information contained in the glossaries themselves is valuable. The glossaries reveal that the census question on nationality does not provide the sole "ethnic" information used to derive the reported total population sizes of nationalities. In fact, the ethnic composition of the Soviet population as reported in the recent censuses is determined in part by the data on native language. For example, the case of the Cossacks in the 1970 census is instructive. The glossary for the 1970 census (USSR, 1969a) states that people who claimed Cossack as their nationality but claimed Russian as their native language were to be classified by nationality as Russians in the census report, while people who claimed Cossack as their nationality but claimed Ukrainian as their native language were to be classified by nationality as Ukrainians. This classification rule could also help to account for the substantial decline in the number of Ukrainians (Ukrainian Cossacks) in some regions between 1926 and later census years: if some Ukrainian Cossacks shifted their native language to Russian while calling themselves Cossack (but not Ukrainian) by nationality, they were classified in the census as having Russian nationality. Moreover, since Ukrainians in the RSFSR lack native-language schools and mass media, their accelerated linguistic russification (given the classification rule just described) would lead to an administrative transformation of Ukrainians into Russians.

Similarly, people who claimed to be Kypchaks by nationality were reclassified by nationality as Uzbeks if they claimed Uzbek as their native language and as Kazakhs if they claimed Kazakh as their native language. In numerous other cases in the glossaries, native-language information is employed to determine nationality. For instance, the problem that confounded the tabulators of the 1897 census of how to classify ethnically the numerous peoples who called themselves "Tyurk" has been solved in recent censuses by use of the information gathered on native language. Tyurks with Azerbaydzhani as their native language are classified by nationality as Azerbaydzhanis, Tyurks with Turkmeni as their native language are classified as Turkmenis, Tyurks with Uzbek as their native language are classified as Uzbeks, and so on.

The glossaries also provide a valuable guide to ways in which the 194 *narodnosti* listed in the 1926 census can be "mapped" onto the approximately 125 *natsional'nosti* listed in the recent Soviet census reports. The 1926 census, for example, listed as separate *narodnosti* the following groups: Tatars, Kryasheny, Mishars, Teptyars, and Nagaybaks. The "Glossary of Nationalities and Languages" for the 1970 census listed Kryasheny, Mishars, Teptyars, and Nagaybaks (among others) as "other names that might be encountered on the census forms" that belong to the Tatar "nationality." Although there are some inconsistencies between the glossaries for 1959 and 1970, these glossaries, in combination with data from other sources, such as Soviet monographs on language (e.g., Isayev, 1970; 1978) and Soviet and Western writings on the ethnography of the Soviet population (e.g., Wixman, 1980; 1984), make it possible to devise a nearly exhaustive mapping of the *narodnosti* from 1926 onto the *natsional'nosti* in the recent census reports. A similar, though crude, mapping between 1897 and 1926 was published in a short compendium (USSR, 1928) to the 1926 census report. Additional information from the 1926 census on the aggregated 1926 *narodnosti* that form part of a given (later) nationality, such as data on literacy, native language, or geographic location, can also be combined to establish a referent or base for measuring change over time.

Uncertainty exists, however, concerning the extent to which the combining of ethnic groups in the glossaries reflects actual assimilation or consolidation of ethnic groups rather than only a paper transfer of ethnic affiliations from smaller to larger groups. In other words, census users are uncertain whether the merging of ethnic groups in the recent census reports registers a social rather than a bureaucratic phenomenon. Furthermore, the extent to which the use of linguistic data to classify people by nationality affects the relative sizes of nationalities cannot be precisely determined. The extent of the administrative transformation of Ukrainian Cossacks into Russians, for example, depends both on how many Ukrainian Cossacks call themselves Cossack rather than Ukrainian during the census and on how many Ukrainian Cossacks have adopted Russian as native language.

A "Soviet" nationality? Prior to the 1979 census, V. I. Kozlov, the leading Soviet ethnic demographer, proposed that a category "Soviet nationality" be added to the 1979 census list of nationalities (Ter-

Izrael'yan, 1979: 190). Kozlov proposed that this category be used for people who had difficulty defining their ethnic affiliation, and he stated that this catagory would most likely be employed by people who had long ago been separated from their nationality and by children of ethnically mixed marriages. Kozlov also maintained that the census instruction to assign nationality of children of mixed marriages according to the nationality of the mother was incorrect because it treated nationality as a biological phenomenon rather than a social phenomenon based on self-consciousness.

No Soviet censuses had ever included a category "Soviet nationality." Nothing akin to the category "Yugoslavs nationally undeclared" employed in recent Yugoslav censuses (Shoup, 1981) had ever been employed in the Soviet censuses. Instead, all citizens had been classified into specific *ethnic* groups (nationalities). Kozlov's proposal for the 1979 census was not adopted. Had his proposal been adopted, it would probably have been difficult to confine the use of the category "Soviet nationality" to cases where respondents had trouble defining their nationality or where children had parents of different nationalities and parents had trouble determining the nationality of their children. Although there is every indication that Kozlov's motivation was to provide an accurate ethnographic accounting of the Soviet population, use of the term "Soviet nationality" would almost inevitably have become politicized, mainly because of the strong official doctrinal emphasis in the past two decades on the emergence of a "new historical community of people—the Soviet people" (*sovetskiy narod*), a form of community that is said to transcend traditional ethnic allegiances.

In view of this doctrinal emphasis, it is interesting that a "Soviet nationality" category was not added to the list of acceptable responses. One reason may have been that addition of a new category could have had very unpredictable or undesirable results (from the government's standpoint). Since historical evidence shows that Russians have assimilated substantial numbers of non-Russians (cf. Kozlov, 1975; Lewis, Rowland, and Clem, 1976; Anderson and Silver, 1983), one can speculate that many people who identified themselves as Russians in the 1979 census and who could trace their ancestry to non-Russian origins might well have chosen the label "Soviet nationality" rather than "Russian" if encouraged to do so. The number of self-identified Russians who chose this label might have exceeded the number of self-identified non-Russians who found it attractive to call themselves "Soviet." Since self-identified Russians amounted to only 52.4 percent of the Soviet population in the 1979 census, providing a "Soviet nationality" category might have eliminated the Russian numerical majority.

Native Language in the Soviet Censuses

All of the general Russian and Soviet population censuses have included a question on *rodnoy yazyk,* sometimes translated in English as "mother tongue" and sometimes as "native language." The term in Russian has not differed across censuses, although, as noted earlier, the instructions to census takers have changed somewhat (see Table 4.2).

The United Nations defines "mother tongue" for census purposes as "the language usually spoken in the individual's home in his early childhood" (Shryock and Siegel, 1976: 157). The UN states that the criterion for determining language for children not yet able to speak should be clearly indicated. Soviet censuses do clearly identify the latter criterion, but the Soviet interpretation of "mother tongue" differs substantially from the UN definition.

"Native language" is not a precise linguistic concept and does not have a clear empirical referent. While most Soviet scholars interpret the term to mean conversational language, many people, including many respondents to the censuses, apparently regard native language as something else—perhaps as the language used in the family when they were children, the language spoken by their mothers, or the language of their nationality. Furthermore, numerous sociolinguistic surveys conducted in the USSR have shown that the language that people claim as their native language is sometimes not the language they use most frequently, use in the family, know best, or occasionally even know at all (e.g., see Bruk and Kozlov, 1967: 10; Arutyunyan, 1973: 292; Klement'yev, 1974: 35).

Soviet scholars have debated the meaning of native language at the All-Union Conferences of Statisticians held on the eve of each of the last three censuses to review the census plans (USSR, 1958b, 1969c; Ter-Izrael'yan, 1979). During each debate, some scholars have proposed substituting a question on "conversational language" for the question on native language or including a separate question on conversational language on the census form. Each time, the proposal has been rejected. Thus, the formulation of the question on native language has gone essentially unchanged for the past five censuses.

The most telling argument against changing the wording of the question on native language was offered in 1967 by the director of the All-Union Census Bureau, P. G. Pod"yachikh, who asserted that the question should remain unchanged for the sake of continuity and comparability with previous census results (USSR, 1969c: 178).[1] At the All-Union Conference of Statisticians held in May 1977, the close subjective link between native language and nationality and the impor-

---

1. This position was challenged by a prominent Soviet ethnographer, S. I. Bruk, on grounds that if earlier data were unsatisfactory, nothing would be lost if there were no comparability with better, later data (USSR, 1969c: 226).

tance of native language as a symbol of national consciousness were also cited as substantial reasons not to drop the question on native language (Ter-Izrael'yan, 1979: 159). Thus, a major accepted rationale for including the native-language question in the Soviet census is the significance of native language as an ethnic rather than a linguistic indicator.

It should not be surprising that a subjective measure of native language turns out not to match a well-defined set of objective linguistic capabilities or behaviors. This does not mean, however, that the indicator is unrelated to linguistic behavior. Even if some people claim a given language as native while they do not use it or know it well, comparing the proportion of the population that claims a given language as native across nationalities still provides a useful comparative indicator of linguistic behavior.

In this vein, some Soviet scholars have suggested that native language can perhaps be most usefully regarded as another measure of ethnic group attachment rather than as a measure of language use (Kozlov, 1969: 299; Guboglo, 1972: 32; Bondarchik, 1980: 214). Change of native language may therefore denote change in one indicator of ethnic attachment rather than change in language use. Although native language cannot serve as a definitive indicator of ethnic attachment, census data on native language can be used for most nationalities to represent a stage in an overall process of assimilation (Kozlov, 1975).

Second Language in the 1970 and 1979 Censuses

The meaning of the question on second language, which was added to the 1970 and 1979 censuses, has been controversial. The formulation of this question in the 1970 and 1979 censuses is given in Table 4.2. This formulation has been challenged on several grounds, the most common criticism being the lack of precision of the term "to freely command" (*svobodno vladet'*). When the question was introduced into the 1970 census plan, Pod"yachikh stated that the phrase "freely command" was generally understood to mean "freely converse," but he conceded that the phrase was in fact "loose" (*rastyazhimyy*), and he invited proposals for a more precise formulation (USSR, 1969c: 239). However, proposals made prior to the 1979 census that the qualifier "freely" be dropped and that the question be rephrased to ask whether people could freely speak, freely read, or freely write were not accepted (Ter-Izrael'yan, 1979: 118, 159–60).

Another criticism of the question has been directed at its restriction to "languages of the peoples of the USSR." One Soviet writer defended this restriction as follows: "Some comrades who were working on the plan of the [1970] census program proposed to ask people about their knowledge of foreign languages, but because of the extreme subjectivity of the personal assessment of such knowledge, the question [on foreign languages] was not included on the census list" (Kolpakov, 1969: 31). Considering the many strong criticisms of the validity of the second-language question in general, this defense cannot be taken seriously. Pod"yachikh offered what appears to have been a definitive justification at the All-Union Conference of Statisticians in 1967 (USSR, 1969c: 314). He stated that he initially preferred not to limit the responses to indigenous languages, but "a judgment was made" to put the words "of the peoples of the USSR" into the formulation in order to help study the rapprochement (*sblizhenie*) among peoples of the USSR.

In the context of the heightened emphasis at that time on spreading knowledge of Russian as a second language among the non-Russian nationalities, and in the context of an ideological campaign to promote rapprochement between Russians and non-Russians, it seems likely that both the inclusion and the formulation of the question on second language were designed to provide the government with measures of its success in spreading Russian-language knowledge and of the level of sympathy for Russians among the non-Russian nationalities. In fact, Soviet officials frequently cited the 1970 census results on the knowledge of Russian language among non-Russians when comparing the performance of different non-Russian republics in teaching the Russian language. Moreover, maintaining the question on second language in the 1979 census protocol was defended at the 1977 All-Union Conference of Statisticians as having "enormous significance, since it allows examination of the spread and functioning of the language of inter-nationality discourse—the Russian language" (Ter-Izrael'yan, 1979: 159).

That the non-Russian populations, or key officials in some of the republics, understand the importance of the message conveyed by the census results on second language perhaps explains the volatility of the second-language figures between 1970 and 1979. For example, between the censuses of those years, the Uzbeks took an enormous leap forward, from 15 percent claiming Russian as a second language in 1970 to 49 percent in 1979, while the Estonians took a long step backward, from 29 percent claiming Russian as a second language to 24 percent. Though not impossible, neither of these shifts seems likely to reflect real change in linguistic competency.

Two other implications of the formulation of the question on second language deserve mention. First, the decision to record only one "other" language means that the census results distort the language facility of many non-Russians in another way. Among certain nationalities, trilingualism is historically very common. Second, how census respondents are to know which languages are "of the peoples of the USSR" is not defined in the census instructions. However, the published census figures for 1970 and 1979 make it clear that although "nonindigenous" peoples can claim their own nationality's traditional language as their native language, they cannot officially "freely command" their group's language as a second language. No Soviet Germans, for example, are recorded as commanding German as a second language.

Relating Census Data and Other Data on Nationality and Language

Data on nationality derived from the Soviet censuses are often used in conjunction with data on nationality developed from other sources. Data from other sources almost always represent a form of official nationality. Most Soviet citizens, for example, have an internal passport that lists their nationality. The passport system (which was created in 1932) and the registration of changes in residence, births, and deaths all rely on the notion of an official nationality. In addition, school records and work records contain information on nationality. These records are the source of such official statistics as data on the nationality composition of professional manpower or of enrollees in institutions of higher education (Feshbach, 1962).

Although some Soviet scholars (e.g., V. I. Kozlov) argue that there is likely to be substantial consistency between "official nationality" and "census nationality," Soviet sources provide no empirical evidence about the extent of such consistency. Because the two notions of nationality are derived in very different ways, statistical distortions can result when data from two sources are combined. For example, if a large proportion of people whose official nationality is non-Russian—and thus are reported as members of a non-Russian nationality by employers—claim to be Russian in the census, then per capita figures on professional manpower in that nationality will be overestimated. Similarly, any statistical rates that rely on both census data on nationality and reports of official nationality, such as marriage registration, births by nationality of the mother, death registration, and migration, could be distorted. Especially for populations experiencing substantial ethnic assimilation, among whom a shift in official nationality is likely to lag behind a shift in census nationality, any statistics that combine official and census nationality data could be very distorted.

Combining census and noncensus information on native language presents a different kind of problem. Soviet sociological studies of language practices often ask respondents to identify their native language as well as, among other things, what language they use in various social spheres (home, workplace, media, and so on). These studies (e.g., Arutyunyan, 1973) are the main source of information about the link between "native language" and actual language behavior. Although a rich fund of information on language use, the studies have not generated data that can be compared directly with census data on language: the samples have not been designed to be representative of population units comparable to those used in the censuses, only a few nationalities have been studied, and none of the studies is USSR-wide. Hence, these studies have limited use for validating or invalidating the census results, and the Soviet censuses remain the only source of information on the language preferences of the entire Soviet population.[2]

Conclusion: General Assessment of the Reliability of Census Nationality and Language Data

Second Language

There is reason to question the reliability of the second-language data from the 1970 and 1979 Soviet censuses. The term "freely command" was not clearly defined. During the administration of the census, the respondents' language ability was not tested. Moreover, census takers were not supposed to prompt or to question the respondents' answers as to whether they did or did not "freely command" a language. In short, the respondents' answers to the question on second language are purely subjective.

Because of the apparent special purpose of the second-language question, many census takers and respondents are likely to have accepted a liberal approach to claiming free command of Russian as a second language. In some cases, as the 1979 data for the Estonians seem to suggest, a certain amount of strategic underreporting of knowledge of Russian as a second language may also have occurred. But in general, the census data on second language probably exaggerate the number of non-Russians who are fluent in Russian.

Assertions by Soviet scholars that the census may underestimate the extent of knowledge of Russian among non-Russians, though based on independent empirical research (e.g., Bruk and Guboglo, 1974; Guboglo, 1978), have not been based on either representative samples of the non-Russian population or an explicit comparison of results using the census wording ("freely command") and results using other questions or

2. In January 1985, the Central Statistical Administration conducted a special "Sample Socio-Demographic Study of the Population." Based on a 5-percent sample, the study covered the entire Soviet population, with the exception of the Far North and a few other regions not readily accessible during January (Troshina, 1984). This "midcensus" study included the standard Soviet question on nationality (Labutova, 1984) but no questions on language. The published results may provide a useful censuslike source of systematic information about the ethnic composition of the USSR.

question formats. The differences in the results between the sociolinguistic surveys and the censuses appear to have two main causes: (1) differences in the level of Russian-language competency measured and (2) differences in the measuring instrument, with the surveys focusing on specific competencies (reading, writing, conversing) and the censuses focusing on a general self-assessment of the respondent's "command" of Russian. Although sociolinguistic surveys suggest that more non-Russians can read or write or converse in Russian than claim to command it freely, the surveys have not shown that more non-Russians think that they "freely command" Russian (using the census formulation) than is revealed by the census data.

It is clear from the debates at the recent All-Union Conferences of Soviet Statisticians that the "freely command" formulation in the 1970 and 1979 censuses is more restrictive than the proposed alternatives, which are analogous to those used in sociolinguistic surveys by Guboglo and others. Consequently, while the data for the second-language question probably underestimate the number of non-Russians who know some Russian, the data could at the same time overestimate the number of non-Russians who can converse fluently in Russian. But the central problem with the second-language question is that the formulation "freely command another language of the peoples of the USSR" is vague.

Native Language

The measure of native language appears to be less volatile than the second-language measure. In addition, any bias in the responses probably runs in the opposite direction from the bias in the responses to the second-language question for several reasons.

First, responses to the census question on native language are likely to be constrained by certain features of the census-taking process itself. Most census takers are likely to be fluent in Russian. Although census takers are not supposed to administer a language test at the doorstep, we expect that they would be skeptical about people who claimed Russian as their native language but did not speak it well. Hence, it seems unlikely, though not impossible, that people who claimed to be non-Russian by nationality would have claimed Russian (or some language other than the language of their nationality) as their native language if they did not at least speak it fluently. Second, with the advent of the second-language question, non-Russians who want to claim knowledge of Russian have another way of doing so. The use of this question could retard the tendency of non-Russians to claim Russian as native language.

Third, to the extent that *rodnoy yazyk* is interpreted by some non-

Russians as "the language of their childhood" (consistent, by the way, with the UN definition), the census figures on native language are likely to underestimate the extent of linguistic russification. It might be more common for non-Russians to claim the traditional language of their nationa.ity as native language even if they do not speak it well than for them to claim Russian as native language if they do not speak Russian fluently.

On balance, then, considering the various potential sources of bias, the bias in the native-language responses seems likely to be toward overestimating use of the traditional language of the respondent's nationality. Similarly, any bias in native language as an indicator of ethnic attachment rather than of language use is likely to be toward greater consistency between self-identified nationality and self-identified native language.

Nationality

Of the three main census items discussed here, the question on nationality appears to be the most reliable. Both Soviet and non-Soviet researchers commonly employ Soviet census data on nationality as key indicators of ethnic-group attachment or identity. Although some problems in enumeration by nationality have been noted, the nationality question on the census forms has evoked little controversy or even discussion in recent years. That the nationalities listed in the census reports represent something of a distillation from a larger set of ethnic self-designations has not been controversial.

References

Anderson, Barbara A. 1977. "Data Sources in Russian and Soviet Demography." In *Demographic Developments in Eastern Europe*, ed. Leszek A. Kosinski, 23–63. New York: Praeger.

Anderson, Barbara A., and Brian D. Silver. 1983. "Estimating Russification of Ethnic Identity among Non-Russians in the USSR." *Demography* 20, no. 4: 461–89.

Armstrong, John A. 1982. *Nations before Nationalism*. Chapel Hill: University of North Carolina Press.

Arutyunvan, Yu. V. 1973. *Sotsial'noye i natsional'noye (Opyt etnosotsiologicheskikh issledovaniy po materialam Tatarskoy ASSR)*. Moscow: Nauka.

Arutyunyan, Yu. V., L. M. Drobizheva, V. S. Kondrat'yev, and A. A. Susokolov. 1984. *Etnosotsiologiya: Tseli, metody i nekotorye rezul'taty issledovaniya*.

Barth, Fredrik, ed. 1969. *Ethnic Groups and Boundaries*. Bergen: Universitetsforlaget.

Bezhkovich, A. S. 1967. "Sovremennyy etnicheskiy sostav naseleniya Krasnodarskogo

kraya." *Doklady po etnografii,* Vypusk 5, 126–42. Leningrad: Geograficheskoye Obshchestvo SSSR, Otdeleniye Etnografii.
Bondarchik, V. K., ed. 1980. *Etnicheskiye protsessy i obraz zhizni (Na materialakh issledovaniya naseleniya gorodov BSSR).* Minsk: Nauka i Tekhnika.
Bromley, Yu. V. 1981. *Sovremennye problemy etnografii (Orcherki teorii i istorii).* Moscow: Nauka.
Bruk, S. I. 1971. "Etnodemograficheskiye protsessy v SSSR (Po materialam perepisi 1970 goda)." *Sovetskaya etnografiya,* no. 4: 8–30.
Bruk, S. I., and M. N. Guboglo. 1974. "Razvitiye i vzaimodeystviye etnodemograficheskikh i etnolingvisticheskikh protsessov v sovetskom obshchestve na sovremennom etape." *Istorya SSSR,* no. 4: 26–45.
Bruk, S. I., and V. M. Kabuzan. 1980a. "Dinamika i etnicheskiy sostav naseleniya Rossii v epokhu imperializma (konets XIX v.–1917 g.)." *Istoriya SSSR,* no. 3.
———. 1980b. "Etnicheskiy sostav naseleniya rossii (1719–1917)." *Sovetskaya etnografiya,* no. 6: 18–33.
Bruk, S. I., and V. I. Kozlov. 1967. "Etnograficheskaya nauka i perepis' naseleniya 1970 goda," *Sovetskaya etnografiya,* no. 5: 3–14.
———. 1968. "Voprosy o national'nosti i yazyke v predstoyashchey perepisi naseleniya." *Vestnik statistiki,* no. 3: 32–37.
Clem, Ralph S. 1980. "The Ethnic Dimension of the Soviet Union." In *Centemporary Soviet Society: Sociological Perspectives,* ed. Jerry G. Pankhurst and Michael Paul Sacks, 11–62. New York: Praeger.
Feshbach, Murray. 1962. *The Soviet Statistical System: Labor Force Recordkeeping and Reporting since 1957.* U.S., Bureau of the Census, International Population Statistics Reports, Series P–90, no. 17. Washington, D.C.: Government Printing Office.
Gozulov, A. I. 1936. *Perepisi naseleniya SSSR i kapitalisticheskikh stran (Opyt istoriko-metodologicheskoy kharakhteristiki proizvodstva perepisey naseleniya).* Moscow: Redaktsionno-izdatel'skoye Upravleniye TsUNKhU Gosplana SSSR and Izdatel'stvo Soyuzorguchet.
Gozulov, A. I., and M. G. Grigoryants. 1969. *Narodonaseleniye SSSR (Statisticheskoye izucheniye chislennosti, sostava i razmeshcheniya).* Moscow: Statistika.
Guboglo, M. N. 1972. "Sotsial'no-etnicheskiye posledstviya dvuyazychiya." *Sovetskaya etnografiya,* no. 2: 26–36.
———. 1978. "Tendentsii razvitiya natsional'no-russkogo dvuyazychiya (Po materialam Uzbekskoy SSR)." *Polevye issledovaniya, 1976,* 12–23. Moscow: Nauka.
Isayev, M. I. 1970. *Sto tridtsat' ravnopravnykh (O yazykakh narodov SSSR).* Moscow: Nauka.
———. 1978. *O yazykakh narodov SSSR.* Moscow: Nauka.
Isupov, A. A. 1964. *Natsional'nyy sostav naseleniya SSSR (Po itogam perepisi 1959 g.).* Moscow: Statistika.
Isupov, A. A., and V. A. Borisov. 1978. *Vsesoyuznaya perepis' naseleniya 1979 goda.* Moscow: Znaniye.
Klement'yev, Ye. I. 1974. "Razvitiye yazykovykh protsessov v Karelii (Po materialam konkretno-sotsiologicheskogo issledovaniya)." *Sovetskaya etnografiya,* no. 4: 26–36.

Kolpakov, B. T. 1969. *Vsesoyuznaya perepis' naseleniya 1970 goda*. Moscow: Sovetskaya Rossiya.
Kozlov, V. I. 1969. *Dinamika chislennosti narodov: Metodologiya issledovaniya i osnovnye faktory*. Moscow: Nauka.
———. 1975. *Natsional'nosti SSSR: Etnodemograficheskiy obzor*. Moscow: Statistika.
———. 1977. *Etnicheskaya demografiya*. Moscow: Statistika.
———. 1982. *Natsional'nosti SSSR (Etnodemograficheskiy obzor)*. 2d ed. Moscow: Finansy i Statistika.
Kuvshinova, L. 1984. "Metod rascheta natsional'nogo sostava naseleniya v mezhperepisnoy periode." *Vestnik statistiki*, no. 4: 23–28.
Labutova, T. 1984. "Vyborochnoye sotsial'no-demograficheskoye obsledovaniye naseleniya 1985 g." *Vestnik statistiki*, no. 12: 41–45.
Lewis, Robert A., Richard H. Rowland, and Ralph S. Clem. 1976. *Nationality and Population Change in Russia and the USSR*. New York: Praeger.
Lorimer, Frank. 1946. *The Population of the Soviet Union: History and Prospects*. Geneva: League of Nations.
Maksimov, G., and A. Isupov. 1960. "Natsional'nosti SSSR po dannym vsesoyuznoy perepisi naseleniya." *Vestnik statistiki*, no. 4: 65–75.
Pod"yachikh, P. G. 1957a. "O proyekte programmy predstoyashchey v yanvare 1959 g. Vsesoyuznoy perepisi naseleniya i osnovnykh polozheniyakh organizatsionnogo plana ee provedeniya." *Vestnik statistiki*, no. 4: 49–76.
———. 1957b. *Vsesoyuznaya perepis' naseleniya 1939 g. (Metodologiya i organizatsiya provedeniya perepisi i razrabotki itogov)*. 2d ed. Moscow: Gosstatizdat.
Polyakov, Yu A., and I. N. Kisilev. 1980. "Chislennost' i natsional'nyy sostav naseleniya rossii v 1917 godu." *Voprosy istorii*, no. 6: 39–49.
Pustokhod, P. I., and V. K. Voblyy. 1936. *Perepisi naseleniya*. Moscow: Gosudarstvennoye Sotsial'noekonomicheskoye Izdatel'stvo.
———. 1940. *Perepisi naseleniya: Istoriya i organizatsiya*. Moscow: Gosplanizdat.
Russian Empire. Tsentral'nyy Statisticheskiy Komitet. 1905a. *Pervaya vseobshchaya perepis' naseleniya Rossiyskoy Imperii, 1897 g.* 89 vols. St. Petersburg.
———. 1905b. *Pervaya vseobschchaya perepis' naseleniya Rossiyskoy Imperii, 1897 g.; obshchiy svod po imperii rezul'tatov razrabotki dannykh pervoy vseobshchey perepisi naseleniya*. 2 parts. St. Petersburg: Izdaniye Tsentral'nogo Statisticheskogo Komiteta Ministerstva Vnutrennykh Del.
———. 1905c. *Pervaya vseobshchaya perepis' naseleniya Rossiyskoy Imperii, 1897 g.: Kratkiye obshchiye svedeniya po imperii. Raspredeleniye naseleniya po glavneyshim sosloviyam, veroispovedaniyam, rodnomu yazyku i po nekotorym zanyatiyam*. St. Petersburg: Izdaniye Tsentral'nogo Statisticheskogo Komiteta Ministerstva Vnutrennykh Del.
Shoup, Paul. 1981. *The East European and Soviet Data Handbook: Political, Social, and Development Indicators, 1945–1975*. New York: Columbia University Press.
Shryock, Henry S., and Jacob S. Siegel. 1976. *The Methods and Materials of Demography*. Condensed ed. by Edward G. Stockwell. New York: Academic Press.
Silver, Brian D. 1975. "Methods of Deriving Data on Bilingualism from the 1970 Soviet Census." *Soviet Studies* 27: 574–97.

Ter-Izrael'yan, T. G., ed. 1979. *Sovershenstvovaniye gosudarstvennoy statistiki na sovremennom etape (Materialy Vsesoyuznogo soveshchaniya statistikov)*. Moscow: Statistika.

Troshina, A. 1984. "Organizatsionnye voprosy vyborochnogo sotsial'no-demograficheskogo obsledovaniya naseleniya 1985 g." *Vestnik statistiki*, no. 6: 34–39.

USSR. Tsentral'noye Statisticheskoye Upravleniye. 1928. *Vsesoyuznaya perepis' naseleniya 17 dekabrya 1926 g., kratkiye svodki*. Vypusk 4: *Narodnost' i rodnoy yazyk naseleniya SSSR*. Moscow: Izdaniye TsSU SSSR.

———. 1929. *Vsesoyuznaya perepis' naseleniya 1926 goda*. 56 vols. Moscow.

———. 1958a. *Vsesoyuznaya perepis' naseleniya 1959 goda*. Moscow: Gosudarstvennoye Izdatel'stvo Politicheskoy Literatury.

———. 1958b. *Vsesoyuznoye soveshchaniye statistikov 4–8 yunya 1958 g.: doklady, vystupleniya v preniyakh i resheniya*. Moscow: Gosudarstvennoye Statisticheskoye Izdatel'stvo.

———. 1959. *Slovari natsional'nostey i yazykov—dlya shifrovki otvetov na 7 i 8 voprosy perepis'nogo lista (O natsional'nosti i rodnom yazyke)*. Moscow: Gosstatizdat.

———. 1963. *Itogi Vsesoyuznoy perepisi naseleniya 1959 goda*. 16 vols. Moscow: Gosstatizdat.

———. 1969a. *Slovari natsional'nostey i yazykov—dlya shifrovki otvetov na 7 i 8 voprosy perepisnykh listov (O natsional'nosti, rodnom i drugom yazyke narodov SSSR) Vsesoyuznoy perepisi naseleniya 1970 g*. Moscow: Statistika.

———. 1969b. *Vsesoyuznaya perepis' naseleniya—vsenarodnoye delo*. Moscow: Statistika.

———. 1969c. *Vsesoyuznoye soveshchaniye statistikov 22–26 aprelya 1968 g.: Stenograficheskiy otchet*. Moscow: Statistika.

———. 1972. *Itogi Vsesoyuznoy perepisi naseleniya 1970 goda*. 7 vols. Moscow: Statistika.

———. 1978. *Vsesoyuznaya perepis' naseleniya—vsenarodnoye delo*. Moscow: Statistika.

Vorob'ev, N. Ya. 1957. *Vsesoyuznaya perepis' naseleniya 1926 g*. 2d ed. Moscow: Gosstatizdat.

Wixman, Ronald. 1980. *Language Aspects of Ethnic Patterns and Processes in the North Caucasus*. Chicago: University of Chicago, Department of Geography Research Paper no. 191.

———. 1984. *The Peoples of Russia and the USSR: An Ethnographic Handbook*. Armonk, N.Y.: M. E. Sharpe.

Zinchenko, I. P. 1976. "Natsional'nyy sostav i yazyki naseleniya SSSR." In *Vsesoyuznaya perepis' naseleniya 1970 goda: Sbornik statey*, ed. G. M. Maksimov, 193–211. Moscow: Statistika.

———. 1984. "Natsional'nyy sostav naseleniya SSSR." In *Vsesoyuznaya perepis' naseleniya 1979 goda: Sbornik statey*, ed. A. A. Isupov and N. Z. Shvartser, 150–61. Moscow: Finansy i statistika.

Chapter 5

Occupations and Work Force Data in Russian and Soviet Censuses

MICHAEL PAUL SACKS

Occupations constitute a classification of activities of individuals which result in the production of economic goods and services. The term "occupations" is commonly distinguished from "industries," defined as a "classification of the activities of organizations" involved in such production (Stinchcombe, 1983: 108). Throughout the world, occupation is a critical determinant of an individual's social status. In preindustrial societies, occupation alone was probably a precise indicator of "dress, recreation, manners, patterns of association, speech, educational level, and other aspects of 'life style'" (Bogue, 1969: 431). In modern societies, income and education are combined with a measure of occupational prestige to create an index of individual socioeconomic achievement (Bogue, 1969: chap. 14).

The occupational composition of the economy reveals much about the characteristics of the total society. It reflects the level of overall economic development and the position of a region or nation within the broader economic system. Data on the occupational structure of the economy can be used to determine the social class divisions within the society. Social inequality is revealed by examining the intergroup differences in occupational structure. Researchers, for example, can study the association between gender or ethnicity and occupational concentration. Data on occupational differences between generations show the extent of upward and downward social mobility.

For Russia and the USSR, detailed data regarding the occupations of the entire work force can only be found in the censuses. The censuses provide a uniform classification of occupations across regions and over time for at least the period between 1939 and 1970 (no such data are currently available for 1979, but their publication would surely extend the longitudinal comparisons that are possible). The censuses also provide enormous potential for studying the association between employment and other social characteristics such as nationality, education, residence, marital status, and family size. This potential varies from one census to the next, but the 1926 census contains by far the most detailed information and the most sophisticated presentation and discussion of occupational data. More recent censuses are extremely disappointing by comparison.

A variety of Soviet economic handbooks provide data on the number of workers by branch of the economy, with additional detail on the branches of industry (USSR, 1981: 135, 357-58). However, each branch includes a wide range of occupations, and the same occupation can fall in many different branches. Further, the occupational composition of branches may change considerably over time and is likely to differ among regions; Feshbach (1972) notes that such problems as changes in the classification of workers and variation in the number of categories impede comparisons of branch data over time. There are also irregular publications containing data on the number of people employed in selected occupations. The categories given are rarely very numerous but may reveal the hierarchy of positions, for example, in the area of industrial management or school administration (Feshbach, 1972: 219-22; Dodge, 1966: chap. 2). In these areas the categories can be more detailed than in the census.

Very few studies have utilized the detailed occupational data from the Soviet censuses. Dodge's (1966) research on women in the USSR has been extremely useful for subsequent study of the subject, but his work is largely descriptive. He presented data on female representation in the occupational categories of the 1939 and 1959 censuses for the USSR as a whole. In *Women's Work in Soviet Russia,* Sacks (1976) used data from the censuses of 1897, 1939, 1959, and 1970 to construct summary measures of the levels of occupational gender differences and to pinpoint and describe where these differences were concentrated. As the title suggests, the book is concerned solely with the RSFSR. More recently, Sacks (1982b) extended this analysis and used detailed occupational data for each of the republics to make both cross-sectional and longitudinal comparisons of gender differences. This work also includes an analysis of age differences in occupations based on 1959 census data and focuses on differences between Muslim ethnic groups and the Russians. Sacks analyzes census data for 1939, 1959, and 1970 to draw conclusions on this subject in the absence of occupational data cross-classified by nationality (the techniques are further elaborated in Sacks, forthcoming).

McAuley (1981) has also used detailed occupational data to analyze gender differences and calculate summary measures. He compares the republics for 1970 and compares the USSR as a whole over the period from 1939 to 1970. McAuley's findings differ from those of Sacks's (1976; 1982a; 1982b) on a number of points, apparently because of their distinct approaches to interpreting the data and to the particular summary measures employed. Unlike Sacks (1982b: chap. 2), McAuley provides little information on the way he has resolved problems of missing occupational categories and of lack of comparability in the number and classification of categories. Thus, the two authors may have differed considerably in their resolution of this matter.

Despite their unquestionable richness, the occupational data from both the 1897 and 1926 censuses have remained almost entirely unutilized. The difficulty in making comparisons with the occupational categories in the more recent censuses has certainly contributed greatly to this neglect. What follows is a discussion of problems common to the Russian and Soviet censuses as well as to most censuses conducted in other areas of the world. Specific features of the 1897 census and the Soviet censuses are then considered separately with a focus on the detail and clarity of occupational categories, the number of variables by which occupational data are cross-classified, the internal comparability of tables of occupational data, and the potential for comparisons with the other censuses.

General Problems Affecting the Census Data

The first problem with occupational data in the censuses concerns the adequacy of coverage of unpaid family labor. Especially in rural areas large numbers of young people and women engaged in economic activity can easily be overlooked by the census informant. Consequently censuses often both understate the share of the work force engaged in agriculture and distort the extent of women's contribution to the household economy. According to a United Nations report pertaining to this subject, "It is commonly true in developing nations that nearly all the able-bodied members of farm households take some part in agricultural work, if only during the seasons of peak labor requirements, but the extent to which women and young people are reported as economically active varies over a wide range" (1968: 74).

This statement leads one to be particularly suspect of low rates of economic activity among rural women and children not in school. At early stages of industrialization, unpaid labor among women and children may also be widespread in cities (Tilly and Scott, 1978). This problem can be illustrated by figures from the 1926 Soviet census. In the RSFSR, one would have expected to find that most rural women in the age group 25–39 combined the bearing and raising of children with agricultural labor of some type. Yet, among families of agricultural workers, the census shows that in this age group 55,986 females were not part of the work force *(nesamodeyatel 'nyy)* and 66,046 were actively engaged in agricultural labor. Among males, on the other hand, the respective figures were 1,062 and 134,876 (USSR, 1930: 41). It does not seem plausible that 46 percent of the females would have been totally excluded from economic activity. To correct for this error, or at least to assess the extent to which it distorts findings based upon the census, the researcher must study other sources such as social science monographs, regional surveys, and even relevant works of fiction that describe the economic activity of all family members. This advice applies as well to the problems mentioned below.

A second problem concerns the adequacy of coverage of the labor of persons engaged in intermittent, temporary, or seasonal employment. Tilly and Scott (1978: 44) find that in preindustrial Europe "the normative family division of labor tended to give men jobs away from the household or jobs which required long and uninterrupted commitments of time or extensive travel, while women's work was performed more often at home and permitted flexible time arrangements." Thus, this second problem can exacerbate the difficulty of measuring unpaid family labor but may clearly apply to other workers as well.

Soviet censuses were conducted in winter, and if census informants were not fully questioned about activity undertaken during other times of the year, there may have been a tendency to undercount workers—especially in agriculture (United Nations, 1968: 74, 76). Noting that persons employed for an incomplete year had no way to specify this in the 1959 Soviet census, Feshbach (1972) contended that this flaw in the questionnaire had resulted in an upward bias in the number shown working within many occupations. He suggested that this might have been rectified in the 1970 census by additional questions directed specifically to those who had worked only during part of 1969.

The subsequent publication of the 1970 census, however, did not bear out Feshbach's prediction, as no information was published regarding employment for part of the year. The 1979 census questionnaire also did not include the additional questions, and instructions to enumerators stated that persons engaged in seasonal work and not employed at the time of the census should record as their occupation the work that they were engaged in during their active season. Likewise, women who had taken leave of absence for the care of children under age one were to record their place of employment as that from which they had taken leave (USSR, 1978: 55). Ideally, occupational data should indicate the number who worked by time intervals for the year preceding the census.

A third and related problem concerns the treatment of individuals engaged in dual economic activities. The 1897 and 1926 censuses contain much extremely detailed data regarding secondary occupations, but subsequent censuses show only primary employment. Instructions from the 1979 census stated that "persons having at the present time two or more places of work and also individuals working part of the year in one enterprise, institution, or organization and part of the year in another, are to write the name of the enterprise, institution or organization where the work is considered by the person to be his primary employment" (USSR, 1978: 55). The consequence of such a procedure, according to a UN report (1968: 76), is likely to be "a tendency to understate the share of manpower in those activities that are frequently subsidiary, and to overstate the share in those which frequently occupy the major part, though less than the whole, of the worker's time."

Several factors contribute to the above problems being more significant for researchers using the earlier censuses. First, a larger proportion of the population was engaged in agriculture, handicrafts, and related activities that were commonly undertaken by the family as a unit. Second, economic activity began at an especially early age, as labor-force entry was rarely delayed by schooling. Thus, in the 1926 census the age group 10–14 actually constituted the first category of the working population. Children probably worked most frequently as unpaid family members, and the quantity or quality of labor viewed as necessary to define children as workers must have varied considerably. In their description of preindustrial Europe, Tilly and Scott (1978: 44) note that "the levels of skill expected of children advanced with age, with young children performing the simplest and crudest chores."

Finally, the extremely low status of women in traditional Russian society may have increased the likelihood that their economic activity would be overlooked. It must have reduced the probability of their being directly interviewed as part of the census. Furthermore, in rural areas women appear to have been the most subordinate and the most insulated from change. Despite the persistence of inequality in a wide range of dimensions, the position of women has improved markedly over the period covered by the censuses (Sacks, 1976; 1982b).

The same factors noted above make it likely that the accuracy of the census results will vary across regions at any single point in time. This is owing to the considerable variation in economic development and in cultural factors influencing female status and the employment level of children and teenagers. The change over time in this level of heterogeneity remains very controversial.

The 1897 Census

Social and occupational categories in the 1897 census differ substantially from those of the Soviet period because of both the dramatic change in the economic structure of society and the distinct influence of political ideology on the conduct of social inquiry. In this latter regard, Lenin complained that the 1897 census lacked the requisite categories to delineate the class structure of the population (USSR, 1958: 11). Looking back at 1897, commentators writing in the 1926 census criticized the lack of information showing the hierarchy of positions within each occupations, and efforts to correct this are obvious in this first complete Soviet census (USSR, 1929b: vii–viii).

The contrast between the 1897 enumeration and those conducted during the Soviet period is immediately evident from the divisions by social strata. For each district and for the major cities, tables in the main volumes of the 1897 census divide the population into such categories as family members of hereditary nobility, church personnel, and petty bourgeoisie. Peasantry is a single category. This framework cannot be used for meaningful comparisons with later census data.

For each guberniya, data are presented for 65 categories of employment, cross-classified by gender and age. Persons active in the labor force are shown separately from nonworking members of the family. As in the 1926 census where this same distinction appears, it is unclear how dependents were classified in cases in which members of the same family were working in different occupations.

The 65 categories constitute an industrial as opposed to an occupational classification (International Labour Office, 1959: 26–39). This classification, therefore, indicates more about where an individual works than what he or she does within a particular area of service or production. Prostitution is one of the categories but, since a small number of both males and females are shown here, it is likely that this too encompasses different occupations (the category does not appear in Soviet censuses).

The industrial classification may not have created serious problems in 1897 because the distinction between occupation and industry was not likely to have been as distinct as it was at a later time. Where the organization of economic activity is not complex, industry is largely equivalent to occupation. "This is particularly the case where agriculture dominates the economy, since even in the most highly developed economies the differentiation of occupations within agriculture has not progressed far" (UN, 1968: 110). The secondary activities of persons engaged in agriculture, hunting, and fishing are shown in remarkable detail. For each district over 150 categories are listed indicating the wealth of material collected in the course of the census and only partially tapped in the actual publications. It is unclear why secondary activities were specified in so much greater detail than were the primary activities of the total population.

Particularly significant additional tables appear in a supplementary volume to the census (Troynitskiy, 1906); these were used to a limited degree in the work of Sacks (1976: chap. 2). The data refer only to "workers," which has a meaning perhaps synonymous with proletariat and includes those in manufacturing, mining, communication, transportation, and some aspects of trade. Twenty-eight of the 65 categories in the main part of the census appear here. In one set of tables, the number in each category is shown for married persons by age and gender and for household heads by gender and number of persons within the household. Thus, there is especially rich potential for study of the relationship between family status and employment.

Another type of table shows data for a substantial number of subcategories of the 28 main categories. These data are cross-classified simultaneously by age, gender, and literacy. The further detail may make this table particularly valuable for regional comparisons of age and gender differences. Cross-sectional rather than longitudinal comparison entailing links with the Soviet census data is surely the most fruitful research agenda.

The 1926 Census

Tables in the 1926 census vary greatly in the detail of the occupational categories, and careful consideration is necessary when deciding upon the geographic units to be compared. The headings of the tables can be confusing and reflect both the intricacy of the occupational classification and the large number of variables by which data are cross-classified. Researchers will find it very useful to become familiar with the number and lettering scheme used in the occupational classification.

The broadest categories are denoted with capital Russian letters. They represent the status in the labor force and include the following:

1. Workers *(rabochii)*
2. Office personnel *(sluzhashchii)*
3. Free professionals
4. Employers with hired labor
5. Household heads with family members working for them or members of producers' collectives
6. Own-account workers (hiring no employees)
7. Family members assisting in an economic enterprise operated by another member of the same household

There are three additional categories for persons not considered to have an occupation:

8. Persons either not having or not stating their occupation
9. Unemployed persons
10. Military personnel

The distinction between the first two categories is especially important. "Worker," the same term used in the 1897 census, refers to "persons employed directly in the production and transference [*peremeshcheniye*] of material value or in the maintenance of production mechanisms." The category of office personnel applies to "persons whose participation in production is in the form of nonmaterial service connected indirectly with production... or in the servicing of population" (USSR, 1929a: 519). The distinction is sometimes difficult to make, as is acknowledged in the statement following these definitions in the 1926 census: "The boundary between both concepts is not fully established, in that it is not possible to posit completely the precise boundaries between 'material' and 'nonmaterial' production. For that reason the placing of specific occupations in the area of worker or office worker is subject to debate. For the great majority of occupations, however, such designation is not difficult" (USSR, 1929a: 519).

The distinction between the first three statuses is best appreciated simply by examining the categories included within them. (Also see the definitions provided in USSR, 1929a: 517-22.) Over time the distribution of occupations among statuses undoubtedly has changed, as is illustrated below by the 1959 and 1970 censuses.

Other status categories are not free of problems. A UN report states that "in the reporting of status the distinction between employers and own-account workers is especially likely to be unreliable; that a self-employed worker hires one or two employees may easily be overlooked by the census informant, with the result that the number of employers is understated and the number of own-account workers overstated" (UN, 1968: 73-74). The status categories are subdivided into a small number of branches of the economy which are assigned uppercase Roman numerals. The third level of divisions (lowercase Russian letters) consists of broad occupational categories. The appearance of a great many of the same occupations across diverse branches of the economy clearly shows the deficiency of branch data alone.

The last subdivisions are of two types—both demarcated with Arabic numbers. The first appears in tables where occupational data are cross-classified by marital status among other variables. This type shows position within the occupation. For workers the positions consist of skilled, semiskilled, and unskilled. Other categories are used for office personnel that number as many as seventeen within a single occupation. Some status categories do not have further subdivisions at this level.

The alternative type of subdivision consists of still more detailed occupations; the tables containing employment data by nationality have this format. The categories are far more numerous and can readily be converted into the categories of the first type. Volume 18 of the 1926 census (USSR, 1929a: 521–38) shows the complete list of occupations in both the full and abbreviated occupational tables of the census and also indicates which occupations fall within each of the hierarchical positions. The level of skill of the worker was not based on a statement by the census informant. Instead, skill levels were established for specific occupations using information from a previous survey and from union handbooks. These levels represent the average or typical level of skill of workers in those occupations (USSR, 1929a: 521). It is therefore quite possible that systematic errors could result, for example, in the understating of differences between male and female skill levels. Unfortunately, it is not possible to convert the first type of subdivisions back into the more detailed occupations from which they were derived.

A brief examination of some of the more significant occupational tables illustrates the richness of the data in the 1926 census and their enormous research potential. One table, for example, distinguishes among males and females who are married, single, widowed, and divorced. For each occupation these categories are further divided into those who are active in the work force and those who are dependent members of the family not gainfully employed. This is the same division found in the 1897 census. There are also between eighteen and twenty age categories, and a distinction is made between urban and rural residents. Furthermore, both age and residence are given not only by gender but also by the literacy or illiteracy of the individuals.

Other tables show occupational data cross-classified by the largest nationality groups in the region, the previous occupation of the unemployed further divided by length of unemployment, city size of current residence along with age and marital status, and place of birth along with place of residence or length of residence in current location. Detailed tables show primary occupation by secondary occupation, and in almost every case the data are also shown separately for males and females.

Obviously the way the variables appear in the tables limits the manner in which they can be combined. For example, researchers cannot examine the impact of marital status on employment while controlling for age, nor can they directly examine the extent to which differences in literacy contribute to the superior position of one nationality group over another. But careful integration of the information on occupational characteristics from several different tables can enable researchers to draw inferences about a wide range of interrelationships.

The 1959 Census

In sharp contrast with the 1926 census, detailed occupational data in the 1959 and 1970 censuses are available only for the republics and not for smaller geographic units. Data are cross-classified only by gender, and the classification of categories is less revealing. Longitudinal comparisons are also complicated by change in occupational characteristics resulting from social and economic changes since 1926—such as the forced collectivization of agriculture and substantial industrial development. The same categories may not represent the same type of activity, and new occupations are present which did not exist in 1926.

The "social groups" within the society are shown to include workers, office personnel, collective farmers and a very small number of independent peasant farmers, and uncollectivized handicraftsmen. Table 30 shows members of the Soviet Army as a separate category within the employed population, but in Table 31 the military is not listed and its members are divided among workers, office personnel, and collective farmers.

The distinction between collective and state farm workers appears to be of far greater significance ideologically than as a sign of very different forms of economic activity, particularly in recent decades (Volin, 1970: 526–31). However, only state farmers are categorized as workers *(rabochii)*. The group that is commonly formed by combining workers and office workers is not equivalent to the nonagrarian work force, although it is often treated this way in Soviet social science literature and statistics.

In Table 45 of the 1959 census, detailed agrarian occupations are shown separately for collective farmers and for a category labeled "workers" *(rabochii)*. These latter must be exclusively state farmers. However, the workers *(rabochii)* shown as having employment in the *branch* of agriculture in Table 33 are not restricted to state farmers.

Persons solely engaged in production for family consumption or for the market on small privately tended plots of land (the private subsidiary economy) are considered to have a source of income but not an occupation. They are clearly not counted as state or collective farm workers (they may also be found among the families of other types of workers). No tables show secondary activities of those in the labor force, but labor in private agriculture frequently takes this form (see Soviet time-budget studies).

Table 44 contains the most detailed occupational categories separately by branch of the economy, but the data are only for the total population. Other tables do not show the breakdown by branch but have data either for 1939 and 1959 or for seven age categories for 1959 only. The table for the USSR as a whole shows only the distribution among age categories, but for each of the republics the number of persons is shown.

Occupations are divided into those that are professional or semiprofessional, defined as requiring "primarily mental exertion," and those that are nonprofessional or requiring "primarily physical exertion." As in the distinction between material and nonmaterial production, there obviously are definitional problems here. This division further confuses matters because it does not correspond to any clear combination of the "social groups" noted above.

Substantially abbreviated occupational tables show the number of females in 1939 and 1959 and their number in the seven age categories (hereafter referred to as the female listing). The number of males must be derived by subtracting the number of females from the corresponding table with the total figure (hereafter referred to as the total listing). This task at times requires some searching and some trial adding together of categories to determine exactly which of the categories in the total listing combine to equal those in the female listing.

Subcategories in the female listing often do not sum to the main category under which they fall. By calculating the residual and then referring to the total listing, the researcher can frequently specify the occupations of those unaccounted for. Some main categories are also missing, and, thus, a residual exists for both major occupational divisions. This can be examined using the same procedure (see Sacks, 1982b: chap. 2).

Table 49 compares the total number of workers in a selected group of occupations for 1959 and 1926. This table is a useful starting point for comparisons between these censuses, but the researcher must study the way in which it was constructed from the categories in the 1926 census. Adding the dimension of gender should be possible for many of the categories.

The 1970 Census

The 1970 census has fewer occupational categories than does the 1959 census, but several new categories appear and added information can be derived from the presentation of data for both 1959 and 1970 in the same tables. Using data for 1959 from both the 1959 census and the 1970 census, the researcher can determine how the occupational classification has changed and also specify categories missing from the female listing in both census publications (see Sacks, 1982b: 30–35). Fully exploiting the analysis of residual categories, the dual set of data for 1959, and other sources of information, Sacks (1982b) shows a definite pattern to categories that are missing or poorly specified in the census tables:

> Occupations that are missing or have been deleted from the 1970 census tend to have distinctly low and/or declining female representation....

Occupations that were added to the listing in the 1970 census showed the opposite trend. In addition, there are many cases in which female overrepresentation is obscured by combining of occupations with a low and high proportion of women. Finally, the nonprofessional female listing clearly omits some of the least desirable occupations and obscures the large numbers of women doing such work. (Sacks, 1982b: 42)

Commenting on the 1970 census, Labutova (1976: 231) notes that the stated occupation was not always the sole basis for classifying the individual as being engaged primarily in either mental or physical work. Social group, education, and answers to questions pertaining to the character of the work were sometimes considered, but these instances would appear to have been rare. The difficulty with this distinction between mental and physical work is shown by changes in occupational classification between 1959 and 1970. In 1959, barbers, manicurists, photographers, and those in the large category of salespeople were considered to be professional or semiprofessional. In 1970 they were reclassified as having occupations that required primarily physical exertion (Sacks, 1982b: chap. 2; Labutova, 1984a). This distinction also influenced the way in which employed persons were distributed between the categories of workers and office personnel, because the numbers given for 1959 differ in the 1959 and 1970 censuses.

The reduction in occupational data in the 1970 census is especially striking in the tables where age categories are shown. The 1970 census contains no absolute figures and no separate data for females. All that appears is the distribution across age groups for the total population. The number of persons can be calculated only imprecisely, as the distribution is to just three decimal places.

Another consequence of the reduction in occupational data is that labor-force participation rates for 1970 cannot be calculated by age and gender. Although subsequently published data show the rates for the USSR as a whole (*Vestnik statistiki*, 1974: 90), they still cannot be determined for each of the republics. In addition, the age group 60 and over is a single category in the 1959 data, and the appropriate population base for calculating the rate for this group is difficult to judge.

A useful set of tables in the 1970 census have greater detail than do their counterpart in 1959. Tables 69–83 in Volume IV show the distribution by educational attainment within each of detailed occupational categories. Whereas in 1959, educational attainment including and beyond incomplete secondary education comprised a single category, in 1970 this was divided into four categories. This arrangement is far better for roughly distinguishing between high and low status occupations (see Sacks, 1982b: chap. 5).

The 1979 Census

The single volume in which the results of the 1979 census were published (USSR, 1984) contains no data whatsoever on even the total number of persons within each occupation. The only pertinent tables show for each republic the proportion in the same four educational-attainment categories as existed in the 1970 census by branch of the economy (Table 42) and by major occupational category (Tables 45 and 46). The occupational categories appear to be the same as those of 1970, and in Tables 45 and 46, data are provided for both 1970 and 1979. Again, there is no distinction between males and females.

Occupational data were obviously collected in the course of the 1979 census, although the questions on this subject were administered to a sample population made up of 25 percent of the population living in their permanent residences (Labutova, 1984a: 10). Perhaps, as was the case with the 1939 census, researchers must await the publication of a future census before more results for 1979 are made available. It is apparent, however, that previously unpublished findings will appear from time to time in Soviet statistical publications and monographs. In a chapter in a book on the 1979 census, Labutova (1984b: 192-93) mentions the percentage of women in a number of occupations. Labutova reveals, for example, that among doctors and head doctors the percentage of women was 69 percent (as opposed to 76 percent in 1970) and among engineers it was 48 percent (up from 42 percent in 1970). This is significant information, but it provides a very paltry basis for analyzing work-force structure and patterns of change.

Conclusion

When working with recent censuses of the United States, researchers commonly use data on the characteristics of individuals for the multivariate analysis of occupational attainment. Computer tapes are available with information on large random samples of the population. For those accustomed to studying social processes with such data, the Soviet census would certainly appear quite useless.

Relative to other sources of information pertaining to Soviet society, however, the censuses constitute a source of hard data that is of enormous value. Furthermore, the 1926 census is surely of exceptional quality compared both to censuses of other countries during this era and to present-day censuses conducted in nations at levels of economic and social development comparable to that of the USSR in 1926. The occupational data from the 1959 and 1970 censuses provide, by comparison, extremely scant data, but they can nevertheless be used for reliable measures of many aspects of Soviet society and of social change. Problems arise primarily from the omission of subcategories and of tables cross-classifying occupational data by additional variables rather than from the publication of false information. This must be considered in the light of the recent reduction in statistical information evidenced by the 1979 census.

Future research might most profitably focus on the following: (1) interregional comparison of occupational differences by gender, nationality, and marital status based on the 1926 census; (2) comparison of the occupational structure of republics in 1926 with that of 1939 through 1970; and (3) intensive study of the characteristics of selected occupations or industries over the entire period from 1897 to 1970. The cumulation of results in the form of a growing data base easily accessible for computer analysis and exchange among scholars is certainly essential. Census data should continue to be used in conjunction with the full range of other sources that, as noted in the section on general problems with the censuses, can help compensate for both possible distortions and omissions. And finally, it is through examining conclusions from research on other countries and applying broader social science theory that the most significant issues warranting further study can be defined and that findings based on Soviet data can be critically evaluated (Sacks and Pankhurst, 1980).

References

Bogue, Donald J. 1969. *Principles of Demography.* New York: Wiley.

Dodge, Norton T. 1966. *Women in the Soviet Economy.* Baltimore: Johns Hopkins University Press.

Feshbach, Murray. 1972. "Soviet Industrial Labor and Productive Statistics." In *Soviet Economic Statistics,* ed. Vladimir G. Treml and John P. Hardt, 195–228. Durham: Duke University Press.

International Labour Office. 1959. *The International Standardization of Labour Statistics.* Studies and Reports, New Ser., no. 53. Geneva.

Labutova, T. S. 1976. "Zanyatiya naseleniya SSSR." In *Vsesoyuznaya perepis' naseleniya 1970 goda,* ed. G. M. Maksimov, 227–46. Moscow: Statistika.

———. 1984a. "Programma perepisi i metodologicheskie osnovy ee provedeniya." In *Vsesoyuznaya perepis' naseleniya 1979 goda,* ed. A. A. Isupov and N. Z. Shvartser, 5–25. Moscow: Finansy i Statistika.

———. 1984b. "Zanyatiya naseleniya SSSR." In *Vsesoyuznaya perepis' naseleniya 1979 goda,* 182–94. See Labutova, 1984a.

McAuley, Alastair. 1981. *Women's Work and Wages in the Soviet Union.* London: George Allen & Unwin.

Sacks, Michael Paul. 1976. *Women's Work in Soviet Russia: Continuity in the Midst of Change.* New York: Praeger.

———. 1982a. Review of *Women's Work and Wages in the Soviet Union*, by Alastair McAuley. *Russian Review* 41, no. 1: 83–84.

———. 1982b. *Work and Equality in Soviet Society: The Division of Labor by Age, Gender, and Nationality.* New York: Praeger.

———. Forthcoming. "The Division of Labor in Central Asia and Its Influence Upon Ethnic and Gender Conflict." In *Soviet Society and Culture: Essays in Honor of Vera S. Dunham*, ed. Richard Sheldon and Terry L. Thompson. Boulder: Westview Press.

Sacks, Michael Paul, and Jerry G. Pankhurst. 1980. "Introduction." In *Contemporary Soviet Society: Sociological Perspectives*, ed. Jerry G. Pankhurst and Michael Paul Sacks, 1–10. New York: Praeger.

Stinchcombe, Arthur L. 1983. *Economic Sociology.* New York: Academic Press.

Tilly, Louise A., and Joan W. Scott. 1978. *Women, Work and Family.* New York: Holt, Rinehart & Winston.

Troynitskiy, N. A., ed. 1906. *Chislennost' i sostav rabochikh v Rossii na osnovaniy dannykh vseobshchiye perepisi Rossiiskoy Imperii 1897.* Moscow: Gosudarstvenniy Ministr Vnutrennykh Delenii.

United Nations. Department of Economic and Social Affairs. 1968. *Methods of Analysing Census Data on Economic Activities of the Population.* Population Studies, no. 43. New York.

USSR. Tsentral'noye Statisticheskoye Upravleniye. 1929a. *Vsesoyuznaya perepis' naseleniya 1926 goda.* Vol. 18. Moscow.

———. 1929b. *Vsesoyuznaya perepis' naselenyia 1926 goda.* Vol. 27. Moscow.

———. 1930. *Vsesoyuznaya perepis' naselenyia 1926 goda.* Vol. 26. Moscow.

———. 1958. *Vsesoyuznaya perepis' naseleniya 1959 goda.* Moscow: Gosudarstvennoye Izdatel'stvo Politicheskoy Literatury.

———. 1978. *Vsesoyuznaya perepis' naseleniya—vsenarodnoye delo.* Moscow: Statistika.

———. 1981. *Narodnoye khozyaystvo SSSR v 1980 g.* Moscow: Finansy i Statistika.

———. 1984. *Chislennost' i sostav naseleniya SSSR (Po dannym Vsesoyuznoy perepisi naseleniya 1979 goda).* Moscow: Finansy i Statistika.

Vestnik statistiki. 1974. No. 12.

———. 1981. No. 5.

Volin, Lazar. 1970. *A Century of Russian Agriculture: From Alexander II to Khrushchev.* Cambridge: Harvard University Press.

Chapter 6

Urbanization and Migration Data in Russian and Soviet Censuses

RICHARD H. ROWLAND

Urbanization and migration, which collectively comprise population redistribution, have been especially important in Russia and the USSR. This region has experienced perhaps the most rapid movement to cities of any major region in history and also some of the most significant long-distance internal migrations of any country (Lewis and Rowland, 1979). Urbanization and migration have an added importance because of their profound influence on Soviet society. Urbanization, for example, has been closely associated with rapid industrialization, modernization, and social change in the USSR, especially in the last half century. Migration is a necessary component of economic development—its chief function is the spatial redistribution of labor—and has resulted in large-scale shifts in the regional distribution of the country's population.

It might be appropriate to define each of these related demographic phenomena more precisely. *Migration* is typically defined as a permanent or semipermanent change in residence. *Urbanization* is the process of population concentration which occurs when the percentage of the total population residing in urban centers (level of urbanization) changes, usually increases. Urbanization is distinguished from urban growth, which involves a change in the urban population per se without any reference to a relative comparison to the total population. Urbanization is, however, greatly influenced by urban growth, as it is the result of urban population change in comparison to that of the total or the residual rural population. In short, urbanization results from a "battle" between urban and rural change, which in turn is the net result of three broad mechanisms: (1) net rural-to-urban migration; (2) urban natural increase vis-à-vis rural natural increase; and (3) reclassification of settlements from rural to urban status. Net rural-to-urban migration has generally been the most important of the three mechanisms in the urbanization process—for both the world as a whole and the USSR in particular—although urban natural increase has loomed larger in recent years in both underdeveloped and developed countries with urban mortality declines. In addition, as a society reaches a high level of urbanization, rural-to-urban migration becomes less important simply because so few rural residents, and thus potential rural-to-urban migrants, remain.

Urbanization

Russian and Soviet census data for the study of urbanization are much more plentiful than are those for migration. Every census contains data on the number of urban and rural residents for all major political units, while some—especially those of 1897 and 1926—also include abundant data on specific characteristics of these populations. The data are of generally high quality, particularly in that urbanization trends portrayed by census figures usually conform to trends as evidenced in other sources.

Census data through 1970 have been used substantially for comprehensive urbanization studies by a number of scholars. In the USSR, perhaps the foremost scholar on urban data is B. S. Khorev, who is the author of numerous works on the subject (e.g., 1975). In the West, major works include Chauncy Harris's (1970a) classic and exhaustive study of the growth of cities of the Soviet Union, particularly from the early 1800s through the late 1960s. In addition, in a recent book the author and Robert Lewis covered numerous facets of the urbanization process (aggregate, regional, and city-size) based on the censuses from 1897 to 1970 and post-1970 estimates (Lewis and Rowland, 1979). Sequel types of works based on the 1979 census have also been recently published (Bond and Lydolph, 1979; Clem, 1980; Khorev, 1982; Rowland and Lewis, 1982).

The chief problem in investigating urban and rural population change and urbanization in Russia and the USSR is the differing and incomparable definitions of "urban" employed in the censuses. The typical procedure of any census is to define certain settlements as urban and to define as a residual all other settlements as rural. Urban settlements are usually distinguished from rural settlements on the basis of size, function, and density; urban centers usually have a larger population, higher density, and are predominately nonagricultural in function. The urban definition of the 1897 Russian census, in particular, was conceptually different from and, in my view, inferior to those employed in censuses of the Soviet period. These definitional problems have been discussed at length elsewhere (Lewis and Rowland, 1969: 776–78; 1979: 162–65; Leasure and Lewis, 1966: xi–xii).

The major problem of the 1897 census in this regard is that it employed an administrative criterion, whereas the Soviet censuses used a more logical size-function criterion. Thus, in the 1897 census, cities consisted solely of "official" or chartered urban places, which in turn consisted mainly of administrative centers (in particular, guberniya and uezd centers), as well as a few other legal cities (*zashtatnyy* and *bezuezdnyy*). The main shortcomings of the definition employed in the 1897 census are that (1) it excluded numerous sizable industrial centers, many of which had populations between 15,000 and 40,000, because they did not enjoy "legal" status; and (2) it included a number of small agricultural villages, some with populations of less than 1,000, simply because they were uezd centers. Thus, if one accepts the contention that an urban center is a relatively large, predominately nonagricultural settlement, the urban definition employed in the 1897 census is somewhat deficient. Despite these deficiencies, the 1897 urban definition is still largely representative of the urban population based on more conventional definitions. The reader is referred to Fedor (1975: 1–17), in particular, for a detailed discussion of urban definitions in late-nineteenth-century Russia.

The censuses of the USSR in 1926 and subsequent years, as noted above, and in contrast to the tsarist practice, employed a size-function criterion. Namely, to be classified as "urban," a settlement had to satisfy minimum standards of both population size and percentage of work force in nonagricultural activities. However, although the censuses of the Soviet period agree in this basic conceptual approach to the definition of an urban center, specific minimum levels have varied by census and even by union republic within a given census; definitions employed in the censuses of 1926, 1939, and 1959 are discussed at length by Leasure and Lewis (1966: 1–17).

Briefly, the urban definition of the 1926 census included both legal cities and other, specialized centers. In the 1926 census, the requirements for a legal city varied significantly by republic. In the RSFSR, for example, a minimum of 1,000 adults and 75 percent nonagricultural work force were required, while in the Ukraine the corresponding requirements were 10,000 and no occupational criterion. In addition, the urban definition in the 1926 census also included industrial centers, railroad stations, and resorts, which were in turn defined by a specific criterion. The urban definition in the 1939 census was apparently the same as that of 1926.

By the 1959 and subsequent censuses, the criteria for urban centers had been changed somewhat, although the basic size-function concept continued to be employed. In these more recent censuses the urban definition consists of two types of settlements: legal cities *(goroda)* and urban-type settlements *(poselki gorodskogo tipa)*. Various legislations around 1959 resulted in revisions of previous laws dealing with urban legal status, except in the Tadzhik and Turkmen SSRs. For instance, the RSFSR definition of a legal city was changed to a minimum of 12,000 people and 85 percent of the work force in nonagricultural activities. The RSFSR definition is the most stringent one used (for example, in Latvia an urban center must have only 8,000 people and 66 percent of the work force in nonagricultural activities). To complicate matters further, the census urban definition does not necessarily conform to the legal definition. According to O. P. Litovka (1976: 12), "due to historical conditions, there exists in the majority of union republics some urban settlements with a population which is less than that stipulated by the corresponding legislation of the republic." In the 1970 census, for example, more than a hundred urban centers of the RSFSR had less than the 12,000 legislated minimum (Khorev and Moiseenko, 1977). Fortunately, however, it appears that these recent definitions have not been changed subsequently. Thus, urban definitional comparability evidently exists among the 1959, 1970, and 1979 censuses, although republic definitional differences obviously remain. Different definitions of urban-type settlements are also employed from republic to republic.

How can the problem of the lack of urban definitional comparability be solved? One approach, adopted by the author and others, employs a uniform size-only definition, because appropriate urban functional data are not available in the post-1926 censuses (Leasure and Lewis, 1966; Lewis and Rowland, 1979). For this approach, a minimum of 15,000 people was selected as the size criterion because all censuses except 1979 list for every region the settlements with 15,000 or more people. Another consideration was that no separate official urban centers below this population are listed for the RSFSR in 1959. For 1897 and 1926, thousands of settlements, officially both urban and rural, many with even only a few hundred people, are individually listed. The 1926 listings come from the main census volumes, while those for 1897 come from a special census volume that lists individually the nearly fifty thousand settlements of the Russian Empire with 500 (actually 485) or more people (Russian Empire, 1905a). The censuses of 1939, 1959, and 1970 list only official urban centers; for these years, the few official rural settlements of 15,000 and over are, unlike for 1897 and 1926, not included. Urban centers with 15,000 or more people for the RSFSR in 1939 are listed in the 1959 census only if their 1959 population exceeded

15,000. Thus, urban centers of the RSFSR which declined from above to below 15,000 between 1939 and 1959 are not listed in the 1959 census.

How valid is the 15,000-plus criterion as an operational definition? Generally, it has been quite useful because in any year it includes the vast majority of the population in centers that were defined as urban by the census, and thus it coincides to a great extent with the urban definition employed in the census. In 1970, for example, over 80 percent of the urban population based on official urban definitions resided in centers of 15,000 and over. Also, patterns of urbanization, and urban and rural population change, both aggregate and regional, generally match known actual patterns (e.g., the recent rapid urban growth in the extreme western region of the USSR is indicated by the 15,000-plus definition).

However, our 15,000-plus definition has some minor shortcomings. First, although it largely overlaps the official urban population, the definition excludes numerous centers that would be included as "urban" by any reasonable definition. Second, because major studies of international urbanization (e.g., United Nations, 1969; Davis, 1972) employ a 20,000-plus criterion, we might have been wise to use this definition. Third, we should have excluded centers of 15,000-plus in 1897 and 1926 which were both predominately agricultural and not official urban centers. Finally, we could not have foreseen that the published results of the 1979 census would not include a list of individual centers below 50,000 in population, thus making the 15,000-plus criterion difficult to employ with 1979 data. Such data may, of course, eventually be published, and, as will be discussed later, it may in any case be possible to estimate the 15,000-plus population in 1979. Fortunately, the most detailed post-1970 listings did include official cities, but not urban-type settlements, of 15,000-plus (USSR, 1974: 636–50), thus making possible a post-1970 census study of urbanization based largely on our comparable definition. In addition, comparative studies of urbanization based on the 1959, 1970, and 1979 censuses can be undertaken using official urban definitions because apparently these definitions have not changed. Indeed, the author and a colleague have employed such data (Rowland and Lewis, 1982).

Four other noteworthy temporal and geographic definitional problems related to an assessment of urbanization and urban population changes in Russia and the USSR are (1) the technical measurement of urbanization over time; (2) changes in city boundaries; (3) the lack of a census "metropolitan" concept; and (4) the general lack of data by internal geographic units (such as "census tracts") *within* cities. To solve the first problem, researchers can measure temporal trends in urbanization by using percentage-point change or percentage change. The former measures changes in urbanization by simply subtracting the earlier level (or percent) of urbanization from the later level, while the latter measurement goes one step further by taking this percentage-point change as a percent of the earlier of the two levels of urbanization. In studies with which the author has been associated, we opted for the first measure, percentage-point change, chiefly because it is less influenced by low base or earlier percentages (Lewis and Rowland, 1979: 162–65). In addition, we used average annual percentage-point changes (overall percentage-point change divided by the number of years in the period) in order to provide comparability between the differing intercensal periods. Of course, average annual percentage change (the calculations for which involve logarithms) should be used when measuring annual percentage changes in the levels of urbanization, and urban and rural populations. A word of caution: irrespective of the measure of change used, the rate of urbanization will inevitably slow over time because urbanization is a finite process; that is, the upper limit is 100 percent, and thus the rate of change will slow as this level is approached.

City boundaries have changed, particularly as large cities have annexed major surrounding areas (e.g., Moscow in the early 1960s). Thus, the reported populations of Moscow in the 1926 census and in the 1979 census are not strictly comparable, as the 1979 area of Moscow was appreciably larger than the 1926 area. Another major type of city boundary change has occurred in the eastern Ukraine, where numerous small mining centers have been annexed to or amalgamated into larger "new" cities. In addition, some cities have been subdivided or "de-annexed" into smaller cities. These problems are covered in detail elsewhere (Harris, 1970a, and 1970b; Lewis and Rowland, 1979: 193–96). In general the overall impact of such changes on urbanization and urban population growth was relatively small, partly because the annexed areas were frequently defined as urban both before and after the boundary change.

Fortunately, the Soviet censuses do provide some degree of urban boundary comparability, especially between two consecutive censuses. The typical "backtracking" procedure used in recent censuses has been to present the populations of a city for the dates of both the census at hand and the preceding census in the boundaries of the city at the later date. In the 1979 census, 1970 and 1979 populations appear to be given in city boundaries existing in 1979 (except for Samarkand). Similarly, in the 1970 census, 1959 and 1970 populations are given in boundaries of 1970, and in the 1959 census, 1939 and 1959 populations are given in boundaries of 1959. A lesser degree of comparability exists between 1926 and 1939, although Lorimer (1946: 250–53) lists the 1926 and

1939 populations of all cities with 50,000 or more people in 1939, apparently both in 1939 boundaries. Unfortunately, no "backtracking" comparability exists between the 1926 and 1897 censuses, although as the urban process was relatively slow during this period, probably few urban boundaries changed significantly.

More annoying, perhaps, and more important for the present and future is the lack of any official census metropolitan definition, that is, a definition including the population of central cities plus suburbs. The United States, in contrast, employs such definitions as the "Metropolitan Statistical Area" (formerly "Standard Metropolitan Statistical Area") and "Urbanized Area." This lack of information on the part of the Soviet censuses is especially disconcerting as metropolitan areas or urban agglomerations continue to evolve. Scholars have put forth different metropolitan definitions; the major and most contentious issue dividing them is the determination of what specific suburban settlements to include within the "orbit" of a major urban center (Lewis and Rowland, 1979: 323-27).

The author and colleague (Lewis and Rowland, 1979: chap. 6) attempted to provide a comparable metropolitan definition for *all* of the censuses between 1897 and 1970 by drawing circles of fifty miles in radius around major Soviet cities in 1970 and summing the populations of settlements with 15,000 or more people within each fifty-mile radius. By this method we determined that in 1970 there were twenty-two "urban regions" with fifty-mile radii which contained 1 million or more people residing in 15,000-plus centers. We then determined the analogous populations residing in centers of 15,000-plus in these twenty-two urban regions in 1897, 1926, 1939, and 1959 and further subdivided the regions into central city, 0–25-mile (excluding the central city), and 25–50-mile zones. Thus, we were able to calculate the population growth of and redistribution within these "metropolitan" regions from 1897 to 1970. However, as this procedure employs a 15,000-plus operational definition, the lack to date of a listing of urban centers of 15,000-plus for the 1979 census precludes a similar investigation of urban region changes from 1970 to 1979, although the author has made similar calculations based on centers of 50,000 and over for this most recent period (Rowland, 1983c: 266).

Finally, virtually no data are available in the Russian and Soviet censuses for the internal parts of cities. Only in the 1897 census are data presented for internal units of cities, and here only for the four largest cities of the Russian Empire (St. Petersburg, Moscow, Warsaw, and Odessa). In contrast, the U.S. censuses present a plethora of data by census tracts and even blocks for all American cities. Therefore, studies of population variations within Russian and Soviet cities are for the most part very difficult to undertake.

Although the availability of specific population characteristics is discussed in other chapters in this volume, I will make some general comments concerning the types of characteristics available for the urban and rural populations in each of the censuses. In this regard, the 1897 and 1926 censuses are clearly superior to those of 1939, 1959, 1970, and 1979. Data presented for urban and rural population by political units in these two earlier censuses include age, sex, work-force composition, language, literacy, and place of birth for migration studies. In addition, the 1897 census includes urban data on social class and religion. A further advantage of the 1897 and 1926 censuses is that these data were presented for hundreds of individual urban centers. A separate volume of the 1897 census lists individually the thousands of settlements of the Russian Empire with 500 or more people and includes data on the number of males, females, and religious groups, which, in general, individually accounted for 10 percent or more of the population of the settlements (Russian Empire, 1905a). Unfortunately, the subsequent censuses of 1939, 1959, 1970, and 1979 presented much less data by urban-rural residence. Not only were available characteristics fewer for the urban and rural populations by political units, but very few data were presented for individual urban centers.

Finally, with respect to the availability of characteristics for the urban and rural populations in recent censuses, researchers should note that additional data have been published in various scholarly works outside of the official census publications. Demographers in the USSR have some access to unpublished census data, and, thus, data not directly available to Western demographers "leak out" through these publications. Two major examples stand out. First, Khorev (1968) presented work-force data from the 1959 census for cities of 50,000 and over. These data allow for the only significant study of the functional classification of Soviet cities since the 1897 and 1926 censuses, and they have been extensively utilized and discussed by Harris (1970a: 54–115).

Second, although 1979 urban-rural ethnic data are generally unavailable from published census results, Kozlov (1982: 100) presented aggregate levels of urbanization for forty major nationalities of the USSR. From these data and the total populations of the nationalities, researchers can determine the 1979 population of each listed nationality residing in urban and rural areas, respectively, for the entire USSR and derive the ethnic composition of the urban and rural populations themselves. Researchers can also determine the 1979 ethnic composition of Moscow, Leningrad, Minsk, Kiev, Tashkent, Alma-Ata, and Ashkhabad by a residual technique applied to available data. Data for 1979, for example, indicate the numbers of Russians and Uzbeks in the Uzbek SSR as a whole and each of its internal units except the city of Tashkent.

Summation of the number of Russians and Uzbeks residing in these political units and subtraction of those sums respectively from the corresponding Uzbekistan total results in a residual, which equals the number of Russians and Uzbeks in Tashkent proper (Rowland, 1983b). A separate publication for Leningrad allows for the derivation of data for Leningrad and Moscow (Leningrad, 1981). Kozlov (1982: 241) also presented 1979 data for thirty-five nationalities on the percentages of the total and urban populations of each which consider the language of their nationality as their native language.

Migration

Data on migration are available in the Russian and Soviet censuses of 1897, 1926, 1970, and 1979 but not in the censuses of 1939 and 1959. Migration studies from the 1897, 1926, and 1979 censuses are based on place-of-birth data, while those for the 1970 census are based on residence change during the two years prior to the census. Major studies employing migration data from the 1897 and 1926 censuses include Rashin (1956), Leasure and Lewis (1967; 1968), Lewis and Rowland (1979), Lorimer (1946: 44–49), Anderson (1980), Rowland (1976; 1982a), and Tikhonov (1978).

Place-of-birth data are perhaps the main indicator of migration found in censuses throughout the world. The underlying rationale is that if a person's place of birth is different from his or her place of residence at the time of the census, a migration has undoubtedly occurred. Thus, such persons are operationally defined as migrants, while all others are not. There are obvious universal conceptual problems with these data as indicators of migration. In particular: (1) they detect at most only one migration (that between place of birth and present place of residence) even though the person may have made many migrations; (2) they do not detect a migration if a person has moved from and then returned to his or her place of birth; and (3) unless specifically indicated, they give no indication of when the migration took place. But despite these shortcomings, place-of-birth data are the basis of most migration studies from censuses.

In the 1897 census, place-of-birth data are available for the eighty-nine guberniyas or equivalent units, for uezds, and for the roughly nine hundred official urban centers listed individually; thus, as a residual, "rural" areas of the uezds can also be derived. Responses to place-of-birth questions are classified in four categories: (1) natives of the same uezd where they lived or "home uezd" *(urozhentsy togo-zhe uezda, gde zhivut)*; (2) natives of other uezds within that guberniya *(urozhentsy drugikh uezdov, toy-zhe gubernii*) or intra-guberniya migrants; (3) natives of other guberniyas (*urozhentsy drugikh guberniy*) or inter-guberniya migrants; and (4) natives of other countries (*urozhentsy drugikh gosudarstv*) or immigrants. The definition of a "migration" must then be operationally specified by the researcher based on migration-defining boundaries. In other words, the researcher determines beforehand which of the available boundaries have to have been crossed for a migration to have taken place. In the 1897 census the first category consists, operationally, of nonmigrants in all situations, while the other three might or might not consist of migrants, depending on the context employed by the researcher. From the broadest perspective, all three categories would be used if a migrant were someone born in another country, guberniya, or uezd. A researcher concerned with internal migration and not international migration, however, would exclude category 4.

The presentation of place-of-birth data in the 1897 census also allows for a more specific investigation of migration streams. In particular, researchers can investigate migration streams between guberniyas, because for the population of a guberniya born in another guberniya or foreign country (as well as rural areas and individual urban centers therein), specific guberniyas or countries of birth are listed. These listings thus allow an investigation not only of in-migration to a guberniya but also of out-migration and thus net and gross migration or migration turnover. Unfortunately, however, particular migration streams *within* guberniyas cannot be determined because specific other uezds of birth are not listed.

It is also unfortunate that very few characteristics of migrants besides the specific guberniya of birth are available from the 1897 census for all three categories of migrants. The only other explicit characteristics available in the general census are sex and social class, although urban and rural origin can be derived from the social class data and crude indicators of distance of migration can be determined based on "home uezd," other uezds, and other guberniyas (Rowland, 1971: 76–91; 1982a: 30). However, a separate, specialized volume provides guberniya-of-birth data for workers and servants (Russian Empire, 1905b), data that have been extensively utilized by Anderson (1980).

Place-of-birth data are also available from the 1926 census. However, the 1926 definition of a migrant is somewhat broader than that of 1897. Whereas a person had to cross an uezd boundary in 1897 to be considered a migrant, in 1926 the individual simply had to have been born in another place *(nemestnyye urozhentsii)*, even if it was in the same uezd. In addition, 1926 place-of-birth data are more comprehensive in terms of available territorial units and migrant characteristics. Indeed, the 1926 census contains the richest source of migration data of any of the Russian and Soviet censuses. In 1926 the political-administrative units were greater in number than in 1897 (about 190 as compared to roughly 90) and different in size and shape. Also, the USSR in 1926 was slightly smaller than the Russian Empire of 1897. In particular, migration data for 1926 are available for approximately 190 units, from guberniyas down to small okrugs in certain cases. Unlike 1897, however, separate place-of-birth data are not available for most uezds and individual urban centers, making the 1897 census superior to that of 1926 at least in these instances. For each of these units, the following migrant characteristics are available: (1) region, guberniya, okrug, etcetera, of birth; (2) sex; (3) current urban-rural residence of the migrant, although the urban definition is different from that of 1897; (4) duration of residence; and—especially important—(5) work-force composition and major ethnic groups, by sex and in borders of both the USSR in 1926 and the Russian Empire. The latter allows a greater degree of comparability between the 1897 and 1926 censuses.

Nearly half a century passed before a Soviet census again included migration data. In the 1970 census, residence-change data during the two years prior to the census were employed instead of place-of-birth data. In particular, the 1970 census asked people, "How long have you continuously resided at this particular residence in 1970?" Those residing in the place of enumeration less than two years were counted and listed in the census, thus providing an operational definition of migrants. Previous place-of-residence data reveal more current migration because they cover recent movements as opposed to those between place of birth and present place of residence, movements that could have taken place decades earlier. Thus, the 1970 migration data are conceptually different from those of 1897 and 1926. The territorial units and urban-rural definitions also differ from those of the earlier censuses. An additional problem is that no other country has employed the operational migration definition used in the 1970 Soviet census, thus impeding comparisons between the migration data in this census and migration data from other countries.

In the 1970 census, migration data are available specifically for total male and female populations and for urban and rural populations for all economic regions, union republics, oblasts, krays, ASSRs, and union republic capitals and the city of Leningrad. It is not possible, however, to assess migration streams in as much detail as it was for either 1897 or 1926 because previous place-of-residence data are presented only for economic regions and union republics and not for oblasts or equivalent units; for 1897 and 1926, it is possible to determine out-migrants by smaller political units. Also, the 1970 census data exclude temporary movers and the military.

In comparison with earlier data, migration data from the 1970 census have two unique advantages. First, using the 1970 data, researchers can determine urban-rural migrations in greater detail. For each political unit available, the 1970 census provides data on either the urban or the rural origin (by economic region or union republic of origin) of both the urban and rural populations of that unit. In 1897 and 1926, no explicit data on the urban-rural origin of the migrants were available (although for 1897 the author, as mentioned before, has shown how available social class data could be used to estimate such origins). Second, the 1970 census allows for a determination of migration flows between various urban size classes by economic region and union republic. The author and a colleague have discussed specific procedures for using these 1970 urban-rural and size-class data, especially the need to include or exclude certain categories of data depending on the unit of reference being employed; for example, for a more realistic determination of the migration to all cities of a particular region, one should exclude migrants from other cities within that region (Lewis and Rowland, 1979: 123–24, 434–35). The 1970 census thus allows for fairly detailed studies of regional total, urban, and rural in- and out-migration and thus total, urban, and rural net and gross migration.

Limited migration data from the 1979 census based on the place-of-birth concept have been published (*Vestnik statistiki*, 1982). Data are presented for the total, urban, and rural populations of the USSR as a whole and of the fifteen union republics. Migrants can be operationally defined as "those who have resided uninterruptedly at their permanent place of residence 'not from birth,'" as opposed to those "nonmigrants" who have resided continuously at their permanent place of residence "from birth." For those in the migrant population, data are also presented on length of residence in seven categories (less than 2 years, 2–5 years, 6–9 years, 10–14 years, 15–19 years, 20–24 years, and 25 or more years). Thus, the migration data from the 1979 census are most comparable to those from the 1926 census, which, as mentioned earlier, employs place-of-birth and length-of-residence data (although the length-of-residence categories are not necessarily exactly the same in each case). However, both the 1970 and 1979 censuses have some comparability in that in each case, data are presented for persons residing in their present place of residence less than two years. Recent works have utilized the 1979 migration data (Moiseenko, 1983; *Naseleniye SSSR*, 1983: 36–53). The latter publication includes "leaked-out" data on mobility by major nationality, data that were not presented in the official census publications.

The study of recent migration in the USSR does not depend solely upon migration data from censuses. Although no migration data are available from the 1959 and 1979 censuses for subrepublic units, net migration for such units can be estimated for the 1959–70 and 1970–79 periods using the vital-statistics, or residual, technique. This method utilizes available data on the number of births and deaths and thus natural increase for individual regions compared to total population change, with the difference between total population change and natural increase being net migration. The application of this technique to the 1959–70 and 1970–79 periods is generally valid, not only because there exists a fairly good—though not complete—array of annual vital statistics but also because it is possible to assess natural increase relatively accurately for the entire period owing to the absence of wars. A number of studies have estimated regional net migration for 1959–70 based on available vital statistics (Lewis and Rowland, 1979; Grandstaff, 1980; Baldwin, 1979).

The author derived estimates of 1970–79 regional and subregional net migration based on available vital statistics for the first half of the 1970s; none have been published for 1975–79 for units other than union republics (Rowland, 1982b). Basically, for units other than union republics, the author used 1974 natural increase, the intercensal midpoint, to estimate natural increase and thus met migration for the entire 1970–79 intercensal period. The continuing publication in *Vestnik statistiki* of the number of births and deaths for twenty-one of the largest Soviet cities (cities of 1 million-plus and/or union republic capitals) for every year of the 1970–79 period enabled the author to assess net migration for these cities during this period, also by means of the vital-statistics technique (Rowland, 1983c: 270).

Recent migration studies are possible using data on the registration of arrivals and departures (Lewis and Rowland, 1979: 34). These data are collected in conjunction with the internal passport system and have been published in a statistical compendium (USSR, 1975: 178–200) and in various issues of *Vestnik statistiki*. They include information on the number of in-migrants and out-migrants for urban centers in general, as well as for union republics and economic regions and individually for cities of 500,000 and over. Unfortunately, these data have not been published for years after 1974 and have other problems connected with their use (Lewis and Rowland, 1979: 111–15; Grandstaff, 1980: 9–17).

A few comments should perhaps be made on the permanent or temporary residence of migrants and the censuses. In the 1897 and 1926 censuses, place-of-birth data are presented for the de facto population, and thus the migrant population includes temporary residents; these residents are listed separately and so can be deleted. In addition, in both censuses it appears that most migrants were permanent, as temporary residents constituted only a very small share of the population. In a study of urban in-migration in 1897, for example, the author concluded that no more than 6 percent of the migrants to cities of the Russian Empire were "temporary" (Rowland, 1983a: 6). In contrast, as was noted earlier, the migrant definition of 1970 and 1979 excludes temporary movers, as they are based on the permanent population.

Future Studies of Urbanization and Migration

In considering future scholarly studies of Russian and Soviet urbanization and migration, I find it useful to recognize two broad categories of studies: (1) those based on potentially available future population data; and (2) those based on population data already published. Recent Soviet cutbacks in published demographic data make it likely that the greater number of future studies will be based on past data.

Studies involving future data seem to hold much greater promise for research on urbanization than for research on migration. Studies of recent national and regional urbanization patterns and city-size trends continue to be possible because the annual *Narodnoye khozyaystvo* series lists the current urban and rural populations of oblasts and equivalent units, as well as the population of cities with 50,000 or more people. A particular study that could be undertaken after urban data are presented in the 1980s and 1990s is an updating of Harris's study of the long-term growth of individual Soviet cities (Harris, 1970a; 1970b). Harris's investigations went through 1967, and new data for the end of the twentieth century would allow for an additional 30–40-year perspective.

Another type of future study in this respect is an assessment of the degree of success of Soviet policies aimed at limiting the growth of large cities (i.e., cities of 100,000 and over). In earlier works, the author and a colleague assessed the "subsequent growth of large cities" from 1959 to the mid-1970s and 1979 (Lewis and Rowland, 1979: 218–89; Rowland, 1983c: 262–64). In addition to investigating changes in the population residing in large and small cities, these studies identified large cities of 1959 and traced the growth of this constant number of cities through the 1970s. Because data on large cities continue to be published in the *Narodnoye khozyaystvo* series, an updating and testing of this policy in the future would seem feasible, barring, of course, any further data cutbacks. Indeed, it could be argued that among *all types* of demographic studies of the future USSR, the brightest prospects are in the area of urbanization.

In contrast, the outlook for studies of current and future migration trends appears to be very limited. First, the 1979 census does not provide migration data for subrepublic units. Second, the cessation of the publication of vital statistics for oblasts and migrant registration data since the mid-1970s limits the study of migration, although it is possible to estimate net migration for the fifteen union republic capitals and other cities with one million or more people based on annually presented population totals and births and deaths. Two important questions concerning future regional migration confront the USSR: (1) will attempts to increase net in-migration to Siberia succeed? and (2) will substantial out-migration from Soviet Central Asia occur? In light of the above comments on potential data availability, prospects seem to be greater for the study of the latter than the former topic because of the availability of vital statistics by union republic and the lack of similar data for areas within republics (e.g., Siberia). Regarding recent migration, a more detailed and rigorous analysis of regional net migration rates estimated in a previously mentioned article by the author would be desirable (Rowland, 1982b).

Given these apparent data limitations, future studies of urbanization and migration may well be based on already existing data that have not been fully tapped, especially those from the censuses of 1897 and 1926. Indeed, the underutilization of these data is suggested by this chapter's list of references, which indicates that most major studies using data of 1897 and 1926 did not occur until the 1960s and 1970s. Studies of urbanization and migration based on existing Russian and Soviet census data are thus still possible; a few examples come to mind. Although the author (Rowland, 1971; 1976; 1982a) has undertaken a study of the migration to Russian cities based on the 1897 census, a similar study based on the 1926 census has yet to be undertaken. It would be interesting to investigate whether the same conditions related to rural-to-urban migration in 1897, especially jobs in personal services, prevailed in 1926. The previously discussed problems of changing city boundaries and metropolitan definitions have not been fully explored; for example, an estimate of the population of Moscow and other cities in 1897, 1926, and other census years in current city boundaries would be useful, although the lack of detailed data may make such a study difficult. Also, the comparable metropolitan definition employed by the author and a colleague was based on agglomerations of 1 million and over in 1970, but clearly a similar delineation of smaller metropolitan areas would be a worthwhile refinement. Regarding comparability, some attempt should be made to estimate the 15,000-and-over population by economic region for 1979. A possible approach might be to estimate the share of the available urban population (census definition) residing in centers of 15,000 and over, based on corresponding available shares by region for 1959 and 1970.

Many studies, particularly those dealing with regional settlement size, are possible based on the roughly fifty thousand individual settlements of

500 and over from the 1897 census. In such a vein, the author recently completed a study involving the settlement-size structure of Jews and non-Jews in the Jewish Pale of Settlement of late-nineteenth-century Russia (Rowland, 1983a). A wealth of data also exist in both 1897 and 1926 on the economic structure of hundreds of urban centers.

A final category of future studies involves regional scale. For the most part, major studies of urbanization and migration using the Russian and Soviet censuses have involved the aggregate national territory of Russia and the USSR and macroregional variations. Future studies could therefore either broaden or narrow the perspective. Further international comparisons involving Russian and Soviet urbanization and migration would be useful in order to assess more precisely the similarities and differences of the Russian and Soviet experience. On the other hand, more detailed studies of urbanization and migration at the microregional level (oblasts and cities) would also be valuable.

In summary, the greatest prospects for future studies of urbanization and migration in Russia and the USSR appear to lie in already existing, rather than future, census data. In this respect the future is in the past, although one must hope that this contention is proven wrong by the publication of much more urbanization and migration data in the future than currently seems reasonable to expect.

References

Anderson, Barbara A. 1980. *Internal Migration during Modernization in Late Nineteenth-Century Russia.* Princeton: Princeton University Press.

Baldwin, Godfrey S. 1979. *Population Projections by Age and Sex: For the Republics and Major Economic Regions of the U.S.S.R., 1970 to 2000.* U.S., Bureau of the Census, International Population Reports, Series P-91. no. 26.

Bond, Andrew A., and Paul E. Lydolph. 1979. "Soviet Population Change and City Growth, 1970-79: A Preliminary Report." *Soviet Geography: Review and Translation* 20: 461-88.

Clem, Ralph S. 1980. "Regional Patterns of Population Change in the Soviet Union, 1959-1979." *Geographical Review* 70: 137-56.

Davis, Kingsley. 1972. *World Urbanization, 1950-1970,* Vol. II; *Analysis of Trends, Relationships, and Development.* Berkeley: University of California, Institute of International Studies.

Fedor, Thomas Stanley. 1975. *Patterns of Urban Growth in the Russian Empire during the Nineteenth Century.* Chicago: University of Chicago, Department of Geography.

Grandstaff, Peter J. 1980. *Interregional Migration in the U.S.S.R.: Economic Aspects, 1959-1970.* Durham: Duke University Press.

Harris, Chauncy D. 1970a. *Cities of the Soviet Union: Studies in Their Functions, Size, Density, and Growth.* Chicago: Rand McNally.

———. 1970b. "Population of Cities of the Soviet Union, 1897, 1926, 1939, 1959, and 1967: Tables, Maps, and Gazetteer." *Soviet Geography: Review and Translation* 11: 307–444.
Khorev, B. S. 1968. *Gorodskiye poseleniya SSSR*. Moscow: Mysl'.
———. 1975. *Problemy gorodov*. 2d. ed. Moscow: Mysl'.
———. 1982. *Urbanizatsiya i demograficheskiye protsessy*. Moscow: Finansy i Statistika.
Khorev, B. S., and V. M. Moiseenko. 1977. "Urbanization and Redistribution of the Population of the U.S.S.R." In *Patterns of Urbanization: Comparative Country Studies*, ed. Sidney Goldstein and David F. Sly, 643–720. Dolhain, Belgium: Ordina Editions.
Kozlov, V. I. 1982. *Natsional'nosti SSSR: Etnodemograficheskiy obzor*. Moscow: Finansy i Statistika.
Leasure, J. William, and Robert A. Lewis. 1966. *Population Changes in Russia and the USSR: A Set of Comparable Territorial Units*. San Diego: San Diego State College Press.
———. 1967. "Internal Migration in the USSR, 1897–1926." *Demography* 4: 479–96.
———. 1968. "Internal Migration in Russia in the Late Nineteenth Century." *Slavic Review* 27: 375–94.
Leningrad. Statisticheskoye Upravleniye Leningradskoy Oblasti i Leningrada. 1981. *Narodnoye khozyaystvo Leningrada i Leningradskoy Oblasti v 10 Pyatiletke: Statisticheskiy sbornik*. Leningrad: Lenizdat.
Lewis, Robert A., and Richard H. Rowland. 1969. "Urbanization in Russia and the USSR: 1897–1966." *Annals of the Association of American Geographers* 59: 776–96.
———. 1976. "Urbanization in Russia and the USSR: 1897–1970." In *The City in Russian History*, ed. Michael F. Hamm. Lexington: University Press of Kentucky.
———. 1979. *Population Redistribution in the USSR: Its Impact on Society, 1897–1977*. New York: Praeger.
Litovka, O. P. 1976. *Problemy prostranstvennogo razvitiya urbanizatsiya*. Leningrad: Nauka.
Lorimer, Frank. 1946. *The Population of the Soviet Union: History and Prospects*. Geneva: League of Nations.
Moiseenko, V. 1983. "Vliyaniye migratsii na formirovaniye naseleniya (po materialam Vsesoyyznoy perepisi naseleniya 1979 g.)." *Vestnik statistiki*, no. 7: 8–14.
Naseleniye SSSR: Spravochnik. 1983. Moscow: Izdatel'stvo Politicheskoy Literatury.
Rashin, A. G. 1956. *Naseleniye Rossii za 100 let*. Moscow: Gosudarstvennoye Statisticheskoye Izdatel'stvo.
Rowland, Richard H. 1971. "Urban In-Migration in Late Nineteenth Century Russia." Ph.D. diss., Columbia University.
———. 1976. "Urban In-Migration in Late Nineteenth Century Russia." In *The City in Russian History*. See Lewis and Rowland, 1976: 115–24.
———. 1982a. *Spatial Patterns of Urban In-Migration in Late Nineteenth Century Russia: A Factor Analytic Approach*. Historical Geography Research Series, no. 10. Norwich, England: Geo Abstracts.

———. 1982b. "Regional Migration and Ethnic Russian Population Change in the USSR (1959–79)." *Soviet Geography: Review and Translation* 23: 557–83.

———. 1983a. "Geographical Patterns of the Jewish Population in the Pale of Settlement of Late Nineteenth Century Russia." Paper presented at the International Conference of Historical Geographers, Oxford, England. Abstract in *Historical Geography* 13: 27–28.

———. 1983b. "Regional Changes in Nationality Composition in the USSR, 1970–79." Paper presented at the Annual Meeting of the Association of American Geographers, Denver, Colo.

———. 1983c. "The Growth of Large Cities in the USSR: Policies and Trends, 1959–79." *Urban Geography* 4: 258–79.

Rowland, Richard H., and Robert A. Lewis. 1982. "Regional Population Growth and Redistribution in the U.S.S.R., 1970–79." *Canadian Studies in Population* 9: 71–93.

Russian Empire. Tsentral'nyy Statisticheskiy Komitet. 1905a. *Naseleniya mesta Rossiyskoy Imperii v 500 i bolee zhiteley s ukazaniyem vsego nalichnago v nikh naseleniya i chisla zhiteley preobladaioshchikh veroispovedanii po dannym pervoy vseobshchey perepisi naseleniya 1897 g.* St. Petersburg.

———. 1905b. *Raspredeleniye rabochikh i prislugi po gruppam zanyatiy i po mestu rozhdeniya na osnovanii dannykh pervoy vseobshchey perepisi naseleniya Rossiyskoy Imperii 28 yanvarya 1897 g.* St. Petersburg.

Tikhonov, B. V. 1978. *Pereseleniya v Rossii vo vtoroy polovine XIXv.* Moscow: Izdatel'stvo "Nauka."

United Nations. Department of Economic and Social Affairs. 1969. *Growth of the World's Urban and Rural Population, 1920–2000.* ST/SOA/Series A, no. 44. New York.

USSR. Prezidium Verkhovnogo Soveta Soyuza Sovetskikh Sotsialisticheskikh Respublik. 1974. *SSSR: Administrativno-territorial'noye deleniye Soyuznykh Respublik na 1 yanvarya 1974 goda.* Moscow.

USSR. Tsentral'noye Statisticheskoye Upravleniye. 1975. *Naseleniye SSSR 1973.* Moscow: Statistika.

Vestnik statistiki. 1982. No. 7: 77–79.

Chapter 7

Marriage, Family, and Fertility Data in Russian and Soviet Censuses

BARBARA A. ANDERSON

Soviet planners are interested in information on the fertility, marriage patterns, and family structure of the Soviet population because of the relevance of these data for monitoring and projecting population growth, for planning the demand for social services such as schools, for assessing social stability, and for studying the household economy. Both Soviet and Western researchers seek information on family and fertility in the Soviet population because of their bearing on questions of social structure and social change. Age of marriage, for example, is often regarded as an indicator of the social progress of women, as a large age gap between spouses can signal a situation in which males are strongly dominant. Also, the disappearance of the extended family has been considered part of the demise of a once traditional way of life.

Fertility differences among regions and among ethnic groups have come to be the major cause of differential rates of population growth. Higher Muslim than non-Muslim fertility generates concerns ranging from the effect of the high fertility of women in traditionally Muslim groups on the women's status to alarm over the "yellowing of the Army" (Ogarkov, 1982) as the proportion of the total population from traditionally Muslim groups increases over time.

The traumas of Soviet history have affected patterns of marriage and family formation. World War II caused a severe male deficit, widowing many women, creating numerous single-parent families, and preventing a large number of women from marrying. These developments in turn affected female labor-force participation rates. Even now, a concern with

Acknowledgments: Work on this paper was supported in part by NICHD Grant No. HD 18027-01. I am grateful also to the Russian Research Center, Harvard University and to the John Simon Guggenheim Memorial Foundation for their support. I also thank Brian Silver, Thomas Burch, Sidney Goldstein, Gur Ofer, Elizabeth Wood, and Kristen Benson.

labor shortage has fueled Soviet interest in the relationship between female labor-force participation, fertility, and child-care arrangements.

Family structure is central to the study of censuses because the way a census treats the individual, the family, and the household determines much of how the census is conducted. Whether family relationships are recorded, whether people need to be coresident to be considered members of the same family, and in what situations people can answer questions about others are all matters that hinge in this issue.

Overview of Family and Fertility Information in Russian and Soviet Census Reports

Table 7.1 summarizes the direct information on marital status, family structure, and fertility available in the published results of the Russian and Soviet censuses from 1897 to 1979. The only items available from all six censuses are marital status by currently married/currently not married, families (or households) by size, and the population by dependency status.

Table 7.1. Availability of family and fertility data in Russian and Soviet census reports, 1897–1979

	1897	1926	1939	1959	1970	1979
Marital status (married/not married)	x	x	x	x	x	x
Single, married, widowed, divorced	x	x				x
Families or households by size	x	x	x	x	x	x
Families/lone individuals		x	x	x	x	x
Families by type		x			x	x
Children ever born						x
Children at home		x			x	x
Crude birthrate				x		
Children under one year of age	x	x		x		
Population by dependent or not	x	x	x	x	x	x
Dependents by type		x	x	x	x	x

The most basic distinction in family structure is between those who live in families and those who do not. Although the definition of a family differs from census to census, a family always must have at least two members. The family members must be related by blood, adoption, or marriage, and there is some requirement of coresidence, sharing of facilities, or sharing of a budget. Soviet censuses classify each member of the population according to whether that person is the head of a family, is not the family head but lives together with other members of his or her family, is a member of a family not living together with the rest of his or her family, or is not a member of a family.

Overall, the 1926 census is the most complete of the six censuses, but the information gathered on family composition and on fertility has improved somewhat in post–World War II censuses. The 1970 and 1979 censuses collected and published more detailed information on the family for the Soviet Union as a whole than did earlier censuses.

Some information on family and fertility in Soviet censuses seldom appears in censuses anywhere. Only the 1979 census collected and published information on the number of children ever born to women. Similarly, crude birthrates rarely appear in censuses. In instances where these rates do appear, as in the 1959 Soviet census report, they had to be calculated by combining census data with vital-statistics data, a practice that usually is not followed.

Information on the dependency status of the population has always appeared in Russian and Soviet censuses. Some discussion of dependency is relevant to family and fertility because dependents are usually supported by other members of the family. Also, the relation between a woman's dependency status and the presence of young children is a topic with great policy relevance.

Census Information on Family and Fertility

It is important to know what information relevant to family and fertility was collected and how the information was used to construct the measures in the census reports. The range of possible census results, of course, is constrained by what was asked. The instructions to interviewers also are helpful for understanding the meaning of the items.

Most questions about family and fertility were asked of the entire Soviet population. In most Soviet censuses, however, some questions were asked of only a part of the total population. Questions directed to a random sample of the population or directed at particular subgroups are often motivated by pressing policy concerns. Besides generating useful data, these special questions provide insight into the concerns of the census planners. In the 1926 census, some questions were asked only of urban residents. In the 1970 and 1979 censuses some questions were asked only of a random sample of the permanent resident families, and special questions were also asked of those working only in the domestic (household) economy or in private auxiliary agricultural employment.

Organization of the census form. The blanks for Russian and Soviet censuses have been published, but the instructions to enumerators usually do not state explicit questions to be asked. Table 7.2 shows the wording of the family and fertility items asked in each census. Every census asked sex and age for every person; sex and age (aside from age in months for those less than one year of age) are not listed in Table 7.2.

Table 7.2. Wording of questions on family and fertility in the Russian and Soviet censuses, 1897–1979

Fertility

1897, 1926, 1939
How many years of age ___ years, or for children less than one year ___ months.
1959
How many years of age, or if less than a year of age, what is the age—in months? (Years ___ Months ___)
1970
Age (Years ___ Months ___)
   For those who desire to work, which of the following would convince you to work: 1) Having children in day care, school-internat or group with an extended day, 2) Obtaining work for part of each day or part of the week, 3) Obtaining work in (my) speciality, 4) Obtaining work near my home, 5) Obtaining further training in my profession, 6) Obtaining work I would enjoy, 7) Other reason
   (In form for those in the working ages who work at home or as private auxiliary workers in the rural economy)

   For women ask: a) the number of children under 16 years of age (Total, number under 1 year of age, 1–2 years of age, 3–6 years of age, 7–13 years of age, 14–15 years of age), b) Of that number, the number in day care, school-internat, or group with an extended day (categories as above)
   (In form for those in the working ages who work at home or as private auxiliary workers in the rural economy)
1979
For women, ask how many children have been born (none, 1, 2, ... 15, or more)
(In 25% sample)
   For those who desire to work, which of the following would convince you to work: 1) Having children in day care, school-internat or group with an extended day, 2) Obtaining work for part of each day or part of the week, 3) Obtaining work in (my) speciality, 4) Obtaining work near my home, 5) Obtaining further training in my profession, 6) Obtaining work I would enjoy, 7) Other reason
   (In form for those in the working ages who work at home or as private auxiliary workers in the rural economy)
   For women ask: a) the number of children under 16 years of age (Total, number under 1 year of age, 1–2 years of age, 3–6 years of age, 7–13 years of age, 14–15 years of age), b) Of that number, the number in day care, school-internat, or group with an extended day (categories as above)
   (In form for those in the working ages who work at home or as private auxiliary workers in the rural economy)

Marital Status

1897
Single, married, widowed, divorced or separated
1926
Marital status (Married, widowed, never married, separated or divorced)
1939
Are you currently married (Yes, no)
1959

Are you currently married? (Yes, no, widowed indicated to interviewer as acceptable answers)
1970
Are you currently married (Yes, no)
1979
Marital status (Married, never married, widowed, divorced/separated)

Relationship to head of family

1897
Write down the head of household or head of family
1926
Relationship to head of family (Wife, son, daughter, etc., [indicate])
Whether the person is the son or daughter of the family head from a previous marriage
Number of family members, including family head, regularly living in the dwelling
(On family card, for the urban population)
Number of servants and members of families of servants regularly living in this dwelling
(On family card, for the urban population)
Number of marital pairs in family
(On family card, for the urban population)
If head of family is a member of a marital pair, number of years married
(On family card, for the urban population)
1939, 1959, 1970
Relationship to head of family (Wife, son, daughter, mother, sister, nephew, etc., [indicate])
1979
Relationship to head of family (Head, wife/husband, daughter/son, mother/father, sister/brother, mother-in-law/father-in-law, daughter-in-law/son-in-law, grandmother/grandfather, granddaughter/grandson, niece/nephew/other relative, lone individual, member of a family that lives elsewhere)

Dependency status

1897
Source of support
1926
If not working, indicate the main source of support
1939
Of what social group are you a member: in a group of workers, service personnel, kolkhozniks, cooperative kustars, individual peasants, a free professional, or a member of a cult or a nonworking element?
1959
If not working, indicate the main source of support
1970, 1979
Primary source of support (Work at an enterprise, in the public sector, work in a kolkhoz, work in own account [for kustars and individual peasants], work as a private individual, free professional, private auxiliary worker in the rural economy, pensioners, on a stipend, other governmental support, dependent, other source)

Although the census is conducted by an enumerator who visits the household and supposedly asks every person (except young children) to answer for himself or herself, the census blank appears similar to one designed for self-enumeration. For example, the census blank contains a heading, such as *Pol* (Sex), and then a blank (M or Zh) to be checked. However, some questions have acceptable responses indicated, and the

1970 and 1979 censuses have precoded categories for the answers to many questions.

The 1897 census was a census of individuals. Unlike later censuses, the basic enumeration unit was the household, rather than the family. Households were tabulated by size, and enumerators recorded whether or not the members of the household were related. The enumeration in the 1926 census and later censuses was based on the family. In fact, the 1926 census included a "family card" for urban residents on which information such as the duration of marriage of the family head was recorded.

Definition of the family head. In the 1926 census and every later census the enumerator had to first determine who the head of the family was. After that was determined, given the definition of family in effect, the information for other family members could be recorded properly.

The definition of family head in Soviet censuses has shifted from being based on economic support to being based on perceptions within the family. The definition was not important in the 1897 census, since that census was based on individuals and developed scanty information about the family. In 1926 and 1939, the family head was to be the person providing the main support for the family (Gozulov and Grigor'yants, 1969: 153; Boyarskiy and Shusherin, 1951: 187; Pustokhod and Voblyy, 1940: 148). In the 1959, 1970, and 1979 censuses the enumerator was instructed to record as family head whoever the family thought was the head, within wide bounds. The family head had to be an adult member of the family whose permanent residence was with the family (Maksimov, 1976; USSR, 1958b; USSR, 1978). Although instructed to accept whoever was designated as head by the family, the enumerator was to give guidance if the respondents had difficulty formulating an answer. In post-World War II censuses, enumerators were advised that the family head should be the person who provided the bulk of support for the family—harking back to the 1926 and 1939 definitions.

Isupov and Borisov (1978: 50–51), in commenting on the 1979 census, state that the designation of the family head is only an heuristic device and that husbands and wives in the Soviet Union have equal legal rights. In addition, they state that the census is not the place to determine whether a single family head exists or whether both marital partners share equally. Some Soviet scholars have complained about the inappropriateness of one person being designated as family head when two spouses share equally or when a family contains more than one marital pair (Ter-Izrael'yan, 1979). Nonetheless, the 1959 and 1970 censuses tabulated some information by the sex of the head of the family.

The recent Soviet definition of family head is generally in line with United Nations recommendations on the designation of the head of household. The UN recommends that

> the *head of the household* is that person in the household who is acknowledged as such by the other household members. Although a more desirable definition for purposes of dependency statistics would be the person who bears the chief responsibility for the economic maintenance of the household, it is not recommended that this definition be applied because of the difficulty of collecting the information needed to determine economic responsibility. (UN, 1967a: 57)

The U.S. definition has differed substantially from UN recommendations. Before 1980, the definition stated:

> The household head is the person reported as the head by members of the group, except that married women are not classified as heads if their husbands are living with them at the time of enumeration. (Shryock and Siegel, 1975: 302)

Since 1980, the United States has tabulated data in relation to a "reference person," who is that person or one of the persons in whose name the housing unit is owned or rented (Bianchi, 1982).

Determining who is a family member. Post–World War II Soviet censuses defined a family as follows:

> A family for the purposes of the censuses includes those individuals, living together, related by blood or marriage[1] and sharing a common budget. Individuals living apart from the family, but who share with the family a common budget or a regular material link (*regularnaya material'naya svyaz'*), are also counted as family members, but as living apart from the family. Individuals not in a family and not sharing support with a family are counted as lone individuals. (USSR, 1974: 4)

The UN recommended definitions and the U.S. definition of family have been more concerned with coresidence than has the Soviet definition. The UN defines a family as

> those members of the household ... who are related to a specified degree, through blood, adoption or marriage. The degree of relationship used in determining the limits of the family is dependent on uses to which the data are to be put and so cannot be precisely set for world-wide use. (UN, 1967a: 48)

---

1. Adopted children are also considered part of the family.

Before 1947, U.S. official usage defined a family as

> all the persons who occupy a housing unit. A house, an apartment or other group of rooms or a single room, is regarded as a housing unit when it is occupied or intended for occupancy as separate living quarters. Separate living quarters are those in which the occupants do not live and eat with any other persons in the structure and in which there is either (1) direct access from the outside or through a common hall, or (2) a kitchen or cooking equipment for exclusive use of the occupants. (United States Bureau of the Census, 1964: LV)

Since 1947, the former U.S. definition of a family has become the definition of a *household,* and the definition of a *family* has become

> the entire group of (two or more) persons in a household who are related by blood, marriage, or adoption. According to this terminology, two related married couples, a couple and a related parent-child group, or any other group of two or more persons related to each other is counted as one family if the members occupy the same living quarters and eat together as one household. (Shryock and Siegel, 1975: 300)

Thus, the United States has moved from enumeration based on households with coresidence as a necessary condition and kinship an unimportant one to enumeration based on households with kinship mattering but coresidence still being required. The Soviet definition of a family concentrates on economic ties—sharing a common budget—for those who are coresident, and on at least the maintenance of a regular material link for family members who are not coresident.

The lack of a coresidence requirement for family membership in Soviet census usage differs from census usage virtually everywhere else in the world. Only in some parts of sub-Saharan Africa does the census definition of family not require coresidence—leading to some families reportedly containing over a hundred members in the case of Portuguese Guinea (Burch, 1967: 356–58). In most parts of the world,

> "Family" refers only to those kin with whom one co-resides.... Kin with whom one does not share the same dwelling unit are not part of one's "family" in the demographic sense, even though they may live close by (sometimes in adjacent dwellings), and even though there may be considerable social and economic integration among them. (Burch, 1979: 174)

Burch (1979: 182–83) notes that a common hypothesis that has received little empirical support is that extended families tend to have higher fertility than nuclear families. According to Burch and Gendell (1970), one reason for this lack of empirical support may be the restriction of consideration to kin who are coresident. The Soviet definition of family is more appropriate for a test of the hypothesized link between fertility and family extension than is the conventional definition of family.

The difference between most census definitions of family and the Soviet census definition of family is essentially the difference between the *family of residence* and the *family of interaction* (Burch, 1967: 348). Most censuses consider the family of residence; the Soviet definition is close to that of the family of interaction.

Even the sub-Saharan African definitions of family that do not require coresidence have assumed close residential proximity of those relatives considered family members (Goody, 1972: 106–10). The Soviet definition of the family does not limit the distance from the rest of the family that the "family members living apart" can reside and does not require that their residential separation be temporary—as long as they maintain a regular material link, they can be family members even though they are permanently resident elsewhere. Also, what constitutes a "regular material link" is a subjective matter determined by the family. There is no requirement that this link involve a majority of the support of the physically separated family member as long as the family considers it "regular."

A. G. Volkov, director of the Scientific Research Institute of the Soviet Central Statistical Administration, complained that the term "regular material link" was not clear and argued at the All-Union Conference of Statisticians convened prior to the 1970 Soviet census that the concept should be clarified. He noted, for example, that a student who had a wife and child at the place of his school but who still received financial aid from his parents could be considered a "family member living separately" in his parents' family. Since the student had his own family, though, Volkov maintained that he should not be thus classified. Despite this appeal, neither the term nor the instructions to interviewers on this point was changed (USSR, 1969: 311–12).

There are several likely consequences of the difference between the Soviet censuses will also contain fewer lone individuals than will American Definitional differences will cause Soviet families to be larger, to contain more dependents, and to be more extended than American families. Soviet censuses will also contain fewer lone individuals than will American censuses.

The difference stemming from the definitional interplay of current residence, place of permanent residence, and family membership can be illustrated by the different way Soviet and American censuses classify college students. According to Soviet convention in 1959 and 1970, students living away from home were classified as having their permanent residence at the place of the school, although they could still be classified as "family members, not living together with the rest of the family." In 1979, the designation of permanent residence at the place of the school applied only to Soviet students at specialized secondary or higher educational institutions. Since 1950, U.S. census procedure has classified college students away from home as permanent residents at the place of the college but secondary school students as permanent residents at the place of residence of their family of origin (Shryock and Siegel, 1975: 96). American students away at a university or college would not be considered members of their family of origin, but Soviet university students would still be members of their family of origin if they maintained a regular material link with that family.

The Soviet census definition affects the classification of families as extended. Imagine that the widowed mother of the family head lives in her own apartment, receives financial aid from her son, and eats with the son's nuclear family on weekends. U.S. definitions would consider the widowed mother a lone individual; Soviet definitions would consider her a member of her son's family. U.S. definitions would consider the son's family to be nuclear; Soviet definitions would consider it to be extended. Now imagine that the mother of the family head lives with her son's family but maintains a separate budget. According to the Soviet census definition of family, she would not be a member of her son's family; according to the American census definition of family, she would be a member of her son's family. On balance, the Soviet definition is more likely to lead to recorded family extension than is the American definition. Volkov (1976: 22-24) notes that both the old and the young disproportionately appear in the categories "family members living apart from their families" and "lone individuals." Those in their 20s tend to be family members living apart, while those over age 50 tend more often to be lone individuals.

Definitions of who is permanently absent as opposed to temporarily absent are also important. In post–World War II Soviet censuses, information on many topics has been reported sometimes for the present population and sometimes for the permanent population; information on family always refers to the permanent population (Anderson and Silver, 1985). Soviet censuses define people as "temporarily absent" if their permanent residence is still with the family and if they have been absent less than six months.[2] People who have been absent less than six months but who (in the opinion of the family) do not intend to return are permanently absent—that is, their permanent residence is elsewhere.

---

2. Students residing at school and members of the military are considered permanently absent even if they have been gone less than six months and even if they intend to return.

Family composition. Soviet censuses have presented information on the composition of the family, including the number of family members, the dependency status of family members, and the sex of the head of the family. Information on the type of family is usually not included in censuses. As Burch (1967: 352) notes, "No convenient international compilations are available on such questions as the number of generations, relationship of household or family members to the head of household, and so forth. Indeed, few nations have comprehensive census data on these more detailed aspects of family composition."

The distribution of families by size has appeared in the published results of each of the five Soviet censuses. This information refers not to all family members but only to the coresident members of the family. For 1970, however, it is possible to estimate the average size of the entire family, including non-coresident members. For the USSR as a whole in 1970, the average number of *coresident* family members was 3.7 (Volume 7, Table 25) and of *all* family members was 3.9 (from the number of family members and the number of lone individuals in Volume 7, Table 22, and from the number of families in Volume 7, Table 25). Although these differences are not large, neither are they trivial.

The lack of a coresidence requirement for family membership probably has more effect on the recorded proportion of families that are extended than on family size. Data on families by type (described below) refer to all family members, not just coresident family members; no data have been located that would allow estimation of the proportion of families that would be extended if coresident family members alone were considered. In 1970, 22.9 percent of families in the USSR as a whole were recorded as extended, that is, were of Types 2, 3, or 4b below (calculated from data in Volume 7, Table 27).

The inclusion of non-coresident family members may be making a large difference in the estimated proportion of families that are extended. If in 1970, for example, every non-coresident family member caused one family to be recorded as extended when that family would not have been recorded as extended based only on coresident family members, then only 6.2 percent of the families in the USSR as a whole would have been recorded as extended based on coresident family members rather than 22.9 percent based on coresident and non-coresident members. The actual effect of inclusion of non-coresident family members in the determination of whether the family is extended is certainly not as great as these calculations suggest is possible, but using the available data to compare the proportion of families that are extended for the USSR and for other countries would be very misleading.

For 1970 and 1979, the distribution of families by size was published according to nationality for families in which all members belonged to the same nationality and also for families of mixed nationality. These data are published by union republic and other nationality areas. They also are published (not by nationality) by oblast. Coale, Anderson, and Härm (1979) used these data to estimate marital fertility by nationality, and Fisher (1980) suggested using them to estimate ethnic intermarriage rates.

The 1926, 1970, and 1979 censuses include interesting information on families by type. The 1926 census classified families as follows:[3]

Type A. Families including a marital pair
  A1. Not including children
    A1a. Without (other) relatives
    A1b. With economically inactive (other) relatives
    A1c. With economically active (other) relatives
  A2. Including children only of the marital pair
    A2a. Without (other) relatives
    A2b. With economically inactive (other) relatives
    A2c. With economically active (other) relatives
  A3. Including children from previous marriages
    A3b. With economically inactive (other) relatives
    A3c. With economically active (other) relatives
Type B. Families without a marital pair, but that include children of the family head
    Ba. Without (other) relatives
    Bb. With economically inactive (other) relatives
    Bc. With economically active (other) relatives
Type C. Families without a marital pair that do not include children of the family head
    Cb. With economically inactive (other) relatives
    Cc. With economically active (other) relatives
Type D. Complex families

The 1970 classification was

1. One marital pair with or without children
2. One marital pair with or without children, but with other relatives
3. Two or more marital pairs with or without children with or without other relatives
4a. A mother/father with children
4b. A mother/father with children, with other relatives
5. Other families

---

3. The letters and numbers assigned to the different types of families in 1926 are as assigned in the 1926 census. No numbers or letters were assigned to the types of families in the 1970 or the 1979 censuses. Numbers and letters are assigned here for convenient reference and comparison.

The 1979 classification was

1. One marital pair with or without children
2a. One marital pair with or without children, but with one of the parents of the marital pair
2b. One marital pair with or without children, but with or without one of the parents of the marital pair but with other relatives
3. Two or more marital pairs with or without children with or without other relatives
4. A mother/father with children
5. Other families

All these typologies focused on the presence or absence of a marital pair, of children, and of nonnuclear relatives. In addition, in 1926 there was a concern with economic activity of nonnuclear kin. The 1979 census was more concerned with whether the family was extended only because of the presence of a parent of the head or a parent of the spouse of the head, while the 1970 census was more concerned with whether a family without a marital pair but with children of the head also included other relatives. The published results of the 1979 census noted that "children" for families classified as Type 1 included "children of all ages, living together with their parents and not married" (*Vestnik statistiki*, 1983: 70). Apparently if married children lived with their parents, the family would then be classified as Type 2b.

The data on dependency status are also interesting. In 1926, family members were classified as to whether or not they were "economically active." The industry in which economically active people worked was cross-classified by the people's marital status and other family characteristics. For those who were not economically active, the cross-tabulations were presented according to the industry in which the person supporting the dependent person worked. The data on dependents in the 1959 census are noteworthy because dependent women in the working ages were classified as to whether or not they had children younger than age 14. The dependency data reported from the 1970 and 1979 censuses did not include information on the presence of children for dependent women.

Currently married versus ever married. Russian and Soviet censuses have varied in the degree of detail for which data on marital status are collected and published. The 1897 and 1926 censuses recorded a full range of marital statuses: single, currently married, widowed, and divorced or separated. The 1939 census recorded only whether or not a person was currently married. In 1959, the interviewers were instructed to record people as married if currently married, widowed if widowed, and not currently married otherwise. In the published 1959 census report, however, the widowed were not separately reported—only a classification by currently married/not currently married was given. In 1970, only current marital status was recorded. The 1979 census returned to the 1897 and 1926 practice of recording a full marital status distribution.

The return to a full marital status distribution in 1979 should allow fuller analysis of marital dissolution in the Soviet Union. However, the published 1979 census results have not yet presented detailed marital status in interesting cross-tabulations. Also, the lack of data by age, including marital status by age, seriously limits the usefulness of the information published to date from the 1979 census.

Who was considered a married person or a divorced person has varied among censuses. In 1897, enumerators were only supposed to record as married those who were legally (officially) married. In later censuses, people were to be recorded as married who considered themselves so, whether the marriage was registered or not. In 1897 and 1926, people were to be recorded as divorced only if the divorce was registered, while in later censuses, people who considered themselves divorced were to be recorded as divorced (or not married) whether or not the divorce was registered (Gozulov and Grigor'yants, 1969: 145).

The initial variant of the 1970 census conducted in 1966 and the test census conducted in 1967 included a full marital status distribution and questions on the duration of marriage for women and the month and year of first marriage and the month and year of dissolution of first marriage (where appropriate) (Gozulov and Grigor'yants, 1969: 163). None of these detailed questions were included in the 1970 census, although the detailed breakdown of marital status appeared in the 1979 census. In their review of the 1979 census methodology, Isupov and Borisov (1978: 52) do not comment on this change in detail on marital status for the 1979 census.

Even though the answer to the question on marital status seems straightforward, the question is subjective. Partners sometimes disagree as to whether or not they are married. For example, comparison of the estimated numbers of Soviet women and men who in 1959 reported themselves as married reveals that larger numbers of women than of men are married at all ages. This discrepancy probably occurs partially because widows sometimes report to census takers that they are married. Also, Goldstein, Goldstein, and Piampiti (1973) found evidence for Thailand that men living apart from their wives sometimes report that they are not married, while their wives more often report themselves as married.

Gozulov and Grigor'yants (1969: 147–48) discuss this phenomenon for those reaching marriageable age in the 1920s through World War II in the Soviet Union. They state that more women than men reported themselves married or divorced (rather than never married) among those who reached marriageable age, even though owing to social turbulence and the shortage of marriageable males, more women than men remained legally unmarried. For the Soviet population as a whole in 1959, based on the reported numbers of men and women aged 16 and over (as published in the 1970 Soviet census report) and the reported proportions of men and women married (as published in the 1959 census report), there were 42,892,500 married men and 43,642,700 married women. Thus, for every 1,000 women reported as married, there were 17 missing husbands, that is, 17 fewer men who reported themselves as married.

In the 1926 census, a larger number of women than men were also reported as currently married. This larger number of currently married women than men for Soviet Central Asia in 1926 has sometimes been interpreted as evidence of polygamy. However, the ratio of the number of married women to married men for Soviet Central Asia in 1926 falls within the range of this ratio for all the Soviet union republics in 1926. Hence, there seems no solid evidence of substantial polygamy in 1926 but only the typical greater tendency of women than men to report themselves as married.

Children present and children ever born. Censuses usually do not record information directly bearing on fertility. Only the 1979 Soviet census includes a direct question on fertility.

The closest that Soviet censuses before 1979 came to recording fertility information was to ask the age in months of children less than one year of age on the census date or to tabulate the number of children of the family head or of the wife of the family head who resided with them. The data on children under one year of age are related to recent fertility but are affected by infant mortality and by the well-known tendency for children under one year of age to be missed by the census or to be reported as one year of age (Ewbank, 1981).

The special questions in the 1926 census for the urban population reflect a concern at that time with urban living conditions and the nature of the urban family. For Moscow, Leningrad, and other large cities in the RSFSR, there are tabulations of the number of children by marital duration and of the number of children by occupation of the family head. However, these 1926 data only include surviving children residing in the same household and are not tabulated for all types of families. The data on children by marital duration only refer to families in which the family head is part of a marital pair and in which there are either no children (Type A1) or all the children in the household are the offspring of the family head's current marriage (Type A2). The data on the number of children by occupation of the family head only refer to families in which the family head is a member of a marital pair (Types A1 and A2) or the family head is not a member of a marital pair but the family includes children of the family head (Type B). For these urban populations, additional data are also presented for families with the head a part of a marital pair and which contain children all of whom are offspring of the current marriage (Type A2). These data provide the average age of the oldest child and the average age of the youngest child, by social group of the family head. With some qualifications, and in combination with data on the number of children in the family, these data can be used to investigate the timing of fertility.

The 1970 Soviet census also included data on the number of children. As in 1926, these data did not refer to all children ever born; they referred only to surviving children residing with their families. Also, the table that presented the number of children by age of mother (Volume 7, Table 32) and the tables that presented the number of children per 1,000 women (Volume 7, Tables 35–37) only referred to children who were coresident with their mother in families that included only one marital pair or a mother living with her children (types 1, 2, 4a, and 4b). In Volume 7, Table 32, the number of families in the USSR as a whole with two children was 14,473,833. In Volume 7, Table 28, which only required that children live with their families, the number of families with two children was 15,490,031. This illustrates the more general point that it is important to understand to what population subgroup any given table refers.

These 1970 data imperfectly reflect age-specific fertility because they are affected by differential mortality, patterns of home-leaving, and differential rates of occurrence of families with more than one marital pair. In Central Asia, for example, extended families might have higher fertility than nuclear families have. If so, these data would underestimate age-specific fertility in Central Asia because they would not include the fertility of women living in extended families that included more than one marital pair.

The inclusion of a question in the 1979 census (in the 25 percent sample) on the number of children ever born was a marked departure from earlier practice. "Children ever born" included living children residing with their mother, living children who resided elsewhere, and children who had died. Tabulations of the number of children of a woman living in the same family are much more common in all countries, because they do not require a special question but only a roster specifying the relationships between family members.

In 1979, the question on children ever born was to be asked of all women aged 16 or older (in the 25 percent sample), regardless of marital status. Information for women younger than age 16 was only supposed to be recorded for those young women who had borne children. It was not clear how the enumerator was to determine whether a woman younger than age 16 had borne children. According to Isupov and Borisov (1978: 57), this question was included because

> obtaining material on the combination by age and other characteristics of the level of fertility of different generations of women by ten-year age groups allows the examination of the differences in fertility in relation to education and nationality. All of this is necessary for the scientific study of the factors related to fertility and the creation of a great furthering of the conditions for the development of Soviet families.

In the 1979 census, the published tabulations from this question report the data for all women aged 15 or older rather than aged 16 or older. Probably the denominator is all women aged 15 or older while the numerator is reported children ever born of all women, even those few children born to women aged 14, 13, or even younger. The lack of agreement between the ages of women who were asked the number of children ever born and the ages used in the publications to date suggests that more fertility was found among women younger than age 16 than the census planners had expected. However, no data on the number of children ever born by age of mother have been published from the 1979 census.

The Soviet definition of a live birth will also make some difference in the number of children ever born. While women were supposed to report all live births, they were not to include stillbirths. The official Soviet definition of a live birth classifies some births as stillbirths that the American definition would classify as live births (United States, Department of Health, Education and Welfare, 1962: 24). If women responded to the Soviet census enumerator in accordance with the Soviet definition of a live birth, then the reported number of children ever born would be somewhat fewer than if the American definition of a live birth had been used.

The identical form was administered to those without public sector jobs in 1970 and 1979. It included items on reasons for not working and on children under age 16 by child-care arrangements. These questions were asked because of the government's strong interest in finding ways to mobilize labor reserves and especially ways to motivate women with young children to take public sector jobs (Isupov and Borisov, 1978). Neither the detailed census results nor research based on these special questions has been published, although the original tabulation plans for the 1970 census included some results using these questions (USSR, 1969: 673). Since plans were originally made to publish some of the data from this special form, something must have happened in the late 1960s or early 1970s which changed that decision.

Data Reliability

In Soviet censuses, as in other censuses and surveys, some rules are more likely to be violated than others. For example, it has commonly been found that more women report themselves as separated or divorced (rather than never married) than do men, even beyond what can be explained by differential remarriage rates. One possible explanation for this phenomenon is that once-married men can plausibly report themselves as single, while women with children have more difficulty doing so. In addition, unwed mothers often report themselves as divorced, separated, or widowed (Shryock and Siegel, 1975: 286). The extent of this misreporting has declined in the United States, possibly owing to a lessening disapproval of illegitimacy (Shryock and Siegel, 1975: 286). At the All-Union Conference of Statisticians held in advance of the 1970 Soviet census, it was noted that differences in the full marital status distribution by sex from the test censuses looked even more implausible than the differences by sex using only the married/not married classification (USSR, 1969: 230). Fuller publication of the detailed marital status data from the 1979 census would allow independent examination of this issue.

The question on temporary absence is certain to cause some difficulty for respondents. People normally have trouble reporting whether events happened more or less than a given length of time in the past. For example, reports on births in the last year are often biased by inaccurate perception of the reference period (Brass, 1975). Also the answer to the question on temporary absence may be affected more by the strength of the feelings of attachment of the rest of the family for the "temporarily absent" member than by the exact length of time the person has been gone or whether the person intends to return.

In addition, in post–World War II censuses the data on family members living apart from the rest of the family are likely to contain some error. For the data to be correct, those living together with the rest of the family and those living apart would need to be in perfect agreement as to whether a person maintained a "regular material link" with the rest of the family. Such agreement is unlikely.

It is well known that older women tend to underreport the number of their children ever born, partially because of omission of dead children and partially because of omission of children who have left home. It would be surprising if this did not happen to some extent in Soviet censuses. Publication of the number of children ever born by age of the mother would provide information that could be used to determine the extent to which such underreporting has occurred (Brass, 1975).

Calculation of Measures Indirectly or in Combination with Noncensus Data

Measures of fertility and family structure can be direct or indirect. On the most direct level, individuals are asked questions, and the distribution of answers is reported. Information obtained by combining answers from more than one respondent is more indirect. For example, censuses sometimes report the distribution of families by type, such as the number of families with one marital pair, with more than one marital pair, and so on. This kind of information is constructed from the set of responses on age, sex, and relationship to the family head from all the respondents in a given family.

Information can be obtained even more indirectly. Usually censuses report information on the status of the population at a given time, such as on the population by marital status by age or the number of women by number of children ever born. Censuses rarely report data on the timing of occurrences of events. For example, censuses rarely report recent births by age of women or recent marriages by age of spouses. Event occurrence data (also called current-accounts data) are usually obtained from the vital-registration system rather than from the census operation. Vital registration obtains information on the number of people to whom some event, such as marriage or birth, has happened in a given time period, but the information from the vital-registration system alone is not sufficient to calculate a rate of occurrence. The vital-registration system cannot provide information on the number of people "at risk" of the event, that is, the number of people to whom the event could have happened—the denominator for a rate. Information on the population at risk is typically obtained from a census. The rate then is calculated from various pieces of information, of which the census provides an important part.

Even more indirect measures can be constructed using census data. Fertility measures are sometimes estimated from census-based population information that does not include items directly referring to fertility at all. For example, the age distribution of the population in combination with a mortality assumption can be used to estimate fertility.

Calculation of marital status. Just as census data are needed to provide denominators for fertility rates when birth data come from vital registration, vital-registration data are necessary to update census estimates of the population by current status between census dates. Naturally, vital-statistics data on births and deaths are used to revise total population estimates. However, vital-registration data on marriages, divorces, and deaths (widowhood) are also used to update estimates of the composition of the population by marital status. For example, using both census and vital-statistics data, the researcher can construct a nuptiality table in the form of a multiple decrement life table for the USSR which is sensitive to period effects on nuptiality (cf. Anderson, 1982; Volkov, 1979).

Results of vital-statistics data collection on marriage and marital dissolution are published by the Soviet Central Statistical Administration in the monthly *Vestnik statistiki*. Marriages and divorces per 1,000 population by sex and age are frequently published for the Soviet population as a whole. Often marriages and divorces per thousand population by sex (not by age) are also published by union republic. Data on divorce by duration of marriage for the total Soviet population are available, but union republic-level data on marriage and divorce by age are more scanty and are found erratically in *Narodnoye khozyaystvo* volumes for union republics.

Models of marriage can be applied to Soviet data on marital status to estimate first-marriage patterns (Coale, Anderson, and Härm, 1979). Such fitted models can be useful for comparing the dynamics of marriage across census dates, unaffected directly by changes in the age distribution.

Calculation of fertility measures. Most conventional fertility measures, such as the crude birthrate or age-specific fertility rates, are calculated through a combination of birth data (or birth data by age of mother) from the vital-registration system and total population data (or data on the female population by age) from the census. Sometimes, however, a lack of fit between census data and vital-statistics data distorts measures. In late-nineteenth-century European Russia, for example, different definitions of urban were used for different purposes (Fedor, 1975). Thus, differences between the urban definition used in the census and that used in vital statistics led to distorted fertility measures for some guberniyas (Coale, Anderson, and Härm, 1979: 212–13).

While in the Soviet Union, as in most countries, the census is under central control, the vital-statistics system is more decentralized. At the All-Union Conference of Statisticians convened before the 1979 Soviet census, R. M. Dmitriyeva, director of the Sector on Statistics of

Population, Health, and Social Welfare of the Soviet Central Statistical Administration, noted that the coverage of vital-statistics data in the Soviet Union is generally less complete than census data and that improvement of the quality of the current-accounts data should be a concern of those involved in the census (Ter-Izrael'yan, 1979: 144–51).

Demographers have long relied on census data by age and sex to obtain fertility estimates. Estimation of recent fertility was clearly the main motivation behind the question on the number of children under one year of age which has been included in some Russian and Soviet censuses. Some evidence suggests that estimates of fertility for 1897 based on the number of children under one year of age are more accurate than estimates based on vital registration (Coale, Anderson, and Härm, 1979: 207–19).

Demographers sometimes employ the child/woman ratio, which is usually the number of children under 5 years of age per 1,000 women aged 15–49, as an indicator of fertility. Researchers using Soviet data have more often used the ratio of children aged 0–9 to women aged 20–49 because of the age categories in which Soviet data are presented (cf. Lewis, Rowland, and Clem, 1976; Mazur, 1967; Silver, 1974). Child/woman ratios are, however, imperfect measures of fertility because they are affected by differential mortality and by differences in the age structure of women within the childbearing ages. We know, for example, that fertility is higher in Central Asia than in the Baltic area. We also know that the age structure is older in the Baltic area than in Central Asia. The higher infant and child mortality in Central Asia will lead the child/woman ratio to underestimate Central Asian fertility in comparison with the Baltic region. On the other hand, the younger age structure in Central Asia will lead to an overestimate of Central Asian fertility in comparison with that of the Baltic. There is no assurance that these countering tendencies will cancel each other out.

Another means of obtaining a fertility estimate involves fitting a population model to the available data by age. For example, a mortality assumption can be used in combination with the proportion of the population under a given age, such as under age 10, in order to fit a model stable population (Brass, 1975; UN, 1967b). A fertility estimate can then be obtained from the fitted model stable population (cf. Coale, Anderson, and Härm, 1979). If the mortality assumption is correct for the given population, and if the population sufficiently fits the other assumptions of stable population models, the mortality level and the age structure will be taken into account by using this method.

The age structure by marital status can also be used to estimate both marital fertility and aspects of the marriage pattern, if certain stable population assumptions are met (Coale and Trussell, 1974). Some regions of the Soviet Union, such as Central Asia, fit these assumptions more closely than other regions, such as European Russia.

Yet another method involves obtaining a regression predictor of fertility from known relationships in order to estimate fertility for groups for which the desired data are not published. Mazur (1976) used this approach in estimating the total fertility rate by nationality from the relation between the Soviet version of the child/woman ratio and the crude birthrate by geographical area of the Soviet Union and between the crude birthrate and the total fertility rate from non-Soviet data. Coale, Anderson, and Härm (1979) used a regression approach to estimate marital fertility in the USSR by nationality in 1970 based on the relation between a measure of marital fertility and the distribution of families by size across provinces.

Both Soviet and Western scholars have been interested in the demography of the Soviet family. The Soviet government has collected extensive data on this topic, although they have not always been published in full. The importance of these data suggest that Soviet statistics on marriage, fertility, and family structure will continue to be collected. It is hoped that they will also continue to be published.

References

Allworth, Edward, ed. 1980. *Ethnic Russia in the USSR*. New York: Praeger.

Anderson, Barbara A. 1982. "Changes in Marriage and Marital Dissolution in the Soviet Union." In *Nuptiality and Fertility*, ed. Ladoslav Ruzicka, 133–50. Liege: ORDINA.

Anderson, Barbara A., and Brian D. Silver 1985. " 'Permanent' and 'Present' Populations in Soviet Statistics." *Soviet Studies* 37: 386–402.

Bianchi, Suzanne M. 1982. "Changing Concepts of Household and Family in the Census and CPS." *Proceedings of the Social Statistics Section—1982*, 13–22. Washington, D.C.: American Statistical Association.

Boyarskiy, A. Ya., and P. P. Shusherin. 1951. *Demograficheskaya statistika*. Moscow: Gosudarstvennoye Statisticheskoye Izdatel'stvo.

Brass, William I. 1975. *Methods for Estimating Fertility and Mortalilty from Limited and Defective Data*. Chapel Hill, N.C.: Carolina Population Center.

Burch, Thomas K. 1967. "The Size and Structure of Families: A Comparative Analysis of Census Data." *American Sociological Review* 32: 347–63.

———. 1979. "Household and Family Demography: A Bibliographic Essay." *Population Index* 45, no. 2: 173–95.

Burch, Thomas K., and Murray Gendell. 1970. "Extended Family Structure and Fertility: Some Conceptual and Methodological Issues." *Journal of Marriage and the Family* 32: 227–36.

Coale, Ansley J., and T. James Trussell. 1974. "Model Fertility Schedules." *Population Index* 40: 185–258.

Coale, Ansley J., Barbara A. Anderson, and Erna Härm. 1979. *Human Fertility in Russia since the Nineteenth Century.* Princeton: Princeton University Press.

Ewbank, Douglas C. 1981. *Age Misreporting and Age-Selective Underenumeration.* Committee on Population and Demography, National Academy of Sciences Washington, D.C.: National Academy Press.

Fedor, Thomas S. 1975. *Patterns of Urban Growth in the Russian Empire during the Nineteenth Century.* Chicago: University of Chicago, Department of Geography.

Fisher, Wesley. 1980. "Comment—The Extent of Intermarriage in the Russian Group." In *Ethnic Russia in the USSR.* See Allworth, ed., 1980: 309–11.

Goldstein, Sidney, Alice Goldstein, and Sauvaluck Piampiti. 1973. "The Effect of Broken Marriage on Fertility Levels in Thailand." *Journal of Social Sciences* (Thailand) 10: 47–87.

Goody, Jack. 1972. "The Evolution of the Family." In *Household and Family in Past Time,* 103–24. See Laslett, ed., 1972.

Gozulov, A. I., and M. G. Grigor'yants. 1969. *Narodonaseleniye SSSR.* Moscow: Statistika.

Isupov, A. A., and V. A. Borisov. 1978. *Vsesoyuznaya perepis' naseleniya 1979 goda.* Moscow: Znaniye.

Laslett, Peter, ed. 1972. *Household and Family in Past Time.* London: Cambridge University Press.

Lewis, Robert A., Richard H. Rowland, and Ralph S. Clem. 1976. *Nationality and Population Change in Russia and the USSR.* New York: Praeger.

Maksimov, G. M., ed. 1976. *Vsesoyuznaya perepis' naseleniya 1970 goda: Sbornik statey.* Moscow: Statistika.

Mazur, D. Peter. 1967. "Fertility among Ethnic Groups in the USSR." *Demography* 4: 172–95.

———. 1976. "Constructing Fertility Tables for Soviet Populations." *Demography* 13: 19–35.

Ogarkov, N. V. 1982. *Vsegda v gotovnosti k zashchite Otechestva.* (All in readiness for the defense of the fatherland.) Moscow: Voyenizdat.

Pustokhod, P. I., and V. K. Voblyy. 1940. *Perepisi naseleniya: Istoriya i organizatsiya.* Moscow: Gosplanizdat.

Shishkina, M. 1969. "Izucheniye sostava sem'i v perepisi naseleniya 1970 g." *Vestnik statistiki,* no. 10: 41–44.

Shryock, Henry S., and Jacob S. Siegel. 1975. *The Methods and Materials of Demography.* Vol. 1. 3d ptg. rev. Washington, D.C.: U.S., Bureau of the Census, U.S. Government Printing Office.

Silver, Brian D. 1974. "Levels of Sociocultural Development among Soviet Nationalities." *American Political Science Review* 68: 1618–37.

Ter-Izrael'yan, T. G., ed. 1979. *Sovershenstvovaniye gosudarstvennoy statistiki na sovremennom etape (Materialy Vsesoyuznogo soveshchaniya statistikov).* Moscow: Statistika.

United Nations. 1967a. *Principles and Recommendations for the 1970 Population Censuses.* Statistical Papers, Series M, no. 44. New York.

———. 1967b. *Manual IV. Methods of Estimating Basic Demographic Measures from Incomplete Data*. Population Studies, Series A, no. 42. New York.
United States. Bureau of the Census. 1964. *U.S. Census of Population: 1960*. Vol. 1, *Characteristics of the Population*, Part 1, *United States Summary*. Washington, D.C.: U.S. Government Printing Office.
———. Department of Health, Education and Welfare. 1962. *Report of the United States Public Health Mission to the Union of Soviet Socialist Republics—August 13 to September 14, 1957*. Washington, D.C.: U.S. Government Printing Office.
USSR. Tsentral'noye Statisticheskoye Upravleniye. 1958a. *Vsesoyuznoye soveshchaniye statistikov 4–8 yunya 1957 g*. Moscow: Gosudarstvennoye Statisticheskoye Izdatel'stvo.
———. 1958b. *Vsesoyuznaya perepis' naseleniya 1959 goda*. Moscow: Gospolitizdat.
———. 1969. *Vsesoyuznoye soveshchaniye statistikov 22–26 aprelya 1968 g*. Moscow: Statistika.
———. 1974. *Itogi vsesoyuznoy perepisi naseleniya 1970 goda. Tom VII. Migratsiya naseleniya, chislo i sostav semey v SSSR, soyuznykh i avtonomnykh respublikakh, krayakh i oblastiyakh*. Moscow: Statistika.
———. 1978. *Vsesoyuznaya perepis' naseleniya—vsenarodnoye delo*. Moscow: Statistika.
Valentey, D. I., ed. 1976. *Demograficheskaya situatsiya v SSSR*. Moscow: Statistika.
Vestnik statistiki. 1983. No. 2.
Volkov, A. 1976. "Izmeneniye velichiny i sostava semey v SSSR." In *Demo graficheskaya situatsiya v SSSR*, 17–33. See Valentey, ed., 1976.
Volkov, A. G. 1979. "Ob ozhidaemoy prodolzhitel'nosti braka i ee demograficheskikh faktorakh." In *Demograficheskoye razvitiye sem'i*, ed. A. G. Volkov, 59–84. Moscow: Statistika.

Chapter 8

Education and Literacy Data in Russian and Soviet Censuses

RONALD D. LIEBOWITZ

Social scientists the world over require a knowledge of the quality and extensiveness of the education made available to, and attained by, individuals in the societies they are investigating. Education plays a pivotal role in shaping and integrating many of the changes that fall beneath the umbrella of "modernization," including increased literacy, urbanization, migration, change in the occupational and work-force structure, and changes in fertility. Quite justifiably, education has been referred to as "the key that unlocks the door to modernization" (Kazamias, 1971: x).

With a large part of social science research rooted in explaining both the reasons for and the consequences of social change, modernization and hence education have become important research frontiers for the social scientist. Moreover, the close relationship between educational attainment and many societal changes brought on by modernization makes the value of education data more attractive to the social scientist. The quality and quantity of education available to a population has a great influence on a society, affecting, for example, labor-force productivity, literacy and political awareness, the allocation and acceptance of available jobs, the mobility of workers, and the spatial patterns of many of its institutions. For these reasons the economist, political scientist, sociologist, geographer, and others have found it helpful to include an analysis of education data in their research and, wherever appropriate, have utilized these data as viable surrogates in specific topical areas beset with scarce or unobtainable data.

Scholars conducting research on the USSR are often confronted with data limitations and thus must employ existing data to solve their problems. Education data can be especially useful in this respect because they are relevant to all disciplines in the social sciences. Writing about

Soviet education, George Counts noted that "the scope of Soviet education is a matter of great importance.... In actuality, education involves the entire process of inducting the young into the life of the group or society. Soviet education embraces the entire cultural apparatus, all of the agencies involved in the molding and the informing of the minds and hearts of both young and old" (Counts, 1969: x).

This chapter addresses the content and coverage of education data in the 1897 Russian census and in the 1926, 1959, 1970, and 1979 censuses of the Soviet Union. These volumes represent a virtually untapped resource for scholars; their contents have gone largely unnoticed and/or unappreciated, although they represent a wide variety of education and literacy data. The major goals of this chapter are to alert researchers to the availability of education data in the Russian and Soviet censuses and to prepare them for some of the problems associated with working with such data.

Educational Attainment Data

Educational attainment is one of the many valuable measures that reflect a society's level of social development. However, unless it is cross-tabulated with selected independent variables (e.g., age, sex, occupation, nationality, time), educational attainment represents a limited measure with which to work. Except for the 1926 census, which contains no education-related data, the Russian and Soviet censuses offer a wealth of educational-attainment information (though the contents of each vary greatly).

Age data are provided in the 1897, 1959, and 1970 censuses, cross-tabulated in all three cases with educational attainment on the secondary administrative level (republic) for 1959 and 1970 and on the tertiary level (uezd) for 1897. Specific levels of educational attainment, described in greater detail below, are provided according to the following categories: higher complete, higher incomplete, secondary special, secondary general, incomplete secondary, elementary, and, in the case of the 1897 census, higher military and secondary military education. The age breakdown across censuses is not as uniform as are the specific levels of educational attainment. In the 1897 census, ten-year cohorts are provided beginning with a 0-9 category and concluding with 60 years of age and over. The 1959 census begins with a 10-19 category and then provides five-year cohorts to age 70, while the 1970 census begins with 10-15 and 16-19 age groups and then switches to ten-year cohorts up to age 60. Some data are presented in absolute numbers and, as has become more common, as a rate per 1,000 people 10 years of age and older. The age data are further cross-tabulated with gender and an urban/rural breakdown in three of the censuses (1897, 1959, and 1970). Thus, in any ten-year cohort the absolute number of people between 10 and 70 years old, male or female, residing in either rural or urban areas, in any republic or guberniya, who have completed one of six levels of schooling can be derived for 1897, 1959, and 1970. In the 1897 census, educational attainment by age is also cross-tabulated with social class. Unfortunately, aside from these, no other age-specific data are available in the census volumes. Age-specific data are the most important type of Soviet census data because of the lack of age-specific Soviet statistical data in general.

Segments of the population with specific characteristics other than age further defined by their educational-attainment levels have been analyzed in conjunction with independent variables. One such variable, gender, is cross-tabulated with all of the characteristics mentioned above in the 1897 census; with oblast-level educational attainment (per 1,000 people over 10 years of age) in the 1959 and 1970 censuses; with the levels of educational attainment of those people employed in the national economy (per 1,000 people employed) in the 1959, 1970, and 1979 censuses;[1] with educational attainment by social group (per 1,000 people over 10 years of age) in the 1959 and 1979 censuses; with the educational-attainment levels of the most populous nationalities (per 1,000 people over 10 years of age) in the 1959 and 1970 censuses by republic; with the educational level of those employed in specific branches of the national economy (per 1,000 people over 10 years of age) in the 1959 and 1979 censuses; and with the education levels of the population employed in manual and intellectual pursuits (per 1,000 people over 10 years of age) in the 1959 and 1979 censuses. An urban/rural breakdown of all of these cross-tabulated variables is also available in whichever years gender-specific data are given. Data for educational attainment (per 1,000 people over 10 years of age) for specific occupations are provided in the 1959 census, but they are not age, gender, or urban/rural-specific.

Literacy Data

Literacy data are more complete than educational-attainment data, for all five censuses offer some information on this subject. The earliest two censuses offer the most complete literacy data. By 1959, virtually the

---

1. Unless otherwise indicated, when reference is made to the 1979 census, it is to the preliminary census results reported in USSR, 1980.

entire Soviet population had achieved literacy,[2] lessening the need for extensive age, gender, area, and other specific literacy data.

The 1897 census offers literacy according to age, class, sex, urban/rural residence, and native language. Age data are provided for each uezd by one-year cohorts up to age 110, cross-tabulated with gender and urban/rural residence. Literacy data cross-tabulated with class association, gender, and urban/rural residence are less age-specific; this information is available for ten-year cohorts up to age 60 and is cross-tabulated by gender and urban/rural residence. Therefore, for 1897, one could determine the number of literate men/women of any age living in either rural or urban areas for any uezd. One could not, however, find the number of literate Tatar native speakers by single years of age or the number of literate clergymen for the same age. Rather, one would have to settle for the number of literate Tatars aged 30–39 (either male or female, rural or urban) and the number of literate clergymen aged 30–39 (residing in urban or rural areas for any guberniya).

The 1926 census volumes offer the greatest amount of space devoted to literacy data, though the utility of such an extensive collection is probably less than that of the 1897 census. Age, urban/rural residence, and gender-specific data are available, although other variables (e.g., nationality and social class) are not age-specific, nor are they offered by an urban/rural breakdown. Consequently, despite extensive data presented for each region, literacy data cross-tabulated with characteristics other than gender and urban/rural residence are not age-specific. It is possible, then, to obtain the number of literate men or women of any age residing in either rural or urban areas of any region. One can not, however, determine the same for any given nationality or social class; literacy crossed with these two variables is only available according to gender.

A feature not available in the 1897 census but provided in the 1926 volumes is an in-depth analysis of the literacy of the populations of cities with more than 200,000 inhabitants. Literacy figures are presented for inhabitants of these cities who are ages 0–19 (by one-year intervals) and ages 20–100 (by five-year intervals); literacy figures are also available for Moscow and Leningrad which take into account class, age, and gender.

The 1959, 1970, and 1979 censuses have far less published literacy data than have earlier enumerations, giving literacy rates for those 9–49 years old by gender and urban/rural residence for each oblast. The extent of the literacy data from the 1959 census is one table. The 1970 census limits literacy coverage to one table as well, providing literacy rates for those 9–49 by gender and urban/rural residence for each republic. This

2. The all-Union literacy rate in 1959 was 98.5 percent. The lowest rate of literacy for any union republic was 95.4 percent in the Turkmen SSR.

table also provides a comparative literacy column, showing 1897, 1920, 1926, 1939, 1959, and 1970 rates of literacy by gender and urban/rural residence for each republic. The 1979 census omits the gender breakdown in its reporting, although it does provide urban and rural rates for 1897, 1926, 1939, 1959, 1970, and 1979. A major limitation, however, is that these rates are given only for the entire Soviet Union; no data below the all-Union level are available. The de-emphasis on literacy reporting in the past three Soviet censuses is more a result of near universal literacy in the Soviet Union than of a conscious data-restricting policy.

Summary of Literacy and Educational Attainment Data

The 1897 and 1959 censuses offer data that is the most in-depth overall on educational attainment and literacy; both censuses provide extensive age-specific educational-attainment data, as well as non-age-specific educational-attainment data. The 1926 census does not include any education-related data, while the 1970 census contains limited data on educational attainment which are age-specific (for each union republic) and non-age-specific (e.g., for those employed in the national economy and by nationality). The 1979 census, at this writing, does not offer any age-specific educational-attainment data, and it is doubtful that any age-specific data will be made available. Miscellaneous data on education from the 1979 census were published in the Soviet journal *Vestnik statistiki*, though none were age-specific. Literacy data are plentiful in the earliest two censuses under investigation. However, illiteracy has virtually been eliminated in the Soviet Union, and the need for such data had lessened by the time of the 1959 census.

Using Education and Literacy Census Data

Much has been written about the problems associated with using published Soviet data. A large portion of the literature addressing these problems has concentrated less on the identification of pitfalls facing the researcher than on the doubts the researcher should have when using Soviet sources. Though one should be made aware of such shortcomings, to discredit all major sources of information dealing with the Soviet Union does little for research in the Soviet field or for bettering the understanding of Soviet society. A far more constructive manner in which to approach Soviet data sources and their associated problems is one that recognizes the potential for certain omissions, deletions, and even the possible manipulation of data but does not take all the above for granted. Accordingly, this chapter addresses the problems confronting the researcher using data available in the Russian and Soviet censuses for an analysis of education. These problems involve the quality of reporting, changes in the definitions of key terms and curriculum, the quality of education across regions, and the questionable practice of grouping education data in certain situations which tends to mislead the user of such data.

Quality of Reporting

The quality of data published in any census is inextricably tied to many factors that cannot be qualitatively assessed. In the Russian and Soviet context, one must assume a degree of error when evaluating census data, for the amount of work done by hand, covering such an extensive land area, undoubtedly led to some inaccuracies. Structurally, in the earlier enumerations (1897 and 1926) the manner in which the census questionnaires were worded would seem to have increased the chances for errors in the reported data; whether the persons completing the questionnaire fully understood the questions is problematic.[3] Aside from the built-in problems that plague censuses conducted in non-industrialized, lesser-educated societies, there is the universal problem of conscious or nonconscious fallacious responses to certain questions. For example, the age data so essential to any analysis of education and literacy are, in many cases, suspect. Falsifying one's age goes beyond vanity; economic advantages are often reason enough for people to claim that they are older than they actually are.

A problem that the researcher can more readily account for and minimize is that of "heaping," typically found in age-specific data. Responses tend to cluster around ages ending in "0" and "5" years, a phenomenon that serves to nullify some of the advantages of having disaggregated age-specific data. In some cases the problem of heaping is so evident that the use of such data would be considered questionable. In 1897, in Samarskaya guberniya, 52,502 people claimed to be 50 years old, while only 12,381 people declared that they were 49 years old, and 8,634 replied that they were 51 years old (Russian Empire, 1904: 8–9). In another example, 25,007 people were reported as being 70 years old, while 2,745 were listed as being 69 years old, and only 1,888 responded on their census forms that they were 71 years old (Russian Empire, 1904: 8–9). Fortunately for those using these data for education analy-

---

3. Although the questions concerning education and literacy have been consistent from one census to another, some census questionnaires yielded more detailed information than others. Unfortunately, much of the potential information that could have been derived from the five published censuses has not been made available.

ses, clustering does not become a major problem until the 20-year cohort. Educational attainment could be assessed without concern over this problem up to age 20, which serves five of the six levels of education covered in the census.[4] Clustering around ages ending in "0" and "5" is common throughout the censuses offering age-specific data for all cohorts over age 20 and is neither gender nor urban/rural specific. The most common way in which researchers have lessened the impact of this problem has been by grouping the data into five-year cohorts and using statistical smoothing techniques.[5]

Errors in calculation and print represent another problem that researchers using census data must anticipate and for which they must adjust accordingly. These errors are more prevalent in the 1897 and 1926 publications than in the later volumes. The frequency of errors of miscalculation and/or print should be on the decline following the new computer tape loadings that started with the 1979 census and will be used in all future censuses (Feshbach, 1981: 7). This method utilizes a coding by mark system for most questions on the census form which eliminates much of the handwritten coding used in the past. Very few answers will be entered onto the computer tapes by words; in these instances, local statistical administrators will code the data before they are entered onto the tapes (Voronitsyn, 1978: 2).

Changes in Curriculum

Education policy in Russia and the Soviet Union has undergone numerous changes since the 1897 census was conducted. Curriculum reforms have resulted from the changing needs of Soviet society in general and from specific branches of the national economy in particular. These curriculum changes, summarized below, have made it difficult to compare data from one year to another without exercising caution during the analysis.

The early policies of the Bolshevik government and the initial policies of Stalin had two major goals. First and foremost was the building of an able intelligentsia from what was an overwhelmingly illiterate society;[6] the second goal was to eliminate all remnants of tsarist and bourgeois idealism. In short, education was to serve the goals of the Party (Zajda, 1980: 14). The move away from the classical education offered in tsarist

---

4. Higher education could not be completed until age 21. Therefore, this level of education is susceptible to the problem of heaping.

5. The Sprague multiplier and Beers smoothing technique are two of the more widely used methods. For more detail, see A. J. Jaffe, *Handbook of Statistical Methods for Demographers* (New York: Gordon, 1977).

6. According to the 1970 Census, the 1920 literacy rate was only 44 percent in Soviet Russia, with areas in Central Asia having less than 4 percent of the population literate.

Russia began in 1918 when the "Declaration on the Single Labor School" was made at the All-Russian Congress on Education. The declaration stressed the political nature of education, and how this was to be the most vital tenet of Soviet pedagogy (Konstantinov, 1974: 14). Since 1918, the basic tenet of this declaration has remained intact, despite numerous reforms in the curriculum.

The first major policy change came in 1920, as a nine-year curriculum replaced the earlier eight-year program. The relatively liberal New Economic Policy influenced the content of the curriculum change, which resulted in the formation of a curriculum that attempted to bridge the gap between society and school life (Zajda, 1980: 20–22). This policy came to an abrupt end as Stalin ascended to power and instituted the curriculum that was to serve as the basis of Soviet education for two decades.

Throughout the 1930s, and lasting into the 1950s, the fundamental basis of the Soviet education system was the seven-year incomplete primary/secondary school and the ten-year completed secondary school. A seven-year factory school and a four-year trade school were also established in order to prepare semiskilled and skilled laborers for all branches of the industrializing economy. The basic educational structure, then, was established for the coming two decades and included the following:[7] (1) primary school (four years); (2) incomplete secondary school (seven years); (3) secondary school (ten years); and (4) trade school (four-year vocational/technical school).

Since the 1926 census offers no data on educational attainment, researchers are not faced with comparative research problems arising from differences between the education structure in 1926 and 1897. The quality of education did, however, change owing to a shift in the emphasis of the curriculum.[8]

By 1959, when the next census offered educational-attainment levels with which comparisons to the 1897 results could be made, compulsory primary education had been introduced and a uniform curriculum established. In the early 1940s, the age at which compulsory education was to begin was lowered from 8 to 7 years. In 1949, compulsory seven-year education was introduced, and in 1969 compulsory secondary education (complete ten-year secondary) for those between the ages of 7 and 18 was required. These changes served to raise the educational-attainment levels of the Soviet population, but the quality of education received was hardly uniform. Many of those included in the data for having completed

---

7. Included in this structural reform, but eliminated in 1934, was the school of the rural youth.

8. Qualitative changes were partially a result of the reintroduction of formal examinations that had been abolished during the 1920s, the use of standardized textbooks, and strict classroom discipline.

primary and secondary education had done so in evening and correspondence schools that serve the goals of the Soviet worker and government well. Workers are able to attain education and skills at higher levels while minimizing the loss of labor/manpower time. It has been suggested, however, that the quality of education received in evening and correspondence schools is markedly lower than that attained by the students studying in the standard day schools (Rosen, 1971: 129). This should be recognized when one evaluates the educational-attainment levels of the Soviet population since the 1950s; enrollments in these institutions have been very high the past twenty years, and their graduates have accounted for a large part of the newly educated segment of the Soviet population.

Another change in the 1950s which serves to hinder comparative studies from one census period to another (especially between 1959 and 1970) was the reinstituting of polytechnical training by way of a 1958 decree. This was done in order to prepare Soviet youth better for work and life; a major criticism of the education system up to that date was that schooling had become too isolated from the real life of the student. This reform was also made in response to a greater need for more trained agricultural and industrial workers. Thus, students were encouraged to continue their education in technical colleges and schools which specialized in preparing students for an extremely wide variety of careers. These matriculants were completing the equivalent of a secondary education, though their training was overwhelmingly specialized and technical. Researchers must take this into account when qualitatively evaluating the Soviet education system solely on the basis of the numbers completing secondary education.[9]

The Khrushchev era, known for its many reforms in general, left its mark on the education system with some major curriculum reforms. In 1958, aside from attempting to improve academic standards, Khrushchev changed the seven-year school to eight years and the ten-year school to eleven years. He also attacked the Soviet school of the 1950s, claiming that the education offered during that time served to divorce students from reality and left them insufficiently prepared for practical life (Tomiak, 1974: 44). As a result, the number of electives was expanded, and a two-year work requirement was instituted for all students before they entered higher education. Secondary specialized schools, which offered more job-related training than the traditional secondary schools, were promoted by Khrushchev, mostly to meet the needs of an expanding industrial sector of the Soviet economy.

---

9. For a discussion of the many ways in which Soviet students are able to attain a secondary education, see, for example, Richard B. Dobson, "Socialism and Social Stratification," in *Contemporary Soviet Society*, ed. Jerry Pankhurst and Michael Paul Sacks (New York: Praeger), 88–114.

The fact that the above reforms were only in practice for six years has led to problems for those using the data in the 1959 and 1970 volumes for comparative purposes. It is virtually impossible to make a qualitative assessment of Soviet secondary education when this education has come to encompass such a wide range of academic/vocational training. In addition, the data corresponding to the 1959–70 intercensal period is difficult to interpret because the Khrushchev reforms did not cover all eleven years. The researcher should be aware of the enrollments in the different types of secondary education institutions before generalizing about the qualitative and quantitative trends in Soviet secondary education.

The past twenty years have seen reforms that could color the face value of education data available in the past two censuses. In 1972, a universal decree was passed which required education for all up to age 17. This served to increase the number of eligible students who continued secondary school beyond grade eight from 80 percent in 1970 to 97.8 percent by 1978 (Zajda, 1980: 37). Thus, the increase in the number of people who had finished secondary education by the time the 1979 census was taken was to a considerable extent a result of this new government policy. This increase in the number of secondary education graduates would probably not have occurred had the decree not been made.

Two other changes should be noted for those using these data over time for comparative purposes. First, in 1969, primary education was reduced from four to three years. This seemingly minor change has had a major impact on data showing primary education completion levels. Instead of completing the first phase of education at age 11, children could now finish primary school by age 10. Because the data in the census volumes are given as the number of people per 1,000 population aged 10 years and older who have completed various levels of education, 10-year-olds who used to deflate the educational-attainment data are now significant contributors to the overall level of primary educational attainment. This reform has served to increase the pool of eligible primary education attainees, for instead of the possible cohort pool being 11-year-olds and older (7-year-olds begin school), it has increased to include the 10-year-olds. Consequently, the researcher should be aware that the rate of primary school completion has increased drastically since 1970 because of the inclusion of 10-year-olds.

The second reform, enacted after the 1970 census, required that all males aged 15 and older obtain preconscription military training. Since military conscription is mandatory, the already compulsory nature of at least an eight-year education has a de facto check and insurance policy. If a male must serve in the military and obtain two years of preconscription training offered predominantly in the school system, the student is almost assured to be in school beyond the eighth grade.

Qualitative changes in the curriculum, as opposed to general structural changes listed above, present a more difficult problem to account for and compensate for when comparing data over time. Since 1970, the courses offered in grades 4 (the first year of secondary school), 6–7, and 9–10 have changed extensively. For example, there has been an increased emphasis on communist indoctrination in grade 4 (Matthews, 1982: 40–66, 153–76). More important to curriculum content, however, have been the extensive changes in mathematics (grades 9–10) and basic sciences (grades 6–7), with linear equations, logarithmic functions, and physics (e.g., molecular kinetic energy) now taught as part of the standard curriculum. These changes would seem to imply that a secondary education completed today is more rigorous than that of the past and hence qualitatively different. Problems could arise if one were to compare attainment levels without evaluating the quality of education offered in each of the periods being compared.

Differences in the quality of education among regions of the country is yet another potential problem researchers might encounter when evaluating education data from the censuses, especially owing to the multiethnic character of the USSR. It is one thing to point out that certain Central Asian nationalities are completing secondary school at a rate equal to or in some cases above that of residents in the RSFSR but quite another to assume that Central Asian education is equal qualitatively to that offered in the RSFSR. Researchers should resolve such questions before using the seemingly objective level of educational-attainment data.

Evaluating the Data as Provided in the Census

The way in which education data are categorized and presented creates problems for both comparative temporal and regional analyses. With regard to educational-attainment data, the Soviet scholar V. Ovsienko believes that reporting data as rates per 1,000 population aged 10 and over understates the level of education (Ovsienko, 1972: 40). Because 10–15-year-olds could not possibly complete secondary education or higher education, Ovsienko maintains that this statistic fails to reflect accurately how well-educated a given population is. Comparing levels of educational attainment across regions whose population structures differ markedly leads to problems as a result of the age 10 and over category used in Soviet statistical sources. On the one hand, if an area has a large portion of its population between the ages of 0 and 20, education attainment could be exaggerated given the large numbers (and large percentage of the total population) finishing school as required by the dictates of the past twenty-five years. On the other hand, regions with older populations (e.g., Estonia, Latvia, Ukraine), which had relatively more men and women pass through the Soviet school system before compulsory secondary education was introduced, and when instability due to World War II limited school participation, would show fewer attainees of secondary education simply because of age structure. It could be argued, however, that if a given region has a large percentage of its population in the 0–9 cohort, a cohort that cannot attain even the lowest level of education, the region's level of education is understated by the current methods of categorizing and presenting the data. The Slavic areas, with the bulk of their populations over age 15, would seem to benefit statistically from the existing guideline used for reporting educational-attainment data as rates per 1,000 population aged 10 years and above. Whichever case is more applicable to given regions of the USSR, one problem is evident: standardization of the data is necessary so that age structure is not the *major* factor for interregional differences in the educational-attainment data used in any serious analysis.[10]

Because 17 is the youngest age by which one could complete secondary education, and because age data are broken into five-year cohorts after a 16–19 cohort (1970 census), Ovsienko suggested a reordering of the age data in order to obtain the most accurate measure of educational attainment. The researcher could simply use the 16–19-year-old cohort and, consulting pertinent volumes of the *Narodnoye khozyaystvo* series, discount the 16-year-old population from the larger cohort by finding the number of births in the given area in question sixteen years before the date of the census being used. What the researcher would be left with, then, is a 17–19-year-old cohort that, when combined with the remaining population (20 years of age and older), gives a far more accurate base population from which to form an education rate (in this case, per 1,000 population). The same correcting techniques could be used when calculating primary educational attainment (with 11 years and older as the base population) and higher educational attainment (with 21 years and older as the base rate). When Ovsienko made adjustments similar to these, the results of the educational-attainment data from the 1970 census changed as follows: instead of 187 per 1,000 completing second-

---

10. For both sides of the issue concerning the differences in the quality of education offered to the Slavic versus non-Slavic regions of the USSR, see Ellen Jones and Fred Grupp, "Dimensions of Ethnic Assimilation in the Soviet Union" (Paper presented at the 1979 Annual Meetings of the American Association for the Advancement of Slavic Studies, New Haven, Conn.); Ellen Jones, "Minorities in the Soviet Armed Forces," *Comparative Strategy* 3, no. 4 (1982): 294–95; Nicolas Poppe, *Introduction to Altaic Linguistics* (Wiesbaden: Otto Horowitz, 1965), 52; and Teresa Rakowska-Harmstone, "Dialectics of Nationalism in the USSR," *Problems of Communism* 23 (1974): 11.

ary education (grade 10, both general and specialized secondary education), 220 per 1,000 finished that level; instead of 42 per 1,000 people reported as having completed higher education, the exclusion of the 10–20-year-old cohort from the base population resulted in a revised ratio of 55 per 1,000 (Ovsienko, 1972: 42).

Another problem associated with the way in which educational-attainment figures are published in the census volumes is the exclusionary characteristic of the level-by-level reporting. For example, those who are listed as having completed higher education are not included in the figures for having attained lower levels of education. Researchers must keep this in mind when analyzing interregional data and data over time.

Other features of statistical reporting methods include the problem of the continuing/discontinuing student. Those students who have completed at least half of the required period of instruction for a higher education are classified as having an "incomplete higher education." Those who have completed less than half of the required course of instruction are listed as secondary education attainees (USSR, 1978: 52). The problem with this method of classification is that it is impossible to discern from the data how many students in these two categories are continuing in education. The same problem holds true for the attainees of an incomplete secondary education. It has been suggested that an additional explanatory column be added to the census data in order to provide the number of those in between levels of instruction as well as the number of continuing students at each level.[11] Thus far, this suggestion has not been acted upon.

Problems facing researchers investigating literacy are twofold. First, when comparing rates from one time period to another, the researcher should recognize that the criterion for establishing literacy has continually changed. In 1897, for example, people who stated that they could read were considered literate; in 1926, people were considered literate if they were able to write their last name; by 1959, the questionnaire asked whether respondents could read and write, only read, or do neither; and by 1970 and 1979, with less emphasis placed on gathering literacy data, the questionnaire merely asked respondents to note if they were unable to read.

The second problem with literacy data concerns the age category used as a population base from which to measure the literacy rates. A. I. Gozulov, the Soviet statistician, is one of the many who have criticized the use of the 9–49-year-old cohort as the population base from which to measure literacy (Gozulov, 1965: 75). The Soviet rationale for limiting the base population to the 9–49-year-old cohort employed in recent

---

11. For a description of what constitutes each level of education as interpreted in the 1979 Soviet census, see USSR, 1978.

censuses revolves around the belief that literacy rates after age 49 do not change significantly, and that by beginning the cohort at age 9, preschoolers and first graders who could not be expected to be literate are rightfully excluded (Ovsienko, 1972: 42). Gozulov maintains that this cohort does not represent the potentially literate (*gramotno-sposobnoye*) population and that the rate should be measured from a population base consisting of those 8 years of age and older. The population aged 50 and over in many parts of the USSR could influence literacy rates, especially in areas where educational-attainment levels have only recently reached all-Union levels. The lower limit of the age cohort used in measuring literacy rates need not be altered nor given close attention by the users of the census volumes for data on literacy. Since all 8-year-olds in the Soviet Union are learning to read and write regardless of which republic they reside in, problems arising as a result of differing age structures across regions are unlikely.

In addition to the data available in the census volumes, statistical journals (*Vestnik statistiki*) and specialized periodicals (e.g., *Sovetskoye obrazovaniye, Uchitel'skaya gazeta, Sovetskaya pedagogika, Vestnik vysshei shkoly*) provide occasional data on educational attainment, school enrollments, and the number of educational institutions in the USSR for various years. All of these statistics are often available in the all-Union and republic-level volumes of the *Narodnoye khozyaystvo* series, and UN publications offer much of this information (in French and English), though in less regular intervals.

Agenda for Research Utilizing Education Data

The use of education data provided in the census volumes should increase in the coming years. Many of the problems and challenges facing Soviet society, as interpreted by those in the West, are closely tied to educational attainment and phenomena related to educational attainment. For example, data on educational attainment could be utilized by the economist who is interested in deriving age-specific data for labor-force estimates (Feshbach, 1982: 27–37). Specifically, the need for skilled and educated labor will inevitably influence enrollments in higher education, and enrollments in higher education will in turn influence the number of available workers. Educational-attainment data could also serve those interested in assessing the quality of the labor force based on the specific type of schooling the graduates have completed.

Analyzing the spatial distribution of educational attainment across the USSR will aid the researcher interested in investigating and projecting migration trends as they relate to the demand for laborers created by economic development programs. Given the spatial breakdown of the number of graduates completing the various types of secondary and higher education, along with plans for economic development throughout the Soviet Union, a researcher could project where gross labor deficits for specific types of employment will be most acute and, with some reservations, predict migration trends. For example, crude migration estimates could be made using education data that show an abundance of trained metallurgical workers for a given year coupled with government plans for the spatial expansion of the iron and steel industry.

Labor participation studies can be aided by the education data provided in the censuses. The acceptance or rejection of a job by a worker could depend upon the level and type of education the worker has completed. With problematic labor shortages surfacing in many branches within the Soviet economy, the education goals (universal secondary education and increased higher educational-attainment levels) and economic goals of the Soviet government appear to be in conflict. With labor becoming less of an available resource, one must assume that the government will urge students, who were previously encouraged to complete higher education, either to work a few years and then return to school or to attend evening or correspondence schools while working in the national economy.

Research on ethnicity and nationalism can be aided by using education data for the union and autonomous republics. Unfortunately, ethnic data for educational attainment have not been available since 1970. Political participation research is another area in which education data should be utilized. The question of whether an increase in the education levels of the Soviet population has led to, or in the future will lead to, increased demands for participation in the state's political process could be further investigated.[12] The success or failure of the Soviet education system as an effective socializer of the educated masses could be determined by answering the above question.

Because education pervades so many institutions of a given society, education data are applicable to most social science research. The census volumes provide an excellent source for education data in spite of the decreasing amount of age-specific data available to the researcher. Virtually the entire Soviet population is literate today, reducing the

---

12. The effect of a population's rising level of educational attainment on the political demands made by that population has become a significant research topic for political scientists and sociologists specializing in ethnicity and nationalism. See, for example, Anthony D. Smith, "Towards a Theory of Ethnic Separatism," *Ethnic and Racial Studies* 2 (January 1979): 21–37; Anthony D. Smith, *The Ethnic Revival* (Cambridge: Cambridge University Press, 1981); and Alexander Gella, ed., *The Intelligentsia and the Intellectuals: Theory, Method, and Case Study* (London: Sage, 1976).

significance and need for literacy data. Nevertheless, the earlier volumes of the censuses are rich with literacy data that make comparative analyses possible and worthwhile.

References

Counts, George S. 1969. *Contemporary Soviet Education*. New York: International Arts & Sciences Press.
Feshbach, Murray. 1981. "Development of the Soviet Census." In *Soviet Population Policy: Conflicts and Constraints,* ed. Helen Desfosses, 3–15. New York: Pergamon Press.
———. 1982. "Between the Lines of the 1979 Census." *Problems of Communism* 31: 27–37.
Gozulov, A. 1965. *Ekonomicheskaya statistika*. Moscow: Finansy Izdatel'stvo.
Kazamias, A. 1971. "Foreword." In *Education and Modernization in the USSR,* ed. Seymour M. Rosen, vii-x. Reading, Mass.: Addison-Wesley.
Konstantinov, N. 1974. *Istoriya pedagogiki*. Moscow: Mysl'.
Matthews, Merwyn. 1982. *Education in the Soviet Union*. London: Allen & Unwin.
Ovsienko, V. 1972. "O statisticheskikh pokazatel'nyakh urovnya obrazovaniya i gramotnosti naseleniya." *Vestnik statistiki,* no. 2: 39–43.
Rosen, Seymour M., ed. 1971. *Education and Modernization in the USSR*. Reading, Mass.: Addison-Wesley.
Russian Empire. Tsentral'nyy Statisticheskiy Komitet. 1904. *Pervaya vseobshchaya perepis' naseleniya Rossiyskoy Imperii*. Vol. 36. St. Petersburg.
Tomiak, J. 1974. "Fifty-five Years of Soviet Education." In *The History of Education in Europe,* ed. T. Cook, 37–51. London: Methuen.
USSR. Tsentral'noye Statisticheskoye Upravleniye. 1929. *Vsesoyuznaya perepis' naseleniya 1926 goda*. 66 vols. Moscow.
———. 1963. *Itogi Vsesoyuznoy perepisi naseleniya 1959 goda*. 16 vols. Moscow: Gosstatizdat.
———. 1972. *Itogi Vsesoyuznoy perepisi naseleniya 1970 goda*. Vol 3. Moscow: Statistika.
———. 1978. *Vsesoyuznaya perepis' naseleniya—Vsenarodnoye delo*. Moscow: Statistika.
———. 1980. *Naseleniye SSSR po dannym Vsesoyuznoy perepisi naseleniya 1979 goda*. Moscow: Izdatel'stvo Politicheskoy Literaturi.
Voronitsyn, S. 1978. "On the Eve of the All-Union Census." *Radio Liberty Research* 230/78: 1–5.
Zajda, Joseph I. 1980. *Education in the USSR*. New York: Pergamon Press.

Part Two

INDEX AND GUIDE TO THE RUSSIAN AND SOVIET CENSUSES, 1897 TO 1979

Peter R. Craumer

CONTENTS

Introduction	177
Format and Use of the Index	177
Materials Included in the Index	178
1897 Census	178
1926 Census	181
1959 Census	183
1970 Census	184
1979 Census	184
List of Census Tables	187
Format of Table Entries	187
Table Titles	188
Table Descriptors	188
Sample Table Entry	190
The First General Census of the Population of the Russian Empire, 1897	191
Vols. 1–89. [Guberniyas and Oblasts of the Russian Empire]	191
General Summaries for the Empire of the Results of Tabulation of Data of the First General Census of Population. Two volumes	195
Distribution of the Population by Type of Chief Occupation and Age Group, for Individual Regions. Table 20. Four volumes	198
Number and Social Composition of Workers in Russia according to the First General Census of Population of the Russian Empire, 1897. Two volumes	199
First General Census of the Population of the Russian Empire, 1897. Short Summaries	200
Number 1. Population of the Empire, according to the Census of January 28, 1897, by Uezd	200
Number 2. Population of Cities, according to the Census of January 28, 1897	200

Number 3. Population of the Cities of St. Petersburg, Moscow, Warsaw, and Odessa according to the Census of January 28th, 1897	200
Number 4. Final Tabulation of the Enumerated [De Facto] Population of the Empire, by Uezd	201
Number 5. Final Tabulation of the Enumerated [De Facto] Population of Cities	201
Number 6. Enumerated [De Facto] Population of Both Sexes by Uezd and City, with Listing of the Predominant Religions and the Main Social Groups	202
Number 7. Enumerated [De Facto] Population of Both Sexes by Uezd, with Listing of the Number of Persons of the Predominant Native Languages	202
Number 8. Percentage Distribution of the Enumerated [De Facto] Population of the Empire of Both Sexes, by the Most Important Occupational Groups Which Provide the Main Means of Livelihood	202
Populated Places of the Russian Empire Having 500 or More Inhabitants.	202
Cities and Population in Uezds Which Have 2000 or More Inhabitants.	202
All-Union Population Census of 1926	**203**
Section 1. Nationality, Native Language, Age, Literacy	203
Rayon Volumes	203
Vol. 9. RSFSR	205
Vol. 11. Ukrainskaya SSR	207
Vol. 17. USSR	209
Section 2. Occupations	211
Rayon Volumes	211
Vol. 26. RSFSR	213
Vol. 28. Ukrainskaya SSR	215
Vol. 34. USSR	216
Section 3. Marital Status, Place of Birth, Length of Residence, Physically Handicapped and Mentally Ill Persons	217
Rayon Volumes	217
Vol. 43. RSFSR	221
Vol. 45. Ukrainskaya SSR	223
Vol. 51. USSR	224
Section 4. Vol. 52. Unemployed in the USSR	227
Section 5. Vol. 53. Properties, Structures, Living and Non-Living Premises in Cities and Urban Settlements of the USSR	228
Section 6. Vol. 54. Living Conditions of the Urban Population of the USSR	229

Section 7. Structure of the Urban Family	233
Vol. 55. USSR. 1. Structure of the Urban Family. Results of the General Tabulation. 2. Social Composition of the Urban Population.	233
Vol. 56. Structure of the Urban Family. Results of a Special Tabulation. Part 1. Moscow. Part 2. Leningrad. Part 3. Cities of the RSFSR.	234
Short Summaries	236
Number 1. Housing Construction in Urban Settlements of the RSFSR, Ukrainskaya SSR, and Belorusskaya SSR	236
Number 2. Unemployment in the City of Moscow	237
Number 3. Population of the USSR	237
Number 4. Nationality and Native Language of the Population of the USSR	238
Number 5. Age and Literacy. European Part of the RSFSR. Belorusskaya SSR	239
Number 6. Housing Stock of the USSR	
Number 7. Age and Literacy of the Population of the USSR	240
Number 8. Social Composition and Occupations of the Population of the City of Moscow	241
Number 9. Social Composition and Occupations of the Population of the City of Leningrad	241
Number 10. Population of the USSR by Position in Occupation and Sector of the Economy	241
Results of the All-Union Population Census of 1959	243
Results of the All-Union Population Census of 1970	251
Vol. 1. Population of the USSR, Union and Autonomous Republics, Krays, and Oblasts	251
Vol. 2. Sex, Age, and Marital Status of the Population of the USSR, Union and Autonomous Republics, Krays, and Oblasts	252
Vol. 3. Level of Education of the Population of the USSR, Union and Autonomous Republics, Krays, and Oblasts	252
Vol. 4. Ethnic Composition of the Population of the USSR, Union and Autonomous Republics, Krays, Oblasts, and National Okrugs	253
Vol. 5. Distribution of the Population of the USSR, Union and Autonomous Republics, Krays, and Oblasts by Social Group, Means of Livelihood, and Sectors of the Economy	255
Vol. 6. Distribution of the Population of the USSR and Union Republics by Occupation	256
Vol. 7. Migration of the Population. Number and Composition of Families in the USSR, Union and Autonomous Republics, Krays, and Oblasts	257

Contents

All-Union Population Census of 1979 — 260
Key-Word Cross Index — 269
  Purpose and Design — 269
  Problems in Using Keywords — 269
  Geographic Codes — 270
  Locating Additional Cross-Tabulations — 272
  Index Subcategories — 272
  Meanings and Limitations of Individual Keywords — 273
  Sample Keyword Index — 276
  Keyword Index to the Russian and Soviet Censuses, 1897 to 1979 — 277
Geographic Units of the Russian and Soviet Censuses — 304
  1897 Census — 304
  1926 Census — 307
  1959 Census — 312
  1970 Census — 316
  1979 Census — 320

INTRODUCTION

The purpose of this guide is to provide a detailed list and description of the contents of all major Russian and Soviet population censuses since 1897, with an index to enable the researcher to locate these census materials by subject. To organize and inventory sets of data as extensive, heterogeneous, and complex as these censuses, it was necessary to make numerous procedural decisions concerning the structure of the index, the level of detail to be included, and the methods to be employed. Since the usefulness of the index depends to a large extent upon these determinations, we would like to make explicit at the outset the format and scope of this work.

Format and Use of the Index

This work consists of three interrelated sections, all of which should be employed by the user to obtain maximum benefit from the index.

Section I is a comprehensive, serialized list of all main census tables for each of the major Russian and Soviet enumerations. The individual table entries consist of a serial number, the table number as it appears in the printed census volume, the translated table title, and a table "descriptor." As is explained in more detail below, this format enables the user to determine the type of information and geographic coverage of data in each individual table.

Section II is a keyword index based on the table titles and descriptors in Section I. By selecting one of seventy keywords, the user can determine the census years, cross-tabulations, and geographic coverage available for each subject. The keyword entries refer directly to the table list in Section I.

Section III is a listing of the main geographic units for which data are given in each of the major Russian and Soviet censuses. This list is useful not only for the purposes of this index but also as an aid to understanding the complex and changing political-administrative structure of the USSR.

Materials Included in the Index

This index covers all of the major population censuses of Russia and the USSR: 1897, 1926, 1959, 1970, and 1979. Data for the 1939 census were not published separately; they are indexed in this guide under the tables in which they appear in the 1959, 1970, and 1979 censuses. Minor censuses or incomplete enumerations conducted during this period are not included here. Of the published census materials, only the main data tables are incorporated into the index. Other potentially useful information, such as descriptions and analyses of the data, maps, and lists of occupational categories or place names, are not included in this index. Minor unnumbered introductory tables that summarize the main tables in the same volume are also not included. The user may want to consult the census volumes directly to ascertain the nature and usefulness of these materials for specific research purposes. In addition, several accessory volumes to the 1897 census are not included; these volumes are listed in the following section on the 1897 census. Aside from these few exceptions, the list of tables here represents a complete inventory of tables for all major population censuses since 1897; thus, it comprises virtually all such data extant.

1897 Census

Volumes included. The decision as to which volumes to include as part of the 1897 census is rather arbitrary. Aside from the eighty-nine main regional volumes, there are two major summary volumes, four volumes of data on occupations by age group (which present greater detail for Table 20 of the regional volumes), two volumes on workers, a series of eight short summary volumes, a list of the populations of all places of 500 or more population, and a list of cities and population in uezds with 2,000 or more population. All of these volumes are in this table list and index. But several brief accessory volumes, typically about forty to fifty pages in length, were not included. Some of those known to have additional census data that are not available in the main volumes are *Distribution of the Population by the Major Social Groups, Religions, Native Language, and Some Occupations* (1905) and *Distribution of Workers and Servants by Groups of Occupations and by Place of Birth* (1905). Other short summary volumes, which are apparently tabulations of census data which are published in the main volumes, include *Distribution of the Population of the Empire by the Main Religions* (1901), *Distribution of Populated Places of the Russian Empire by Population Size* (1902), and *Number and Social Composition of Blind Persons in Russia* (1905).

Format of regional and summary volumes. The format of the tables in the eighty-nine regional (guberniya) volumes is sufficiently similar that only one entry is used in the index to represent the same table number in all eighty-nine volumes. The tables in the two main summary volumes have nearly the same format as those in the eighty-nine regional volumes, but there are significant differences between the introductory, unnumbered tables in the guberniya volumes and those in the summary volumes, including, of course, major differences in the level of geographic units. Therefore, a separate set of entries is given (Nos. 30–57) for the tables in these two summary volumes. In most cases, the entries in the summary volumes first indicate the level of units given (e.g., "by guberniya") and then provide a reference to the regional volume table of the same format.

Although these two summary volumes have the same basic table list as most of the regional volumes, eighteen of the regional volumes have a slightly different format from both the other regional volumes and the main summary volumes. After these eighteen had been published, the format of the census was changed slightly to eliminate unnecessary tables and to speed up the tabulation and publishing of the census. Therefore, six volumes were published in three *tetrady* (parts), while twelve others were published in two *tetrady*. The remaining seventy-one regions each have a single volume. All tables presented here have the format of those seventy-one volumes. The major difference between the earlier multiple-*tetrad'* volumes and the final census format is that the multiple-*tetrad'* volumes contain duplicates of some tables and more of the tables give data for both the permanent (de jure) and the enumerated (de facto) population. In addition, the multiple-*tetrad'* volumes have a map of the guberniya at the end of the first *tetrad'*, giving literacy and population density by uezd. The volumes that are published in three parts also have (in the second part) three extra tables on children younger than one year old ("Children Younger than One Year Old by Social Group of the Parents and by Monthly Age Groups," "Children Younger than One Year Old by Native Language of the Parents and by Monthly Age Groups," and "Children Younger than One Year Old by Religion and by Monthly Age Groups"). The unit list for the 1897 census included with this index shows the guberniyas that have two or three *tetrady*.

An appendix to the first main summary volume has forty-four tables (each with an accompanying map) that were not indexed here. Each table consists of a particular demographic characteristic, given in percent, for each guberniya. These relationships are presented by guberniya on a schematic map of the Russian Empire. Examples of these tables and maps include the number of women per 100 men, the city population as a percent of total population, and the percent literate of the male population. All of these data either are found in other census tables or can easily be calculated from them; nevertheless, they provide a very interesting spatial representation of the major demographic characteristics of the population of the empire.

Other parts of the empire. In most cases, regional data of the 1897 census cover only the eighty-nine guberniyas and do not include outlying parts of the empire such as Finland or some parts of Central Asia. Major exceptions to this pattern are noted in the individual entries, such as tables in which data are also given for the principalities of Finland. The two main summary volumes, however, often contain data for the following populations in addition to the eighty-nine guberniyas: the Russian population in Finland, military personnel abroad serving on warships, the Russian population in Bukhara, and the Russian population in Khiva. In most cases these data are aggregated into one group and thus are of little interest. Cases where each of the four is given separately are noted in the table descriptor.

Urban and rural data. The way in which these data are given in the 1897 census differs substantially from the way in which they are presented in the other censuses. Urban data usually consist of the population of the largest town or city in each uezd only; in some uezds with many settlements more than one town is listed. All remaining population in each uezd is classified as rural by the census. Usually the rural population is referred to as simply the population "in the uezd." Most of the tables in the eighty-nine guberniya volumes give data by uezd for the population of the main town or towns and then for the remaining population. The entries give the specific urban and rural categories—rather than the category "urban-rural"—to minimize confusion. In the Keyword Index, however, these entries are indexed as urban-rural. Since the urban population is represented by individual settlements, the data for which are also given, these entries are coded in the index with a "c" for city (see the Keyword Index).

1926 Census

Limitations of the entries. This census is by far the most detailed and complex of all of the Russian or Soviet censuses. More than a third of the entries and more than half of the pages of descriptions in this index are devoted to 1926. In spite of this detail, however, the descriptors can give only an overview of the contents of some of these complex tables. Whereas in the recent censuses, and generally also in 1897, tables represent simple cross-tabulations of several categories, in 1926 a large number of tables contain ten or more different categories, not all of which are completely cross-tabulated. With minor exceptions, these discrepancies in the cross-tabulations are noted in the descriptors. In a few cases, it was necessary to simplify the descriptions; therefore, a few cross-tabulations that are implied in the descriptors may not be found in the actual tables.

Census sections 1–3. The heart of the 1926 census consists of the fifty-one volumes that make up the first three sections (*otdely*). Each section contains a series of tables on a particular subject or subjects; each series of tables is published separately in seventeen different regional and summary volumes. (See the unit list in this guide for the particular regions [rayons] that each volume contains.) One of the main reasons for the difficulty in describing fully the contents of each of the tables is the relative lack of uniformity among the regional tables. While the description given here may apply to most of the rayon tables, there are often significant discrepancies among them. Major systematic discrepancies are noted in the descriptors, but some rayon tables may not have the detail that is given in the entry. Usually, rayon data are most detailed in the rayons of the European USSR and least detailed in some ethnic units of the Urals, Siberia, or Central Asia. Age data are a notable example of this. Nationality data, however, are least detailed in the European RSFSR and sometimes are omitted entirely because of the uniformity of the population (Russians). Many rayon volumes contain special tables, (usually as supplements [*dopolneniya*] to the main tables) which often contain data for a major city or cities in the rayon; these extra tables are included in the index. Nearly all of the extra tables on cities include Moscow and Leningrad, but Moscow and Leningrad are not listed by name unless they are the only cities given. In the Russian Republic volumes, including the summary volume, lists of data by guberniya often include four cities: Moscow, Leningrad, Grozniy, and Vladikavkaz (now Ordzhonikidze). In these cases only Moscow and Leningrad are listed in the table entries here.

Supposedly, the summary volumes for the first three sections of the census, covering the RSFSR, Ukrainskaya SSR, and the entire USSR, merely summarize data that are presented in the rayon volumes. The number of tables, their titles, their table numbers, and their formats, however, often are significantly different from each other and from those in the rayon volumes. Therefore, to avoid confusion and to simplify the amount of description that would have been required in each entry to explain the differences among these summary volumes, each of the three summary volumes for each of the first three *otdely* of the census was indexed, in addition to the rayon volumes. In many of the tables in these summary volumes, the table format is the same as that of the rayon volume, and in these cases there is a reference to the appropriate rayon table. In other cases, the tables for Ukrainskaya SSR or the USSR have the same format as the ones in the RSFSR summary volume; a reference to the appropriate Russian Republic table is indicated for these entries.

Census sections 4–7. The remaining main sections of the 1926 census, *otdely* 4–7, are not divided into regional volumes but consist of only one volume for each particular subject; one entry is therefore sufficient to describe each table. In section 7, Volume 56 is divided into three *vypuska* (parts), but these are combined here into one set of entries because they have the same table titles and formats. One part presents data for Moscow, one is for Leningrad, and one is for cities of the RSFSR. This third part consists of the results of a sample of 453 cities and urban-type settlements of different sizes and types, weighted to represent all of the cities of the republic. The sample does not include Moscow and Leningrad. The data are aggregates of all the sample cities, not results for any individual cities.

Short summaries. In addition to these fifty-six main volumes, the ten short summary (*Kratkiye svodki*) volumes are also a vital part of the census. These volumes are not all merely summaries or retabulations of data from the main volumes: some of the 1926 summary volumes contain data that were not published in the main census volumes. Each of these ten summaries is included in this index separately with the exception of Numbers 8 and 9 (Moscow and Leningrad), which were combined into one set of entries.

Occupational data and social groups. Another major difference between the 1926 census and the other censuses is the way in which occupational data are presented. Occupational data are usually divided into gainfully employed and nongainfully employed, and the gainfully employed are then divided into various positions in occupations, separate sectors of the economy in which they work, and, often, specific occupations. These occupation data by position are sometimes referred to in the census as

Introduction 183

exactly that (*polozheniye v zanyatii*), but sometimes they are referred to as social groups (*sotsial'nyye gruppy*) instead. In the other censuses, the term "social group" refers more to a social classification than to a work classification, so social group data from the 1926 census are not comparable with other censuses. In the table entries here, 1926 data are presented both as occupation data by position and as social group data, depending upon the original Russian wording used in the particular table in which they appear. Therefore, for 1926 it is necessary to look at both sets of entries to get a complete list of the tables that contain these kinds of data.

1959 Census

Volumes. This census contains one regional volume for each union republic and a summary volume for the entire USSR. The summary volume is sufficiently similar to the format of the republic volumes that it was not necessary to include a separate list of tables from the USSR summary volume alone. Differences between this volume and the republic volumes are noted in the entries where these differences apply. The USSR summary volume has a number of tables that do not appear in the individual republic volumes; these additional tables appear in the census as subparts a or b to the main tables in the summary volume and are listed in this index in the order in which they are given in the census. Therefore, a letter after a table number in the entries here means that the table is from the USSR summary volume only, except where noted otherwise.

As a guide to the geographic units that are included in the summary volume versus those given only in the individual republic volumes, it can usually be assumed that if data are given only by republic, the USSR volume contains data for the entire USSR only and each regional volume contains republic-level data only. When data are given by oblast, the summary volume usually contains data by republic and the republic volumes contain the oblast data (for those republics that are divided into oblasts). Not all of the republic volumes contain all of the tables that are listed here. Tables with oblast-level data are omitted for republics where there are no oblasts, provided that these data have already been given for that republic at the republic level. In some republics where there are no oblasts, the oblast table is used to present data for the capital city of that republic or for areas subject to republic-level administration. Republics that have oblasts, however, have these city data in addition to the oblast data. In some republics, such as Moldavia, either data for years before the region was incorporated into the USSR (notably 1939) are omitted or the entire table is omitted.

184 *Index and Guide*

1970 Census

Volumes. The 1970 census consists of seven volumes, each on a particular topic or topics; it does not contain any regional or summary volumes. All of the entries here represent the tables exactly as they appear in the census, with one major exception. For many topics a separate table is given in the census for each republic or even for different administrative levels within the same republic. For example, one table might be given for the entire USSR, one for each republic, one for the oblasts of the RSFSR, one for the oblasts of the Ukrainskaya SSR, and one for the minor ethnic units within the RSFSR. These tables always have similar titles, which mention the particular regional units shown in each table. These tables were combined into one entry, with brackets enclosing the particular regional units that are included. The brackets indicate that the wording for these units is paraphrased; therefore, the title is not exactly as it appears in the census.

1979 Census

Sources. At the time this index was prepared, results of the 1979 census had been published only in various issues of the journal *Vestnik statistiki* (between no. 2, 1980 and no. 12, 1983). Therefore, the table entries here are given in the order in which they appeared in that journal, with a citation to the corresponding issue number and year. Many of these tables are not numbered because there are no table numbers for those *Vestnik statistiki* tables.

In 1984 a census volume was finally published (Tsentral'noye Statisticheskoye Upravleniye SSSR, 1984. *Chislennost' i sostav naseleniya SSSR. Po dannym Vsesoyuznoy perepisi naseleniya 1979 goda.* Moscow: Finansy i Statistika). In the table entries here, this volume is referred to as TsSU SSSR, 1984. The data in this volume are essentially the same as those published in *Vestnik statistiki*, but some significant differences are worth noting. There is no correspondence in the number and order of tables between the two sources. In *Vestnik statistiki*, initial tables on a subject were typically followed in subsequent issues by more detailed tabulations as further results of the census became available. Therefore, the journal contains more tables, but with much duplication of data among them. Many tables in the book encompass the data from two or more tables in *Vestnik statistiki*. Some of the extra tables in *Vestnik statistiki*, however, contain data from earlier censuses which were not repeated in the corresponding book tables.

In a few cases, data from the 1979 census appear in only one of these sources. *Vestnik statistiki* has all-Union population data by sex by urban-rural (no. 704) as well as literacy data (no. 706). The book has population data for cities of 50,000 or greater (vs. 100,000 in *Vestnik statistiki*, no. 703), de facto versus de jure population by republic for urban-rural and by sex (nos. 759–60), and all-Union education data for census years since 1939 (no. 761).

Following each entry from *Vestnik statistiki* in the table list, a note in parentheses gives the citation to the number of the corresponding table or tables from the book which contain the same data. Whenever a single table number is listed with no comment, it can be assumed that the book table is essentially identical in content to the *Vestnik statistiki* table. The table title, however, is not necessarily the same nor is the number of digits in the data (many initial *Vestnik statistiki* tables on a subject, most commonly at the all-Union level, are rounded to the nearest thousand). In the numerous cases in which a table in the book contains data from more than one journal table, the number of the book table is followed by "contains these data." Where a book table has data that were not given anywhere in *Vestnik statistiki*, or lacks data that were given in the journal, a note describes the differences.

With the exception of book tables 5–7, which were given separate entries in the table list here, all tables in the book are referenced under one or more *Vestnik statistiki* entries. In cases where these book tables include data that are not in the related journal table, these data are included in the cross-index under the *Vestnik statistiki* entry in which this difference is explained. Therefore, checking the cross-index by subject will lead the researcher to *all* data from the TsSU SSSR volume as well as to all data from *Vestnik statistiki*.

In addition to the data from *Vestnik statistiki* and TsSU SSSR, small amounts of data from the census which have been published in other sources are included here. These are data on population by sex by urban-rural residence compiled by Theodore Shabad from Soviet regional press reports (no. 755), urban nationality data (no. 756), data on bilingualism by nationality (no. 757), and education data by nationality (no. 758).

List of Census Tables

Format of Table Entries

For each entry, the number ("no.") at the left side represents the sequential order in which that table appears in a particular census. The first digit of the entry number is keyed to the individual census as follows:

1897 census	Nos. 1–90
1926 census	Nos. 100–414
1959 census	Nos. 500–581
1970 census	Nos. 600–680
1979 census	Nos. 700–761

Because not all census volumes are numbered, some operational decisions were made regarding the order in which volumes were listed. Generally, the regional volumes were listed first, followed by any summary volumes and other accessory parts of the census. The second number for each entry represents the number (or numbers) of the table as it appears for many in the 1979 census. There is not necessarily a separate entry to represent each individual table in every census. In many cases, particularly in the 1970 census, the census contains a series of tables with the same title, each for a different administrative unit. These tables were combined into one entry in each case where this occurs; each of these entries includes all of the census table numbers. For the 1897, 1926, and 1970 censuses—in which table numbers are unique to each particular topical volume—the user will need to read up the serial table-number list to determine which volume of the census contains a given table. The 1897, 1926, and 1959 censuses comprise multiple regional volumes, each of which has essentially the same format. These volumes were represented by only one table when possible, but when there were very wide discrepancies among these table titles and/or contents, extra entries were included as needed to account for these differences.

All table numbers and letters used to denote parts of tables are given exactly as they appear in the census, with the letters transliterated. For example, in transliterations from Russian to English, the first four parts are given here as a, b, v, and g; they are not given as a, b, c, and d. This is necessary to avoid confusion, since in a few cases some parts are deliberately or inadvertently left out of the tables in the census volumes. Thus, the second section of a table may have a letter "v" in the census, rather than a "b." Roman numerals, which are used extensively throughout the censuses for table numbers and in volume or section titles, were converted here to Arabic numerals.

Table Titles

Each table title is translated from the Russian as literally as possible, so that the user can more easily determine the original terminology of a particular table. Often, there are slight differences between the title of a table as presented in the table of contents of the census volume and the title that appears at the top of the table itself. When the discrepancies are great, this is noted in the individual entries; otherwise, the title used is the one that best describes the contents of the table. In some cases the table titles consist of several parts and subparts. These are usually given in the entry, although some parts were not included when they became too repetitious (e.g., "rural population," "urban population," "USSR population," "Population by Union Republic"). When these parts were omitted, information was included in the descriptor to account for them. Brackets in the titles indicate paraphrasing and not a direct translation of the original. Brackets were necessary mainly when regional tables on the same subject were combined into one entry; brackets enclose the types of units that were included. Parentheses in the titles are part of the original title.

Table Descriptors

Titles of all of the tables as they appear in the censuses are generally indicative of the contents, but they are usually incomplete. Accordingly, a "descriptor" was included for each entry, enclosed in parentheses below the title. In a few cases, the title is sufficient to describe the contents, and no descriptor was used. The purpose of the descriptor is not only to provide information that is not contained in the title itself but also to clarify vague or misleading information in the title. Therefore, the descriptors often repeat some of the title categories and give greater detail. For example, if a title included the words "by age," the descriptor would tell how many age groups there were and give a better idea of the usefulness of the table. The number of categories that are indicated for a particular factor such as age or marital status is often approximate because the number depends upon whether categories such as "total," "all," "other," or "not specified" are included. Generally, these summary or other categories were not counted in listing the number of categories or groups.

Many of the descriptors are very detailed, especially for 1926 entries; nevertheless, they often do not indicate all of the information in the table. One of the most common categories that appears in the title but not in the descriptor is "by sex." Thus, it is necessary to look at both the title and the descriptor to get a complete understanding of all of the categories. When neither the title nor the descriptor includes the year or years represented by the data, then the data are for the year of that particular census only. The combination of title and descriptor includes virtually all categories in all tables with the exception of some tables for 1897 and 1926 where it was necessary to generalize some categories. Sections of the tables which are essentially repetition of other data in the same table (such as "percent urban" when the urban and rural populations are both given) were not included. That is, when a category can easily be calculated from other categories in the same table, it is usually not mentioned. This also applies in the numerous cases where the total population and then the urban population are given. These are described simply as "urban-rural."

The descriptors are generally limited to explaining *categories* of data that are included in the tables; other subtleties that the reader must understand before intelligent use of the data can be made are beyond the scope of this work. A good example of this is the use of "de facto" and "de jure" population data. The Russian and Soviet censuses employ both types of data (depending upon the particular census and particular table), both in reporting population totals and in reporting population characteristics. Many of the table titles in the censuses indicate whether the data are for the de facto (*nalichnoye*) or de jure (*postoyannoye*) population; this information is thus provided here for those tables. In cases where the table title does not specify de facto or de jure, it is the responsibility of the reader to examine the censuses and determine the type of data being presented. For example, while the nationality data in the 1979 census represented the permanent population, previous censuses generally gave nationality data in terms of the present population.

Another peculiarity of the census data which is not included in the descriptors is the use of both the preannexation and postannexation boundaries (depending upon the table) to represent the 1939 population.

This applies mainly to the 1959 census, where most of the 1939 census data that are available were published. The user should be aware that both types of data are used in the censuses; again, examination of the censuses themselves is necessary in order to determine which data are being used before comparability among tables can be attempted. Data presented for the postannexation boundaries in the censuses are not actual census data: they represent adjustments made by the Central Statistical Administration to estimate the population characteristics for the postannexation boundaries. Data for age distributions in 1939 which were published in the 1959 census represent the postannexation boundaries; comparison of age distributions with the preannexation boundaries can be made by reference to preannexation data published in *Vestnik statistiki*, no. 6, 1956.

Sample Table Entry

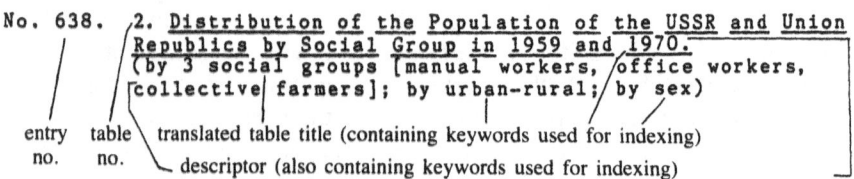

In this sample, the table serial number (no. 638) indicates that this table is from the 1970 census, while the table number (2) shows that it is labeled Table 2 in the census volume. Again, for the 1897, 1926, and 1970 censuses, the reader should read up the serial list of table entries to locate the appropriate census volume (in this example, Volume 5). The translated table title is then given, followed by the table descriptor, which provides supplementary information as to the actual table contents. Examples are also shown here of typical keywords in the table title and descriptor; these words were used for preparing the keyword cross index.

THE FIRST GENERAL CENSUS OF THE POPULATION OF THE RUSSIAN EMPIRE, 1897

Volumes 1-89. [Guberniyas and Oblasts of the Russian Empire].

No. 1. Suburban Settlements and Villages of [Name of Guberniya]. a. Those Included in the Tabulation as Parts of the Cities. b. Those Located Close to the Cities but Not Included as Parts of Them.
(population of each of these points by sex)

No. 2. Title (by Uezd with Cities and by Cities), with Indication of the Area, Population Density, and Percent Literacy.
(this is the title in the table of contents [title of the table itself is the name of the guberniya only]; data are for the whole uezd and then for the largest city [sometimes for more than one city] in the uezd; the area and population density are of the whole uezd only, not of the city also; enumerated [de facto] population, by sex; of the enumerated population [not by sex], the number of persons who were there temporarily at the time of the census, and the number of foreign citizens; percent literate [this is only by uezd and city, is not cross-tabulated with any other category])

No. 3. Summary--Composition of the Enumerated [De Facto] Population of Both Sexes (by Uezd with Cities and by Cities), with Division by Place of Birth, Social Group, Religion, and Native Language.
(this is the title in the table of contents [title of the table itself is simply Composition of the Enumerated Population of Both Sexes]; data are for the whole uezd and for the largest city [sometimes for more than one city] in the uezd; number of persons by place of birth [locally born, born in another uezd in the same guberniya, born in another guberniya, or born in another state]; number of persons by 5 social groups, plus foreigners; number of persons by native language [about 8 categories]; number of persons by religion [about 6 to 8 categories]; none of these categories is cross-tabulated by any other, and none of the categories is by sex)

No. 4. 1. Enumerated [De Facto] and Permanent [De Jure] Population.
(data are for each whole uezd and for the largest city [sometimes for more than one city] in the uezd, plus the uezd population without the cities; enumerated population is by Russian and foreign [each is divided into the permanent population and the population that was temporarily present at the time of the census]; permanent population is for the total and the number of persons who were temporarily absent at the time of the census; by sex)

No. 5. 2. Distribution of the Population by Households and Their Composition.
(data are for each whole uezd and for the largest city [sometimes for more than one city] in the uezd, plus the uezd population without the cities; total number of households, private households [divided into many

subcategories for households of related persons, households of persons living alone, households with servants, and households of unrelated persons (each of these categories have further subcategories, some of which are by sex)], and households of enterprises [by sex of members])

No. 6. 3a. Population by Ten-Year Age Groups.
(data are for each whole uezd and for the largest city [sometimes for more than one city] in the uezd, plus the uezd population without the cities; by sex)

No. 7. 3b. Distribution of the Population by Age (in Years), and Literacy.
(data are for each whole uezd and for the largest city [sometimes for more than one city] in the uezd, plus the uezd population without the cities; by sex)

No. 8. 4. Children Younger than One Year Old by Monthly Age Groups.
(data are for each whole uezd and for the largest city [sometimes for more than one city] in the uezd, plus the uezd population without the cities; by sex)

No. 9. 5. Distribution of the Population by Marital Status and Age Group.
(data are for each whole uezd and for the largest city [sometimes for more than one city] in the uezd, plus the uezd population without the cities; 4 categories of marital status; by 10 age groups; by sex)

No. 10. 6. Distribution of the Population by Social Group and Place of Birth.
(data are for each whole uezd and for the largest city [sometimes for more than one city] in the uezd, plus the uezd population without the cities; number of persons who were born in the uezd where they now live, born elsewhere in the same guberniya, born in another guberniya, or born in another country; by 3 different social groups; by sex)

No. 11. 7. Distribution of the Non-Locally Born Population by Place of Birth.
(place of birth [by guberniyas in Russia, principalities in Finland, and foreign states] by place of location at the time of the census [by guberniyas, uezds (not including their city populations), and one or two cities in each uezd]; by sex)

No. 12. 8. Distribution of the Population by Social Group.
(data are for each whole uezd and for the largest city [sometimes for more than one city] in the uezd, plus the uezd population without the cities; by about 9 social groups, plus the total for all social groups of those born in Finland, all Russian subjects, and all foreign citizens; by sex)

No. 13. 9. Distribution of the Population by Literacy, Education, Social Group, and Age Group.
(data are for each uezd, without the city population, and then for the largest city [sometimes for more than one city] in the uezd; number literate and the number who are studying in 6 different kinds of schools; by about 5 social groups, plus the total of all social

List of Census Tables   193

groups for those born in Finland and for foreign citizens; by seven 10-year age groups; by sex)

No. 14.   10. <u>Distribution of the Population by Social Group and Marital Status (by Guberniya and the Major Cities)</u>.
(data for each guberniya are for the whole guberniya, the population without the cities, the city population, and several individual cities; by 4 types of marital status; by about 5 social groups, plus the total of all social groups for those born in Finland and for foreign citizens; by sex)

No. 15.   11. <u>Distribution of Foreign Citizens by State (by Guberniya and the Major Cities)</u>.
(data for each guberniya are for the whole guberniya, the population without the cities, the city population, and several individual cities; by about 18 categories of foreign countries, depending upon the guberniya; by sex)

No. 16.   12. <u>Distribution of the Population by Religion.</u>
(data are for each whole uezd and for the largest city [sometimes for more than one city] in the uezd, plus the uezd population without the cities; for about 15 categories of religions; by sex)

No. 17.   13. <u>Distribution of the Population by Native Language.</u>
(data are for each whole uezd and for the largest city [sometimes for more than one city] in the uezd, plus the uezd population without the cities; by about 40 or more different languages, depending upon the guberniya; by sex)

No. 18.   14. <u>Distribution of the Population by Religion and Native Language.</u>
(data are for each uezd and for the largest city [sometimes for more than one city] in the uezd, plus the uezd population without the cities; by about 20 different languages; by about 15 different categories of religions; by literacy; by sex)

No. 19.   15. <u>Distribution of the Population by Native Language, Literacy, and Age Group (by Uezd with Cities and by the Major Cities)</u>.
(data for each guberniya are for the whole guberniya, the population without the cities, the whole city population, and several major cities; data at the uezd level are only for the whole uezd; by about 20 different languages; by 8 mostly 10-year age groups; by 3 measures of literacy [literate in Russian, literate in another language, having education higher than primary level]; by sex)

No. 20.   16. <u>Distribution of the Population by Marital Status and Native Language (by Guberniya and the Major Cities)</u>.
(data for each guberniya are for the whole guberniya, the population without the cities, the whole city population, and several major cities; 4 types of marital status; for about 20 different languages; by sex)

No. 21.   17. <u>Distribution of Persons with Physical Handicaps by Age Group.</u>
(data are for each uezd [without the city population] and for the major city [sometimes for more than one city] in the uezd; by 5 different types of physical

handicaps; by 8 mostly 10-year age groups; by marital status [married or not]; by sex)

No. 22. 18. **Distribution** of **Persons** with **Physical** **Handicaps** by **Native** **Language.**
(data are for each whole uezd and for the major city [sometimes for more than one city] in the uezd, plus the uezd population without the cities; by 5 types of physical handicaps; by about 15 native languages, depending upon the guberniya; by sex)

No. 23. 19. **Distribution** of **Persons** with **Physical** **Handicaps** by **Social** **Group.**
(data are for each whole uezd and for the largest city [sometimes for more than one city] in the uezd, plus the uezd population without the cities; by 5 types of physical handicaps; by 4 different social groups, plus the total of all social groups for those born in Finland and for foreigners; persons born in Finland are not by different types of handicaps [only the total handicaps] and foreigners are only by 3 types of handicaps; by sex)

No. 24. 20. **Results** by **Guberniya** for the **Population** by **Occupational** **Group** and **Age** **Group.**
(number of self-supporting persons in each of 65 occupational groups, by 7 age groups; number of their family members, by members younger than 15 years old, or 15 years and older; by sex)

No. 25. 21. **Distribution** of the **Population** by **Occupational** **Group.**
(data are by uezd [without the cities] and for the major city [sometimes for more than one city] in each uezd; number of self-supporting persons in each of 65 occupational groups, and the number of their family members; by sex)

No. 26. 22. **Distribution** of the **Population** by **Occupational** **Group** and by **Nationality,** on the **Basis** of **Native** **Language.**
(this table has the same format as Table 21, but each category is also by about 25 to 35 different languages; by sex)

No. 27. 23. **Distribution** of the **Population** by **Persons** **Engaged** in **Agricultural** or **Nomadic** **Economy,** **Fishing,** and **Hunting,** by **Part-Time** **Occupations.**
(by uezd: total number of self-supporting persons who are in all of the occupations listed above [together], and number of their family members; number of these self-supporting persons and number of their family members who have part-time occupations; by sex)
(subtitle: **Of** **Them,** **Persons** **with** **Part-Time** **Occupations.**;
by uezd: number of self-supporting persons and number of family members in each of more than 200 part-time occupations; by sex)

No. 28. 24. **Distribution** of the **Population** by **Native** **Language** and **Social** **Group.**
(data are by uezd [without the cities] and for the major city [sometimes for more than one city] in each uezd; by about 20 different languages; by 9 social groups, plus the total of all social groups for those born in Finland and for foreigners; by sex)

List of Census Tables 195

No. 29. 25. **Distribution of the Population by Religion and Ten-Year Age Groups.**
(data are by uezd [without the cities] and for the major city [sometimes for more than one city] in each uezd; by about 15 different religious groups; by sex)

General Summaries for the Empire of the Results of Tabulation of Data of the First General Census of Population. Volumes 1-2.

Volume 1.

No. 30. **Area, Enumerated [De Facto] Population, and Population Density.**
(by guberniya; by sex)

No. 31. **Enumerated [De Facto] Population in Cities.**
(by guberniya; urban population, by sex)

No. 32. 1. **Enumerated [De Facto] and Permanent [De Jure] Population.**
(by guberniya, for the whole population and for the city population; data are also given for 4 special categories that are not included in guberniyas [Russian population in Finland, military personnel who are abroad on warships, Russian population in Bukhara, and Russian population in Khiva], but these categories are only for the whole population, not for cities also; same format as Table 1 in the guberniya volumes [No. 4])

No. 33. 2. **Distribution of the Population by Households and Their Composition.**
(by guberniya, for the whole population and for the city population; data are also given for the 4 special categories that are not included in guberniyas [see Table 1], but for the whole population only; same format as Table 2 in the guberniya volumes [No. 5])

No. 34. 3a. **Population by Sex, Ten-Year Age Groups, and Literacy.**
(by guberniya, for the whole population and for the city population; data are also given for the 4 special categories that are not included in guberniyas [see Table 1], but for the whole population only)

No. 35. 3b. **Distribution of the Population by Sex, Age (in Years), and Literacy.**
(by main divisions of the Russian Empire)

No. 36. 4. **Children Younger than One Year Old by Monthly Age Groups.**
(by guberniya, for the whole population and for the city population; data are also given for the 4 special categories that are not included in guberniyas [see Table 1], but for the whole population only; by sex; same format as Table 4 in the guberniya volumes [No. 8])

No. 37. 5. **Distribution of the Population by Marital Status and Age Group.**
(by main divisions of the Russian Empire, for the population without the cities and for the city

population; by 10 age groups; by marital status [married, single, not in a family, widowed]; by sex; same format as Table 5 in the guberniya volumes [No. 9])

No. 38.   6. <u>Distribution of the Population by Social Group and Place of Birth.</u>
(by guberniya, for the whole population and for the city population; data are also given for the 4 special categories that are not included in guberniyas [see Table 1], but for the whole population only; same format as Table 6 in the guberniya volumes [No. 10])

No. 39.   7. <u>Distribution of the Non-Locally Born Population by Place of Birth.</u>
(first part: place of birth [by guberniyas in Russia, principalities in Finland, and foreign states] by place of enumeration in the census [by main divisions of the Russian Empire, for the whole division and for the city population]; by sex)
(second part: place of enumeration in the census [by guberniyas in Russia, principalities of Finland, and foreign states] by place of birth [by guberniyas in Russia, Finland, and foreign states]; by sex)

No. 40.   8. <u>Distribution of the Population by Social Group.</u>
(by guberniya, for the whole population and for the city population; data are also given for the 4 special categories that are not included in guberniyas [see Table 1], but for the whole population only; same format as Table 8 in the guberniya volumes [No. 12])

No. 41.   9. <u>Distribution of the Population by Literacy, Education, Social Group, and Age Group.</u>
(by main divisions of the Russian Empire, for the whole population and for the city population; same format as Table 9 in the guberniya volumes [No. 13])

No. 42.   10. <u>Distribution of the Population by Social Group and Marital Status.</u>
(by guberniya, for the whole population and for the city population; data are also given for the 4 special categories that are not included in guberniyas [see Table 1], but for the whole population only; same format as Table 10 in the guberniya volumes [No. 14])

No. 43.   11. <u>Distribution of Foreign Citizens by State.</u>
(by guberniya, for the whole population and for the city population; data are also given for the 4 special categories that are not included in guberniyas [see Table 1], but for the whole population only; same format as Table 11 in the guberniya volumes [No. 15])

No. 44.   12. <u>Distribution of the Population by Religion.</u>
(by guberniya, for the whole population and for the city population; data are also given for the 4 special categories that are not included in guberniyas [see Table 1], but for the whole population only; same format as Table 12 in the guberniya volumes [No. 16])

<u>Volume 2.</u>

List of Census Tables 197

No. 45. 13. <u>Distribution of the Population by Native Language.</u>
(by guberniya, for the whole population and for the city population; data are also given for the 4 special categories that are not included in guberniyas [see Table 1, <u>Volume 1.</u>], but for the whole population only; same format as Table 13 in the guberniya volumes [No. 17], but for more than 100 languages)

No. 46. 14. <u>Distribution of the Population by Religion and Native Language.</u>
(by main divisions of the Russian Empire, for the whole population and for the city population; same format as Table 14 in the guberniya volumes [No. 18])

No. 47. 15. <u>Distribution of the Population by Native Language, Literacy, and Age Group.</u>
(by main divisions of the Russian Empire, for the whole population and for the city population; same format as Table 15 in the guberniya volumes [No. 19])

No. 48. 16. <u>Distribution of the Population by Marital Status and Native Language.</u>
(by main divisions of the Russian Empire, for the whole population, for the population without the cities, and for the city population; same format as Table 16 in the guberniya volumes [No. 20])

No. 49. 17. <u>Distribution of Persons with Physical Handicaps by Age Group.</u>
(by main divisions of the Russian Empire, for the whole population and for the city population; same format as Table 17 in the guberniya volumes [No. 21])

No. 50. 18. <u>Distribution of Persons with Physical Handicaps by Native Language.</u>
(by main divisions of the Russian Empire, for the whole population and for the city population; same format as Table 18 in the guberniya volumes [No. 22], but for 97 languages)

No. 51. 19. <u>Distribution of Persons with Physical Handicaps by Social Group.</u>
(by guberniya, for the whole population and for the city population; data are also given for the 4 special categories that are not included in guberniyas [see Table 1, <u>Volume 1.</u>], but for the whole population only; same format as Table 19 in the guberniya volumes [No. 23])

No. 52. 20. <u>Distribution of the Population by Occupation and Age Group.</u>
(for the whole Russian Empire: number of self-supporting persons in each of 65 occupational groups [and in numerous subcategories of these groups], by 7 age groups; number of their family members, by members younger than 15 years old, or 15 years and older; by sex)
(by main divisions of the Russian Empire: for the population without the cities and for the city population; number of self-supporting persons in each of the same 65 occupational groups and subgroups, and number of their family members; by sex)

No. 53. 21. <u>Distribution of the Population by Occupational Group.</u>

(by guberniya [Moscow, St. Petersburg, Warsaw, and Odessa not included]; number of self-supporting persons in each of 65 occupational groups, and the number of their family members; by sex; data are also given by main divisions of the empire for these same categories, but these data are for the population without the cities and then for the city population)

No. 54. 22. **Distribution of the Population by Occupational Group and by Nationality, on the Basis of Native Language.**
(for the whole Russian Empire only; number of self-supporting persons in each of 65 occupational groups, and the number of their family members; by more than 100 different languages; by sex)

No. 55. 23. **Distribution of the Population by Persons Engaged in Agricultural or Nomadic Economy, Fishing, and Hunting, by Part-Time Occupations.**
(first part: by main divisions of the Russian Empire; same format as the first part of Table 23 in the guberniya volumes [No. 27])
(subtitle: **Of Them, Persons with Part-Time Occupations.**; by main divisions of the Russian Empire; number of self-supporting persons and number of family members in each of 47 groups [and detailed subgroups] of part-time occupations; by sex)
(third part: by guberniya; number of self-supporting persons and number of family members in agricultural or nomadic economy, fishing and hunting [total of all these occupational categories]; number of these persons [by self-supporting persons and family members] who have part-time occupations; by sex)

No. 56. 24. **Distribution of the Population by Native Language and Social Group.**
(by main divisions of the Russian Empire, for the whole population and for the city population; same format as Table 24 in the guberniya volumes [No. 28])

No. 57. 25. **Distribution of the Population by Religion and Ten-Year Age groups.**
(by main divisions of the Russian Empire; same format as Table 25 in the guberniya volumes [No. 29])

Distribution of the Population by Type of Chief Occupation and Age Group, for Individual Regions. Table 20. Volumes 1-4.

No. 58. 20. **Distribution of the Population by Occupations and Age Groups.**
(these volumes present a more detailed version of Table 20; they consist of 20 regions, each of which contains separate data for several guberniyas)
(by region: for 65 occupational groups, most of which have many subdivisions; number of persons who are self-supporting in each of these occupational categories [by 7 age groups], and the number of their family members [by younger than 15 years old, or 15 and older]; number of these self-supporting persons and of their family members by population not in cities and population in cities [generally the city population represents only all cities in each region, but data for St. Petersburg, Moscow, Warsaw, and Odessa are included in their

respective regions, in addition to the total city population in those regions]; by sex)
(by guberniya: for the whole guberniya, for all cities together, and for one or more specific cities; by the same 65 occupational groups as for the region level data, but with fewer subcategories; number of persons who are self-supporting in each of these occupational categories, and the number of their family members; data are also given for each uezd [not by urban-rural], but only for the number of self-supporting persons in each occupational category [not for family members]; all of the data in this table are by sex)

Number and Social Composition of Workers in Russia according to the First General Census of Population of the Russian Empire, 1897. Volumes 1-2.

Volume 1.

No. 59. 1. Distribution of Workers by Group and Type of Occupation (by Guberniya).
(data for 10 cities also [Ivanovo-Voznesensk, Rostov-na-Donu, Kiev, Riga, Moscow, St. Petersburg, Khar'kov, Odessa, Warsaw, Lodz']; for all workers and for those 15 years old or younger; by sex; by 149 different occupations)

No. 60. 2. Distribution of Workers by Sex, Marital Status, and Relation to the Family (by Occupational Group and by Guberniya).
(data for 10 cities also [see Table 1]; total number of workers, number of married workers in each of 5 age groups, number of workers who are heads of families [by 6 size groups of the number of family members]; by 28 occupational groups)

No. 61. 3. Distribution of Workers by Type of Occupation, Sex, Age, and Literacy (General Summary for the Empire, European Russia, Privislinskiy Guberniyas, Caucasus, Siberia, and Central Asia).
(by 7 age groups; by 149 different occupations)

Appendix. Number and Composition of Agricultural Workers, Workers in Forest Industries and Forestry, in Fishing and Hunting, Day Laborers, Unskilled Workers, and Servants.

No. 62. 1. Distribution of Workers, Day-Laborers, Unskilled Workers, and Servants by Type of Occupation (by Guberniya).
(data for 10 cities also [see Table 1]; number of all workers and of those aged 15 and younger; by 10 occupations, from the types listed above; by sex)

No. 63. 2. Distribution of Workers and Servants by Sex, Marital Status, and Relation to the Family.
(by main divisions of the empire; number of married workers, by 5 age groups; number of married workers who head families, by 6 size groups of the families they head; by the same 10 occupational groups as Table 1)

No. 64. 3. **Distribution of Workers and Servants by Sex, Marital Status, and Relation to the Family.**
(same title as Table 2, but it is apparently a typographical error, because the contents are unrelated to the title: by main divisions of the empire; for the same 10 occupational groups as in Table 1, this table gives literacy by 7 age groups and by sex [there are no data on marital status or relation to the family])

Volume 2.

No. 65. 3. **Distribution of Workers by Type of Occupation, Sex, Age, and Literacy.**
(this table is the same title and format as the main Table 3 in **Volume 1.**, but it is by guberniya rather than by major divisions of the empire; data are also included for the 10 cities [see Table 1, **Volume 1.**])

First General Census of the Population of the Russian Empire, 1897. Short Summaries. Numbers 1-8.

Number 1. Population of the Empire, according to the Census of January 28, 1897, by Uezd.

No. 66. 1. **Population of the Russian Empire, according to the 1897 Census, by Uezd.**
(permanent population, by sex; urban population, not by sex)

No. 67. 2. **Population of the Russian Empire, according to the 1897 Census, by Guberniya.**
(permanent population, by sex; urban population, not by sex)

Number 2. Population of Cities, according to the Census of January 28, 1897.

No. 68. 1. **Population of Cities of the Russian Empire, according to the 1897 Census.**
(by guberniya, the population of individual cities [about 5 to 25 cities, depending upon the guberniya]; by sex)

No. 69. 2. **Enumerated [De Facto] Population in Cities, according to the 1897 Census, by Guberniya.**
(urban population, by sex)

Number 3. Population of the Cities of St. Petersburg, Moscow, Warsaw, and Odessa, according to the Census of January 28th, 1897.

No. 70. 1. **Population of St. Petersburg, according to the 1897 Census.**
(by police districts and their subdivisions ["uchastki"] for the city and the suburbs; by sex; enumerated population in 1890 and 1897; permanent population [de

jure] in 1897)

No. 71. 2. <u>Population of St. Petersburg, according to the 1897 Census.</u>
(by the same districts and uchastki as in Table 1; for the years 1890 and 1897; by peasant and non peasant social groups; by sex)

No. 72. 3. <u>Population of Moscow, according to the 1897 Census.</u>
(exactly the same format as Table 1, but the years are 1882 and 1897)

No. 73. 4. <u>Population of Moscow, according to the 1897 Census.</u>
(exactly the same format as Table 2, but the years are 1882 and 1897)

No. 74. 5. <u>Population of Odessa, according to the 1897 Census.</u>
(exactly the same format as Table 3)

No. 75. 6. <u>Population of Odessa, according to the 1897 Census.</u>
(exactly the same format as Table 4)

No. 76. 7. <u>Population of Warsaw, according to the 1897 Census.</u>
(by districts of the city; unlike the other tables in this volume, it is for 1897 only; enumerated [de facto] and permanent [de jure] population; enumerated peasant and non peasant population; by sex)

Number 4. <u>Final Tabulation of the Enumerated [De Facto] Population of the Empire, by Uezd.</u>

No. 77. 1. <u>Enumerated [De Facto] Population of the Empire, by Uezd.</u>
(total population, by sex; urban population; number of persons who were born in the guberniya in which they were enumerated)

No. 78. 2. <u>Enumerated [De Facto] Population of the Empire, by Guberniya.</u>
(same format as Table 1, but by guberniya only)

Number 5. <u>Final Tabulation of the Enumerated [De Facto] Population of Cities.</u>

No. 79. 1. <u>Enumerated Population of Cities of the Russian Empire, according to the 1897 Census.</u>
(by guberniya and by the populations of individual cities in each guberniya [about 5 to 25 cities, depending upon the guberniya]; total population of each unit, by sex; suburban population and preliminary city population figures [not by sex])

No. 80. 2. <u>Enumerated Population of Cities of the Russian Empire, according to the 1897 Census, by Guberniya.</u>
(same format as Table 1, but data are only at the guberniya level, not for individual cities)

Number 6. Enumerated [De Facto] Population of Both Sexes by Uezd and City, with Listing of the Predominant Religions and the Main Social Groups.

No. 81.   1. Enumerated Population of Both Sexes by Uezd and City, with Listing of the Predominant Religions and the Main Social Groups.
(by urban-rural in each uezd [data are not given for individual cities]; not by sex; data on religions and social groups are not cross-tabulated by each other)

Number 7. Enumerated [De Facto] Population of Both Sexes by Uezd, with Listing of the Number of Persons of the Predominant Native Languages.

No. 82.   [see title of Number 7.]
a. By Guberniya and Oblast.
(for the total population and for the urban population; not by sex)
b. By Uezd and Okrug.
(not by sex)

Number 8. Percentage Distribution of the Enumerated [De Facto] Population of the Empire of Both Sexes, by the Most Important Occupational Groups Which Provide the Main Means of Livelihood.

No. 83.   1. Distribution of the Enumerated Population by the Main Occupational Groups -- in Percentages (%) -- Summary.
(for main divisions of the empire only; for the total population and for the urban population; for 20 occupational groups; not by sex)

No. 84.   2. Distribution of the Enumerated Population by Main Occupational Group -- in Percentages (%) -- By Guberniya.
(same format as Table 1, but by guberniya)

Populated Places of the Russian Empire Having 500 or More Inhabitants, with Listing of the Total Enumerated Population and the Number of Inhabitants Who Belong to the Predominant Religious Groups, according to Data of the First General Census of the Population, 1897.

No. 85.   Supplement. Number of Populated Places of 500 Inhabitants or More, by Guberniya.
(also gives, for each guberniya, the total population in places with 500 inhabitants or more and the number and total population of other settlements)

No. 86.   - Same title as volume title -.
(by guberniya; the total population of each place is by sex, but data on religion are not by sex; each settlement is also coded as to its type and function)

Cities and Population in Uezds that Have 2000 or More Inhabitants.

List of Census Tables 203

No. 87. Cities.
(by guberniya; number of cities and their total population in each of 5 size groups)

No. 88. Settlements in Uezds.
(by guberniya; number of population points in the uezds [i.e., other than the cities included above] and their total population in each of 6 size groups)

No. 89. Cities that Have Fewer than 2000 Inhabitants.
(by guberniya; population of each of these cities)

No. 90. Distribution of Settlements of 2000 or More Inhabitants, Excluding Cities, by the Population of Both Sexes.
(by guberniya; population of each of these settlements; total population and number of settlements in each of 6 size groups; not by sex)

ALL-UNION POPULATION CENSUS OF 1926

Section 1. Nationality, Native Language, Age, Literacy.

Rayon Volumes.

No. 100. 1. Urban Soviets, Volosts, and Rayons by Population Size.
(data are generally by guberniya [in many units, especially those not in European RSFSR or Ukrainskaya SSR, data are only at the whole ASSR or SSR level]; number of urban soviets and number of volosts and rayons [together] and their population, by 15 population-size groups)

No. 101. 2. Rural Soviets [Councils] by Population Size.
(by guberniya and [in most guberniyas] by uezd; population in rural soviets and volosts [together]; number of volosts; number of rural soviets and their total population, by 6 population-size groups)

No. 102. 3. Number of Rural Soviets, Populated Places, Rural Households, and Enumerated [De Facto] Population by Volost, with an Apportionment of Those Registered in Urban Settlements.
(in some units data are given only at the rayon [equivalent to uezd] level, not for volosts; in addition to the rural population in the categories listed above, population of urban soviets that are included in the volost soviets is also given)

No. 103. 4. Distribution of Urban and Rural Populated Places by Population Size.
(part a, by guberniya, gives the number of urban and of rural populated places and the total population in them, by 14 size groups; part b, by guberniya and [in most guberniyas] by uezd, gives similar data but by 11 size groups)

No. 104.   5. **Enumerated [De Facto] and Permanent [De Jure] Population of Urban Settlements.**
(by guberniya, data for each urban settlement; by sex)

No. 105.   6. **Population by Nationality, Native Language, and Literacy.**
(by guberniya, and for individual large cities [usually 1 or more cities in each major census rayon, and sometimes 1 city in each guberniya]; number of persons by relationship of nationality and native language [native language is the language of their nationality, is not of their nationality (by Russian, one or two local languages, or other)]; total number of literate persons and number of those who are literate in the language of their nationality; for 190 different categories of nationalities; by urban-rural; by sex; the total foreign population and the number of them who are literate is also given, by sex and urban-rural only)

No. 106.   6a. **Literate Persons by Sex and Language of Literacy.**
(only about half of the major census rayons have this table; in some rayons the table covers only one ethnic administrative unit, while in others it covers all guberniya-level units and [especially in Ukrainskaya SSR] even some major cities; number of persons literate in each of several different languages; by two or more ethnic groups; by sex; by urban-rural; language and nationality data are especially detailed in Ukrainskaya SSR)

No. 107.   7. **Foreigners by Sex and State.**
(by guberniya and for most major cities; for 47 different states or groups of states; by urban-rural)

No. 108.   8. **Population (Citizens of the USSR and Foreigners) by Native Language.**
(by guberniya and for most major cities; for 153 different language categories; by urban-rural; by sex; data are aggregate, not by citizenship)

No. 109.   9. **Population by Sex, Age, Main Nationalities, and Literacy.**
(by guberniya and for most major cities; nationality is usually by Russian or other [in areas with wide ethnic diversity or in non-Russian republics it is for several or more nationalities, while in areas that are mostly Russian nationality data are often not given]; by single-year ages; by sex; by urban-rural)

No. 110.   9a. **Children Younger than One Year Old by Sex and Age.**
(by guberniya and for most major cities; by nationality [usually Russian and other, or several different ethnic groups]; by 5 age groups; by urban-rural [in some units urban-rural data are not by nationality])

No. 111.   9b. **Ukrainians by Native Language and Sex, Age, and Literacy.**
(this table is in the 6 Ukrainian sub-rayons only; by okrug and for most major cities; total number of Ukrainians and the number literate; number of Ukrainians whose native language is Ukrainian, Russian, or other, and the number of each of those groups who are literate; by single-year ages to age 19, and then by

List of Census Tables 205

5- and 10-year age groups; by urban-rural)

No. 112. 10. **Population by Sex, Nationality, and Native Language by Individual Urban Settlements and Volosts.**
(by guberniya and uezd; for the major ethnic groups and for the major languages only [commonly 5-10 of each], not cross-tabulated by each other)

No. 113. 11. **Population by Age, Sex, and Literacy, by Uezd, Volost, and Individual Urban Settlements.**
(for 26 age groups; also by nationality in most units [from 2 to about 6 or 8 groups, depending upon the unit], but ethnic data are often not given when the population in the guberniya is mainly Russian; within guberniyas where ethnic data are given, they are generally included for most uezds and for many volosts and cities, but not all; often, ethnic data that are given for the whole uezd are not by urban-rural)

Volume 9. **RSFSR.**

No. 114. 1. **Populated Places. Enumerated [De Facto] Urban and Rural Population.**
(generally by guberniya and uezd, but some units are not subdivided [i.e., data are only at the ASSR, AO, or guberniya level]; area of each unit and population density [total, rural]; number of populated places and total population, by sex and urban-rural)

No. 115. 2. **Urban Soviets [Councils], Volosts, and Rayons, by Population Size.**
(by guberniya; same format as Rayon Table 1 [No. 100])

No. 116. 3. **Rural Soviets [Councils] by Population Size.**
(by guberniya; same format as Rayon Table 2 [No. 101])

No. 117. 4. **Distribution of Urban and Rural Populated Places by Population Size.**
(for the main rayons [19 of them]; same format as Rayon Table 4 [No. 103], part a)

No. 118. 5. **Enumerated [De Facto] and Permanent [De Jure] Population of Urban Settlements.**
(by guberniya, data for each urban settlement; same format as Rayon Table 5 [No. 104])

No. 119. 6. **Population by Sex, Nationality, Native Language, and Literacy (in Absolute Numbers).**
(whole RSFSR only; same format as Rayon Table 6 [No. 105], but native language is only for 2 categories [Russian and other])

No. 120. 7. **Population by Sex, Nationality, Native Language, and Literacy (in Relative Numbers).**
(whole RSFSR only; in spite of the title, this table is not exactly the same format as Table 6; number of women per 1000 men, percent of the population of each nationality whose native language is the language of that nationality, percent literate by nationality, percent of literate persons who are literate in the language of their nationality; for 190 different ethnic groups; by urban-rural; literacy of all foreigners is

also given, by sex and urban-rural only)

No. 121. 8. **Foreigners by State.**
(the format of this table at the whole RSFSR level is the same as that of Rayon Table 7 [No. 107], including data by sex and urban-rural; data also given for each of the 19 census rayons and for Moscow and Leningrad, but those regional and city data are not by sex or urban-rural)

No. 122. 9. **Population (Citizens of the USSR and Foreigners) by Native Language.**
(whole RSFSR; same format as Rayon Table 8 [No. 108])

No. 123. 10. **Ethnic Composition of the Population of Individual Territorial Units of the RSFSR.**
(by guberniya plus Moscow and Leningrad; number of different ethnic groups given for each region varies from 3 to about 35; by urban-rural and by sex [data are not cross-tabulated by urban-rural and sex])

No. 124. 11. **Distribution of Nationalities in the Territory of the RSFSR.**
(for 190 different ethnic categories; for each ethnic group the number of that group living in each ethnic unit or guberniya [plus Moscow and Leningrad] of the RSFSR is given, with the units listed in decreasing order of the number of that group living there; by urban-rural)

No. 125. 12. **Population of Individual Territorial Units of the RSFSR by Native Language (Including Foreign Citizens).**
(exactly the same administrative units and format as Table 10 [No. 123] but for native language)

No. 126. 13. **Distribution of Languages in the Territory of the RSFSR.**
(exactly the same administrative units and format as Table 11 [No. 124] but for language)

No. 127. 14. **Population by Sex, Age, and Literacy. a. In the RSFSR. b. In the RSFSR without Kazakhskaya ASSR, Kirgizskaya ASSR, Dagestanskaya ASSR, and Autonomous Oblasts of the North Caucasus.**
(for the whole RSFSR and for the RSFSR without the units noted above only; by single-year ages; for urban, rural, cities with more than 100,000 population [total, not individual cities], cities with populations of 50,000 to 99,999 [also total], and other urban)

No. 128. 15. **Population by Sex, Age, and Literacy, according to the Censuses of December 17, 1926 and February 9, 1897.**
(by 19 census rayons of the RSFSR; by single-year ages 1-19, then by 5-year age groups; by urban-rural)

No. 129. 16. **Children Younger than One Year Old by Sex and Age. a. In the RSFSR. b. In the RSFSR without Kazakhskaya ASSR, Kirgizskaya ASSR, Dagestanskaya ASSR, and Autonomous Republics of the North Caucasus.**
(for the whole RSFSR and the RSFSR without the units noted above only; by 5 age groups; for urban, rural, cities with more than 100,000 population [total], cities with populations of 50,000 to 99,999 [also total], other urban)

No. 130. 17. **Age Composition of the Population according to the Censuses of 1926 and 1897, in Relative Numbers (in %).**
(by 19 census rayons of the RSFSR; by single-year ages 1-19, then by 5-year age groups; by urban-rural; by sex)

No. 131. 18. **Literacy of the Population by Age, according to the Censuses of 1926 and 1897, in Relative Numbers (in %).**
(by 19 census rayons of the RSFSR; by single-year ages 5-19, then by 5-year age groups; by urban-rural; by sex)

No. 132. 19. **Literacy of the Population of Individual Territorial Units with Apportionment of the Most Numerous Nationalities, in Relative Numbers (in %).**
(by guberniya and uezd [many units do not give uezd data], plus Moscow and Leningrad; number of nationalities given ranges from about 2 to 35; by sex; by urban rural; data at the uezd level are not by nationality)

Volume 11. Ukrainskaya SSR.

No. 133. 1. **Populated Places. Enumerated [De Facto] Urban and Rural Population.**
(by okrug, same format as RSFSR Table 1 [No. 114])

No. 134. 2. **Urban Soviets [Councils] and Rayons by Population Size.**
(by 6 sub-rayons; number of urban soviets and of rayons and their total populations, by 11 population-size groups)

No. 135. 3. **Rural Soviets by Population Size.**
(by 6 sub-rayons; number of rural soviets and their total population, by 6 population-size groups)

No. 136. 4. **Distribution of Urban and Rural Populated Places by Population Size.**
(by 6 sub-rayons; same format as Rayon Table 4 [No. 103], part a)

No. 137. 5. **Enumerated [De Facto] and Permanent [De Jure] Population of Urban Settlements.**
(by 6 sub-rayons; data for all urban settlements only [not individual ones]; by sex)

No. 138. 6. **Population By Sex, Nationality, Native Language, and Literacy (in Absolute Numbers).**
(whole republic only; same format as Rayon Table 6 [No. 105])

No. 139. 6a. **Literate Population by Sex and Language of Literacy (in Absolute Numbers). a. Ukrainians. b. Russians. c. Jews.**
(whole republic only; number of persons literate in each of several different languages [see title] by native language [Russian, Ukrainian, other]; Table 7a gives the same information, but in relative numbers [%])

No. 140. 7. **Population by Sex, Nationality, Native Language, and Literacy (in Relative Numbers).**
(whole republic only; same format as RSFSR Table 7 [No. 120])

No. 141. 8. **Foreigners by State.**
(data for the whole republic are for 39 categories of states, by sex and by urban-rural; data for these same categories are also given for the 6 sub-rayons and for Kiev, Kharkov, and Odessa, but these data are not by sex or by urban-rural)

No. 142. 9. **Population (Citizens of the USSR and Foreigners) by Native Language.**
(whole republic only; same format as Rayon Table 8 [No. 108])

No. 143. 10. **Ethnic Composition of Individual Territorial Units of the Ukrainskaya SSR.**
(by okrug; same format as RSFSR Table 10 [No. 123], but the number of different ethnic groups given for each unit varies from about 4 to 11)

No. 144. 11. **Distribution of Nationalities in the Territory of the Ukrainskaya SSR.**
(same format as RSFSR Table 11 [No. 124], but data are given for fewer languages and are not provided for any cities)

No. 145. 12. **Population of Individual Territorial Units of the Ukrainskaya SSR by Native Language.**
(by okrug; exactly the same format as Table 10 [No. 143] but for native language)

No. 146. 13. **Distribution of Languages in the Territory of the Ukrainskaya SSR.**
(exactly the same format as Table 11 [No. 144], but for languages)

No. 147. 14. **Population by Sex, Age, Main Nationalities, and Literacy.**
(whole republic only; number of persons who are Ukrainians, Russians, Jews, or others, and the number of each of these nationalities who are literate [for Ukrainians and Jews the data also include the number of literate persons whose native langauge is Ukrainian or Russian (for Jews, the number whose language is a native European language)]; by urban, rural, cities of more than 100,000 population [total, not individual cities], cities of 50,000 to 99,999 population [also total], and other urban; by single-year ages)

No. 148. 15. **Children Younger than One Year Old by Sex and Age.**
(whole republic only; by Ukrainian, Russian, Jew, other; by 5 age groups; by urban, rural, cities of more than 100,000 population [total, not individual cities], cities of 50,000 to 99,999 population [also total], and other urban)

No. 149. 16a. **Ukrainians by Native Language and Age (in Relative Numbers).**
(whole republic only; percent of Ukrainians whose native language is Ukrainian, Russian, or other; by single-year ages to age 19 and then by 5-year age

groups; by urban-rural; by sex)

No. 150. 16b. **Jews by Native Language and Age (in Relative Numbers).**
(same format as Table 16a, but percent of Jews whose native language is a European language)

No. 151. 17. **Population by Sex, Age, and Literacy, according to the Censuses of 1926 and 1897 (in Absolute Numbers).**
(whole republic only; by single-year ages 1-19 and then 5-year age groups; by urban-rural)

No. 152. 18. **Population by Sex, Age, and Literacy, according to the Censuses of 1926 and 1897 (in Relative Numbers).**
(same format as Table 17, but in %)

Volume 17. **USSR.**

No. 153. 1. **Populated Places. Enumerated [De Facto] Urban and Rural Population.**
(by rayon; same format as RSFSR Table 1 [No. 114])

No. 154. 2. **Urban Soviets [Councils], Volosts, and Rayons, by Population Size.**
(by Union Republic; same format as Rayon Table 1 [No. 100])

No. 155. 3. **Rural Soviets [Councils] by Population Size.**
(by Union Republic; population which is included in rural soviets and that which is not included; number of rural soviets and the population in them, by 6 population-size groups)

No. 156. 4. **Distribution of Urban and Rural Populated Places by Population Size.**
(by Union Republic; same format as Rayon Table 4 [No. 103], part a)

No. 157. 5. **Enumerated [De Facto] and Permanent [De Jure] Population of Urban Settlements.**
(for whole USSR, RSFSR, Belorusskaya SSR, and Ukrainskaya SSR only; by sex; data for all [not individual] urban settlements in each unit)

No. 158. 6. **Population by Sex, Nationality, Native Language, and Literacy (in Absolute Numbers).**
(whole USSR only; same format as Rayon Table 6 [No. 105], but native language is only for 2 categories [Russian and other])

No. 159. 7. **Population by Sex, Nationality, Native Language, and Literacy (in Relative Numbers).**
(whole USSR only; same format as RSFSR Table 7 [No. 120])

No. 160. 8. **Foreigners by State.**
(the format of this table at the whole USSR level is the same as that of Rayon Table 7 [No. 107], including data by sex and urban-rural; data are also given by Union Republic, but data for those units are only the total number of foreigners of each state, they are not by sex or urban-rural)

No. 161. 9. Population (Citizens of the USSR and Foreigners) by Native Language.
(whole USSR only; same format as Rayon Table 8 [No. 108])

No. 162. 10. Ethnic Composition of the Population of the Union Republics.
(for 190 different ethnic categories; by urban-rural)

No. 163. 11. Distribution of the Population of the Union Republics by Language.
(for 153 different language categories; by urban-rural)

No. 164. 12. Population by Sex, Age, and Literacy. a. In the USSR. b. In the RSFSR (without Kazakhskaya ASSR, Kirgizskaya ASSR, Dagestanskaya ASSR, and Autonomous Oblasts of the North Caucasus), Belorusskaya SSR, and Ukrainskaya SSR.
(whole USSR and whole RSFSR [without the units listed above] only; same format as RSFSR Table 14 [No. 127])

No. 165. 13. Children Younger than One Year Old by Sex and Age. a. In the USSR. b. In the RSFSR (without Kazakhskaya ASSR, Kirgizskaya ASSR, Dagestanskaya ASSR, and Autonomous Republics of the North Caucasus), Belorusskaya SSR, and Ukrainskaya SSR.
(whole USSR and whole RSFSR [without the units listed above] only; same format as RSFSR Table 16 [No. 129])

No. 166. 14. Population by Sex, Age, and Literacy, according to the Censuses of December 17, 1926, and February 9, 1897.
(by Union Republic; same format as RSFSR Table 15 [No. 128])

No. 167. 15. Age Composition of the Population, according to the Censuses of 1926 and 1897, in Relative Numbers (in %).
(by Union Republic; same format as RSFSR Table 17 [No. 130])

No. 168. 16. Literacy of the Population by Age, according to the Censuses of 1926 and 1897, in Relative Numbers (in %).
(by Union Republic; same format as RSFSR Table 18 [No. 131])

No. 169. 17. Age and Literacy of the Population by Nationality (Absolute Data).
(whole USSR only [figures for each nationality are the USSR total, based on the ethnic populations in selected regional units only]; by 53 different ethnic categories; by single-year ages 1-19, then by 5-year age groups; by sex)

No. 170. 18. Age Composition of the Population by Nationality, in Relative Numbers (in %).
(whole USSR only; by 53 different ethnic categories; by single-year ages 1-19, then by 5-year age groups; by sex)

No. 171. 19. Literacy of the Population by Nationality and Age, in Relative Numbers (in %).
(whole USSR only; by 53 different ethnic categories; by single-year ages 5-19, then by 5-year age groups; by sex)

Section 2. Occupations.

Rayon Volumes.

No. 172. 1. **Population by Position in Occupation and Sector of the Economy.**
(by guberniya, and also for many major cities; by gainfully employed and non-gainfully employed; by urban-rural; by sex; most guberniyas are also by 2 or 3 different nationalities [most cities, except for Moscow and Leningrad, are not by nationality]; nationality data are not by urban-rural)

No. 173. 2. **Sex, Age, Literacy, and Marital Status by the Main Divisions of the Occupational Classification.**
(by main census rayons, but some rayons are divided by guberniyas [Moscow and Leningrad are also included]; by position in occupation and sector of the economy; by gainfully employed and non-gainfully employed; by 17 age groups; by marital status [4 types] of the whole population aged 15 and older [not by age]; by urban-rural [this is cross-tabulated with everything except age and marital status]; this table for the rayons of Belorusskaya SSR, Sibirskiy kray, and Dal'ne-Vostochnyy kray is based not on the main divisions of the occupational classification, but on the short occupational classification [i.e., the occupational data are more detailed])

No. 174. 2a. **Farmers and Agricultural Workers in Peasant-Type Enterprises.**
(by rayon; for all farmers and agricultural workers together, by position in occupation; by 15 age groups; by sex; by number literate [literacy is only for the total by age and sex, not by position in occupation]; this table is numbered 2b for the rayons listed in No. 175)

No. 175. 2a. **Supplementary Data on the Age Composition of Gainfully Employed Persons by Separate Types of Occupations. The Most Numerous Types of Occupations, Except Farmers.**
(this table presents rayon data for Belorusskaya SSR, Severo-Kavkazskiy kray, the republics of Zakavkazskaya SFSR, Ural'skaya oblast, Sibirskiy kray, and Dal'ne-Vostochnyy kray; for about 360 occupations [not all of them are included in every rayon] by position in occupation; by 15 age groups; by sex; by literacy [this is by all of the categories except age])

No. 176. 2b. **Distribution of Underage Workers (10-15 Years Old) Who Help in Agriculture, Are Personal Servants, or Are Indigents, by Age.**
(by rayon, plus Leningrad; by single-year ages 10-15; by sex; by urban-rural; this table is numbered 2g or 2d for the rayons listed in No. 175)

No. 177. 3. **Gainfully Employed Persons by Their Main Occupations, and the Non-Gainfully Employed by the Main Occupations of the Breadwinners.**
(by guberniya, and also for most major cities; by position in occupation, sector of the economy, and 242

occupations; by urban-rural; by sex)

No. 178. 4. <u>Main</u> <u>and</u> <u>Part-Time</u> <u>Occupations</u> <u>of</u> <u>the</u> <u>Gainfully</u> <u>Employed</u> <u>by</u> <u>the</u> <u>Complete</u> <u>Occupational</u> <u>Classification.</u>
(by guberniya, and also for one or more cities in some guberniyas; by position in occupation, sector of the economy, and 373 occupations; by agricultural or non-agricultural of part-time occupation, for those also having a full-time occupation [this category given at the rayon level only]; by sex; by urban-rural of location of main or part-time occupation; for most guberniyas data are also given for main occupations only by 2 or 3 nationalities [these data are cross-tabulated with everything except urban-rural])

No. 179. 4. <u>Main</u> <u>and</u> <u>Part-Time</u> <u>Occupations</u> <u>of</u> <u>Gainfully</u> <u>Employed</u> <u>Persons</u> <u>and</u> <u>Their</u> <u>Age</u> <u>Composition,</u> <u>by</u> <u>the</u> <u>Complete</u> <u>Occupational</u> <u>Classification.</u>
(this table is for Moscow and Leningrad only, and appears in their respective rayon volumes; number of gainfully employed persons by position in occupation, sector of the economy, and 373 occupational categories of their main and of their part-time occupations, by sex; data for main occupations are by all of the above and also by 15 age groups; data for main occupations are also by nationality [Russians and Jews], and these nationality data are by all categories except age)

No. 180. 4a. <u>Main</u> <u>and</u> <u>Part-Time</u> <u>Occupations</u> <u>of</u> <u>Manual</u> <u>and</u> <u>Office</u> <u>Workers.</u> <u>Results</u> <u>for</u> <u>All</u> <u>Sectors</u> <u>of</u> <u>the</u> <u>Economy.</u>
(by guberniya, and also for Moscow and Leningrad; number of persons by main occupation, part-time occupation, and [for the unemployed] most recent occupation; by 289 occupations; by sex)

No. 181. 4b. <u>Supplementary</u> <u>Data</u> <u>on</u> <u>Management</u> <u>Personnel</u> <u>of</u> <u>Institutions.</u> <u>Directors</u> <u>of</u> <u>Agricultural,</u> <u>Medical-</u> <u>Sanitary,</u> <u>and</u> <u>Cultural</u> <u>Institutions,</u> <u>Corresponding</u> <u>to</u> <u>Numbers</u> <u>190</u> <u>and</u> <u>204</u> <u>of</u> <u>the</u> <u>Full</u> <u>Occupational</u> <u>Classification.</u>
(by guberniya, and also for some major cities; number of employed persons who are directors of the types of institutions listed above; each of the main categories is divided by several or more specific kinds of institutions; by urban-rural; by sex)

No. 182. 4v. <u>Age</u> <u>Composition</u> <u>of</u> <u>Persons</u> <u>Who</u> <u>Are</u> <u>Gainfully</u> <u>Employed</u> <u>in</u> <u>the</u> <u>Major</u> <u>Types</u> <u>of</u> <u>Occupations</u> <u>of</u> <u>the</u> <u>Handicraft</u> <u>Industry,</u> <u>Construction,</u> <u>and</u> <u>Local</u> <u>Transport</u> <u>in</u> <u>the</u> <u>City</u> <u>of</u> <u>Moscow.</u> <u>Comparative</u> <u>Data</u> <u>for</u> <u>Individual</u> <u>Positions</u> <u>in</u> <u>Occupations.</u>
(this table is in <u>Volume 19</u>; for 15 different occupations, organized under the sectors listed above; each occupation is by 5 different positions in occupation; by 15 age groups; by sex [only one sex is given for each occupation, but a different sex is given depending upon the occupation]; a table with the same format but entitled <u>Major</u> <u>Types</u> <u>of</u> <u>Occupations</u> <u>of</u> <u>the</u> <u>Handicraft</u> <u>Industry,</u> <u>Building,</u> <u>and</u> <u>Local</u> <u>Transport</u>, appears as Table 2v or 2g in rayons of Belorusskaya SSR, the republics of Zakavkazskaya SFSR, Severo-Kavkazskiy kray, Ural'skaya oblast, Sibirskiy kray, and Dal'ne-Vostochnyy kray [data are at the rayon level])

No. 183. 5. **Persons with Part-Time Occupations by the Position in Occupation and Sector of the Economy of Their Main Occupations.**
(by rayon; for each position in occupation and sector of the economy of persons having part-time occupations, the table gives the number of persons who have main occupations, by position in occupation and sector of the economy of those main occupations)

No. 184. 5a. **Persons with Part-Time Occupations by the Position in the Main Agricultural Occupation and by Group and Type of Part-Time Occupation.**
(by rayon; for each part-time occupation [by position in occupation, sector of the economy, and about 360 occupations] the table gives the number of persons having an agricultural occupation as their main occupation [by 5 positions in occupation] and the number of persons who do not [total, number of them in urban settlements])

No. 185. 6. **Unemployed by Sector of the Economy and Position in Most Recent Occupation.**
(by guberniya [in most rayons, although some of them are only the whole rayon] and most major cities; number of unemployed in 4 categories [previously worked for hire, previously worked not for hire, looking for work for the first time, other], each category by several positions in occupations and/or sectors of the economy; by sex; by urban-rural)

No. 186. 7. **Population of the Uezds of the Guberniyas of [Name of Rayon] by Position in Occupation and Sector of the Economy.**
(some rayons do not have this table; by gainfully employed and non-gainfully employed; by sex; by urban-rural)

Volume 26. RSFSR.

No. 187. 1. **Population by Position in Occupation and Sector of the Economy. RSFSR.**
(whole RSFSR; by gainfully employed and non-gainfully employed; by sex; by urban-rural)

No. 188. 2. **Population by Position in Occupation and Sector of the Economy. Rayons of the RSFSR.**
(by gainfully employed and non-gainfully employed)

No. 189. 3. **Population by Position in Occupation and Sector of the Economy. Oblasts, Guberniyas, Okrugs, and Uezds of the RSFSR.**
(data are also given for many large cities; position in occupation and sector of the economy are not cross-tabulated [unlike nearly all other occupational tables]; data at the guberniya level or higher are by urban-rural)

No. 190. 4. **Sex, Age, Literacy, and Marital Status by Group of Occupations of the Short Classification.**
(whole RSFSR only; by position in occupation, sector of the economy, and some specific occupations [241 numbered categories]; by gainfully employed and non-

gainfully employed; by 17 age groups [19 groups for non-gainfully employed]; marital status [4 categories] and urban-rural are also by all of the occupational categories and by literacy, but they are not by age)

No. 191. 4a. **Supplementary Data on the Age Composition of Gainfully Employed Persons by Separate Types of Occupations. The Most Numerous Types of Occupations, except Farmers.**
(whole RSFSR; same format as the second Rayon Table 2a [No. 175])

No. 192. 4b. **Agricultural Workers, Farmers, and Cattle Raisers.**
(by 19 rayons; by each of the main occupational categories listed above; by age composition [%] in 15 age groups; by literacy [%]; by sex; farmers and cattle raisers are also by position in occupation, but the position in occupation data are not by rayon, only for the whole RSFSR)

No. 193. 4v. **Major Types of Occupations of the Small-Scale and Domestic Handicraft Industries, Construction, and Local Transport. Comparative Data for Various Positions in Occupations.**
(whole RSFSR; for about 18 occupations, among the categories listed above; by position in occupation; by 15 age groups; by sex and urban-rural [not all occupations are for both sexes or for urban-rural]; by literacy [not by sex and urban-rural in some cases])

No. 194. 4g. **Distribution of Underage (10-15 Years Old) Persons Who Are Helping in Agriculture, Are Personal Servants, or Are Declasse, by Age.**
(whole RSFSR; by about 10 different occupations from the categories above; by single-year ages; by sex; by urban-rural)

No. 195. 5. **Main and Part-Time Occupations of Persons Who Are Gainfully Employed, by the Main Divisions of the Occupational Classification.**
(whole RSFSR; number of persons with main occupations, number with part-time occupations, and number of unemployed [by most recent position in occupation and sector]; by position in occupation and sector of the economy; by urban-rural; by sex)

No. 196. 6. **Main and Part-Time Occupations of Persons Who Are Gainfully Employed, by the Full Occupational Classification.**
(whole RSFSR; same format as Table 5, but also by 373 occupational categories)

No. 197. 6a. **Supplementary Data on Management Personnel of Institutions. Directors of Agricultural, Medical-Sanitary, and Cultural Institutions, Corresponding to Numbers 190 and 204 of the Full Occupational Classification.**
(whole RSFSR; same format as Rayon Table 4b [No. 181])

No. 198. 7. **Main and Part-Time Occupations of Manual and Office Workers. Results for All Sectors of the Economy.**
(whole RSFSR; number of persons with main occupations, number with part-time occupations, and number of unemployed [by most recent occupation]; by 289

occupational categories, but not by individual sectors; by sex; by urban-rural)

No. 199. 8. **Persons with Part-Time Occupations by Position in Occupation and Sector of the Economy of Their Main Occupation.**
(whole RSFSR; same format as Rayon Table 5 [No. 183])

No. 200. 9. **Relation between Agricultural and Nonagricultural Occupations of Persons Having Part-Time Occupations.**
(whole RSFSR; number of persons with a main occupation [by agricultural and nonagricultural] and number of persons with a part-time occupation [by position in occupation of agricultural occupations]; by position in occupation, sector of the economy, and 361 occupational categories)

Volume 28. **Ukrainskaya SSR.**

No. 201. 1. **Population by Position in Occupation and Sector of the Economy. Whole Republic.**
(by gainfully employed and non-gainfully employed; by nationality [Ukrainian, Russian, Jew, other]; by sex; by urban-rural)

No. 202. 2. **Population by Position in Occupation and Sector of the Economy. By Sub-Rayons.**
(by gainfully employed and non-gainfully employed [same format as RSFSR Table 2 (No. 188)])

No. 203. 3. **Population by Position in Occupation and Sector of the Economy. By Okrug.**
(units also include 6 cities; position in occupation is only for manual workers, office workers, and other; sector of economy data are not cross-tabulated with position in occupation; number of gainfully employed and non-gainfully employed in each okrug are also given)

No. 204. 4. **Sex, Age, Literacy, and Marital Status by Group of Occupations of the Short Classification.**
(whole republic; same format as RSFSR Table 4 [No. 190])

No. 205. 4a. **Supplementary Data on the Age Composition of Gainfully Employed Persons by Separate Types of Occupations. The Most Numerous Types of Occupations, except Farmers.**
(whole republic; same format as the second Rayon Table 2a [No. 175])

No. 206. 4b. **Agricultural Workers in Peasant-Type Enterprises, and Farmers.**
(whole republic; by the two categories listed above; by 15 age groups; by literacy; by sex; the farmers category is also by position in occupation, but the position in occupation data are not by literacy)

No. 207. 4v. **Major Types of Occupations of the Small-Scale and Domestic Handicraft Industry, Construction, and Local Transport. Comparative Data for Various Positions in Occupations.**

(whole republic; same format as RSFSR Table 4v [No. 193], but for fewer occupations)

No. 208. 4g. <u>Distribution of Underage (10-15 Years Old) Persons Who Are Helping in Agriculture, Are Personal Servants, or Are Declasse, by Age.</u>
(whole republic; same format as RSFSR Table 4g [No. 194], but for a slightly different list of occupations)

No. 209. 5. <u>Main and Part-Time Occupations of Persons Who Are Gainfully Employed, by the Main Divisions of the Occupational Classification.</u>
(whole republic; same format as RSFSR Table 5 [No. 195])

No. 210. 6. <u>Main and Part-Time Occupations of Persons Who Are Gainfully Employed, by the Full Occupational Classification, Apportioned by the Main Nationalities.</u>
(whole republic; number of persons with a main occupation [by Ukrainian, Russian, Jew], number of persons with a part-time occupation, number of unemployed [by most recent occupation]; by position in occupation, sector of the economy, and 373 occupational categories; by sex; by urban-rural)

No. 211. 6a. <u>Supplementary Data on Management Personnel of Institutions. Directors of Agricultural, Medical-Sanitary, and Cultural Institutions.</u>
(by 6 sub-rayons, and also for 6 cities; same format as Rayon Table 4b [No. 181])

No. 212. 7. <u>Main and Part-Time Occupations of Manual and Office Workers. Results for All Sectors of the Economy.</u>
(whole republic; same format as RSFSR Table 7 [No. 198])

No. 213. 8. <u>Persons with Part-Time Occupations by Position in Occupation and Sector of the Economy of Their Main Occupation.</u>
(whole republic; same format as Rayon Table 5 [No. 183])

No. 214. 9. <u>Relation between Agricultural and Nonagricultural Occupations of Persons Having Part-Time Occupations.</u>
(whole republic; same format as RSFSR Table 9 [No. 200])

Volume 34. USSR.

No. 215. 1. <u>Population by Position in Occupation and Sector of the Economy. USSR.</u>
(same format as RSFSR Table 1 [No. 187])

No. 216. 2. <u>Population by Position in Occupation and Sector of the Economy. Union Republics.</u>
(same format as RSFSR Table 2 [No. 188])

No. 217. 3. <u>Sex, Age, Literacy, and Marital Status by Group of Occupations of the Short Classification.</u>
(whole USSR; by position in occupation, sector of the economy, and some specific occupations [241 numbered categories]; by gainfully employed and non-gainfully employed; by 17 age groups [19 groups for non-gainfully employed]; by urban-rural; marital status of persons aged 15 and older [in 4 categories] is by all of the above except age and urban-rural)

No. 218. 3a. Supplementary Data on the Age Composition of Gainfully Employed Persons by Separate Types of Occupations. The Most Numerous Types of Occupations, except Farmers.
(whole USSR; same format as the second Rayon Table 2a [No. 175])

No. 219. 3b. Agricultural Workers, Farmers, and Cattle Raisers.
(whole USSR; each of the groups listed above is by 15 age groups, by sex, and by literacy; farmers and cattle raisers are also by position in occupation, but the position in occupation data are not by literacy)

No. 220. 3v. Major Types of Occupations of the Small-Scale and Domestic Handicraft Industry, Construction, and Local Transport. Comparative Data for Various Positions in Occupations.
(whole USSR; same format as RSFSR Table 4v [No. 193])

No. 221. 3g. Distribution of Underage (10-15 Years Old) Persons Who Are Helping in Agriculture, Are Personal Servants, or Are Declasse, by Age.
(whole USSR; same format as RSFSR Table 4g [No. 194], but the occupations listed under the three categories above are slightly more detailed)

No. 222. 4. Main and Part-Time Occupations of Persons Who Are Gainfully Employed, by the Main Divisions of the Occupational Classification.
(whole USSR; same format as RSFSR Table 5 [No. 195])

No. 223. 5. Main and Part-Time Occupations of Persons Who Are Gainfully Employed, by the Full Occupational Classification.
(whole USSR; same format as RSFSR Table 6 [No. 196])

No. 224. 5a. Supplementary Data on Management Personnel of Institutions. Directors of Agricultural, Medical-Sanitary, and Cultural Institutions, Corresponding to Numbers 190 and 204 of the Full Occupational Classification.
(whole USSR; same format as Rayon Table 4b [No. 181])

No. 225. 6. Main and Part-Time Occupations of Manual and Office Workers. Results for All Sectors of the Economy.
(whole USSR; same format as RSFSR Table 7 [No. 198])

No. 226. 7. Persons with Part-Time Occupations by Position in Occupation and Sector of the Economy of Their Main Occupation.
(whole USSR; same format as Rayon Table 5 [No. 183])

No. 227. 8. Relation between Agricultural and Nonagricultural Occupations of Persons Having Part-Time Occupations.
(whole USSR; same format as RSFSR Table 9 [No. 200])

Section 3. Marital Status, Place of Birth, Length of Residence, Physically Handicapped and Mentally Ill Persons.

Rayon Volumes.

No. 228. 1. **Population by Marital Status, Sex, Age, and Nationality.**
(by guberniya and some major cities; by 4 different categories of marital status; by several nationalities [nationality data are not given for some guberniyas or cities, but are given only at the rayon level]; by single-year ages 15-29, then by 5-year age groups; by urban-rural [in many units nationality data are by urban-rural only at the rayon level, and are not given for some or all guberniyas]; Uzbekskaya SSR and Turkmenskaya SSR have a supplement to this table which gives similar data for single-year ages 10-14, at the whole SSR level and not by urban-rural)

No. 229. 2. **Population by Marital Status, Sex, Age, and Position in Occupation.**
(by rayon; by gainfully employed and non-gainfully employed; by single-year ages 15-29, then by 5-year age groups; by 4 different categories of marital status; position in occupation data for private employers, self-employed, and assisting family members [these categories together] who work in agriculture are also included, in addition to the other position in occupation categories, and these data are by all categories listed above)

No. 230. Supplement to Table 2. **Population by Marital Status, Sex, Age, and Position in Occupation. [Name of City or Cities].**
(this table appears in the census volumes for 15 rayons and covers 28 cities; format is the same as that of Table 2, but the last category on agricultural workers is not included)

No. 231. 3. **Population by Place of Birth, Nationality, Position in Occupation, and Sector of the Economy.**
(first part: by rayon; number of persons born in the USSR [without Bessarabia], by urban-rural of place of residence and urban-rural of place of birth [cross-tabulated]; number of persons born in Bessarabia and number born abroad; by gainfully employed [by position in occupation and sectors] and non-gainfully employed; by 10 age groups [for all ages] for the entire population and for the non-gainfully employed population, but by 8 age groups [for ages 10 and older] for the gainfully employed population and its occupational categories [in some rayons the position in occupation and sector data are not by age]; also by several different nationalities for most rayons, but nationality data are only for the entire population [i.e., they are by all of the above except the occupational categories]; by sex)
(second part: by guberniya and also for Moscow and Leningrad; same format as the rayon-level data but there are no age data)

No. 232. Supplement 1 to Table 3. **Persons Who Were Born Abroad and Are Permanent Residents at the Place of the Census, by Position in Occupation and Sector of the Economy.**
(by rayon; total number of persons born abroad and the number of them born outside the borders of the Russian Empire, by urban-rural of place of current residence; by gainfully employed [by position in occupation and

sectors] and non-gainfully employed; by sex)

No. 233. Supplement 2 to Table 3. <u>Office Workers of Sectors 1-8 by Place of Birth and Age (Women)</u>.
(by guberniya, and also for Moscow and Leningrad; number of women born in the USSR [without Bessarabia] by urban-rural of place of residence and urban-rural of place of birth [cross-tabulated], number born in Bessarabia, number born abroad; by 8 age groups of those aged 10 and older [age data are only at the rayon level, not for guberniyas and cities]; the rayons of Dagestanskaya ASSR, Buryato-Mongol'skaya ASSR, Yakutskaya ASSR, Kazakskaya ASSR, Kirgizskaya ASSR, Uzbekskaya SSR, and Turkmenskaya SSR do not have this table)

No. 234. 4. <u>Population by Length of Residence, Nationality, Position in Occupation, and Sector of the Economy</u>.
(first part: by rayon; number of temporary residents, number of locally born [of them, number of temporary residents], and number of non-locally born [by number of temporary residents and by 9 lengths of residence of permanent residents]; number of married persons, by locally and non-locally born; by gainfully employed [by position in occupation and sectors] and non-gainfully employed; by 10 age groups [all ages] of the total population, of the nationalities, and of the non-gainfully employed, and by 8 age groups [ages 10 and older] for all categories of the employed population; in most rayons, also by several nationalities [these data are by all of the above except the occupational categories]; by sex; by urban-rural)
(second part: by guberniya, and also for Moscow; same format as the rayon-level data, but there are no age data)

No. 235. Supplement 1 to Tables 3-4. <u>Population by Place of Birth, Length of Residence, Age, Nationality, Position in Occupation and Sector of the Economy for [Name of City or Cities]</u>.
(this table is in 17 of the rayon volumes and covers 33 cities; for the Tsentral'no-Promyshlennyy rayon these data are also in a Supplement 4 to Tables 3-4; number of persons born in the USSR [without Bessarabia], by urban-rural; number born in Bessarabia; number born abroad [of them, number of temporary residents]; number of locally born [of them, number of temporary residents]; number of non-locally born, by number of temporary residents and by 9 lengths of residence of permanent residents; number of married persons, by locally and non-locally born; by sex; by 10 age groups [age is not by nationality or occupational categories]; by gainfully employed [by position in occupation and sector] and non-gainfully employed; by several nationalities [these data are not by age or by occupational categories]; tables for Moscow and Leningrad contain age data for all categories listed above)

No. 236. Supplement 2 to Tables 3-4. <u>Non-Gainfully Employed Persons of Moscow by Length of Residence and by Position in Occupation and Sector of the Economy of Their Breadwinners</u>.
(this table is found in the Tsentral'no-Promyshlennyy

rayon volume; number of temporary residents, number of permanent residents [of them, number born in Moscow and 9 lengths of residence of those not born there]; by 10 age groups; by sex)

No. 237. Supplement 3 to Tables 3-4. <u>Gainfully Employed Population of Moscow by Place of Birth and Length of Residence, by the Short Occupational Classification.</u>
(this table, under a similar title, appears as Supplement 2 in Leningradsko-Karel'skiy rayon and in Levoberezhnyy podrayon [for Leningrad and Kharkov]; number of persons born in Moscow, born in other parts of the USSR [by urban-rural], born in Bessarabia; number of temporary residents; number of permanent residents [of them, number born in Moscow and 9 lengths of residence of those not born there]; by sex; by position in occupation, sector of the economy, and 228 occupational categories)

No. 238. 5. <u>Non-Locally Born Persons Who Are Permanent Residents at the Place of the Census, by Place of Birth and Place of Residence, Indicated in Detail.</u>
(first part: by rayon; number of non-locally born persons who are living in the rayon, by urban-rural of place of residence; number of locally born persons who are living in other rayons; by the specific rayons of place of birth of the non-locally born and the rayons of place of residence of the locally born who are living in other rayons; by gainfully employed [by position in occupation and sector of the economy] and non-gainfully employed; by sex)
(second part: by guberniya, and for Moscow and Leningrad; same format as the first part, but the places of birth and of residence are given at the guberniya level and also include Moscow and Leningrad)

No. 239. Supplement to Table 5. <u>Non-Locally Born Persons Who Are Permanent Residents in [Name of City or Cities] by Place of Birth, Denoted in Detail.</u>
(this table is given in 15 rayon volumes and covers 28 cities [the cities are not exactly the same ones as in the Supplement to Table 2 or Supplement 1 to Tables 3-4]; number of non-locally born residents by each of the major rayons, guberniyas, or other units [Moscow and Leningrad included, depending upon the city] where they were born; by position in occupation, some of which are divided by several sectors of the economy; by sex)

No. 240. 6. <u>Physically Handicapped and Mentally Ill Persons by Guberniya and Uezd.</u>
(in many rayons [especially those not in European RSFSR] the data are only by guberniya or okrug, not by uezd; data are presented for many major cities also; usually, data for the smallest regional units [uezd] consist of the number of physically handicapped persons by 8 categories and the number of mentally ill by 2 categories, by sex; at the guberniya level, data are, in addition, by urban-rural; for some guberniyas [and for Moscow and Leningrad] and for all nearly all rayons data are also by several or more nationalities)

No. 241. 7. <u>Physically Handicapped and Mentally Ill Persons by Cause of Disability.</u>
(by guberniya [for many units, data are only by rayon]

and for some major cities; by 4 categories of
causes; by 6 categories of handicaps, plus mental
illness; by sex)

No. 242. 8. **Physically Handicapped and Mentally Ill Persons by Place of Birth.**
(by rayon and guberniya [some rayons are not divided], plus Moscow and Leningrad; number of persons by 8 categories of physical handicaps and 2 categories of mental illness; by urban-rural of place of birth for those living in urban and those living in rural areas [these data are only given at the rayon level]; by sex; by the number who live in a unit who were born there [these data given only at the guberniya level])

No. 243. 9. **Physically Handicapped and Mentally Ill Persons by Age.**
(by rayon; number of persons by 8 categories of physical handicaps, 2 categories of mental illness, 3 categories of war invalids, and labor invalids; by single-year ages to age 4, then by 5-year age groups; by sex)

No. 244. 10. **Physically Handicapped and Mentally Ill Persons by Age and Literacy.**
(by guberniya and many major cities [for many units data are given only at the rayon level]; number of persons by 5 categories of physical handicaps, and mental illness; by 6 age groups; by urban-rural; by sex)

No. 245. 11. **Physically Handicapped and Mentally Ill Persons by Main Means of Livelihood.**
(by rayon: number of persons by 8 categories of physical handicaps, 2 categories of mental illness, war invalids, and labor invalids; by gainfully employed and non-gainfully employed; by sex; the total number of persons with physical handicaps and mental illness [together] is also by urban-rural)
(by guberniya and many major cities: the total number of all handicapped persons [physically and mentally together]; by all of the other categories above, including urban-rural)

Volume 43. **RSFSR.**

No. 246. 1. **Population by Marital Status, Sex, and Age.**
(whole RSFSR: 4 categories of marital status; by urban [total, cities with populations of more than 100,000, other urban] and rural; by single-year ages 15-29, then by 5-year age groups)
(by rayon: same format as whole republic data, but urban-rural does not include any extra categories of urban)

No. 247. 2. **Population by Marital Status, Sex, Age, Position in Occupation, and Sector of the Economy.**
(whole RSFSR; marital status is by 4 types for the total of gainfully employed and of non-gainfully employed, but by 2 types for the specific positions in occupations and sectors; by gainfully employed and non-gainfully employed; by single year ages 15-29, then by

222 Index and Guide

5-year age groups; by urban-rural)

No. 248.   3. <u>Population by Place of Birth, Position in Occupation, and Sector of the Economy. a. Results for the RSFSR and Rayons. b. Results for the RSFSR without These ASSRs: Dagestanskaya, Kazakhskaya, Kirgizskaya, and Yakutskaya.</u>
(whole RSFSR and whole republic without the units listed above: number of persons born in the USSR, without Bessarabia [total, born in urban settlements, registered in urban settlements (of them, locally born; born in other urban settlements of the USSR; born in rural settlements)], number born in Bessarabia, number born abroad; by gainfully employed and non-gainfully employed; by 8 age groups [everything is by age except the position in occupation and sector data]; by sex)
(by rayon: same format as RSFSR data, but none of the categories is by age)

No. 249.   Supplement 1 to Table 3. <u>Persons Who Were Born Abroad and Are Permanent Residents at the Place of the Census, by Position in Occupation and Sector of the Economy.</u>
(whole RSFSR; same format as Supplement 1 to Table 3 in the Rayon volumes [No. 232])

No. 250.   Supplement 2 to Table 3. <u>Office Workers of Sectors 1-8 by Place of Birth and Age. Results for the RSFSR without These ASSRs: Dagestanskaya, Kazakhskaya, Kirgizskaya, and Yakutskaya (Women).</u>
(whole RSFSR without the units listed above; same format as Supplement 2 to Table 3 in the Rayon volumes [No. 233], including the age data)

No. 251.   4. <u>Population by Length of Residence, Position in Occupation, and Sector of the Economy.</u>
<u>a. Results for the RSFSR and Rayons.</u>
(a. whole RSFSR: total population [of them, temporary residents], locally born [of them, temporary residents], non-locally born [total, number of temporary residents, number of permanent residents by 9 different lengths of residence]; by 10-year age groups [age is by all categories except the specific positions in occupations and sectors]; by gainfully employed and non-gainfully employed; by sex; by urban-rural)
(a. by rayon: same format as whole RSFSR, but there are no age data)
b. <u>Results for the RSFSR without These ASSRs: Dagestanskaya, Kazakhskaya, Kirgizskaya, and Yakutskaya.</u>
(b. whole RSFSR without units listed above: same format as whole RSFSR in part a, but all categories [including all positions in occupations and sectors] are by age)

No. 252.   5. <u>Physically Handicapped and Mentally Ill Persons by Rayon, Autonomous Republic, Guberniya, Okrug, and Autonomous Oblast.</u>
(data are also included for Moscow and Leningrad; by 8 categories of physical handicaps and 2 categories of mental illness; by sex)

No. 253.   6. <u>Physically Handicapped and Mentally Ill Persons by Nationality.</u>
(whole RSFSR; by 8 categories of physical handicaps and 2 categories of mental illness; by about 70 different nationalities; by sex)

No. 254.   7. **Physically Handicapped and Mentally Ill Persons by Age, Literacy, and Marital Status.**
(whole RSFSR; 8 categories of physical handicaps, 2 categories of mental illness, 3 categories of war invalids, labor invalids; by 5-year age groups; by urban-rural; by sex; marital status [number married] and literacy are each by all of the above categories except war and labor invalids, but they are not cross-tabulated by each other)

No. 255.   8. **Physically Handicapped and Mentally Ill Persons by Means of Livelihood.**
(whole RSFSR; same format as whole rayon-level data in Rayon Table 11 [No. 245], but the means of livelihood data are more detailed, and all categories are by urban-rural)

No. 256.   9. **Physically Handicapped and Mentally Ill Persons by Cause of Disability.**
(whole RSFSR; same format as Rayon Table 7 [No. 241])

No. 257.   10. **Physically Handicapped and Mentally Ill Persons by Place of Birth.**
(whole RSFSR; same format as the rayon-level data in Rayon Table 8 [No. 242])

Volume 45. Ukrainskaya SSR.

No. 258.   1. **Population by Marital Status, Sex, Age, and Nationality.**
(whole republic; 4 categories of marital status; by single-year ages from 15-29, then 5-year age groups; by nationality [Ukrainian, Russian, Jew]; by urban-rural)

No. 259.   2. **Population by Marital Status, Sex, Age, and Position in Occupation.**
(whole republic; 4 categories of marital status; by single-year ages 15-29, then by 5-year age groups; by gainfully employed and non-gainfully employed; occupation data are not only by position in occupation, but also by sectors of the economy; by urban-rural)

No. 260.   3. **Population by Place of Birth, Nationality, Position in Occupation, and Sector of the Economy.**
(whole republic; same format as Rayon Table 3 [No. 231]; all occupational data are by age)

No. 261.   Supplement 1 to Table 3. **Persons Who Were Born Abroad and Are Permanent Residents at the Place of the Census, by Position in Occupation and Sector of the Economy.**
(whole republic; same format as Supplement 1 to Table 3 in the Rayon volumes [No. 232])

No. 262.   Supplement 2 to Table 3. **Office Workers of Sectors 1-8 by Place of Birth and Age (Women).**
(whole republic; same format as Supplement 2 to Table 3 in the Rayon volumes [No. 233])

No. 263.   4. **Population by Length of Residence, Nationality, Position in Occupation, and Sector of the Economy.**
(whole republic; same format as the rayon-level data in

Rayon Table 4 [No. 234]; nationality data are by Ukrainian, Russian, and Jew)

No. 264. 5. <u>Physically Handicapped and Mentally Ill Persons in the Republic.</u>
(whole republic; for 8 categories of physical handicaps and 2 categories of mental illness; by 10 different ethnic groups; by sex; by urban-rural [cross-tabulated by everything except nationality])

No. 265. 6. <u>Physically Handicapped and Mentally Ill Persons by Cause of Disability.</u>
(whole republic; same format as Rayon Table 7 [No. 241])

No. 266. 7. <u>Physically Handicapped and Mentally Ill Persons by Place of Birth.</u>
(whole republic; for 8 categories of physical handicaps and 2 categories of mental illness; by urban-rural of place of birth for those living in urban and those living in rural areas; by sex)

No. 267. 8. <u>Physically Handicapped and Mentally Ill Persons by Age.</u>
(whole republic; same format as Rayon Table 9 [No. 243], but ages are all 5-year age groups)

No. 268. 9. <u>Physically Handicapped and Mentally Ill Persons by Age and Literacy.</u>
(whole republic; same format as Rayon Table 10 [No. 244])

No. 269. 10. <u>Physically Handicapped and Mentally Ill Persons by Main Means of Livelihood.</u>
(whole republic; same format as Rayon Table 11 [No. 245])

Volume 51. <u>USSR.</u>

No. 270. 1a. <u>Population by Marital Status, Sex, and Age. Results for the USSR and Union Republics.</u>
(whole USSR: 4 types of marital status; by single-year ages 15-29, then by 5-year age groups; by urban [total, population in cities of more than 100,000 persons, other urban] and rural)
(by republic: same format as whole USSR, but urban-rural data do not include any other categories of urban)

No. 271. 1b. <u>Population by Marital Status and Nationality. Results for the USSR.</u>
(4 types of marital status; by about 50 ethnic groups; by same age groups as Table 1a; by sex)

No. 272. 2. <u>Population by Marital Status, Sex, Age, Position in Occupation, and Sector of the Economy.</u>
(whole USSR; 4 types of marital status; by gainfully and non-gainfully employed; by single-year ages 15-29, then by 5-year age groups; by urban-rural)

No. 273. 3a. <u>Population by Place of Birth and Age. Results for the USSR.</u>
(number of persons born in the USSR, without Bessarabia

List of Census Tables 225

[of them, number born in cities], number registered in cities [by locally born, born in another city, born in a rural area], number of persons born in Bessarabia, number born abroad; by gainfully employed and non-gainfully employed; by 10 age groups; by sex)

No. 274. 3b. <u>Population by Place of Birth, Position in Occupation, and Sector of the Economy. Results for the USSR and Union Republics.</u>
(number of persons born in USSR, without Bessarabia [of them, born in urban settlements], number registered in urban settlements [by locally born, born in another urban area, born in a rural area], number born in Bessarabia, number born abroad [in Russian Empire, outside the empire]; by sex)

No. 275. Supplement to Table 3b. <u>Persons Who Were Born Abroad and Are Permanent Residents at the Place of the Census, by Position in Occupation and Sector of the Economy. Results for the USSR.</u>
(whole USSR; same format as Supplement 1 to Table 3 in the Rayon volumes [No. 232])

No. 276. 3v. <u>Population by Place of Birth, Age, Position in Occupation, and Sector of the Economy. Results for the USSR without These Republics: Uzbekskaya SSR, Turkmenskaya SSR, Dagestanskaya ASSR, Kazakhskaya ASSR, Kirgizskaya ASSR, and Yakutskaya ASSR.</u>
(whole USSR without these republics; number of persons born in USSR, by urban-rural of place of residence and urban-rural of place of birth [cross-tabulated]; number born in Bessarabia; number born abroad; by 10 mostly 10-year age groups; by sex)

No. 277. Supplement to Table 3v. <u>Office Workers (Women) of Sectors 1-8 by Place of Birth and Age. Results for the USSR without These Republics: Uzbekskaya SSR, Turkmenskaya SSR, Dagestanskaya ASSR, Kazakhskaya ASSR, Kirgizskaya ASSR, and Yakutskaya ASSR.</u>
(same format as Table 3v, but only for female office workers, and by 8 age groups)

No. 278. 4a. <u>Population by Length of Residence and Age. Results for the USSR.</u>
(total population, number locally born, and number non-locally born, each of these categories by the total and the number of temporary residents; number of permanent residents by 9 lengths of residence; by gainfully employed and non-gainfully employed; by 10 age groups; by sex; by urban-rural)

No. 279. 4b. <u>Population by Length of Residence, Position in Occupation, and Sector of the Economy. Results for the USSR and Union Republics.</u>
(RSFSR is not included; total population, number locally born, number non-locally born, each of these categories by the total and the number of temporary residents; number of permanent residents by 9 lengths of residence; by sex; by urban-rural)

No. 280. 4v. <u>Population by Length of Residence, Age, Position in Occupation, and Sector of the Economy. Results for the USSR without These Republics: Uzbekskaya, Turkmenskaya,</u>

Dagestanskaya, Kazakhskaya, Kirgizskaya, and Yakutskaya.
(whole USSR without these republics; same format as
Table 4b, but by 10 age groups in addition)

No. 281. 5. **Persons Born in the USSR Who Are Permanent Residents at the Place of the Census, by Place of Birth and Place of Residence, Indicated in Detail.**
(by guberniya, and also for Moscow and Leningrad; number of persons registered in each unit as of the census [total permanent residents (of them, number born in that unit, number born in other regions of the USSR)], number born in the unit who live in another region of the USSR, and total number of locally born persons, all of these categories by sex; number born in each unit who live in that unit and the number living in another unit of the USSR, number who live in each unit who were born in another unit, all of these categories by gainfully employed [by position in occupation and sectors of the economy] and non-gainfully employed; the first section [by sex] and the second section [by occupations] are not cross-tabulated)

No. 282. 6a. **Persons Born in Other Republics and Rayons by Place of Birth. Results for the Urban and Rural Population. Union Republics.**
(number of persons born in each republic, number born in Bessarabia, number born abroad, all of these categories by sex; by republic of current residence, by urban-rural)

No. 283. 6b. **Persons Born in Other Republics and Rayons by Place of Birth. Results for the Urban and Rural Population by Sex. Rayons.**
(number of persons by 29 rayons of place of birth [not by sex or urban-rural], cross-tabulated by 29 rayons of place of residence [this is by sex and by urban-rural])

No. 284. 6v. **Persons Born in Other Republics and Rayons by Place of Birth. Results by Social Group. Union Republics.**
(number of persons born in each republic, by gainfully employed [by position in occupation and sector of the economy] and non-gainfully employed; by republic of current residence)

No. 285. 6g. **Persons Born in Other Republics and Rayons by Place of Birth. Results by Social Group. Rayons.**
(number of persons born in each of the 29 rayons, by gainfully employed [by position in occupation and sector of the economy] and non-gainfully employed; by the rayon of current residence)

No. 286. 7. **Physically Handicapped and Mentally Ill Persons. Results for the USSR and Union Republics.**
(8 categories of physical handicaps and 2 categories of mental illness; by sex)

No. 287. 8. **Physically Handicapped and Mentally Ill Persons by Nationality.**
(whole USSR; 8 categories of physical handicaps and 2 categories of mental illness; by about 100 nationalities; by sex)

No. 288. 9. **Physically Handicapped and Mentally Ill Persons by**

Age, Literacy, and Marital Status. USSR.
(8 categories of physical handicaps, 2 categories of mental illness, 3 categories of war invalids, labor invalids; by 5-year age groups; by sex; by urban-rural; only the 8 categories of physical handicaps and the total for mental illness are also by literacy and marital status [married or not]; literacy and marital status are not cross-tabulated)

No. 289. 10. Physically Handicapped and Mentally Ill Persons by Main Means of Livelihood.
(whole USSR; same format as Rayon Table 11 [No. 245])

No. 290. 11. Physically Handicapped and Mentally Ill Persons by Cause of Disability. Results for the USSR.
(same format as Rayon Table 7 [No. 241])

No. 291. 12. Physically Handicapped and Mentally Ill Persons by Place of Birth.
(whole USSR; same format as the rayon-level data in Rayon Table 8 [No. 242])

Section 4. Volume 52. Unemployed in the USSR.

No. 292. 1. Unemployed by Length of Unemployment, Age, and Marital Status. Based on the Short Classification of Occupations. USSR (without Turkmenskaya SSR).
(data are for the whole USSR, Moscow, Leningrad, other cities of 100,000 population and greater as a group [by industrial centers and other], other cities and urban settlements as a group, and agricultural localities as a group; number of unemployed by 2 main types of unemployment [previously worked for hire, did not work for hire]; by 4 lengths of unemployment; by 8 age groups [age is by all categories except marital status and the individual cities and settlement types listed above]; by position in occupation, sector of the economy, and 228 occupational categories; by sex; by marital status [married or not], which is not by age)

No. 293. 2. Unemployed by Length of Unemployment, Age, and Marital Status. According to the Main Divisions of the Classification of Occupations. Results for the USSR, Union Republics, and Rayons (without Turkmenskaya SSR).
(number of unemployed by 4 main categories of unemployment and several subcategories [including some sectors of the economy and positions in occupations of previously employed persons]; by 4 lengths of unemployment; by 8 age groups [age is by all categories except length of unemployment and marital status]; by sex; by marital status [married, other], which is not by age)

No. 294. 3. Unemployed by Length of Unemployment, Place of Birth and Length of Residence. According to the Main Divisions of the Classification of Occupations. Results for the USSR.
(data are given for the units and city types listed in Table 1; by 3 place-of-birth and residence categories [temporary residents; non-locally born, by 4 categories of length of residence and by urban-rural of place of

birth (these are not cross-tabulated); locally born];
by 4 lengths of unemployment; by position in occupation
and sector of the economy; by sex)

No. 295. 4. <u>Unemployed by Place of Birth and Length of
Residence. Results for the Union Republics and Rayons.</u>
(for the same 3 place-of-birth and residence categories
used in Table 3; by sex; by urban-rural)

Section 5. Volume 53. <u>Properties, Structures, Living and Non-
Living Premises in Cities and Urban Settlements of the USSR.</u>

No. 296. 1. <u>Number of Properties, Their Population, and the Area
of Land Parcels.</u>
(for Union Republics, rayons, and 30 cities of 100,000
population or greater; by 4 city-size groups; by 3 main
types of building ownership)

No. 297. 2. <u>Buildings.</u>
(for Union Republics, rayons, and 30 cities of 100,000
population or greater; number of living structures by
type of material, construction status, and number of
floors; number of non-living structures, by type; by 4
city-size groups; by 3 main types of building ownership)

No. 298. 3. <u>Living Premises (Apartments and Dormitories).</u>
(for Union Republics, rayons, and cities of 100,000
population or greater; number of apartments, the number
of inhabitants in them, number of kitchens, number of
living rooms, and living area by type of building
material; number of dormitories, the number of
inhabitants in them, and living area by type of
building material; number of living structures which
have electricity, and the number of inhabitants in
them; by 4 city-size groups; by 3 main types of
building ownership)

No. 299. 4. <u>Non-Living Premises in Living Structures.</u>
(for Union Republics, rayons, and cities of 100,000
population or greater; number and floor space of non-
living premises by type of building material and by
kinds of use; by 4 city-size groups; by three main
types of building ownership)

No. 300. 5. <u>Characteristics of Properties, Buildings, and
Premises by Individual Urban Settlements.</u>
(by rayon, and for the major cities in each unit [about
2000 cities]; total number of built properties and
their floor space; living structures by type of
building material and number of floors; living premises
by type [apartments and dormitories], characteristics
[living space, number of rooms, number of inhabitants,
kitchens, etc.], type of building material, and supply
of electricity)

No. 301. 6. <u>Living Structures, Living Area, and Number of
Inhabitants by Category of Property (Results by
Individual Urban Settlements).</u>
(for same units as Table 5; by 3 main types of building
ownership and several subcategories; by the number of
living structures, the living space in square meters,
and the number of inhabitants)

List of Census Tables 229

No. 302. 7. **Properties that Are Connected to the Water Supply.**
(for each Union Republic and for 266 population centers; number of buildings, number connected to water supply, and number of inhabitants in buildings with water supply; by types of building ownership)

No. 303. 8. **Properties that Are Connected to the Sewage System.**
(for 36 cities, in the RSFSR, Ukrainskaya SSR, and Zakavkazskaya SSR only; number of buildings, number connected to sewage system, and number of inhabitants in buildings that are connected to the sewage system; by types of building ownership)

Section 6. Volume 54. **Living Conditions of the Urban Population of the USSR.**

No. 304. 1. **Distribution of Families and Persons Living Alone by Character of Occupied Premises.**
a. **Results for the USSR and Union Republics.**
(type of lodging of families and persons living alone [house, separate apartment, part of an apartment (part of a room, 1 room, more than 1 room), dormitory, non-living premises (kitchen, other)]; by social group and sector of the economy)
b. **Results by Type of Urban Settlement.**
(same format as part a, but whole USSR only; settlement type is divided into Moscow, Leningrad, and about 25 other types [by size and function]; 19 of these categories [settlements with populations of 50,000 or fewer] are not subdivided by social group or sector of the economy)

No. 305. 2. **Distribution of Families and Persons Living Alone by the Character of Use of the Living Area; Average Living Area per Inhabitant.**
a. **Results for the USSR and Union Republics.**
(character of use of living space is divided into those not having their own living area [living with other people, living in kitchen or other non-living space, living in dormitory] and those having their own living space [including the average area per person]; by social group and sector of the economy)
b. **Results by Type of Urban Settlement.**
(same format as part a, but whole USSR only; data by settlement type have the same format and limitations as Table 1b)

No. 306. 3. **Distribution of Families and Persons Living Alone by the Number of Square Meters of Living Area per Inhabitant.**
a. **Results for the USSR and Union Republics.**
(living space per person is by 8 size groups; by social group and sector of the economy)
b. **Results by Type of Urban Settlement.**
(same format as part a, but whole USSR only; data by settlement type have the same format and limitations as Table 1b)

No. 307. 4. **Distribution of Families and Persons Living Alone by Number of Inhabitants per Room.**
a. **Results for the USSR and Union Republics.**
(by 5 size groups of the number of persons per room; by social group and sector of the economy)

No. 308.   5. Distribution of Families by Number of Occupied Rooms and Use of Kitchens.
a. Results for the USSR and Union Republics.
(number of rooms per family is in 3 categories [part of a room, 1 room, more than 1 room]; use of kitchens includes number of families having a separate kitchen [and whether it is used for living], those sharing a kitchen, those not having use of a kitchen; by social group and sector of the economy)
b. Results by Type of Urban Settlement.
(same format as part a, but whole USSR only; data by settlement type have the same format and limitations as Table 1b)

b. Results by Type of Urban Settlement.
(same format as part a, but whole USSR only; data by settlement type have the same format and limitations as Table 1b)

No. 309.   6. Conditions of the Use of Dwellings and Rent.
a. Results for the USSR and Union Republics.
(number of families and persons living in their own houses, number of families and persons who are renters [number paying rent, size of living area, rent paid, etc.]; by social group and sector of the economy)
b. Results by Type of Urban Settlement.
(same format as part a, but whole USSR only; data by settlement type have the same format and limitations as Table 1b)

No. 310.   7. Social Composition of the Population by Category of Proprietorship.
a. Results for the USSR and Union Republics.
(proprietorship divided by state, cooperative, and private, and by additional subcategories of these; by sector of the economy)
b. Results by Type of Urban Settlement.
(same format as part a, but whole USSR only; data by settlement type have the same format and limitations as Table 1b)

No. 311.   8. Distribution by Type of Proprietorship of the Living Area, by Separate Social Groups.
a. Results for the USSR and Union Republics.
(proprietorship divided by state, cooperative, and private, and by additional subcategories of these; by sector of the economy, but sectors are not as detailed as in Tables 1-7)
b. Results by Type of Urban Settlement.
(same format as part a, but whole USSR only; data by settlement type have the same format and limitations as Table 1b)

No. 312.   9. Distribution of Families and Persons Living Alone by Character of Occupied Premises. Results by Rayon and for Cities with More than 100,000 Inhabitants.
(types of occupied premises include separate houses, separate apartments, part of an apartment, dormitory, non-living space [kitchen, other]; by 4 main social groups)

No. 313.   10. Distribution of Families and Persons Living Alone by the Character of Use of the Living Area; Average Living Area per Inhabitant. Results by Rayon and for

Cities with More than 100,000 Inhabitants. (character of use of living space has the same categories as Table 2a; by 4 main social groups)

No. 314. 11. **Distribution of Families and Persons Living Alone by Number of Square Meters of Living Area per Inhabitant. Results by Rayon and for Cities with More than 100,000 Inhabitants.**
(living space per person is by 8 size groups; by 4 main social groups)

No. 315. 12. **Distribution of Families and Persons Living Alone by Number of Inhabitants per Room. Results by Rayon and for Cities with More than 100,000 Inhabitants.**
(by 5 size groups of the number of persons per room; by 4 main social groups)

No. 316. 13. **Distribution of Families by Number of Occupied Rooms and Use of Kitchens. Results by Rayon and for Cities with More than 100,000 Inhabitants.**
(number of rooms per family is in 3 categories [see Table 5a]; use of kitchens is also by the same categories as Table 5a; by 4 main social groups)

No. 317. 14. **Conditions of the Use of Dwellings and Rent. Results by Rayon and for Cities with More than 100,000 Inhabitants.**
(number of families and persons living in their own houses, number of families and persons who are renters [number paying rent, size of living area, rent paid, etc.]; by 4 main social groups)

No. 318. 15. **Social Composition of the Population by Category of Proprietorship. Results by Rayon and for Cities with More than 100,000 Inhabitants.**
(proprietorship divided by state, cooperative, and private, and by additional subcategories of these; by 4 main social groups)

No. 319. 16. **Distribution by Type of Proprietorship of the Living Area, by Separate Social Groups. Results by Rayon and for Cities with More than 100,000 Inhabitants.**
(proprietorship divided by state, cooperative, and private, and by additional subcategories of these; by 4 main social groups)

No. 320. 17. **Apartment Rent by Category of Proprietorship. Results by Rayon and for Cities with More than 100,000 Inhabitants.**
(proprietorship divided by state, cooperative, and private, and by additional subcategories)

No. 321. 18. **Characteristics of Living Conditions of the Population by Individual Urban Settlements.**
(data are by all census units at the guberniya level or above, and for all major cities and urban type settlements [approximately 2000 population points]; number of families and number of people living in non-living premises, in dormitories, in their own living areas, or with others; total living space; average living space per person for families and for persons living alone; number of occupied living rooms; number of kitchens used for living; number of people per 100

No. 322. 19. **Total Living Area by Social Group. Results for Rayons and for Cities of More than 20,000 Population.**
(for about 225 individual cities; total living space and average living space per person; social groups include several subcategories, usually by sectors of the economy)

Living Conditions of the Workers of the Factory-and-Works Industries.

No. 323. 20. **Distribution of Families and Persons Living Alone by Type of Premises Occupied.**
(see section title above; by rayon, and for major cities [about 70]; by same types of lodging as in Table 1; by several separate types of workers [metalworkers, textile workers, miners])

No. 324. 21. **Distribution of Families and Persons Living Alone by the Character of Use of the Living Area.**
(see section title above; same regional units and cities as Table 20; by those not having their own living space [living with others, living in non-living space, living in dormitory] and those having their own living space [total living space and average living space per person]; by several separate types of workers)

No. 325. 22. **Distribution of Families and Persons Living Alone by Number of Square Meters of Living Area per Inhabitant.**
(see section title above; same regional units and cities as Table 20; living space per person is by 8 size groups; by several separate types of workers)

No. 326. 23. **Distribution of Families and Persons Living Alone by Number of Inhabitants per Room.**
(see section title above; same regional units and cities as Table 20; by 5 size groups of the number of persons per room; by several separate types of workers)

No. 327. 24. **Distribution of Families by Number of Occupied Rooms and Use of Kitchens.**
(see section title above; same regional units and cities as Table 20; number of rooms per family and use of kitchens have the same categories as Table 5a; by several separate types of workers)

No. 328. 25. **Conditions of the Use of Dwellings and Rent.**
(see section title above; same regional units and cities as Table 20; number of families and persons living in their own houses, number of families and persons who are renters [number paying rent, size of living area, rent paid, etc.]; by several separate types of workers)

No. 329. 26. **Distribution of Workers of the Factory-and-Works Industry by Category of Proprietorship.**
(same regional units and cities as Table 20; proprietorship divided by state, cooperative, and private, and by additional subcategories of these; by

several separate types of workers)

Section 7. **Structure of the Urban Family.**

Volume 55. **Union of Soviet Socialist Republics. 1. Structure of the Urban Family. Results of the General Tabulation. 2. Social Composition of the Urban Population.**

1. Structure of the Urban Family.

No. 330.   1. **Composition of the Family. Number of Members, Employment. Connection with Agriculture.**
(whole USSR only; total number of families, families with male head of family, families with female head of family, each of these categories divided by employment status of family members; connection with agriculture [families having land, families with members who participate in field work and the number of those members]; number of persons living alone, by sex; connection of persons living alone with agriculture; by position in occupation, sector of the economy, and 375 occupations)

No. 331.   2. **Distribution of Families by Total Number of Members and by Number of Actively Employed Members. Employment. Connection with Agriculture.**
(by rayon, plus Moscow and Leningrad; number of persons living alone, by sex; number of families by 9 size groups, by sex of head of family, and by number of actively occupied members; employment status of family members, in 3 categories; connection of families with agriculture [by categories given in Table 1]; connection of persons living alone with agriculture [number who have land and number who participate in field work]; by position in occupation of head of family and sector of the economy in which he or she works)

No. 332.   2. Supplement. **Composition of the Families of Metalworkers, Miners, and Textile Workers.**
(essentially the same as Table 2, but covers only these specialized occupations)

No. 333.   3. **Social Characteristics of the Actively Employed Members in Relation to the Social Characteristics of the Head of the Family.**
a. **Results for the USSR.**
(whole USSR only; social characteristics of heads of families by sector of the economy in which they work, by social characteristics and sectors of actively employed family members)
b. **Results by Rayons.**
(number of families by social group and sector of the economy in which the head of the family works, and the social group [and, in some cases, also the sector of the economy] of family members of these heads of families)

2. **Social Composition of the Urban Population.**

No. 334. 4. Social Composition of the Population of Cities and Urban Type Settlements.
a. Results by Union Republic.
(number of persons living alone, number of heads of families, and number of family members; by social composition and sector of the economy)
b. Results for Individual Urban Settlements.
(by guberniya, for all cities and urban-type settlements in each unit [more than 2000 altogether]; social group [position in occupation] and sector of the economy of gainfully employed persons; other persons [unemployed, pensioners, students])

Volume 56. Structure of the Urban Family. Results of a Special Tabulation. Part 1. Moscow. Part 2. Leningrad. Part 3. Cities of the RSFSR.

No. 335. 1. Types of Families by Age of the Head of the Family.
(number of families headed by males and by females, and the number of persons in them; by about 15 different family types and subtypes; by social group [by some sectors of the economy] and 10 age groups of the head of the family)

No. 336. 2. Occupation by Type and Subtype of Families.
(number of families, number of persons in them, number of occupied persons, number of unemployed, number of non-gainfully employed persons; by about 15 different family types and subtypes, by sex of head of family; by social group and some sectors of the economy)

No. 337. 3a. Families with Actively Employed Members. Distribution by Total Number of Family Members and by Number of Actively Employed Family Members.
(number of families and number of actively employed family members, by 9 family-size groups; by sex of head of family; by 4 main family types; by social group and some sectors of the economy)

No. 338. 3b. Families without Actively Employed Members. Distribution by Number of Persons.
(number of families by sex of head of family and by 9 family-size groups; by social group and some sectors of the economy; by 3 family types)

No. 339. 3v. Distribution of Families by Total Number of Family Members and by Number of Actively Employed Family Members, in %.
(by 7 family-size groups; by sex of head of family; by social group and some sectors of the economy)

No. 340. 4. Composition of Families in Relation to the Age of the Head of the Family.
(number of families by 9 family-size groups, and number of persons in them; number of family members by employment [gainfully employed, unemployed, non-gainfully employed], sex, and 3 age groups; number of children of head of family and number of relatives [by 3 categories of employment]; by age [in 10 age groups] and sex of head of family; by 4 main family types; by social group and some sectors of the economy)

List of Census Tables 235

No. 341. 5. **Average Number of Family Members, Children of the Head of the Family, and Relatives, per Family.**
(by 4 main family types; by sex and 10 age groups of head of family; by social group and some sectors of the economy)

No. 342. 6. **Distribution of Family Members by Age, in %.**
(percentage of family members younger than 16 years of age and of those aged 16-59; by sex and 10 age groups of head of family; by 4 main family types; by social group and some sectors of the economy)

No. 343. 7. **Percentage of Occupied Members and of Actively Employed Members of the Family.**
(by sex and 10 age groups of family head; by 4 main family types; by social group and some sectors of the economy)

No. 344. 8. **Employment of Members of Married Couples in Relation to Their Ages. Families of Type A.**
(number of families; number of families where both spouses have occupations; number of families where one spouse has an occupation and the other [by sex] has another source of income, is unemployed, or is dependent; by 10 age groups of the husband [for each of these age groups by age groups of the wife]; by social group and some sectors of the economy)

No. 345. 9. **Employment of Mothers in Relation to the Number of Children. Families of Types A1 and A2.**
(number of families in each of 9 size groups by number of children; each size group includes data on the total number of families and the number of families in which the mother is gainfully employed, is unemployed, or is non-gainfully employed; by social group and some sectors of the economy)

No. 346. 10. **Employment of Children of Heads of Families. Families of Types A and B.**
(number of children who have their own sources of income [those having occupations, having another source of income, unemployed]; number of children who do not have their own source of income; by sex; by single-year ages 10-25; by social group and some sectors of the economy)

No. 347. 11. **Distribution of Children of the Head of the Family by Position in Occupation. Families of Types A and B.**
(number of children by 7 different positions in occupations, by sex, and by 6 age groups [for children aged 16-25]; all of these categories are by the social group and sector of the economy of the family heads)

No. 348. 12. **Distribution of Families of Types A1 and A2 by Number of Children.**
(number of children by 9 size groups; by 7 age groups of the age of the mother at marriage; by length of marriage, in 33 groups; by social group and some sectors of the economy)

No. 349. 13. **Average Number of Children per Family.**
(by length of marriage, in 33 groups; by social group and some sectors of the economy)

No. 350.   14. Distribution of Families of Type A by Number of Children, in %.
(number of families and the number of children in 4 size groups; by length of marriage, in 3 groups; by social group and some sectors of the economy)

No. 351.   15. Average Age of the Oldest and the Youngest Child in Families of Type A2.
(by the age of the mother at marriage, in 4 groups; by social group and some sectors of the economy)

All-Union Population Census of 1926. Short Summaries.

Number 1. Housing Construction in Urban Settlements of the RSFSR, Ukrainskaya SSR, and Belorusskaya SSR.

No. 352.   1. Number of Living Structures Which Were Newly Constructed, Completed, and Renovated during the Years 1923-26 in Cities and Urban-Type Settlements, and the Living Area of These Buildings (Results for Main Rayons).
(for individual years 1923, 1924, 1925, 1926; number of buildings and their area in square meters by construction categories listed above; by type of building ownership [state, cooperative, private]; by type of building material [wood, stone, mixed, other], but only at the republic level; for RSFSR, Ukrainskaya SSR, and Belorusskaya SSR rayons only)

No. 353.   2. Number of Living Structures Which Were Newly Constructed, Completed, and Renovated during the Years 1923-26 in Cities and Urban-Type Settlements, and the Living Area of These Buildings (Results for Autonomous Republics and Oblasts, Guberniyas and Okrugs).
(units also include Moscow and Leningrad; same as Table 1 except data are for these smaller units; type of building material data are at the rayon level)

No. 354.   3. Distribution of Living Structures Which Were Newly Constructed, Completed, and Renovated during the Years 1923-26, by Material of the Walls.
(number of buildings; for the entire period, not by individual years; by type of building ownership; by rayons in RSFSR, Ukrainskaya SSR, and Belorusskaya SSR only, plus Moscow and Leningrad)

No. 355.   4. Distribution of Living Area in Structures Which Were Newly Constructed, Completed, and Renovated during the Years 1923-26, by Material of the Walls.
(same subcategories as Table 3, and also by rayons in RSFSR, Ukrainskaya SSR, and Belorusskaya SSR [plus Moscow and Leningrad], but for square meters of living area)

No. 356.   5. Quantity of Living Area per Building, by Category of Builder and Material of the Walls, in Structures Which Were Newly Constructed, Completed, and Renovated during the Years 1923-26.
(by rayons in RSFSR, Ukrainskaya SSR, and Belorusskaya SSR, plus Moscow and Leningrad; for the entire period,

No. 357. 6. **Living Area per 1000 Inhabitants in Structures Which Were Newly Constructed, Completed, and Renovated during the Years 1923-26, by Category of Builder.**
(for 1923-26 total and for 1926; by autonomous republics and oblasts, guberniyas, and okrugs in RSFSR, Ukrainskaya SSR, and Belorusskaya SSR, plus Moscow and Leningrad; category of builder refers to building ownership or proprietorship)

not by individual years; category of builder refers to building ownership or proprietorship; for each category data are given for number of buildings and the living area in them)

No. 358. 7. **Living Area in Structures Which Were Completed, Renovated, and Newly Constructed in 1924, 1925, and 1926, in Relation to the Living Area of Buildings Which Were Completed, Renovated, and Newly Constructed in 1923, with 1923 Given as 100.**
(for individual years 1924, 1925, 1926; by rayon in the RSFSR, Ukrainskaya SSR, and Belorusskaya SSR, plus Moscow and Leningrad)

Number 2. **Unemployment in the City of Moscow.**

No. 359. 1. **Unemployed in the City of Moscow by Sex, Age, and Marital Status.**
(by 4 categories of unemployment; by 4 types of marital status; by 16 age groups of persons aged 10 and older)

No. 360. 2. **Unemployed in the City of Moscow by Sex, Previous Occupation, and Length of Unemployment (Excluding Workers Who Are Seeking Work for the First Time).**
(number of unemployed persons, by 7 lengths of unemployment; by previous position in occupation, sector of the economy, and 377 different occupations)

Number 3. **Population of the USSR.**

No. 361. 1. **Territory. Administrative Units. Populated Places. Population. Results for Rayons and Sub-Rayons.**
(area of each unit in square kilometers; number of rural and city soviets; number of volosts and rayons; number of rural and urban populated places; population by urban-rural; average population size of cities and of rural populated places; population density per square kilometer by total and rural)

No. 362. 2. **Territory. Administrative Units. Populated Places. Population. Results for Uezds and Okrugs.**
(this table is the same as Table 1, but data are at the uezd level [okrug level in some units])

No. 363. 3. **Distribution of Populated Places by Number of Inhabitants. Results by Republic, Rayon, and Sub-Rayon.**
(number of rural and urban populated places and the population in them, by 14 size groups)

No. 364. 4. **Rural and Urban Population by Sex.**
(by guberniya)

No. 365. 5. **Permanent (De Jure) and Temporary (De Facto) Urban Population. Results by Republic, Oblast, and Guberniya.**
(by sex)

No. 366. 6. **Permanent (De Jure) and Temporary (De Facto) Population. Cities with More than 50,000 Inhabitants.**
(data for 91 cities; by sex)

Number 4. **Nationality and Native Language of the Population of the USSR.**

No. 367. Introductory Table 1. **Comparison of the Results of the 1897 and 1926 Censuses on Nationality and Language (in Thousands of People).**
(for 80 ethnic groups; 1897 data are by language only; 1926 data give the number of each nationality as determined by both nationality and by native language; for those living in European USSR, Transcaucasus, Central Asia, other)

No. 368. Introductory Table 2. **Relative Change in the Populations of Ethnic Groups since 1897 (1897 Data Given as 100).**
(for 51 ethnic groups, as determined by both nationality and by language in 1926; for those living in European USSR, Transcaucasus, Central Asia, other)

No. 369. 1. **Population by Sex, Nationality, and Category of Populated Places by Union Republic.**
(for 188 ethnic groups; category of places means that data are by urban-rural)

No. 370. 2. **Population by Sex, Native Language, and Category of Populated Places by Union Republic.**
(for 147 languages; category of places means that data are by urban-rural)

No. 371. 3. **Distribution of the Population by Nationality and Language.**
(by guberniya; number of persons of each nationality; number of persons speaking each language; for the major nationalities and languages in each unit; by sex; by urban-rural)

No. 372. 4. **Sex Composition of the Population of the USSR by Nationality (Number of Females per 1000 Males).**
(whole USSR; by urban-rural)

No. 373. Supplement 1a. **Distribution of the Population of Dal'ne-Vostochnyy Kray by Nationality (Final Count).**
(for about 150 nationalities; by sex; by urban-rural)

No. 374. Supplement 1b. **Distribution of the Population of Dal'ne-Vostochnyy Kray by Native Language (Final Count).**
(for about 75 languages; by sex; by native language)

No. 375. Supplement 2. **Distribution of the Population of the Tobolsk North by Nationality and Native Language.**
(for about 28 nationalities and 22 languages, not cross-tabulated; by sex)

Number 5. Age and Literacy. European Part of the RSFSR. Belorusskaya SSR.

No. 376.   1. Population of the European Part of the RSFSR by Sex, Age, and Literacy, according to Data of the 1926 Census.
(for whole European RSFSR, not disaggregated; by individual year ages; by urban-rural)

No. 377.   2. Population by Sex, Age, and Literacy by Rayons of the European Part of the RSFSR, according to Data of the 1926 Census.
(by individual year ages through age 19, then by 5-year age groups; by urban-rural)

No. 378.   3. Population of Moscow, Leningrad, Rostov-na-Donu, and Saratov by Sex, Age, and Literacy, according to Data of the 1926 Census.
(by same age groups as Table 2)

No. 379.   4. Population of Belorusskaya SSR by Sex, Age, and Literacy, according to Data of the 1926 Census.
(by individual year ages; by urban-rural)

No. 380.   5. Population by Sex, Age, and Literacy, according to Data of the Censuses of 1897, 1920, and 1926 (Data for 8 Rayons of the European Part of the RSFSR).
(by single-year ages to age 19, then by 5- and 10-year age groups)

No. 381.   6. Population Aged 20 Years and Older by Sex, Literacy, and Single-Year Age-Groups, according to Data of the 1897 and 1926 Censuses (Data for 8 Rayons of the European Part of the RSFSR).

No. 382.   7. Literacy of the Population of the European Part of the RSFSR by Sex and Nationality, according to Data of the 1926 Census.
(whole European RSFSR, not disaggregated; for about 60 nationalities)

No. 383.   8. Literacy by Republic, Guberniya, Autonomous Oblast and Okrug of the European Part of the RSFSR, according to Data of the 1926 Census.
(units include Moscow and Leningrad; by sex; by urban-rural; in many units where the population is ethnically diverse, data are also given for several nationalities by sex and by literacy, but not by urban-rural)

No. 384.   9. Literacy of the Population of Belorusskaya SSR by Sex and Nationality, according to Data of the 1926 Census.
(for 8 ethnic groups)

No. 385.   10. Literacy by Okrug of Belorusskaya SSR, according to Data of the 1926 Census.
(by sex; by urban-rural)

Number 6. Housing Stock of the USSR.

No. 386. 1. <u>Living Structures by Material of the Walls and Number of Floors.</u>
(by republic; by category of building ownership [state, cooperative and social, private])

No. 387. 2. <u>Living Area and Area of Non-Living Premises by Category of Ownership.</u>
(by republic; by 4 types of construction materials)

No. 388. 3. <u>Number of Rooms and Living Area in Apartments and Dormitories.</u>
(by republic; by 3 categories of building ownership)

No. 389. 4. <u>Area of Living and Non-Living Premises in Living Structures by Republic and Rayon.</u>
(by 3 categories of building ownership; by 4 types of construction materials)

No. 390. 5. <u>Distribution of Built Properties by Category of Ownership.</u>
(by rayon, and also for about 240 cities; by 3 categories of building ownership)

No. 391. 6. <u>Living Structures and Living Premises.</u>
(by rayon, and also for about 225 cities; by 3 categories of building ownership)

Number 7. <u>Age and Literacy of the Population of the USSR.</u>

No. 392. 1-10. <u>Population of the [USSR, Union Republics, and Rayons] by Sex, Age, and Literacy.</u>
(data for all republics, the Asiatic part of the RSFSR, rayons of the Asiatic RSFSR, and rayons of Ukrainskaya SSR and Zakavkazskaya SSR; age data are given as single-year ages for the republics, but as single-year ages from 1-19 and as 5-year age groups from ages 20-100 for rayons; by urban-rural)

No. 393. 11. <u>Population of Cities of More than 200,000 Inhabitants by Sex, Age, and Literacy.</u>
(data for Kiev, Baku, Odessa, Khar'kov, Tashkent, Tbilisi, Dnepropetrovsk; Moscow and Leningrad are not included; by single-year ages 1-19 and 5-year age groups from 20-100)

No. 394. 12. <u>Population of the USSR by Sex, Age, and Literacy, according to Data of the 1897 and 1926 Censuses.</u>
(whole USSR only; by single-year ages)

No. 395. 13. <u>Population of the USSR by Sex, Nationality, and Literacy.</u>
(whole USSR only; for about 110 ethnic groups)

No. 396. 14-18. <u>Literacy of the Population of the [Union Republics, Guberniyas, Autonomous Oblasts, and Okrugs].</u>
(data for the RSFSR are only for the Asiatic part, because data for the European part were given in Number 5 of the <u>Short Summaries</u>; by several [up to as many as 8 or 9] of the most numerous nationalities in each unit; by sex; by urban-rural)

No. 397. Appendix. **Population of Uralskaya Oblast by Sex, Age, and Literacy.**
(same format as Tables 1-10)

Number 8. Social Composition and Occupations of the Population of the City of Moscow.

Number 9. Social Composition and Occupations of the Population of the City of Leningrad.

No. 398. 1. **Gainfully Employed Population of [Moscow and Leningrad] by Position in Main Occupation (Comparative Data from the 1926, 1923, and 1920 Censuses). a. Absolute Number. b. Relative Number (%).**
(by sex)

No. 399. 2. **Occupations and Other Means of Livelihood of the Gainfully Employed (by Main Occupation) and Non-Gainfully Employed (by Main Occupation of the Breadwinner) Population of [Moscow and Leningrad].**
(by position in occupation, sector of the economy, and 237 numbered occupational categories; by sex)

No. 400. 3. **Gainfully Employed Population of [Moscow and Leningrad] by Sex, Branch of Labor, Position in Main Occupation, and Types of Occupations (%).**
(i.e., by position in occupation, sector of the economy, and 337 numbered occupational categories; by sex)

No. 401. 4. **Gainfully Employed Population of [Moscow and Leningrad] Older than 10 Years of Age by Sex and by Groups according to Position in Chief Occupation, Age, and Literacy (Relative Numbers).**
(by 19 age groups)

No. 402. 5. **Population of [Moscow and Leningrad] by Sex, Employment, Chief Occupation, Age, and Literacy.**
(by gainfully employed and non-gainfully employed; by position in occupation, sector of the economy, and more than 100 occupations; by 19 age groups)

No. 403. 6. **Comparative Table of Data from the Censuses of 1926, 1923, and 1920 on Occupations of the Population of [Moscow and Leningrad].**
(by position in occupation and about 250 occupations; by sex)

Number 10. Population of the USSR by Position in Occupation and Sector of the Economy.

Part 1.

No. 404. 1-4. **Population of the [USSR, Union Republics, Rayons of the RSFSR and Ukrainskaya SSR, and Republics of Zakavkazskaya SFSR] by Sex and Employment.**
(by urban-rural; for population younger than 10 years old and for population aged 10 and older; population 10 and older by gainfully employed [employed, unemployed, other] and non-gainfully employed)

No. 405. 5. **Population of the Major Cities of the USSR by Sex and Employment.**
(same format as Tables 1-4 but for 35 large cities)

No. 406. 6. **Persons Who Have Occupations, by Sector of the Economy and by Position in Occupation (Republics, Rayons, Sub-Rayons.**
(by sex; by urban-rural)

No. 407. 7. **Persons Who Have Occupations, by Sector of the Economy and by Position in Occupation (Major Cities).**
(same format as Table 6 but for 35 large cities)

No. 408. 8. **Persons Who Have Occupations, by Sector of the Economy and by Position in Occupation (Autonomous Republics, Guberniyas, and Okrugs).**
(this table format is not quite the same as Table 6, because only the position in occupation is by sex; only sector of economy and the total of all males with occupations and all females with occupations are by urban-rural)

No. 409. 9. **Distribution of Persons Working in Separate Sectors of the Economy by Position in Occupation (in %).**
(by republic and by rayon; by urban-rural at the republic level but not at the rayon level)

Part 2.

No. 410. 1. **Population by Sex and Employment (USSR without Yakutskaya ASSR).**
(by republic and by rayon; number of gainfully employed persons aged 10 and older [by those with occupations, unemployed, other], number of non-self-supporting persons [dependents (with occupations, unemployed, other) and children younger than 10 years old who are registered as gainfully employed; by urban-rural)

No. 411. 2. **Population by Sex and Employment in the RSFSR (without Yakutskaya ASSR), Ukrainskaya SSR, and Zakavkazskaya SFSR, by Rayons.**
a. **Results for Persons Who Are Gainfully Employed and Their Dependents.**
(number of employed and unemployed; number of chidren less than 10 years old who are registered as gainfully employed; by urban-rural)
b. **Non-Gainfully Employed Persons by the Occupations of Those Supporting Them.**
(same format as part a, but for dependent persons; by status of dependents [having occupation, unemployed, other])

No. 412. 3-11. **Population by Position in Occupation and Sector of the Economy. USSR. RSFSR. European Part of the RSFSR. Asiatic Part of the RSFSR. Belorusskaya SSR. Ukrainskaya SSR. Zakavkazskaya SFSR. Uzbekskaya SSR. Turkmenskaya SSR.**
a. **Gainfully Employed Persons Who Have Occupations, and Their Dependents.**
(by sex; by urban-rural)
b. **Gainfully Employed Persons Who Have Occupations.**
(same categories as part a, without data on dependents; only the tables for the USSR, RSFSR, and the Asiatic Part of the RSFSR have this section)

v. Dependents of Gainfully Employed Persons Who Have Occupations.
(same categories as part a, but for dependents only)

No. 413. 12. Non-Gainfully Employed Persons Who Are Dependents of Persons Having Occupations, by Sector of the Economy and by Position in Occupation of the Breadwinner (Results for Rayons.)
(by republic and rayon; the position in occupation is by sex but data for sectors of the economy are not by sex)

No. 414. Appendix. Part-Time Occupations of the Population of the USSR (without Yakutskaya ASSR).
(whole USSR only; number of persons with part-time occupations [agricultural, not agricultural], number of unemployed persons by most recent occupation, and number of persons with a part-time occupation whose main occupation is in agriculture [by position in occupation of main occupation] or not in agriculture [by position in occupation in part-time occupation]; by position in occupation and sector of the economy of the main occupation)

RESULTS OF THE ALL-UNION POPULATION CENSUS OF 1959

No. 500. 1. Change in Population of the [USSR and Union Republics].
(summary table for the USSR gives the population in 1913, 1917, 1920, 1926, 1939, 1959, and 1962, while for the republics data are usually given for fewer years [commonly 1913, 1926, 1939, 1959, 1962]; by urban-rural)

No. 501. 2. Population of the [USSR and Union Republics] in 1917, 1920, 1926, 1939, 1959, and 1962 in Percentages of the 1913 Population.
(years above are for the whole USSR, while for republics only 1926, 1939, 1959, and 1962 are included; by urban-rural; where applicable, by current borders and by pre-1939 borders)

No. 502. 3. Administrative-Territorial Divisions of the [USSR, Republics, Krays, and Oblasts].
(data are given for 1959 and 1962 on the number of administrative divisions of all types in each unit, down to the oblast level, including all Union Republic capitals; area and population density in each unit are also given; USSR population density is in Table 4a.)

No. 503. 4. Number of Enumerated [De Facto] and Permanent [De Jure] Population in the [USSR, Republics, Krays, and Oblasts].
(by sex; by urban-rural)

No. 504. 4a. Number and Density of Population by Union Republic.
(this table is in the USSR summary volume only; also includes population of the capital of each republic)

No. 505. 5. Enumerated [De Facto] Population of the [USSR, Republics, Krays, and Oblasts] in 1939 and 1959.
(units include 10 of the SSR capitals; by urban-rural; USSR summary volume also gives republic data by sex)

No. 506. 5a. Enumerated [De Facto] Population of the Republics, Krays, and Oblasts in 1939 and 1959.
(by urban-rural; this table is in the USSR summary volume only)

No. 507. 6. Population of Cities Which Are Administrative Centers of Union and Autonomous Republics, Krays, and Oblasts, and Also Other Cities with Populations of More than 50,000 in 1939 and 1959.
(this is the title of the table in the USSR summary volume; in most republic volumes this table includes the populations of all cities and urban-type settlements, although in several republics with many large cities only those greater than 10,000 or 15,000 population are given)

No. 508. 7. Grouping of Cities and Urban-Type Settlements by Population Size in 1926, 1939, and 1959.
(by republic; data for cities give the number of populated places and their total population in each of 7 or 8 size groups; data for urban-type settlements are in 5 size groups)

No. 509. 8. Grouping of Cities and Urban-Type Settlements by Population Size in the [USSR, Republics, Krays, and Oblasts].
(number of cities, in 7 or 8 size groups, and number of urban-type settlements, in 5 size groups)

No. 510. 9. Grouping of Rural Populated Places by Type and Population Size.
(by republic; number of places and their total population, by 12 population-size groups and 6 types [generally by function]; as of January 1961)

No. 511. 9a. Grouping of Rural Populated Places by Type and Population Size (in Percentages of the Total).
(this table is in the USSR summary volume only; whole USSR; same format as Table 9, but in percentages)

No. 512. 9b. Grouping of Rural Populated Places by Population Size by Union Republic.
(this table is in the USSR summary volume only; number of populated places and the total population in each of 12 size groups; data are for 1961)

No. 513. 10. Grouping of Rayons by Population Size in the [USSR, Republics, Krays, and Oblasts].
(number of rayons in each of 9 size groups; as of January 1962; data for Union Republic capitals not given)

No. 514. 11. Grouping of Rural Soviets by Population Size in the [USSR, Republics, Krays, and Oblasts].
(number of soviets in each of 10 size groups; as of January 1962)

No. 515. 12. Distribution of the Population by Age in 1939 and 1959.

(by republic; for 13 age groups)

No. 516. 13. **Distribution of the Population by Sex and Age.**
(by republic; by 14 age groups to age 100, then 5 age groups of population aged 100 and older; by urban-rural)

No. 517. 14. **Distribution of Children Younger than One Year Old by Sex and Age.**
(by republic; by ages in months, in 12 age groups; by urban-rural)

No. 518. 15. **Distribution of the Population of the [USSR, Republics, Krays, and Oblasts] by Sex and Age.**
(by 12 age groups; by urban-rural)

No. 519. 16. **Number of Males and Females by Separate Age Groups per 1000 Population of a Given Age.**
(by republic; by 12 age groups; by urban-rural)

No. 520. 17. **Number of Married Persons per 1000 Population by Age and Sex.**
(by republic; for population aged 16 and older; by 12 age groups; by urban-rural)

No. 521. 18. **Number of Married Persons per 1000 Population by Age and Sex in 1939 and 1959.**
(by republic; for population aged 16 and older; by 12 age groups)

No. 522. 19. **Number of Married Persons per 1000 Population Aged 16 and Older by Sex in the [USSR, Republics, Krays, and Oblasts].**
(units include only 10 of the SSR capitals; by urban-rural)

No. 523. 20. **Level of Education of the Population.**
(by republic; for population aged 10 and older; by 6 levels of education; by 12 age groups; by sex; by urban-rural)

No. 524. 21. **Number of Persons with Higher and Secondary Education in 1939 and 1959.**
(by republic; for all population with education and for all population of able-bodied ages with education; by sex; by urban-rural)

No. 525. 22. **Distribution of the Population of the [USSR, Republics, Krays, and Oblasts] by Level of Education.**
(by 6 levels of education; by sex; by urban-rural)

No. 526. 23. **Number of Persons with Higher and Secondary Education in the [USSR, Republics, Krays, and Oblasts] in 1939 and 1959.**
(units include only 10 of the SSR capitals; in the republic volumes the title includes **per 1000 Population**; data in the republic volumes are by sex and by urban-rural for all units; data in the USSR summary volume are at the republic level, by sex only)

No. 527. 24. **Number of Persons of Able-Bodied Ages with Higher and Secondary Education per 1000 Population in the [USSR, Republics, Krays, and Oblasts].**
(units include only 10 of the SSR capitals; by sex; by

urban-rural)

No. 528. 25. **Literacy of the Population Aged 9-49 in 1897, 1926, 1939, and 1959.**
(by republic; by sex; by urban-rural)

No. 529. 26. **Literacy of the Population Aged 9-49 in 1897, 1926, 1939, and 1959 in the [USSR, Republics, Krays, and Oblasts].**
(units include only 10 of the SSR capitals; the USSR summary volume has data for all years given above, at the Union Republic level, while data in the republic volumes are only for 1939 and 1959; literacy given in percentages; by sex; by urban-rural)

No. 530. 27. **Distribution of the Population by Social Group.**
(by republic; 4 categories of social groups; by sex; by urban-rural)

No. 531. 28. **Distribution of Population by Social Group in 1939 and 1959 (in Percentages of the Total).**
(by republic; 4 categories of social groups)

No. 532. 29. **Distribution of the Population of the [USSR, Republics, Krays, and Oblasts] by Social Group.**
(4 categories of social groups; by sex)

No. 533. 29a. **Distribution of the Working Population by Social Group by Union Republic.**
(this table is in the USSR summary volume only; 4 categories of social groups)

No. 534. 30. **Distribution of Population by Means of Livelihood.**
(by republic; by 9 categories of means of livelihood; by sex; by urban-rural)

No. 535. 31. **Distribution of the Population by Means of Livelihood in 1939 and 1959 (in Percentages of the Total).**
(by republic; by 6 categories of means of livelihood; by sex)

No. 536. 32. **Distribution of the Population of Able-Bodied Ages by Means of Livelihood in the [USSR, Republics, Krays, and Oblasts].**
(by 5 categories of means of livelihood; some of the categories are by sex; by urban-rural)

No. 537. 32a. **Distribution of the Population of Able-Bodied Ages by Means of Livelihood by Union Republic (in %).**
(this table is in the USSR summary volume only; by 5 categories of means of livelihood; by urban-rural)

No. 538. 33. **Distribution of the Working Population by Sector of the Economy and Social Group.**
(by republic; 4 categories of social groups; by sex; by urban-rural)

No. 539. 34. **Distribution of the Working Population by Sectors of the Economy in 1939 and 1959 (in Percentages of the Total).**
(by republic; by sex)

No. 540. 35. __Level of Education of the Population by Social Group.__
(per 1000 population with education; by republic; by 3 categories of social groups; by 4 levels of education; by sex; by urban-rural)

No. 541. 35a. __Level of Education of the Population by Social Group and Age.__
(this table is in the USSR summary volume only; whole USSR; per 1000 population of 3 different social groups with education; by 4 levels of education; by 12 age groups; by sex; whole USSR)

No. 542. 36. __Level of Education of the Working Population by Social Group.__
(by republic; per 1000 working population of 3 different social groups with education; by 4 levels of education; by sex; by urban-rural)

No. 543. 37. __Level of Education of Manual Workers, Office Workers, and Collective Farmers in 1939 and 1959.__
(by republic; per 1000 working population with higher and secondary education [together]; by sex; by urban-rural)

No. 544. 38. __Level of Education of Manual Workers, Office Workers, and Collective Farmers in 1939 and 1959 in the [USSR, Republics, Krays, and Oblasts].__
(this title is of the table in the USSR summary volume; USSR summary data are per 1000 working population with higher and secondary education [together], by republic; data in the republic volumes are for the same educational categories but are given down to the oblast level [units include only 10 of the SSR capitals] by sex and by urban-rural, for 1959 only)

No. 545. 39. __Age Structure of the Working Population by Separate Sectors of the Economy and Industries.__
(by republic; per 1000 working population; by 8 age groups; for about 70 different sectors and industries; by sex)

No. 546. 40. __Level of Education of the Working Population by Separate Sectors of the Economy and Industries.__
(by republic; per 1000 working population with education; by 4 levels of education; for about 85 different sectors and industries; by sex)

No. 547. 40a. __Level of Education of the Working Population by Separate Sectors of the Economy.__
(this table is in the USSR summary volume only; whole USSR; per 1000 population with education; by sex)

No. 548. 41. __Number of People Employed in Physical and Mental Labor in 1939 and 1959.__
(by republic; by sex)

No. 549. 41a. __Number of People Employed in Physical and Mental Labor in 1939 and 1959 by Union Republic.__
(this table is in the USSR summary volume only; by urban-rural)

No. 550. 42. __Distribution of the Population by Occupation and Age.__

(by republic; in USSR summary volume per 1000 population, but in republic volumes by numbers of people; by 7 age groups; for about 450 different occupations, by those of primarily physical and those of primarily mental labor; when combined with Table 43, some of these data can be calculated by sex)

No. 551. 43. Distribution of Females by Occupation and Age.
(this table is the same as Table 42, except it is only for females and covers only about 125 different occupations)

No. 552. 44. Distribution of the Population by Occupation, in Separate Sectors of the Economy.
(by republic; number of workers in each of about 1000 occupations)

No. 553. 45. Distribution of the Population Engaged in Physical Labor in the Agricultural Sector, by Social Group.
(by republic; number of workers in each of 27 occupations; by worker and collective farmer [social group]; when combined with Table 46, some of these data can be calculated by sex)

No. 554. 46. Distribution of Females Engaged in Physical Labor in the Agricultural Sector, by Social Group.
(by republic; number of women in each of 21 occupations; by worker and collective farmer [social group])

No. 555. 47. Distribution of the Population by Occupation in 1939 and 1959.
(by republic; number of people employed in each of about 235 different occupations, grouped by those of primarily physical and those of primarily mental labor; when combined with Table 48, data for some of these occupations can be calculated by sex)

No. 556. 48. Distribution of Females by Occupation in 1939 and 1959.
(by republic; number of females employed in each of about 125 different occupations, grouped by those of primarily physical and those of primarily mental labor)

No. 557. 49. Distribution of the Population by Occupation in 1926 and 1959.
(by republic; number of people employed in each of about 85 different occupations, grouped by those of primarily physical and those of primarily mental labor)

No. 558. 50. Level of Education of the Population Engaged in Physical and Mental Labor.
(by republic; per 1000 persons with education; by higher and by secondary education; by sex; by urban-rural)

No. 559. 50a. Level of Education of the Population Engaged in Physical and Mental Labor, by Republic.
(this table is in the USSR summary volume only; per 1000 persons with education; by 3 levels of education)

No. 560. 51. Number of Persons with Higher and Secondary Education Engaged in Physical and Mental Labor in 1939 and 1959.

(by republic; per 1000 persons with higher and
secondary education; by sex; by urban-rural)

No. 561. 52. **Level of Education of the Population by Separate Occupation in 1939 and 1959.**
(by republic; per 1000 persons with higher and
secondary education employed in a given occupation; for
each of about 250 different occupations, grouped by
those of primarily physical and those of primarily
mental labor)

No. 562. 53. **Distribution of the Population by Nationality and Native Language.**
(by republic; number of persons of each nationality by
native language [language of that nationality, of the
titular nationality of the Union Republic, Russian, or
other]; by sex; by urban-rural)

No. 563. 54. **Distribution of the Population of the Union and Autonomous Republics, Autonomous Oblasts, and National Okrugs by the Most Numerous Nationalities.**
(Table 54 with this title is in the USSR summary volume
only; number of people of each nationality in all
ethnic units listed above)

No. 564. 54. **Distribution of Population of the [Republics, Krays, and Oblasts] by the Most Numerous Nationalities and Native Language.**
(Table 54 with this title is in the republic volumes
only; data given for all census units, including Union
Republic capitals; number of persons in each
nationality, by native language [language of that
nationality, language of the titular nationality of the
Union Republic that the unit is located in, Russian, or
other]; by sex; by urban-rural)

No. 565. 54a. **Distribution of the Titular Nationalities of the Union Republics by Republic of Their Primary Residence.**
(this table is in the USSR summary volume only; number
of people of each Union Republic nationality living in
each Union Republic)

No. 566. 54b. **Distribution of Titular Nationalities of the [Union and Autonomous Republics] by Age and by Percentage of the Nationality Who Consider That Nationality To Be Their Native Language.**
(Table 54b. [which gives data for the titular
nationalities of the SSRs] is in the USSR summary
volume only; Table 54a. of the RSFSR volume contains
the same data, but for the titular nationalities of the
ASSRs in that republic only; for 12 age groups; by sex;
by urban-rural)

No. 567. 55. **Distribution of the Population by Native Language.**
(by republic; number of people who consider each
language to be their native language [for most
languages, not for only the major ones]; by sex; by
urban-rural)

No. 568. 56. **Number of Married Persons by the Titular Nationalities of the Union Republics.**
(by republic; in the republic volumes the title is by
the Most Numerous Nationalities; per 1000 married
population; by 10 mostly 5-year age groups of the

population aged 16 and older; by sex)

No. 569. 57. **Level of Education of the Population of the Titular Nationalities of the Union Republics in 1939 and 1959.**
(by republic; this title is for the table in the USSR summary volume only; in the republic volumes this table is for the most numerous nationalities, while for the RSFSR it also includes the nationalities of the ASSR's; per 1000 persons with higher and secondary education [together]; by sex; by urban-rural; data for 1959 are given for all population and for the employed population)

No. 570. 57a. **Level of Education of the Population of the Titular Nationalities of the [Union and Autonomous Republics] by Age Group.**
(this table is in the USSR summary volume [where it gives data for the Union Republic nationalities] and the RSFSR volume [where it gives data for the titular nationalities of the ASSR's in the Russian Republic] only; per 1000 persons with higher and secondary education; by 10 mostly 5-year age groups of the population aged 16 and older; by urban-rural)

No. 571. 58. **Number of Family Members and Persons Living Alone in the [USSR, Republics, Krays, and Oblasts].**
(number of persons living in families, number living separately but included in family budgets, number of persons living alone who do not have families; by sex; by urban-rural)

No. 572. 59. **Grouping of Families by Size in the [USSR, Republics, Krays, and Oblasts].**
(number of families by sex of family head; number of families in each of 9 size groups; average family size; by urban-rural)

No. 573. 60. **Number of Families, Family Members, and Persons Living Alone per 1000 Permanent Population in 1939 and 1959.**
(by republic; by sex [for families it is the sex of the family head]; by urban-rural)

No. 574. 60a. **Sex and Age of Family Members by Family Size.**
(this table is in the USSR summary volume only; whole USSR; number of family members per 100 families; by 9 family-size groups; by 11 mostly 5-year age groups; by sex; by urban-rural)

No. 575. 61. **Grouping of Families by Number of Members Living Together in 1939 and 1959.**
(by republic; per 1000 families; by 9 family-size groups; by urban-rural)

No. 576. 62. **Number of Family Members Living Separately from the Family, and Persons Living Alone, by Age Group.**
(by republic; by 6 mostly 10-year age groups; by urban-rural)

No. 577. 63. **Number of Family Members Living Separately from the Family, and Persons Living Alone, by Social Group.**
(by republic; by 3 social groups; by sex; by urban-rural)

No. 578. 64. Grouping of Families by Social Group of the Family Head and Family Size.
(by republic; number of families by sex of family head; number of families in each of 9 size groups; average family size; by 3 social groups; by urban-rural)

No. 579. 64a. Grouping of Single-Nationality Families of the Titular Nationalities of the Union Republics by Size.
(this table is in the USSR summary volume only; whole USSR; per 1000 families of each nationality who are living together; by 9 family-size groups, and average family size; by urban-rural)

No. 580. 64b. Distribution of Family Members by Means of Livelihood and Family Size.
(this table is in the USSR summary volume only; whole USSR; per 100 families; by 4 categories of means of livelihood; by 9 family-size groups; by sex; by urban-rural)

No. 581. Appendix. Tables of Mortality and Average Life Expectancy of the Urban and Rural Population (1958-1959).
(by sex and by individual-year ages)

RESULTS OF THE ALL-UNION POPULATION CENSUS OF 1970

Volume 1. Population of the USSR, Union and Autonomous Republics, Krays, and Oblasts.

No. 600. 1. Enumerated [De Facto] Population of the USSR and Union Republics in 1913, 1939, 1959, and 1970.
(by urban-rural)

No. 601. 2. Enumerated [De facto] Population of the Republics, Krays, and Oblasts in 1959 and 1970.
(by urban-rural; also includes the population of the administrative center of each unit for 1959 and 1970)

No. 602. 3. Population of Cities and Urban-Type Settlements with Populations of 15,000 or Greater in Republics, Krays, and Oblasts in 1959 and 1970.
(cities and settlements in AO's and NO's are listed not under those units but under the krays and oblasts which contain those units)

No. 603. 4. Grouping of Cities and Urban-Type Settlements in the USSR and Union Republics by Population Size in 1939, 1959, and 1970.
(8 size groups; number and total population of cities and of settlements in each size group)

No. 604. 5. Grouping of Cities and Urban-Type Settlements in the Republics, Krays, and Oblasts by Population Size.
(8 size groups; number and total population of cities and of settlements in each size group)

No. 605. 6. Grouping of Rayons in the Republics, Krays, and Oblasts by Population Size.

(number of rayons in each of 9 size groups only [not the total population in each of those rayons]; units that contain only urban rayons, such as Union Republic capitals, are not included)

No. 606.   7. **Grouping of Rural Soviets in the Republics, Krays, and Oblasts by Population Size.**
(number of soviets [not the population in them] by 10 population-size groups)

No. 607.   8. **Grouping of Rural Populated Places in the Republics, Krays, and Oblasts by PopulationSize.**
(number of populated places and the total population in each of 12 size groups)

Volume 2.   **Sex, Age, and Marital Status of the Population of the USSR, Union and Autonomous Republics, Krays, and Oblasts.**

No. 608.   1. **Distribution of the Population of the USSR and Union Republics by Sex in 1939, 1959, and 1970.**
(by urban-rural)

No. 609.   2. **Number of Males and Females per 1000 Population of the USSR and Union Republics in 1939, 1959, and 1970.**
(by urban-rural)

No. 610.   3. **Distribution of the Population of the USSR and Union Republics by Sex and Age in 1959 and 1970.**
(by 5-year age groups; by urban-rural)

No. 611.   4. **Distribution of the Population of the ASSR's, Krays, and Oblasts by Age in 1959 and 1970.**
(by 10-year age groups; by urban-rural)

No. 612.   5. **Number of Males and Females Aged 100 and Older in the USSR and Union Republics in 1959 and 1970.**
(by 5-year age groups; by urban-rural)

No. 613.   6. **Number of Married Persons per 1000 Population by Age and Sex in the USSR and Union Republics in 1959 and 1970.**
(by 12 [mostly 5-year] age groups; by urban-rural)

Volume 3.   **Level of Education of the Population of the USSR, Union and Autonomous Republics, Krays, and Oblasts.**

No. 614.   1. **Distribution of the Population of the USSR and Union Republics by Education.**
(for all population, by 6 levels of education; by 8 age groups; by sex; by urban-rural)

No. 615.   2. **Distribution of the Population of the USSR, Union and Autonomous Republics, Krays, and Oblasts by Education.**
(for population aged 10 and older, by 6 levels of education; by sex; by urban-rural)

No. 616.   3. **Level of Education of the Population of the USSR, Union and Autonomous Republics, Krays, and Oblasts in 1959 and 1970.**

(per 1000 educated persons aged 10 and older; by 6
levels of education; by sex;by urban-rural)

No. 617. 4. **Population with Higher and Secondary Education in the USSR and Union Republics in 1939, 1959, and 1970.**
(by higher and by secondary education; by sex; by urban-rural)

No. 618. 5. **Number of Persons with Higher and Secondary Education per 1000 Population Aged 10 and Older in the USSR, Union and Autonomous Republics, Krays, and Oblasts in 1939, 1959, and 1970.**
(by higher and by secondary education; by sex; by urban-rural)

No. 619. 6. **Level of Education of the Working Population in the USSR, Union and Autonomous Republics, Krays, and Oblasts in 1959 and 1970.**
(per 1000 working persons with education; by 6 levels of education; by sex; by urban-rural)

No. 620. 7. **Level of Education of the Working Population of the USSR and Union and Autonomous Republics in 1939, 1959, and 1970.**
(per 1000 working persons with education; by higher and by secondary education; by sex; by urban-rural; contains data only for SSR's and ASSR's)

No. 621. 8. **Literacy of the Population Aged 9-49 in the USSR and Union Republics (according to the Data of the Censuses; in %).**
(by sex; by urban-rural; for 1897, 1920, 1926, 1939, 1959, 1970)

Volume 4. **Ethnic Composition of the Population of the USSR, Union and Autonomous Republics, Krays, Oblasts, and National Okrugs.**

No. 622. 1. **Distribution of the Population of the USSR by Nationality and Language in 1959 and 1970.**
(population of each of 104 nationalities; percentage of that population who consider the language of that nationality to be their native language; for 1970 only, percentage of each nationality who speak either Russian or another national language of the USSR fluently)

No. 623. 2. **Change in the Population of Individual Nationalities by Union Republic.**
(population of the most numerous nationalities in each SSR in 1959 and 1970)

No. 624. 3. **Change in the Population of Individual Nationalities by Autonomous Republic.**
(population of the most numerous nationalities in each ASSR in 1959 and 1970)

No. 625. 4-29. **Distribution of the Population of the [USSR, Republics, Krays, and Oblasts] by Nationality and Language.**
(for 104 nationalities at the USSR and Union Republic level, where present; data for units below the Union Republic level are only for the most numerous nationalities; for each nationality is given its

population, the number of these persons who consider their native language to be this language, Russian, or other, and the number who speak a second national language of the USSR [Russian, the language of the unit, or other]; by urban-rural; by sex, at the Union Republic level only)

No. 626. 30. **Distribution of Population of the Titular Nationalities of the Union and Autonomous Republics.**
(the number of each of the 15 nationalities of the Union Republics living in each Union Republic; the population of the titular nationalities of the ASSR's by the major SSR's, ASSR's, krays, oblasts, and cities [Moscow and Leningrad] in which they live)

No. 627. 31. **Distribution of the Population of the USSR and Union and Autonomous Republics by Native Language and Second National Language of the USSR.**
(number of people in each unit who speak each of the major languages spoken in that unit and the number of these who speak a second national language; by sex; by urban-rural)

No. 628. 32. **Age and Language of the Population of Individual Nationalities of the USSR.**
(for 15 languages of Union Republics only; number speaking each language as their native language and number of these who speak a second national language [Russian, the language of their nationality, or other]; by 8 age groups; whole USSR)

No. 629. 33. **Age and Language of the Population of Individual Nationalities by Union Republic.**
(in each Union Republic the number of people speaking each of the 15 titular languages and each of the languages of the ASSRs, AOs, or NOs in that Republic as their native language; number of these who speak a second national language [Russian, the language of their nationality, and other]; by 8 age groups)

No. 630. 34. **Number of Married Men and Women of Individual Nationalities in the USSR in 1959 and 1970.**
(per 1000 married population; for 15 titular nationalities; by 6 [mostly 10-year] age groups of persons aged 16 and older)

No. 631. 35. **Number of Married Men and Women by Individual Nationalities by Union Republic in 1959 and 1970.**
(per 1000 married population; for the most numerous nationalities and nationalities of the ASSR's in each Republic; by 6 age groups)

No. 632. 36-53. **Level of Education of the Population of Individual Nationalities in the [USSR, Union and Autonomous Republics, Autonomous Oblasts, and National Okrugs] in 1959 and 1970.**
(per 1000 educated persons aged 10 and older; for the most numerous nationalities in each ethnic unit plus for all nationalities of the ASSRs, AOs, and NOs that are located within those units; generally, data for Russians, Ukrainians, Belorussians, and Tatars are for the population in each unit respectively, while data for other nationalities are for the ethnic unit in which most of that group lives; by 7 levels of

education; by sex; by urban-rural)

No. 633. 54. **Level of Education and Age of the Population of Individual Nationalities in the USSR.**
(whole USSR; per 1000 educated persons; for 15 titular nationalities; by 3 levels of education; by 8 age groups; by urban-rural)

No. 634. 55. **Level of Education and Age of the Population of Individual Nationalities by Union Republic.**
(per 1000 educated persons; in each Union Republic, for the titular nationality and the nationalities of all ASSR's; by 3 levels of education; by 8 age groups; by urban-rural)

No. 635. 56. **Level of Education of the Whole Population and of the Working Population of Individual Nationalities in the USSR and Union Republics in 1959 and 1970.**
(for the major nationalities and the nationalities of ASSRs in each Union Republic; per 1000 persons aged 10 and older and per 1000 working population, with higher and secondary education [together, not by type of education]; by sex; by urban-rural)

No. 636. 57-72. **Level of Education of the Working Population of Individual Nationalities of the [USSR and Union Republics].**
(one table for the USSR and one for each Union Republic; per 1000 educated working persons; for 7 educational levels; for 15 titular nationalities at the whole USSR level; within each Union Republic, for the most numerous nationalities and for the nationalities of intra-Republic ASSRs, AOs, and NOs; by sex; by urban-rural)

Volume 5. **Distribution of the Population of the USSR, Union and Autonomous Republics, Krays, and Oblasts by Social Group, Means of Livelihood, and Sectors of the Economy.**

No. 637. 1. **Enumerated [De Facto] and Permanent [De Jure] Population of the USSR and Union Republics.**
(by sex; by urban-rural)

No. 638. 2. **Distribution of the Population of the USSR and Union Republics by Social Group in 1959 and 1970.**
(by 3 social groups [manual workers, office workers, collective farmers]; by urban-rural; by sex)

No. 639. 3. **Distribution of the Population of the Republics, Krays, and Oblasts by Social Group in 1959 and 1970.**
(by 3 social groups)

No. 640. 4. **Distribution of the Working Population of the USSR and Union Republics by Social Group in 1959 and 1970.**
(by 3 social groups; by sex; by urban-rural)

No. 641. 5. **Distribution of the Working Population of the Republics, Krays, and Oblasts by Social Group in 1959 and 1970.**
(by 3 social groups)

256   *Index and Guide*

No. 642. 6. Level of Education of the Population of the USSR and Union Republics by Social Group in 1959 and 1970.
(per 1000 educated persons; by 3 social groups; by 4 levels of education; by sex; by urban-rural)

No. 643. 7. Level of Education of the Working Population of the USSR and Union Republics by Social Group in 1959 and 1970.
(per 1000 educated working persons; by 3 social groups; by 4 levels of education; by sex; by urban-rural)

No. 644. 8. Level of Education of the Working Population of the Republics, Krays, and Oblasts by Social Group in 1959 and 1970.
(per 1000 working persons with higher and secondary education [together]; by 3 social groups; by sex; by urban-rural)

No. 645. 9. Distribution of the Population of the USSR and Union Republics by Means of Livelihood.
(by 9 categories of means of livelihood; by sex; by urban-rural)

No. 646. 10. Distribution of the Population of the USSR and Union Republics by Means of Livelihood in 1959 and 1970 (in Percentages of the Whole Population).
(means of livelihood is by 6 categories; by sex; by urban-rural)

No. 647. 11. Distribution of the Population of the USSR and Union Republics by Means of Livelihood and Social Group.
(means of livelihood is by 6 categories; by sex; by urban-rural)

No. 648. 12-27. Distribution of the Working Population of the [USSR and Union Republics] by Sector of the Economy and Social Group.
(one table for the whole USSR and one for each Union Republic; by 3 social groups; by sex; by urban-rural)

No. 649. 28. Distribution of the Working Population of the USSR and Union Republics by Sector of the Economy and Social Group in 1959 and 1970 (in %).
(by 3 social groups)

Volume 6. Distribution of the Population of the USSR and Union Republics by Occupation.

No. 650. 1. Population Occupied by Physical and Mental Labor in the USSR and Union Republics in 1959 and 1970.
(by sex; by urban-rural)

No. 651. 2-17. Distribution of the Population of the [USSR and Union Republics] by Occupation in 1959 and 1970.
(one table for the whole USSR and one for each Union Republic; number of workers in each of approximately 330 different occupations, grouped by those of primarily physical and those of primarily mental labor)

No. 652. 18-33. Distribution of Women of the [USSR and Union Republics] by Occupation in 1959 and 1970.

(these tables have the same format as Tables 2-17, except they apply only to women and cover only about 130 different occupations)

No. 653. 34-49. **Distribution of the Population of the [USSR and Union Republics] by Occupation and Sector of the Economy.**
(one table for the whole USSR and one for each Union Republic; number of workers in each of about 760 different occupations and sectors of the economy)

No. 654. 50-65. **Age Structure of the Population by Individual Occupations, for the [USSR and Union Republics].**
(one table for the whole USSR and one for each Union Republic; per 1000 persons employed in a given occupation; for about 320 different occupations, grouped by those of primarily physical and those of primarily mental labor; for 7 age groups)

No. 655. 66. **Level of Education of the Population Occupied by Physical and Mental Labor in the USSR and Union Republics.**
(per 1000 employed persons with education; by higher and by secondary education; by sex; by urban-rural)

No. 656. 67. **Number of Persons with Higher and Secondary Education among Workers Occupied by Physical and Mental Labor in the USSR and Union Republics in 1959 and 1970.**
(per 1000 persons having higher and secondary education [together]; by sex; by urban-rural)

No. 657. 68-83. **Level of Education of the Population of the [USSR and Union Republics] by Individual Occupations in 1959 and 1970.**
(one table for the whole USSR and one for each Union Republic; per 1000 educated persons employed in a given occupation; for about 320 different occupations, grouped by those of primarily physical and those of primarily mental labor; by 4 educational levels for 1970, but only higher and secondary education [together] for 1959)

Volume 7. **Migration of the Population. Number and Composition of Families in the USSR, Union and Autonomous Republics, Krays, and Oblasts.**

No. 658. 1. **Distribution of the Population by Region of In-Migration and Out-Migration during the Two Years before the Census.**
(number of out-migrants from each Union Republic and the number of them migrating to each other Republic; number of migrants within each Republic)

No. 659. 2. **Distribution of the Population of the USSR Which Has Migrated, by Place of Previous Permanent Residence.**
(number of persons who migrated within 2 years prior to the census, by Union Republic or Economic Region of previous residence and by sex; second part of the table gives for these same units the number of in-migrants to urban and to rural areas, by urban-rural of the place of out-migration, but not by sex)

No. 660. 3-17. **Distribution of In-Migrants to the [Republics, Krays, and Oblasts] by Place of Previous Permanent Residence.**
(number of in-migrants to each unit in the period within 2 years prior to the census, by economic region and Union Republic of their place of previous residence, and by sex; second part of the table gives for these same units the number of in-migrants to urban and to rural areas, by urban-rural of the place of previous residence, but not by sex)

No. 661. 18. **Number of In-Migrants and Out-Migrants by Republic, Kray, and Oblast.**
(number of in-migrants and out-migrants who moved within 2 years prior to the census and the number who moved within the boundaries of the unit; data for cities are not included except for Moscow, Leningrad, Kiev, Minsk, Tashkent, and Alma-Ata)

No. 662. 19. **Distribution of the Population in the USSR, Union Republics, and Economic Regions of the RSFSR and Ukrainskaya SSR Which Has Migrated, by City and Settlement Size.**
(number of migrants within the 2 years prior to the census, by urban-rural of the populated place in which they currently live [number of those living in urban areas is given by 5 population-size groups of city or urban settlement] and urban-rural of the populated place in which they formerly lived [by the same 5 urban-size groups])

No. 663. 20. **Distribution of Migrants in the USSR, Union Republics, and Economic Regions of the RSFSR and Ukrainian SSR, by Age Group.**
(number of migrants within the 2 years prior to the census, by 3 age groups [younger than able-bodied, able-bodied, older than able-bodied]; by sex; by urban-rural of the previous place of residence of the migrants to urban areas and of those to rural areas)

No. 664. 21. **Distribution of Migrants by Separate Nationalities of the USSR.**
(whole USSR; number of migrants within the 2 years prior to the census; for the 15 major titular nationalities; by sex; by urban-rural of the previous place of residence of the migrants to urban areas and of those to rural areas)

No. 665. 22. **Number of Family Members and Persons Living Alone in the USSR and Union Republics.**
(number of persons living in families, those living separate from the family but included in the family budget, and persons living alone; by sex; by urban-rural)

No. 666. 23. **Number of Family Members and Persons Living Alone by Autonomous Republic, Kray, and Oblast.**
(number of persons living in families, those living separate from the family but included in the family budget, and persons living alone; by urban-rural)

No. 667. 24. **Number of Families, Family Members, and Persons Living Alone per 1000 Permanent Population of the USSR and Union Republics in 1959 and 1970.**
(the above categories also include the number of

families by sex of head of family; by urban-rural; by sex)

No. 668. 25. **Number of Families by Size Groups in the USSR, Union and Autonomous Republics, Krays, and Oblasts.**
(number of families [by 9 size groups], number of families by sex of head of family, and average family size; by urban-rural)

No. 669. 26. **Grouping of Families by the Number of Members Living Together, for the USSR and Union Republics in 1959 and 1970.**
(per 1000 families; number of families [by 9 family-size groups] and average family size; by urban-rural)

No. 670. 27. **Distribution of Families in the USSR and Union Republics by Type.**
(number of families, number of family members living together, average family size; by 5 types; by urban-rural)

No. 671. 28. **Grouping of Families in the USSR and Union Republics by the Number of Children Living in the Family.**
(number of families without children and 5 size groups of those with children; by urban-rural)

No. 672. 29. **Grouping of Families in the USSR and Union Republics by Size and by Social Group of Family Members.**
(number of families in each of 3 social groups, and total number of families which consist of more than one social group; by 9 family-size groups, and average family size; by urban-rural)

No. 673. 30. **Grouping of Families in the USSR and Union Republics by Size and by Nationality of Family Members.**
(for the most numerous nationalities in each Union Republic and the titular nationalities of any ASSRs, AOs, or NOs in that Republic; by 9 family-size groups; by urban-rural)

No. 674. 31. **Grouping of Families by Size and by Nationality of Family Members, in the Autonomous Republics, Autonomous Oblasts, and National Okrugs.**
(same as Table 30 but for the most numerous nationalities in each of the ethnic units below the Union Republic level)

No. 675. 32. **Distribution of Families in the USSR and Union Republics by Number of Children and Age of the Mother.**
(number of children per family in 4 groups [no children, 1, 2, 3 or more] by eight 5-year groups of mothers' ages; by urban-rural)

No. 676. 33. **Distribution of Families in the USSR and Union Republics by the Number of Working Family Members and Number of Dependents.**
(number of families where 1, 2, or 3 or more members are working, number of families that do not have a working member; by number of dependents [none, 1, 2, 3 or more]; by urban-rural)

No. 677. 34. Distribution of Family Members and Persons Living Alone in the USSR and Union Republics by Age Group.
(number of family members living together, number of them living separately, and number of persons living alone; by 7 age groups; by sex; by urban-rural)

No. 678. 35. Number of Children by Mothers Who Are Manual Workers, Office Workers, and Kolkhoz Workers in the USSR and Union Republics.
(per 1000 mothers of each social group; by urban-rural)

No. 679. 36. Number of Children by Mothers Who Have Various Means of Livelihood in the USSR and Union Republics.
(number of children per 1000 mothers; by those engaged in physical labor, mental labor, personal agriculture, other; by urban-rural)

No. 680. 37. Number of Children by Mothers Who Have Various Levels of Education in the USSR and Union Republics.
(per 1000 mothers with education; by 4 levels of education; by urban-rural)

ALL-UNION POPULATION CENSUS OF 1979

1. Population of the USSR, Republics, Krays, Oblasts, Autonomous Okrugs, and Large Cities.

No. 700. Change in the Population of the USSR.
(population by urban-rural; for 1913, 1939, 1959, 1970, 1979) in Vest. stat. No. 2, 1980 (TsSU SSSR, 1984: Table 1 has same format, but also includes 1897, 1920, 1926)

No. 701. Population of the Union Republics.
(for 1970, 1979) in Vest. stat. No. 2, 1980 (TsSU SSSR, 1984: Table 2 has union republic population by urban-rural for 1939, 1959, 1970, 1979)

No. 702. Population of the Union and Autonomous Republics, Krays, Oblasts, and Autonomous Okrugs.
(by urban-rural; see 1979 unit list for the specific units included) in Vest. stat. No. 2, 1980 (TsSU SSSR: Table 3 has same format but units are listed in different order)

No. 703. Cities with a Population of 100,000 or More.
(whole USSR; in thousands; cities listed in decreasing order by size) in Vest. stat. No. 2, 1980 (TsSU SSSR, 1984: Table 4 has cities of 50,000 population or larger, in alphabetical order, to nearest person)

No. 704. 2. Number of Men and Women.
(whole USSR; by urban-rural; for 1939, 1959, 1970, 1979) in Vest. stat. No. 2, 1980 (TsSU SSSR, 1984: urban-rural population cross-tabulated by sex does not appear at all in this volume)

3. Married Population. Number and Size of Families.

List of Census Tables 261

No. 705. **Number of Families by Family-Size Group.**
(by republic; 6 size groups; average family size) in
Vest. stat. No. 2, 1980 (TsSU SSSR, 1984: Table 48
includes these data)

4. Level of Education.

No. 706. **Literacy of the Population Aged 9-49 (in %).**
(whole USSR; by urban-rural; for 1897, 1926, 1939,
1959, 1970, 1979) in **Vest. stat.** No. 2, 1980 (TsSU
SSSR, 1984: no tables in this volume contain literacy
data)

No. 707. **Growth of the Population Having Higher and Secondary Education.**
(whole USSR; total number and per 1000 population aged
10 and older; by 5 levels of education; for 1970, 1979)
in **Vest. stat.** No. 2, 1980 (TsSU SSSR, 1984: Table 7
includes these data [see No. 761])

No. 708. **Number of People Having Higher and Secondary Education Among the Working Population.**
(whole USSR; total number and per 1000 workers; by 5
levels of education; for 1970, 1979) in **Vest. stat.**
No. 2, 1980 (TsSU SSSR, 1984: Table 7 includes these
data [see No. 761])

No. 709. **Comparative Data on the Level of Education for the Period between the 1939 and 1979 Censuses.**
(whole USSR; per 1000 working population with
education; for population aged 10 and older and for all
working population; by higher and by secondary
education; for 1939, 1959, 1970, 1979) in **Vest. stat.**
No. 2, 1980 (TsSU SSSR, 1984: Table 7 includes these
data [see No. 761])

No. 710. **Level of Education of Males and Females.**
(whole USSR; per 1000 population with education; for
population aged 10 and older and for all working
population; by higher and by secondary education; for
1939, 1959, 1970, 1979) in **Vest. stat.** No. 2, 1980
(TsSU SSSR, 1984: Tables 9 and 11 include these data,
except all data for 1939 and 1959 data per 1000 working
population)

No. 711. **Changes in the Level of Education of the Urban and Rural Population.**
(whole USSR; per 1000 population with education; for
population aged 10 and older and for all working
population; by higher and secondary education; for
1939, 1959, 1970, 1979) in **Vest. stat.** No. 2, 1980
(TsSU SSSR, 1984: Tables 9 and 11 include these data,
except all data for 1939 and 1959 data per 1000 working
population)

No. 712. **Growth of the Level of Education of the Population of the Union and Autonomous Republics.**
(per 1000 population aged 10 and older and per 1000
working population, with higher and secondary education [together]; for 1959, 1970, 1979) in **Vest. stat.**
No. 2, 1980 (TsSU SSSR, 1984: Tables 9-12 include these
data, except 1959 and 1970 data by ASSR and 1959 union
republic data per 1000 working population)

No. 713. **Distribution of the Population of the USSR by Nationality and Language.**
(whole USSR; population of each nationality, for 92 ethnic groups; percentage who consider this national language to be their native language; percentage who speak another national language of the USSR fluently [by Russian and other]; for 1970, 1979) in **Vest. stat.** No. 2, 1980 (TsSU SSSR, 1984: Table 13 includes these data, but for 1979 only)

No. 714. **Population of Individual Nationalities by Union Republic.**
(for the most numerous nationalities in each republic) in **Vest. stat.** No. 2, 1980 (TsSU SSSR, 1984: Tables 13-35 include these data)

No. 715. 6. **Distribution of the Population by Means of Livelihood.**
(whole USSR; 5 categories of means of livelihood; for 1970, 1979) in **Vest. stat.** No. 2, 1980 (TsSU SSSR, 1984: Table 37 includes these data, but for 1979 only)

Level of Education of the Population of the USSR, Union and Autonomous Republics, Krays, and Oblasts.

No. 716. 1. **Distribution of the Population of the USSR and Union Republics by Education (Thousand People).**
(by 6 levels of education; by urban-rural) in **Vest. stat.** No. 6, 1980 (TsSU SSSR, 1984: Table 8)

No. 717. 2. **Level of Education of the Population of the USSR and Union Republics in 1959, 1970, and 1979 (per 1000 Population Aged 10 and Older).**
(by 6 levels of education; by sex; by urban-rural) in **Vest. stat.** No. 6, 1980 (TsSU SSSR, 1984: Table 9)

No. 718. 3. **Level of Education of the Population of the USSR, Republics, Krays, and Oblasts (per 1000 Population Aged 10 and Older).**
(includes data for all union republic capitals and Leningrad; by 6 levels of education) in **Vest. stat.** No. 6, 1980 (TsSU SSSR, 1984: Table 10)

No. 719. 4. **Level of Education of the Working Population of the USSR, Republics, Krays, and Oblasts (per 1000 Working Population).**
(includes data for all union republic capitals and Leningrad; by 6 levels of education) in **Vest. stat.** No. 6, 1980 (TsSU SSSR, 1984: Table 12)

Ethnic Composition of the Population of the USSR.

No. 720. 1-23. **Distribution of the Population of [the USSR, Republics, Krays, and Oblasts] by Nationality and Language.**
(Table 1, for the whole USSR, gives data for 101 nationalities, while tables for the lesser administrative divisions give data only for the most numerous nationalities and the nationalities of ASSR's, Autonomous Oblasts and Autonomous Okrugs located in those units; number of each ethnic group who consider their

native language to be the language of their nationality, Russian, the language of the corresponding ethnic unit, or other; number of each group who are fluent in a second national language of the USSR [by Russian, the language of the corresponding ethnic unit, or other]; data are not given for any cities) in Vest. stat. Nos. 7-11, 1980 (TsSU SSSR, 1984: Tables 13-35)

No. 721. 24. **Distribution of Population of the Titular Nationalities of the Union Republics by Place of Residence.**
(number of each of the 15 major nationalities living in each Union Republic) in Vest. stat. No. 11, 1980 (TsSU SSSR, 1984: Table 36)

Marital Status. Number and Size of Families.

No. 722. 1. **Distribution of the Population Aged 16 and Older by Marital Status in the USSR and Union Republics (per 1000 Persons of the Corresponding Sex).**
(4 categories of marital status; by urban-rural) in Vest. stat. No. 12, 1980 (TsSU SSSR, 1984: Table 47)

No. 723. 2. **Number of Families in the USSR and Union Republics by Family Size.**
(number of families in each of 9 size groups; average family size; by urban-rural) in Vest. stat. No. 12, 1980 (TsSU SSSR, 1984: Table 48)

No. 724. 3. **Grouping of Families in the USSR and Union Republics by Number of Members Living Together in 1970 and 1979.**
(per 1000 families; number of families in each of 9 size groups; average family size; by urban-rural) in Vest. stat. No. 12, 1980 (TsSU SSSR, 1984: Table 49)

Means of Livelihood and Social Groups.

No. 725. 1. **Distribution of the Population of the USSR and Union Republics by Means of Livelihood.**
(5 categories of means of livelihood; by urban-rural) in Vest. stat. No. 1, 1981 (TsSU SSSR, 1984: Table 37 includes these data)

No. 726. 2. **Distribution of Population of the USSR and Union Republics by Means of Livelihood in 1970 and 1979 (in %).**
(5 categories of means of livelihood; by urban-rural) in Vest. stat. No. 1, 1981 (TsSU SSSR, 1984: Table 38 includes these data, but for 1979 only)

No. 727. 3. **Distribution of the Population of the USSR and Union Republics by Social Group.**
(3 categories of social groups [manual worker, office worker, collective farmer]; by urban-rural) in Vest. stat. No. 1, 1981 (TsSU SSSR, 1984: Table 39)

No. 728. 4. **Distribution of Working Population of the USSR and Union Republics by Social Group.**
(3 social groups; by urban-rural) in Vest. stat. No. 1, 1981 (TsSU SSSR, 1984: Table 40)

No. 729. **Level of Education of the Working Population of the USSR and Union Republics by Social Group (per 1000 Working Population).**

(3 social groups; by 4 levels of education; by sex; by urban-rural; for 1970 and 1979) in Vest. stat. No. 2, 1981 (TsSU SSSR, 1984: Table 41)

No. 730. **Level of Education of the Working Population by Sectors of the Economy, in the USSR and Union Republics.**
(per 1000 working population with education; by sectors of the economy [by productive sectors (9 categories) and non productive sectors (8 categories)]; by 4 levels of education) in Vest. stat. No. 4, 1981 (TsSU SSSR, 1984: Table 42)

No. 731. **Population of the USSR and Union Republics Engaged in Physical and Mental Labor, in 1970 and 1979.** in Vest. stat. No. 5, 1981 (TsSU SSSR, 1984: Table 43)

No. 732. **Level of Education of the Population Engaged in Physical and Mental Labor in the USSR and Union Republics in 1970 and 1979.**
(per 1000 working population with education; by 3 levels of education) in Vest. stat. No. 5, 1981 (TsSU SSSR, 1984: Table 44)

No. 733. **Level of Education of the Population Engaged in Physical and Mental Labor in the USSR in 1970 and 1979, by Separate Occupations.**
(per 1000 educated persons having a given occupation; by about 50 different occupations; by 3 levels of education) in Vest. stat. No. 5, 1981 (TsSU SSSR, 1984: Tables 45 [physical labor] and 46 [mental labor] together encompass these data; Table 46 is by 4 levels of education)

Family Composition.

No. 734. **Distribution of Families by Type and Size in the USSR and Union Republics.**
(number of families by 5 family types and by 6 family sizes; average family size is also by family type) in Vest. stat. Nos. 11-12 1981 (TsSU SSSR, 1984: Table 51 includes these data)

No. 735. 2. **Distribution of Families in the USSR by Size and Nationality of Family Members.**
(for families living together; number of families in which all members belong to one nationality [by 15 titular nationalities]; number of families in which the members belong to different nationalities; by 6 family-size groups; by urban-rural) in Vest. stat. No. 12, 1981 (TsSU SSSR, 1984: Table 52 includes these data)

No. 736. 3. **Distribution of Families in the USSR by Size and Social Group of Family Members.**
(number of families in which members belong to one social group [by manual workers, office workers, collective farmers], and number of families in which members belong to different social groups; by 6 family-size groups; by urban-rural) in Vest. stat. No. 12, 1981 (TsSU SSSR, 1984: Table 53 includes these data)

Number of Children Ever Born.

No. 737. 1. **Distribution of All Women in the USSR and Union Republics by the Number of Children Ever Born** (per 1000

Women Aged 15 and Older).
(number of women by number of children ever born, in 8 size groups; average number of children ever born) in Vest. stat. No. 1, 1982 (TsSU SSSR, 1984: Table 55)

No. 738. 2. **Distribution of Married Women in the USSR and Union Republics by the Number of Children Ever Born (per 1000 Married Women).**
(number of women by number of children ever born, in 8 size groups; average number of children ever born) in Vest. stat. No. 1, 1982 (TsSU SSSR, 1984: Table 56)

No. 739. 3. **Number of Children Ever Born in the USSR and Union Republics by Women with Various Levels of Education.**
(per 1000 women aged 15 and older who have had children; by 7 levels of education) in Vest. stat. No. 1, 1982 (TsSU SSSR, 1984: Table 57)

No. 740. 4. **Number of Children Ever Born to Women of Various Nationalities in the USSR (per 1000 Women Aged 15 and Older, by Nationality).**
(number of women by number of children ever born, in 8 size groups; average number of children ever born; for 15 titular nationalities) in Vest. stat. No. 1, 1982 (TsSU SSSR, 1984: Table 58)

No. 741. **Length of Residence of the Population of the USSR and Union Republics in Their Place of Permanent Residence.**
(number of persons who live constantly in the place of permanent residence [with parents, not with parents]; number of non-locally born by 7 different lengths of residence in their place of permanent residence; by urban-rural) in Vest. stat. No. 7, 1982 (TsSU SSSR, 1984: Table 59)

Means of Livelihood.

No. 742. 1. **Distribution of All Population in the USSR and Union Republics, Male and Female, by Means of Livelihood.**
(6 categories of means of livelihood) in Vest. stat. No. 9, 1982 (TsSU SSSR, 1984: Table 37 includes these data)

No. 743. 2. **Distribution of All Population in the USSR and Union Republics, Male and Female, by Means of Livelihood (in %).**
(6 categories of means of livelihood) in Vest. stat. No. 9, 1982 (TsSU SSSR, 1984: Table 38 includes these data)

No. 744. **Number of Families Grouped by Size in Autonomous Republics, Krays, and Oblasts.**
(city data given only for Moscow and Leningrad; for families living together; by 9 family sizes; average family size; by urban-rural; data for the RSFSR only) in Vest. stat. No. 10, 1982 (TsSU SSSR, 1984: Table 50 includes these data)

No. 745. 1. **Number of Families Grouped by Size in Autonomous Republics and Oblasts.**
(for families living together; by 9 family sizes; by urban-rural; data for all autonomous republics, autonomous oblasts, oblasts, and all Union Republic capital cities, except those units in the RSFSR) in Vest. stat.

No. 2, 1983 (TsSU SSSR, 1984: Table 50 includes these data)

2. Family Composition. [Nos. 746-749]

No. 746. 1. <u>Distribution of Families in the USSR and Union Republics by the Number of Children Younger than Age 18.</u>
(number of families, grouped by number of children [1, 2, 3 or more]; average family size of families having children younger than 18) in <u>Vest. stat.</u> No. 2, 1983 (TsSU SSSR, 1984: Table 54)

No. 747. 2. <u>Distribution of Families in the USSR and Union Republics by Type and Size.</u>
(number of families of each type [5 types plus other] by 6 size groups; average family size [by type]; by urban-rural; see No. 734 for all population) in <u>Vest. stat.</u> Nos. 2 and 4, 1983 (TsSU SSSR, 1984: Table 51)

No. 748. <u>Distribution of Families in the USSR and Union Republics by Size and by Nationality of Family Members.</u>
(number of families in each of 6 size groups, plus average family size; by number of families in which members belong to one nationality [by nationality] and number of families in which members belong to different nationalities [not by nationality]; by urban-rural) in <u>Vest. stat.</u> Nos. 6 and 7, 1983 (TsSU SSSR, 1984: Table 52)

No. 749. <u>Distribution of Families by Size and Social Group of Family Members by Union Republic.</u>
(data by republic but not for USSR as a whole [see No. 736 for whole USSR]; number of families in each of 6 size groups, plus average family size; by number of families in which members belong belong to one social group [by 3 social groups] and number of families in which members belong to different social groups [not by social group]; by urban-rural) in <u>Vest. stat.</u> No. 8, 1983 (TsSU SSSR, 1984: Table 53 data are for whole USSR and also by union republic)

No. 750. <u>Level of Education of the Working Population of the USSR and Union Republics in 1970 and 1979.</u>
(per 1000 working persons with education; 6 levels of education; by sex; by urban-rural) in <u>Vest. stat.</u> No. 9, 1983 (TsSU SSSR, 1984: Table 11)

No. 751. <u>Distribution of Men and Women in the USSR and Union Republics by Means of Livelihood, by Urban-Rural.</u>
(6 categories of means of livelihood) in <u>Vest. stat.</u> No. 10, 1983 (TsSU SSSR, 1984: Table 37)

No. 752. <u>Distribution of Men and Women in the USSR and Union Republics by Means of Livelihood, by Urban-Rural (in %).</u>
(6 categories of means of livelihood) in <u>Vest. stat.</u> No. 10, 1983 (TsSU SSSR, 1984: Table 38)

No. 753. <u>Level of Education of the Population Engaged in Physical Labor by Individual Occupations by Union Republic, in 1970 and 1979.</u>
(data are by republic but not for USSR as a whole [see No. 733 for whole USSR]; per 1000 working population

with education; 3 levels of education; by about 30 types of occupations) in Vest. stat. No. 11, 1983 (TsSU SSSR, 1984: Table 45 data are for whole USSR and also by union republic)

No. 754. Level of Education of the Population Engaged in Mental Labor by Individual Occupations by Union Republic, in 1970 and 1979.
(data include USSR as a whole; per 1000 working population with education; 4 levels of education; by about 17 types of occupations) in Vest. stat. No. 12, 1983 (TsSU SSSR, 1984: Table 46)

No. 755. Changes in Male Percentage of Population (1959-1979).
(by republic; for 1959, 1979, and 1979, by urban-rural; data for Moldavskaya SSR, Latviyskaya SSR, Litovskaya SSR, and Tadzhikskaya SSR in 1979 are only for the total percent male, not by urban-rural); these 1979 data on population by sex and urban-rural were compiled by Theodore Shabad from Soviet regional press reports and appear on p. 444 of "News Notes: Preliminary Results of the 1979 Soviet Census," Soviet Geography: Review and Translation (September 1979), 440-56.

No. 756. Share of the Urban Population of the Most Numerous Nationalities of the USSR in 1970 and 1979, %.
(percent urban of about 40 different nationalities in 1970, for the nationalities in their own titular republics and in the whole USSR; percent urban of the same 40 nationalities in 1979, in the whole USSR only); on p. 100 of V.I. Kozlov (1982), Natsional'nosti SSSR: Etnodemograficheskiy obzor. 2d ed. Moscow: Finansy i statistika.

No. 757. Distribution of Bilingualism in Various Groups of the Population by Nationalities of the USSR (according to Data of the 1970 and 1979 Censuses, in %).
(for 68 different nationalities, percentage of population which speak Russian freely as a second language; by sex; by urban rural [sex and urban-rural not cross-tabulated]; for these same nationalities, the percentage which speak another national language of the USSR [besides Russian] freely as a second language, by urban-rural); on pp. 114-15 of M.N. Guboglo (1984), Sovremennyye etnoyazykovyye protsessy v SSSR. Moscow: Nauka.

No. 758. Level of Education of the Population of Separate Nationalities.
(per 1000 population aged 10 and older; total number having higher or secondary [complete or partial] education together; for 38 nationalities of SSR's and ASSR's; for 1959, 1970, 1979); on p. 160 of A.A. Isupov and N.Z. Shvartsev, eds. (1984), Vsesoyuznaya perepis' naseleniya 1979 goda. Sbornik statey. Moscow: Finansy i statistika.

No. 759. Table 5. Number of De Facto and De Jure Population by Union Republic.
(by urban-rural); p. 20 in TsSU SSSR (1984), Chislennost' i sostav naseleniya SSSR. Po dannym Vsesoyuznoy perepisi naseleniya 1979 goda. Moscow: Finansy i statistika.

No. 760. Table 6. Distribution of the De Facto and De Jure Population of the Union Republics by Sex.
p. 20 in TsSU SSSR, 1984 (see No. 759 for citation)

No. 761. Table 7. Distribution of the Population of the USSR by Education in 1939, 1959, 1970, and 1979.
(total number and number per 1000 population, for all population with education and for working population with education; by 5 levels of education)
p. 23 in TsSU SSSR, 1984 (see No. 759 for citation)

Keyword Cross-Index

Purpose and Design

Since the entries in this index are all listed in the order in which they appear in the censuses without regard to the subjects contained in the individual tables, some means is needed to locate these entries by subject. The system used here is a modified keyword index; entries are indexed not only on the words in the table title or in the table descriptor but also to some extent on the subject. A number of keywords, ranging from two to as many as fifteen, were selected for each entry, based on both the specific words used in the table entry and the subject material of the table. Generally, however, the keywords were taken from actual words in the entry itself. For most of the tables in the 1959, 1970, and 1979 censuses, one set of keywords was used. This was possible because there are complete cross-tabulations of all of the data in most of these tables. The complex tables in the 1926 census and to a much lesser extent in the 1897 census, along with many incomplete cross-tabulations of the data in those censuses, required as many as twenty sets of keywords in a few cases. As is discussed below, representing every possible cross-tabulation in all of these tables was not always practicable.

Problems in Using Keywords

When sets of keywords are used for a cross-index, a computer search will find a match (and thus an apparent cross-tabulation) between any two words that appear in the same set. One table, for example, may contain data on marital status, age, nationality, sex, and urban-rural residence. If there are complete cross-tabulations of these data, the keywords will be "age," "marital status," "nationality," "sex," and "urban-rural." If, however, marital status and nationality are not cross-tabulated, two sets of keywords will be needed to represent this table. One set will have the words "marital status," "age," "sex," and "urban-rural"; the other set will have the words "nationality," "age," "sex," and "urban-rural." The number of sets needed to represent a table with ten different subjects and very incomplete cross-tabulations is too large to be practicable in an index such as this one.

A further complication here is that—as will be explained—all entries are coded with a letter to represent the level of units which are covered in the table. If, in the example above, data at the republic level contain all of the categories, while those at the guberniya level do not include age, the number of sets of keywords needed to represent the table will be doubled.

In all, a thousand sets of keywords were used to represent the 630 entries in the table list, with 60 percent of the sets representing the 1926 census alone. Nevertheless, for the most complex tables in the 1926 census it was necessary to generalize somewhat in setting up the sets of keywords which were used by the computer to find the cross-tabulations. That is, *all* keywords were still included for each entry (so the entries can be found by looking at the "all entries" subheading under each main heading), but sometimes two keywords that were not cross-tabulated in the census itself were included in the same set of keywords. Most of these "false" cross-tabulations in the 1926 census deal with occupational-type data or with characteristics of the family (since many tables on the family have categories of data for the head of the family which are different from the categories given for family members). The majority of misleading cross-tabulations have been eliminated by using fewer subcategories under these subjects than under the other subject headings. Furthermore, this is not a serious problem because any false cross-tabulations in the index will quickly be discovered by turning to the table entries themselves.

Geographic Codes

Each of the sets of keywords is identified by the entry number that it represents, along with a geographic code to indicate the level of units which it contains. The geographic code should make it possible to scan much more rapidly through the index to find the level of units desired. Since the detail of categories given within a single table and the particular cross-tabulations may vary considerably depending upon the geographic level, many tables require more than one set of geographic codes to represent them. Therefore, the index may contain several entries in a row with the same entry number, but with different geographic codes.

The code represents the lowest or most detailed unit level for each set of cross-tabulations; one can assume that the same data are available for higher order units. For example, a table in which the data are given by republic and by guberniya will be coded only with a "g," not also with an "r." If, however, data presented at the republic level are slightly different in format from those at the guberniya level, an additional set of keywords, coded with an "r," will be used to represent the republic-level data in the index.

The following geographic codes were used in the index (see the unit list for more detail on these administrative divisions):

u	USSR or Russian Empire
r	Union Republic
s	RSFSR
k	Ukrainskaya SSR
b	Belorusskaya SSR
y	rayon (large units in 1926 census)
d	main division of the Russian Empire
e	economic region (1970)
a	ASSR
n	NO or AO
g	guberniya (or similar level unit)
o	oblast (or similar level unit)
z	uezd
v	volost
c	city or settlement
m	Moscow
l	Leningrad or St. Petersburg

The codes represent one or more units at those levels, not necessarily all such units in the USSR. For example, a table for a single rayon will be coded as "y," as will tables that contain data for all rayons. A table that contains one or more cities will be coded as "c," even if that list also contains Moscow and Leningrad. If Moscow and Leningrad are specifically names in the table title or descriptor, then the codes "m" and "l" are used. Therefore, to look for data on Moscow and Leningrad, the user must look at all three of these letter codes. Furthermore, to find city data, the user must also look at the codes for guberniyas and oblasts. This is obvious from the unit lists (see the unit list section) because in many censuses cities are included as standard census units. In the 1970 census, for example, unless otherwise noted, all tables that give data at the oblast level also include all capital cities of union republics plus Leningrad. Since these cities are part of the standard census unit list, they are found whenever the lowest level units (oblasts) are given.

Locating Additional Cross-Tabulations

All of the cross-tabulations given in the index are two-way cross-tabulations. It is possible to identify additional three-way, four-way, or higher cross-tabulations by comparing the two-way cross-references with other categories. Under the main index heading "marital status," for example, are three entries for the year 1970 under the subcategory "all entries." Therefore, the only entries containing data on marital status for 1970 are numbers 613r, 630u, 631r. A glance at the same subcategory for 1959 shows that these three numbers are also listed there; these listings indicate that all of these tables in the 1970 census contain data for 1959 as well. A further comparison with the subcategory "age" shows that all of these tables are also by age, and a comparison with "nationality" shows that 630u and 631r are also by that category. Finally, these three entries are listed under "sex." Therefore, entries 630u and 631r give marital status by nationality, age, and sex for both 1959 and 1970, while entry 613r gives marital status by age and sex for those two years.

This procedure works very well for the 1959, 1970, and 1979 censuses and fairly well for the 1897 census (because there are complete cross-tabulations in most of those census tables). Some of the complex tables in the 1926 census are not as amenable to this method of identifying additional cross-tabulations because these census tables have too many categories that are not cross-tabulated. For all entries, however, the years that each table represents were included as keywords, so the user can always compare table entry numbers to find out which years of data are included in a given table. In many cases, it may be easier for the user to look up all of the table entries under the "all entries" subcategory (discussed below) to determine what the tables actually contain rather than to undertake a complex comparison of index entry numbers.

Index Subcategories

Most of the major headings in the index contain an "all entries" subcategory, which provides a complete list of the table entries containing data on that subject (based on the sets of keywords used for each entry) for each census year. The other subcategories are two-way cross-tabulations between the main heading and other subjects (keywords) used in this index. It is very important to remember that the list of subcategories given under a particular main category is not always comprehensive. The category "marital status," for example, contains only ten subcategories in addition to "all entries." This does not mean that only ten other keywords are cross-tabulated with marital status but rather that these are ten of the most important ones. Therefore, to

Keyword Index   273

compile a complete list of all of the possible table entries under a main subject heading, the user must look at the "all entries" category.

Meanings and Limitations of Individual Keywords

Since this index is not a true subject index, it is not always possible to find all of the entries that contain information on a particular topic by looking at one keyword heading alone. Many of the keywords represent subjects very clearly, and with these words the keyword and the subject coincide. These include education, family, foreign born, foreigners, literacy, mental illness, marital status, mothers, nationality, native language, physically handicapped, persons living alone, religion, and Soviets (councils). For other keywords, there is more ambiguity between the word and what it might represent in the index. The keywords use the terminology of the tables and the descriptors as closely as possible, so the index headings will coincide with the particular terminology used in each census. Therefore, when the terminology of the censuses has changed over the years, the terminology used here to represent these topics changes also. Uses of some of the major keywords are as follows:

Age. An entry has the keyword "age" only when three or more age groups are in the table. While the entry itself might indicate, for example, that the data are for the population aged 10 and older, or for the population younger than 15 and that aged 15 and older, these are not listed in the index as being by age because they have two or fewer age groups. Exceptions are the occasional use of the term "able-bodied ages" and the term "ages 9–49," which is used only with literacy.

Agriculture. Only tables that have data on agriculture either as the main subject or as a major part of the table are listed here. Most of the tables that contain data on agriculture do so as occupational categories, as a sector of the economy, or as a means of livelihood. Therefore, most of the data on agricultural work force and population will be found only by looking under those general categories.

Children. This term is used as a keyword when it is a major part of the table itself, not when the subject of the table merely encompasses children or when children are listed as one category among dependents or non-self-supporting persons. Other keywords under which children may be found are "dependents," "family," "non-gainfully employed," "occupation, position in," and "means of livelihood."

Cities. This word is used generically; it does not conform to official Soviet definitions as to what constitutes a "city." Use of the word "city" in the keywords is generally based on the wording of the table title or of the descriptor. Therefore, many entries that are translated as "urban" or as "urban settlements" appear not in this category but under the heading "settlements." Entries here also include those in which other data are given by city size or city type.

Dependents. The paucity of entries under this category is due to the small number of census tables in which the word "dependents" (*izhdiventsy*) appears and not to a lack of census tables on this subject. ("Means of livelihood" categories, however, also contain this word.) A very large number of tables containing data on dependent or non-self-supporting persons are found under "non-gainfully employed" and "occupation, position in."

Gainfully employed. This term in the 1926 census is a translation of "*samodeyatel'nyy*." Tables from the 1897 census which use the term "*samostoyatel'nyy*" are also indexed under "gainfully employed." For other tables with data on employed persons, see also "actively employed," "agriculture," "labor," "occupations," "means of livelihood," "workers," and "working population."

Industry. Nearly all census tables that contain data on industry are found only under "occupations" or "economy, sectors of." Few census tables are devoted to that subject alone or even to one particular industry.

Labor. Only the three most recent censuses use this term to describe occupations or employment. Related terms in earlier censuses include all of the categories related to occupations and employment, although none of these terms is precisely equivalent.

Leningrad. These entries represent all subjects; they are included to facilitate finding entries that include data on Leningrad or St. Petersburg. Only entries in which Leningrad would not normally be expected to appear (i.e., where Leningrad is not on the unit list) are given. Other entries in which Leningrad is included as only one among many cities are coded with a "c," not with an "l"; therefore, these entries are not on this list. Most entries with the code "c," however, do include Leningrad.

Marital status. Entries that have different types of marital status and entries that have only "married" or "not married" are both listed under this heading.

Means of livelihood. This term is synonymous with "sources of support" (*istochniki sredstv sushchestvovaniya*).

Moscow. The explanation for the use of the term "Leningrad" applies to the term "Moscow" also.

Nationality. Natsional'nost' and *narodnost'* are both indexed under this term.

Non-gainfully employed. This is a translation of *"nesamodeyatel'nyy,"* and could alternatively be translated in many cases as "non-self-supporting." In most tables it is used to mean non-gainfully employed persons, but in some tables it also included persons who are gainfully employed but are, nevertheless, dependent.

Occupations. This category is *not* a general heading representing all occupational data. Entries are listed here only if they contain one or more specific occupations or groups of occupations.

Occupation, position in. All entries with this subject are for the 1926 census. In some parts of that census the position in occupation data are referred to as "social groups" (*sotsial'nyye gruppy*). When that term is used, the entries are found under the heading "social groups," not under "occupation, position in."

Population. Entries that contain data only by age, sex, or urban-rural residence are indexed under this category. All of these entries that contain age data are also indexed under the main category "age." Some entries with keywords "cities" and "settlements" also appear under this heading if these urban data are only by sex and/or age.

Settlements. Some overlap occurs between this category and the "cities" category. Entries for populated places or settlements are usually classified under settlements when the word "city" is not used in the title or in the table itself. In some ambiguous cases the entry is classified under both categories.

Sex. Although some tables that are specifically about women are indexed under "women" or "mothers," all other tables that include any data by sex are listed by this subcategory, which appears under most of the main subject headings.

Social groups. The entries given under this category for 1926 represent only a small portion of all of the tables that contain these data. Most of the 1926 entries are indexed under the term "occupation, position in." Only 1926 tables that use the term *"sotsial'nyye gruppy"* appear under this category, and even some of those tables (one that emphasize occupational data alone) are only indexed under "position in occupation."

Unemployment. Tables that are devoted solely to unemployment data or for which these data are mentioned in the table descriptor are listed here. Many more tables containing unemployment data for 1926 are found under the "position in occupation" heading, because data on position in occupation often include a category for unemployment.

Urban and rural. Entries that give data by both urban and rural populations have the keyword "urban-rural"; they appear under this subcategory below most of the main subject categories. Data by urban-rural residence are usually not indexed by each of the two parts separately, so they do not appear automatically under the subcategories "urban" and "rural." Furthermore, entries that are only by urban or only by rural generally are not listed under the subcategory "urban-rural." Entries that give data for particular cities, either because those cities are a part of the unit list or because they have special city data (entries coded with the letter "c," "m," or "l"), are *not* automatically indexed as urban. Therefore, urban data in these entries are usually in addition to any urban data found under the subcategories "urban-rural" or "urban."

Working population. This term refers to tables in the 1959, 1970, and 1979 censuses only. It is used as a keyword and not as a subject category. That is, this term is used to index the tables in which it appears, not to index all of the tables that give data on the employed population. Therefore, the user must also consult related headings such as "labor," "means of livelihood," and "occupations." Most of the entries under this heading are related to education of the working population.

Sample Keyword Index

```
SOCIAL GROUPS─────────────── main subject heading
    all entries
        1897  3zc, 10zc,
              41d, 42g,
    persons living alone ──── subheading
        1926  304r, 304um1,
              307um1, 312yc,  entry number [300's = 1926 census]
        1959  577r
    sex                       code for geographical units (r = republic)
       ┌1897  10zc, 12zc,
       │      42g, 51g, 56d,  ┌ year of data that the entry includes (limited
       └                        to main census years)
```

Keyword Index   277

KEYWORD INDEX TO THE RUSSIAN AND SOVIET CENSUSES, 1897 TO 1979

ACTIVELY EMPLOYED
   all entries
      1926   331ym1, 332ym1, 333u, 333y, 337m1, 338m1, 339m1,
             343m1
ADMINISTRATIVE UNITS, AREA
   all entries
      1897   2z
      1926   114sz, 133kg, 153y, 361y, 362z
      1959   502o
AGE
   all entries (see also the categories below for able-bodied
             ages; literacy, ages 9-49; and migration)
      1897   6zc, 7zc, 8zc, 9zc, 13zc, 19gc, 19z, 21zc, 24g,
             29zc, 34g, 35d, 35g, 36g, 37d, 41d, 47d, 49d, 52u,
             57d, 58y, 60gc, 61d, 63d, 64d, 65gc, 151k, 152k,
             300sy, 381sy, 394u
      1926   109gc, 110gc, 111kgc, 113zvc, 127s, 128sy, 129s,
             130sy, 131sy, 147k, 148k, 149k, 150k, 151k, 152k,
             164u, 165u, 166r, 167r, 168r, 169u, 170u, 171u,
             173gm1, 174y, 175y, 176y1, 179m1, 182m, 182y, 190s,
             191s, 192s, 192sy, 193s, 194s, 204k, 205k, 206k,
             207k, 208k, 217u, 218u, 219u, 220u, 221u, 228gc,
             229y, 230c, 231y, 233y, 234y, 235c, 235m1, 236m,
             243y, 244gc, 246sy, 247s, 248s, 250s, 251s,
             254s, 258k, 259k, 260k, 262k, 263k, 267k, 268k,
             270u, 270r, 271u, 272u, 273u, 276u, 277u, 278u,
             280u, 288u, 292u, 293y, 335m1, 340m1, 341m1, 342m1,
             343m1, 344m1, 346m1, 347m1, 351m1, 359m, 376s,
             377sy, 378m1c, 379b, 380sy, 381sy, 392y, 393c,
             394u, 397y, 401m1, 402m1
      1939   515r, 521r
      1959   515r, 516r, 517r, 518o, 519r, 520r, 521r, 523r,
             541u, 545r, 550r, 551r, 566u, 566s, 568r, 570u,
             570s, 574u, 576r, 581u, 610r, 611o, 612r, 613r,
             630u, 631r
      1970   610r, 611o, 612r, 613r, 614r, 628u, 629r, 630u,
             631r, 633u, 634r, 654r, 675r, 677r
   able-bodied ages
      1939   524r
      1959   524r, 527o, 536o, 537r
      1970   663re
   birth, place of
      1926   231y, 233y, 234y, 235c, 235m1, 236m, 248s, 250s,
             251s, 260k, 262k, 263k, 273u, 276u, 277u, 278u,
             280u
   children
      1897   8zc, 36g
      1926   110gc, 129s, 148k, 165u, 340m1, 346m1, 347m1,
             351m1, 411sky
      1959   517r
   "dolgozhiteli" (persons aged 100 or older)
      1959   516r, 612r
      1970   612r
   education
      1897   13zc, 19gc, 19z, 41d, 47d
      1959   523r, 541u, 570u, 570s
      1970   614r, 633u, 634r
   family, head of
      1926   335m1, 340m1, 341m1, 342m1, 343m1

278 Index and Guide

foreigners
   1897   13zc, 41d
gainfully employed
   1897   24g, 52u, 58y
   1926   173gml, 175y, 179ml, 182m, 182y, 190s, 191s, 204k,
              205k, 217u, 218u, 229y, 230c, 231y, 234y, 235ml,
              247s, 248s, 251s, 259k, 260k, 263k, 272u, 273u,
              278u, 340ml, 344ml, 346ml, 401ml, 402ml
labor (physical and mental)
   1959   550r, 551r
   1970   654r
language, native
   1897   19gc, 19z, 47d
   1926   111kgc, 149k, 150k
   1959   566u, 566s
   1970   628u, 629r
life expectancy
   1959   581u
literacy
   1897   7zc, 13zc, 19gc, 19z, 34g, 35d, 41d, 47d, 61d, 64d,
              65gc, 151k, 152k, 380sy, 381sy, 394u
   1926   109gc, 111kgc, 113zvc, 127s, 128sy, 131sy, 147k,
              151k, 152k, 164u, 166r, 168r, 169u, 171u, 173gml,
              174y, 190s, 192s, 192sy, 193s, 204k, 206k, 207k,
              217u, 219u, 220u, 244gc, 254s, 268k, 288u, 376s,
              377sy, 378mlc, 379b, 380sy, 381sy, 392y, 393c,
              394u, 397y, 401ml, 402ml
literacy, ages 9-49 (one age group)
   1897   528r, 529r, 621r, 706u
   1926   528r, 529r, 621r, 706u
   1939   528r, 529r, 529o, 621r, 706u
   1959   528r, 529r, 529o, 621r, 706u
   1970   621r, 706u
   1979   706u
marital status
   1897   9zc, 21zc, 37d, 49d, 60gc, 63d
   1926   228gc, 229y, 230c, 234y, 235c, 235ml, 246s, 246sy,
              247s, 254s, 258k, 259k, 263k, 270u, 270r, 271u,
              272u, 288u, 359m
   1939   521r
   1959   520r, 521r, 568r, 613r, 630u, 631r
   1970   613r, 630u, 631r
marriage, age of mother at
   1926   348ml, 351ml
mentally ill
   1926   243y, 244gc, 254s, 267k, 268k, 288u
migration (able-bodied ages)
   1970   663re
mortality
   1959   581u
mothers
   1970   675r
nationality
   1926   109gc, 110gc, 111kgc, 113zvc, 147k, 148k, 149k,
              150k, 169u, 170u, 171u, 228gc, 231y, 234y, 235ml,
              258k, 260k, 263k, 271u
   1959   566u, 566s, 568r, 570u, 570s, 630u, 631r
   1970   630u, 631r, 633u, 634r
occupation, position in (for 1926 see also Age, social group)
   1926   173gml, 174y, 175y, 179ml, 182m, 182y, 190s, 191s,
              192s, 204k, 205k, 206k, 207k, 217u, 218u, 219u,
              220u, 229y, 230c, 231y, 233y, 234y, 235ml, 236m,
              247s, 250s, 251s, 259k, 260k, 262k, 272u, 276u,
              277u, 280u, 292u, 293y, 347ml, 401ml, 402ml

Keyword Index

occupations
  1897 24g, 52u, 58y, 60gc, 61d, 63d, 64d, 65gc
  1926 174y, 175y, 179ml, 182m, 182y, 190s, 191s, 192sy, 193s, 194s, 204k, 205k, 206k, 207k, 208k, 217u, 218u, 219u, 220u, 221u, 247s, 292u, 402ml
  1959 550r, 551r
  1970 654r

persons living alone
  1959 576r
  1970 677r

physically handicapped
  1897 21zc, 49d
  1926 243y, 244gc, 254s, 267k, 268k, 288u

population
  1897 6zc
  1926 130sy, 167r
  1939 515r
  1959 515r, 518o, 610r
  1970 610r

religion
  1897 29zc, 57d

sex
  1897 6zc, 7zc, 8zc, 9zc, 13zc, 19gc, 19z, 21zc, 24g, 29zc, 34g, 35d, 36g, 37d, 41d, 47d, 49d, 52u, 57d, 58y, 60gc, 61d, 63d, 64d, 65gc, 151k, 152k, 380sy, 381sy, 394u
  1926 109gc, 110gc, 111kgc, 113zvc, 127s, 128sy, 129s, 130sy, 131sy, 147k, 148k, 149k, 150k, 151k, 152k, 164u, 165u, 166r, 167r, 168r, 169u, 170u, 171u, 173gml, 174y, 175y, 176yl, 179ml, 182m, 182y, 190s, 191s, 192sy, 192s, 193s, 194s, 204k, 205k, 206k, 207k, 208k, 217u, 218u, 219u, 220u, 221u, 228gc, 229y, 230c, 231y, 234y, 235c, 235ml, 236m, 243y, 244gc, 246s, 246sy, 247s, 248s, 251s, 254s, 258k, 259k, 260k, 263k, 267k, 268k, 270u, 270r, 271u, 272u, 273u, 276u, 278u, 280u, 288u, 292u, 293y, 340ml, 344ml, 346ml, 347ml, 359m, 376s, 377sy, 378mlc, 379b, 380sy, 381sy, 392y, 393c, 394u, 397y, 401ml, 402ml
  1939 521r
  1959 516r, 517r, 518o, 519r, 520r, 521r, 523r, 541u, 545r, 550r, 551r, 566u, 566s, 568r, 574u, 581u, 610r, 612r, 613r, 630u, 631r
  1970 610r, 612r, 613r, 614r, 630u, 631r, 677r, 677r

social group (for 1926, see mainly, Age, occupation, position in)
  1897 13zc, 41d
  1926 335ml, 340ml, 341ml, 342ml, 343ml, 344ml, 346ml, 347ml, 348ml, 351ml
  1959 541u

urban-rural
  1897 6zc, 7zc, 8zc, 9zc, 13zc, 19gc, 21zc, 29zc, 34g, 36g, 37d, 41d, 47d, 49d, 57d, 151k, 152k
  1926 109gc, 110gc, 111kgc, 113zvc, 127s, 128sy, 129s, 130sy, 131sy, 147k, 148k, 149k, 150k, 151k, 152k, 164u, 165u, 166r, 167r, 168r, 176yl, 193s, 194s, 207k, 208k, 217u, 220u, 221u, 228gc, 231y, 233y, 234y, 235c, 235ml, 244gc, 246s, 246sy, 247s, 248s, 250s, 251s, 254s, 258k, 259k, 260k, 262k, 263k, 268k, 270u, 270r, 272u, 273u, 276u, 277u, 278u, 280u, 288u, 376s, 377sy, 379b, 392y
  1959 516r, 517r, 518o, 519r, 520r, 523r, 566u, 566s, 570u, 570s, 574u, 576r, 581u, 610r, 611o, 612r, 613r

280   *Index and Guide*

        1970   610r, 611o, 612r, 613r, 614r, 633u, 634r, 675r, 677r
  working population
        1959   545r
AGRICULTURE (see also ECONOMY, SECTORS OF; LABOR; OCCUPATIONS; MEANS OF LIVELIHOOD)
  all entries
        1897   27z, 55d, 55g, 62gc, 63d, 64d
        1926   174y, 176yl, 178y, 181gc, 184y, 192s, 192sy, 194s, 197s, 200s, 206k, 208k, 211kyc, 214k, 219u, 221u, 224u, 227u, 229y, 330u, 331yml, 332yml, 414u
        1959   553r, 554r
        1970   679r
  age
        1897   63d, 64d
        1926   174y, 176yl, 192s, 192sy, 194s, 206k, 208k, 219u, 221u, 229y
  occupation, position in
        1926   174y, 178y, 184y, 192s, 200s, 206k, 214k, 219u, 227u, 229y, 330u, 414u
  occupations
        1897   27z, 55d, 55g, 62gc, 63d, 64d
        1926   174y, 178y, 181gc, 184y, 192s, 192sy, 194s, 197s, 200s, 206k, 208k, 211kyc, 214k, 219u, 221u, 227u, 330u, 414u
        1959   553r, 554r
  persons living alone
        1926   330u, 331yml, 332yml
  sex
        1897   27z, 55d, 62gc, 63d, 64d
        1926   174y, 176yl, 178y, 181gc, 192sy, 194s, 197s, 206k, 211kyc, 219u, 224u, 229y, 331yml, 332yml
        1959   553r, 554r
BIRTH, PLACE OF
  all entries
        1897   3zc, 10zc, 11g, 11zc, 38g, 39d, 39g, 77z, 78g
        1926   231y, 231gml, 232y, 233gml, 233y, 234y, 234gm, 235c, 235ml, 236m, 237mlc, 238gml, 239c, 239gml, 242gml, 242y, 248s, 248sy, 249s, 250s, 251s, 251sy, 257s, 260k, 261k, 262k, 263k, 266k, 273u, 274r, 275u, 276u, 277u, 278u, 279r, 280u, 281gml, 282r, 283y, 284r, 285y, 291u, 294uml, 295y
  age
        1926   231y, 233y, 234y, 235c, 235ml, 236m, 248s, 250s, 251s, 260k, 262k, 263k, 273u, 276u, 277u, 278u, 280u
  foreign born
        1897   3zc, 10zc, 11g, 38g, 39g
        1926   231y, 231gml, 232y, 233y, 233gml, 235c, 235ml, 238s, 248sy, 249s, 250s, 260k, 261k, 262k, 273u, 274r, 275u, 276u, 277u, 282r
  locally born
        1897   3zc, 10zc, 38g, 39g, 77z, 78g
        1926   234y, 234gm, 235c, 235ml, 236m, 237mlc, 238gml, 248s, 248sy, 251s, 251sy, 263k, 273u, 274r, 278u, 279r, 280u, 281gml, 282r, 284r, 285y
  non-locally born
        1897   3zc, 10zc, 11g, 11zc, 38g, 39g
        1926   234y, 234gm, 235c, 235ml, 236m, 237mlc, 238gml, 239c, 239gml, 242gml, 248s, 248s, 248sy, 251s, 251sy, 263k, 273u, 274r, 278u, 279r, 280u, 281gml, 294uml, 295y
  sex
        1897   10zc, 11g, 11zc, 38g, 39d, 39g

Keyword Index 281

    1926   231y, 231gm1, 232y, 234y, 234gm, 235c, 235m1, 236m, 237m1c, 238gm1, 239c, 239gm1, 242gm1, 242y, 248s, 248sy, 249s, 251s, 251sy, 257s, 260k, 261k, 263k, 266k, 273u, 274r, 275u, 276u, 278u, 279r, 280u, 281gm1, 282r, 291u, 294um1, 295y

  urban-rural
    1897   3zc, 10zc, 11zc, 38g, 39d
    1926   231y, 260k, 231gm1, 232y, 249s, 261k, 275u, 233gm1, 233y, 250s, 262k, 277u, 234y, 263k, 234y, 263k, 234gm, 235c, 235m1, 237m1c, 238gm1, 242y, 257s, 291u, 248s, 248sy, 251s, 251sy, 266k, 273u, 274r, 276u, 278u, 279r, 280u, 294um1, 295y

BUILDINGS (all of these tables are from the 1926 census; they are listed in the table list as Nos. 296-329, 352-58, 386-91)

  apartments (see also BUILDINGS, living premises)
    1926   298yc, 300yc, 304r, 304um1, 305r, 312yc, 313yc, 320yc, 323yc, 388r

  buildings
    1926   302rc, 303c

  construction
    1926   297yc, 352skby, 352skb, 353skbgm1, 353skby, 354skbym1, 355skbym1, 356skbym1, 357skbgm1, 358skbym1

  dormitories (see also BUILDINGS, living premises)
    1926   298yc, 300yc, 304r, 304um1, 305r, 305um1, 312yc, 313yc, 321gc, 323yc, 324yc, 388r

  electricity, supply of
    1926   298yc, 300yc

  floors, number of
    1926   297yc, 300yc, 386r

  inhabitants
    1926   296yc, 298yc, 300yc, 301yc, 302rc, 303c, 307r, 307um1, 315yc, 357skbgm1

  kitchens (see also BUILDINGS, non-living space and non-living premises)
    1926   298yc, 300yc, 304r, 304um1, 305r, 305um1, 308r, 308um1, 312yc, 313yc, 316yc, 321gc, 323yc, 324yc, 327yc

  land parcels
    1926   296yc

  living area
    1926   298yc, 300yc, 301yc, 305r, 305um1, 306r, 306um1, 309r, 309um1, 311r, 311um1, 313yc, 314yc, 317yc, 319yc, 321gc, 322yc, 324yc, 325yc, 328yc, 352skby, 352skb, 353skbgm1, 353skby, 355skbym1, 356skbym1, 357skbgm1, 358skbym1, 387r, 388r

  living premises
    1926   296yc, 298yc, 300yc, 304r, 304um1, 321gc, 388r, 389y, 391yc

  living structures
    1926   297yc, 298yc, 299yc, 300yc, 301yc, 352skby, 352skb, 353skbgm1, 353skby, 354skbym1, 356skbym1, 386r, 389y, 391yc

  material of construction
    1926   297yc, 298yc, 299yc, 300yc, 352skb, 353skby, 354skbym1, 355skbym1, 386r, 387r, 389y

  non-living premises
    1926   299yc, 304r, 304um1, 321gc, 323yc, 387r, 389y

  non-living space
    1926   305r, 305um1, 312yc, 313yc, 324yc

  non-living structures
    1926   297yc

ownership (proprietorship)
    1926 296yc, 297yc, 298yc, 299yc, 301yc, 302rc, 303c,
          310r, 310um1, 311r, 311um1, 318yc, 319yc, 320yc,
          329yc, 352skby, 352skb, 353skbgm1, 353skby,
          354skbym1, 355skbym1, 356skbym1, 357skbgm1, 386r,
          387r, 388r, 389y, 390yc, 391yc
properties
    1926 296yc, 300yc, 302rc, 303c, 390yc
rent
    1926 309r, 309um1, 317yc, 320yc, 321gc, 328yc
rooms
    1926 298yc, 300yc, 307r, 307um1, 308r, 308um1, 315yc,
          316yc, 321gc, 326yc, 327yc, 388r
settlement type and size, buildings and housing conditions by
    1926 297yc, 299yc, 305um1, 306um1, 307um1, 308um1,
          309um1, 310um1, 311um1
sewage system, connected to
    1926 303c
social group, housing conditions by
    1926 304r, 304um1, 305r, 305um1, 306r, 306um1, 307r,
          307um1, 308r, 308um1, 309r, 309um1, 310r, 310um1,
          311r, 311um1, 312yc, 313yc, 314yc, 315yc, 316yc,
          317yc, 318yc, 319yc, 322yc
water supply, connected to
    1926 302rc
CHILDREN (see also DEPENDENTS; FAMILY; NON-GAINFULLY EMPLOYED)
    all entries
        1897 8zc, 36g
        1926 110gc, 129s, 148k, 165u, 340m1, 341m1, 345m1,
              346m1, 347m1, 348m1, 349m1, 350m1, 351m1, 411sky
        1959 517r
        1970 671r, 675r, 678r, 679r, 680r
        1979 737r, 738r, 739r, 740u, 746r
    age (all entries)
        1897 8zc, 36g
        1926 110gc, 129s, 148k, 165u, 340m1, 346m1, 347m1,
              351m1, 411sky
        1959 517r
    age (younger than one year)
        1897 8zc, 36g
        1926 110gc, 129s, 148k, 165u
        1959 517r
    children ever born
        1979 737r, 738r, 739r, 740u
    gainfully employed
        1926 346m1
    occupation, position in
        1926 347m1
    sex
        1897 8zc, 36g
        1926 110gc, 129s, 148k, 165u, 340m1, 346m1, 347m1,
              411sky
        1959 517r
    urban-rural
        1897 8zc, 36g
        1926 129s, 148k, 165u, 411sky
        1959 517r
        1970 671r, 675r, 678r, 679r, 680r
CHILDREN YOUNGER THAN 1 YEAR OLD (see CHILDREN, age)
CHILDREN EVER BORN (see CHILDREN, children ever born)
CITIES (see also POPULATION; SETTLEMENTS; entries include
        other subjects that are by city size or type)
    all entries
        1897 1gc, 87g, 89gc

Keyword Index 283

```
              1926   127s, 129s, 147k, 148k, 164u, 165u, 292um1, 294um1,
                     296yc, 297yc, 298yc, 299yc, 352skb, 353skbgm1,
                     353skby, 366c, 393c, 508r
              1939   507c, 508r, 603r
              1959   507c, 508r, 509o, 601oc, 602oc, 603r
              1970   601oc, 602oc, 603r, 604o, 662re
              1979   703c
DEPENDENTS (see also CHILDREN; MEANS OF LIVELIHOOD; NON-GAINFULLY
              EMPLOYED)
     all entries
              1926   344m1, 346m1, 411sky, 412r, 413y
              1970   676r
ECONOMY, SECTORS OF (see also AGRICULTURE; INDUSTRY)
     all entries
              1926   172gc, 172gm1, 173gm1, 177gc, 178y, 178gc, 178g,
                     179m1, 182m, 182y, 183y, 184y, 185gc, 186z, 187s,
                     188sy, 189sgc, 189sz, 190s, 193s, 195s, 196s, 199s,
                     200s, 201k, 202ky, 203kgc, 204k, 207k, 209k, 210k,
                     213k, 214k, 215u, 216r, 217u, 220u, 222u, 223u,
                     226u, 227u, 231y, 231gm1, 232y, 233gm1, 233y, 234y,
                     234gm, 235c, 235m1, 236m, 237m1c, 238gm1, 239c,
                     239gm1, 247s, 248s, 248sy, 249s, 250s, 251s, 251sy,
                     259k, 260k, 261k, 262k, 263k, 272u, 274r, 275u,
                     276u, 277u, 279r, 280u, 281gm1, 284r, 285y, 292um1,
                     292u, 293y, 294um1, 304r, 304um1, 305r, 305um1,
                     306r, 306um1, 307r, 307um1, 308r, 308um1, 309r,
                     309um1, 310r, 310um1, 311r, 311um1, 322yc, 330u,
                     331ym1, 332ym1, 333u, 333y, 334r, 334gc, 335m1,
                     336m1, 337m1, 338m1, 339m1, 340m1, 341m1, 342m1,
                     343m1, 344m1, 345m1, 346m1, 347m1, 348m1, 349m1,
                     350m1, 351m1, 360m, 399m1, 400m1, 402m1, 406y,
                     407c, 408g, 409y, 409r, 412r, 413y, 414u
              1939   539r
              1959   538r, 539r, 545r, 546r, 547u, 552r, 649r
              1970   648r, 649r, 653r
              1979   730r
     sex
              1926   172gc, 172gm1, 173gm1, 177gc, 178y, 178gc, 178g,
                     179m1, 182m, 182y, 185gc, 186z, 187s, 190s, 193s,
                     195s, 196s, 201k, 204k, 207k, 209k, 210k, 215u,
                     217u, 220u, 222u, 223u, 231y, 231gm1, 232y, 234y,
                     234gm, 235c, 235m1, 236m, 237m1c, 238gm1, 239c,
                     239gm1, 247s, 248s, 248sy, 249s, 251s, 251sy, 259k,
                     260k, 261k, 263k, 272u, 274r, 275u, 276u, 279r,
                     280u, 292um1, 292u, 293y, 294um1, 330u, 331ym1,
                     332ym1, 335m1, 336m1, 337m1, 338m1, 339m1, 340m1,
                     341m1, 342m1, 343m1, 344m1, 346m1, 347m1, 360m,
                     399m1, 400m1, 402m1, 406y, 407c, 412r
              1939   539r
              1959   538r, 539r, 545r, 546r, 547u
              1970   648r
     urban-rural
              1926   172gc, 173gm1, 177gc, 178y, 178gc, 185gc, 186z,
                     187s, 189sgc, 190s, 193s, 195s, 196s, 201k, 204k,
                     207k, 209k, 210k, 215u, 217u, 220u, 222u, 223u,
                     232y, 233y, 233gm1, 234y, 234gm, 235c, 235m1,
                     237m1c, 247s, 248s, 248sy, 249s, 250s, 251s, 251sy,
                     259k, 262k, 261k, 263k, 272u, 274r, 275u, 276u,
                     277u, 279r, 280u, 292um1, 294um1, 406y, 408g, 409r,
                     412r
              1959   538r
              1970   648r
     working population
              1939   539r
```

         1959   538r, 539r, 545r, 546r, 547r, 649r
         1970   648r, 649r
         1979   730r
EDUCATION (see also LITERACY)
    all entries
         1897   13zc, 19gc, 19z, 41d, 47d
         1939   524r, 526o, 543r, 544r, 560r, 561r, 569r, 617r,
                618o, 620ra, 709u, 710u, 711u, 761u
         1959   523r, 524r, 525o, 526o, 527o, 540r, 541u, 542r,
                543r, 544r, 544o, 546r, 547r, 558r, 559r, 560r,
                561r, 569r, 570u, 570s, 616o, 617r, 618o, 619o,
                620ra, 632ran, 635r, 642r, 643r, 644o, 656r, 657r,
                709u, 710u, 711u, 712ra, 717r, 758u, 761u
         1970   614r, 615o, 616o, 617r, 618o, 619o, 620ra, 632ran,
                633u, 634r, 635r, 636r, 642r, 643r, 644o, 655r,
                656r, 657r, 680r, 707u, 708u, 709u, 710u, 711u,
                712ra, 717r, 729r, 732r, 733u, 750r, 753r, 754r,
                758u, 761r
         1979   707u, 708u, 709u, 710u, 711u, 712ra, 716r, 717r,
                718o, 719o, 729r, 730r, 732r, 733u, 739r, 750r,
                753r, 754r, 758u, 761u
    age
         1897   13zc, 19gc, 19z, 41d, 47d
         1959   523r, 541u, 570r, 570s
         1970   614r, 633u, 634r
    labor (physical and mental)
         1939   560r, 561r
         1959   558r, 559r, 560r, 561r, 656r, 657r
         1970   655r, 656r, 657r, 732r, 733u, 753r, 754r
         1979   732r, 733u, 753r, 754r
    language, native
         1897   19gc, 19z, 47d
    mothers
         1970   680r
         1979   739r
    nationality
         1939   569r
         1959   569r, 570u, 570s, 632ran, 635r, 758u
         1970   632ran, 633u, 634r, 635r, 636r, 758u
         1979   758u
    occupations
         1939   561r
         1959   561r, 657r
         1970   657r, 733u, 753r, 754r
         1979   733u, 753r, 754r
    sex
         1897   13zc, 19gc, 19z, 41d, 47d
         1939   524r, 526o, 543r, 560r, 569r, 617r, 618o, 620ra,
                710u
         1959   523r, 524r, 525o, 526o, 527o, 540r, 541u, 542r,
                543r, 544o, 546r, 547u, 558r, 560r, 569r, 616o,
                617r, 618o, 619o, 620ra, 632ran, 635r, 642r, 643r,
                644o, 656r, 710u, 717r
         1970   614r, 615o, 616o, 617r, 618o, 619o, 620ra, 632ran,
                635r, 636r, 642r, 643r, 644o, 655r, 656r, 710u,
                717r, 729r, 750r
         1979   710u, 717r, 729r, 750r
    social group
         1897   13zc, 41d
         1939   543r, 544r
         1959   540r, 541u, 542r, 543r, 544r, 544o, 642r, 643r,
                644o
         1970   642r, 643r, 644o, 729r
         1979   729r

Keyword Index   285

```
urban-rural
     1897   13zc, 19gc, 41d, 47d
     1939   524r, 526o, 543r, 560r, 569r, 617r, 618o, 620ra,
            711u
     1959   523r, 524r, 525o, 526o, 527o, 540r, 542r, 543r,
            544o, 558r, 560r, 569r, 570u, 570s, 616o, 617r,
            618o, 619o, 620ra, 632ran, 635r, 642r, 643r, 644o,
            656r, 711u, 717r
     1970   614r, 615o, 616o, 617r, 618o, 619o, 620ra, 632ran,
            633u, 634r, 635r, 636r, 642r, 643r, 644o, 655r,
            656r, 680r, 711u, 717r, 729r, 750r
     1979   711u, 716r, 717r, 729r, 750r
working population
     1939   543r, 544r, 620ra, 709u, 710u, 711u, 761u
     1959   542r, 543r, 544r, 546r, 547u, 569r, 619o, 620ra,
            635r, 643r, 644o, 709u, 710u, 711u, 712ra, 761u
     1970   619o, 620ra, 635r, 636r, 643r, 644o, 708u, 709u,
            710u, 711u, 712ra, 729r, 732r, 750r, 753r, 754r, 761u
     1979   708u, 709u, 710u, 711u, 712ra, 719o, 729r, 730r,
            732r, 750r, 753r, 754r, 761u
EMPLOYED (see GAINFULLY EMPLOYED)
ETHNIC GROUPS (see NATIONALITY)
FAMILY
  all entries
     1897   24g, 25zc, 26zc, 27z, 52u, 52d, 53g, 53d, 54u, 55d,
            55g, 58y, 58gc, 60gc, 63d
     1926   304r, 304um1, 305r, 305um1, 306r, 306um1, 307r,
            307um1, 308r, 308um1, 312yc, 313yc, 314yc, 315yc,
            316yc, 317yc, 321gc, 323yc, 324yc, 325yc, 326yc,
            327yc, 328yc, 330u, 331ym1, 332ym1, 333u, 333y,
            334r, 335m1, 336m1, 337m1, 338m1, 339m1, 340m1,
            341m1, 342m1, 343m1, 344m1, 345m1, 346m1, 347m1,
            348m1, 349m1, 350m1, 351m1
     1939   573r, 575r
     1959   571o, 572o, 573r, 574u, 575r, 576r, 577r, 578r,
            579u, 580u, 667r, 669r
     1970   665r, 666o, 667r, 668o, 669r, 670r, 671r, 672r,
            673r, 674ar, 675r, 676r, 677r, 724r
     1979   705r, 723r, 724r, 734r, 735u, 736u, 744so, 745o,
            746r, 747r, 748r, 749r
  children
     1926   340m1, 341m1, 345m1, 346m1, 347m1, 348m1, 350m1,
            351m1
     1970   671r, 675r
     1979   746r
  head of (all entries)
     1897   60gc, 63d
     1926   330u, 331ym1, 332ym1, 333u, 333y, 334r, 335m1,
            336m1, 337m1, 338m1, 339m1, 340m1, 341m1, 342m1,
            343m1, 344m1, 347m1
     1939   573r
     1959   572o, 573r, 578r, 667r
     1970   667r, 668o
  head of (age)
     1926   335m1, 340m1, 341m1, 342m1, 343m1
  head of (sex)
     1897   63d
     1926   330u, 331ym1, 332ym1, 335m1, 336m1, 337m1, 338m1,
            339m1, 340m1, 341m1, 342m1, 343m1
     1939   573r
     1959   572o, 573r, 578r, 667r
     1970   667r, 668o
  nationality
     1959   579u
```

  1970 673r, 674an
  1979 735u, 748r
 size
  1897 60gc, 63d
  1926 331yml, 332yml, 337ml, 338ml, 339ml, 340ml, 345ml, 348ml, 350ml
  1939 575r
  1959 572o, 574u, 575r, 578r, 579u, 580u, 669r
  1970 668o, 669r, 670r, 671r, 672r, 673r, 674an, 724r
  1979 705r, 723r, 724r, 734r, 735u, 736u, 744so, 745o, 747r, 748r, 749r
 social group
  1926 304r, 304uml, 305r, 305uml, 306r, 306uml, 307r, 307uml, 308r, 308uml, 312yc, 313yc, 314yc, 315yc, 316yc, 317yc, 330u, 331yml, 332yml, 333u, 333y, 334r, 335ml, 336ml, 337ml, 338ml, 339ml, 340ml, 341ml, 342ml, 343ml, 344ml, 345ml, 346ml, 347ml, 348ml, 349ml, 350ml, 351ml
  1959 577r, 578r
  1970 672r
  1979 736u, 749r
 type
  1926 335ml, 336ml, 337ml, 338ml, 340ml, 341ml, 342ml, 343ml, 344ml, 345ml, 346ml, 347ml, 348ml, 350ml, 351ml
  1970 670r
  1979 734r, 747r
 urban-rural
  1897 25zc, 26zc, 52d, 53d, 58y, 58gc
  1939 573r, 575r
  1959 571o, 572o, 573r, 574u, 575r, 576r, 577r, 578r, 579u, 580u, 667r, 669r
  1970 665r, 666o, 667r, 668o, 669r, 670r, 671r, 672r, 673r, 674an, 675r, 676r, 677r, 724r
  1979 723r, 724r, 735u, 736u, 744so, 745o, 747r, 748r, 749r

FOREIGN BORN (see BIRTH, PLACE OF, foreign born)
FOREIGNERS (see also BIRTH, PLACE OF, foreign born)
 all entries
  1897 2zc, 3zc, 4zc, 12zc, 13zc, 14gc, 15gc, 23zc, 28zc, 32g, 40g, 41d, 42g, 43g, 51g, 56d
  1926 105gc, 107gc, 119s, 120s, 121s, 121syml, 138k, 140k, 141k, 141kyc, 158u, 159u, 160u, 160r
 age
  1897 13zc, 41d
 education
  1897 13zc, 41d
 literacy
  1897 13zc, 41d
  1926 105gc, 119s, 120s, 138k, 158u, 159u
 sex
  1897 4zc, 12zc, 13zc, 14gc, 15gc, 23zc, 28zc, 32g, 40g, 41d, 42g, 43g, 51g, 56d
  1926 105gc, 107gc, 119s, 120s, 121s, 140k, 141k, 159u, 160u
 state
  1897 15gc, 43g
  1926 107gc, 121s, 121syml, 141k, 141kyc, 160u, 160r
 urban-rural
  1897 2zc, 3zc, 4zc, 12zc, 13zc, 14gc, 15gc, 23zc, 28zc, 32g, 40g, 41d, 42g, 43g, 51g, 56d
  1926 105gc, 107gc, 119s, 120s, 121s, 138k, 140k, 141k, 158u, 159u, 160u

Keyword Index 287

GAINFULLY EMPLOYED (see also ACTIVELY EMPLOYED; LABOR; MEANS OF
          LIVELIHOOD; WORKERS; WORKING POPULATION)
     all entries
          1897   24g, 25zc, 26zc, 27z, 52u, 52d, 53g, 54u, 55d, 55g,
                 58y, 58gc, 58z
          1926   172gc, 172gml, 173gml, 175y, 177gc, 178y, 178gc,
                 178g, 179ml, 182m, 182y, 186z, 187s, 188sy, 190s,
                 191s, 195s, 196s, 201k, 202ky, 203kgc, 204k, 205k,
                 209k, 210k, 215u, 216r, 217u, 218u, 222u, 223u,
                 229y, 230c, 231y, 231gml, 232y, 234y, 234gm, 235c,
                 235ml, 237mlc, 238gml, 245y, 245gc, 247s, 248s,
                 248sy, 249s, 251s, 251sy, 255s, 259k, 260k, 261k,
                 263k, 269k, 272u, 273u, 275u, 278u, 281gml, 284r,
                 285y, 289u, 334gc, 336ml, 340ml, 344ml, 345ml,
                 346ml, 398ml, 399ml, 400ml, 401ml, 402ml, 404y,
                 405c, 408g, 410y, 411sky, 412r
     age
          1897   24g, 52u, 58y
          1926   173gml, 175y, 179ml, 182m, 182y, 190s, 191s, 204k,
                 205k, 217u, 218u, 229y, 230c, 231y, 234y, 235ml,
                 247s, 248s, 251s, 259k, 260k, 263k, 272u, 273u,
                 278u, 340ml, 344ml, 346ml, 401ml, 402ml
     sex
          1897   24g, 25zc, 26zc, 27z, 52u, 52d, 53d, 53g, 54u, 55d,
                 55g, 58y, 58gc, 58z
          1926   172gc, 172gml, 173gml, 175y, 177gc, 178y, 178gc,
                 178g, 179ml, 182m, 182y, 186z, 187s, 190s, 191s,
                 195s, 196s, 201k, 204k, 205k, 209k, 210k, 215u,
                 217u, 218u, 222u, 223u, 229y, 230c, 231y, 231gml,
                 232y, 234y, 234gm, 235c, 235ml, 237mlc, 238gml,
                 245y, 245gc, 247s, 248s, 248sy, 249s, 251s, 251sy,
                 255s, 259k, 260k, 261k, 263k, 269k, 272u, 273u,
                 275u, 278u, 289u, 340ml, 344ml, 346ml, 398ml,
                 399ml, 400ml, 401ml, 402ml, 404y, 405c, 408g,
                 411sky, 412r
     urban-rural
          1897   25zc, 26zc, 52d, 53d, 58y, 58gc
          1926   172gc, 173gml, 177gc, 178y, 178gc, 186z, 187s,
                 190s, 195s, 196s, 201k, 204k, 209k, 210k, 215u,
                 217u, 222u, 223u, 232y, 234y, 234gm, 235c, 235ml,
                 237mlc, 245gc, 247s, 248s, 248sy, 249s, 251s,
                 251sy, 255s, 259k, 261k, 263k, 269k, 272u, 273u,
                 275u, 278u, 289u, 404y, 408g, 410y, 411sky, 412r
HEAD OF FAMILY (see FAMILY, head of)
HOUSEHOLDS (see also FAMILY; PERSONS LIVING ALONE)
     1897   5zc, 33g
     1926   102v
HOUSING (see BUILDINGS)
INCOME, SOURCE OF (see MEANS OF LIVELIHOOD)
INDUSTRY (see mainly ECONOMY, SECTORS OF; OCCUPATIONS)
     age of workers
          1926   182m, 182y, 193s, 207k, 220u
          1959   545r
     education of workers
          1959   546r
     handicrafts
          1926   182m, 182y, 193s, 207k, 220u
     living conditions of workers
          1926   323yc, 324yc, 325yc, 326yc, 327yc, 328yc, 329yc
LABOR (Physical and Mental)
     all entries
          1939   548r, 549r, 555r, 556r, 560r, 561r
          1959   548r, 549r, 550r, 551r, 553r, 554r, 555r, 556r,
                 557r, 558r, 559r, 560r, 561r, 650r, 651r, 652r,

288 *Index and Guide*

```
                      656r,  657r
             1970     650r,  651r,  652r,  654r,  655r,  656r,  657r,  679r,
                      731r,  732r,  733u,  753r,  754r
             1979     731r,  732r,  733u,  753r,  754r
       age
             1959     550r,  551r
             1970     654r
       education
             1939     560r,  561r
             1959     558r,  559r,  560r,  561r,  656r,  657r
             1970     655r,  656r,  657r,  732r,  733u,  753r,  754r
             1979     732r,  733u,  753r,  754r
       occupations
             1939     555r,  556r,  561r
             1959     550r,  551r,  553r,  554r,  555r,  556r,  557r,  561r,
                      651r,  652r,  657r
             1970     651r,  652r,  654r,  657r,  733u,  753r,  754r
             1979     733u,  753r,  754r
       physical labor only (no data on mental labor)
             1959     553r,  554r
             1970     753r
             1979     753r
       sex
             1939     548r,  555r,  556r,  560r
             1959     548r,  550r,  551r,  553r,  554r,  555r,  556r,  558r,
                      560r,  650r,  652r,  656r
             1970     650r,  652r,  655r,  656r
       social group
             1959     553r,  554r
       urban-rural
             1939     549r,  560r
             1959     549r,  558r,  560r,  650r,  656r
             1970     650r,  655r,  656r,  679r
LANGUAGE, NATIVE
       all entries
             1897     3zc,  17zc,  18zc,  19gc,  19z,  20gc,  22zc,  26zc,  28zc,
                      45g,  46d,  47d,  48d,  50d,  54u,  56d,  82g,  82z
             1926     105gc,  106gc,  108gc,  111kgc,  112zvc,  119s,  120s,
                      122s,  125sgm1,  126sgm1,  138k,  139k,  140k,  142k,
                      145kg,  146kg,  149k,  150k,  158u,  159u,  161u,  163r,
                      367d,  368d,  370r,  371g,  374y,  375g
             1959     562r,  564o,  566u,  566s,  567r,  622u
             1970     622u,  625r,  625o,  627ra,  628u,  629r,  713u
             1979     713u,  720o
       age
             1897     19gc,  19z,  47d
             1926     111kgc,  149k,  150k
             1959     566u,  566s
             1970     628u,  629r
       education
             1897     19gc,  19z,  47d
       literacy
             1897     18zc,  19gc,  19z,  46d,  47d
             1926     105gc,  106gc,  111kgc,  119s,  120s,  138k,  139k,  140k,
                      158u,  159u
       marital status
             1897     20gc,  48d
       nationality
             1926     105gc,  106gc,  111kgc,  119s,  120s,  138k,  140k,  149k,
                      150k,  158u,  159u
             1959     562r,  564o,  566u,  566s,  622u
             1970     622u,  625r,  625o
             1979     713u,  720o
```

Keyword Index 289

occupations
   1897   26zc, 54u
religion
   1897   18zc, 46d
sex
   1897   17zc, 18zc, 19gc, 19z, 20gc, 22zc, 26zc, 28zc, 45g,
            46d, 47d, 48d, 50d, 54u, 56d
   1926   105gc, 106gc, 108gc, 111kgc, 112zvc, 119s, 120s, 122s,
            125sgml, 138k, 139k, 140k, 142k, 145kg, 149k, 150k,
            158u, 159u, 161u, 370r, 371g, 374y, 375g
   1959   562r, 564o, 566o, 566s, 567r
   1970   625r, 627ra
social group
   1897   28zc, 56d
urban-rural
   1897   3zc, 17zc, 18zc, 19gc, 20gc, 22zc, 26zc, 28zc, 45g,
            46d, 47d, 48d, 50d, 56d, 82g, 82z
   1926   105gc, 106gc, 108gc, 111kgc, 119s, 120s, 122s,
            125sgml, 126sgml, 138k, 140k, 142k, 145kg, 146kg,
            149k, 150k, 158u, 159u, 161u, 163r, 370r, 371g

LANGUAGE, SECOND
   all entries
      1970   622u, 625r, 625o, 627ra, 628u, 629r, 713u
      1979   713u, 720o, 757u
   age
      1970   628u, 629r
   nationality
      1970   622u, 625r, 625o, 713u
      1979   713u, 720o, 757u
   sex
      1970   625r, 627r
      1979   757u
   urban-rural
      1970   625r, 625o, 627ra
      1979   757u

LENINGRAD (tables with geographic code "l")
   1897 census
            701, 701, 711
   1926 census
            121syml, 123sgml, 124sgml, 125sgml, 126sgml,
            132szml, 132sgml, 172gml, 173gml, 176yl, 179ml,
            180gml, 231gml, 233gml, 235ml, 237mlc, 238gml,
            239gml, 240gml, 242gml, 252sgml, 281gml, 292uml,
            294uml, 304uml, 305uml, 306uml, 307uml, 308uml,
            309uml, 310uml, 311uml, 331yml, 332yml, 335ml,
            336ml, 337ml, 338ml, 339ml, 340ml, 341ml, 342ml,
            343ml, 344ml, 345ml, 346ml, 347ml, 348ml, 349ml,
            350ml, 351ml, 353skbgml, 354skbyml, 355skbyml,
            356skbyml, 357skbgml, 358skbyml, 378mlc, 383sgml,
            398ml, 399ml, 400ml, 401ml, 402ml, 403ml

LIFE EXPECTANCY
   1959   581u

LITERACY (see also EDUCATION)
   all entries
      1897   2zc, 7zc, 13zc, 18zc, 19gc, 19z, 34g, 35d, 41d,
            46d, 47d, 61d, 64d, 65gc, 151k, 152k, 300sy, 381sy,
            394u, 528r, 529r, 621r, 706u
      1926   105gc, 105gc, 109gc, 111kgc, 113zvc, 119s, 120s,
            127s, 128sy, 131sy, 132szml, 132sgml, 138k, 139k,
            140k, 147k, 151k, 152k, 158u, 159u, 164u, 166r,
            169u, 171u, 173gml, 174y, 175y, 190s, 191s, 192sy,
            192s, 193s, 204k, 205k, 206k, 207k, 217u, 218u,
            219u, 220u, 244gc, 254s, 268k, 288u, 376s, 377sy,
            378mlc, 379b, 380sy, 381sy, 382s, 383sgml, 384b,

                    385bg, 392y, 393c, 394u, 395u, 396g, 397y, 401ml,
                    402ml, 528r, 529r, 621r, 706u
         1939   528r, 529r, 529o, 621r, 706u
         1959   528r, 529r, 529o, 621r, 706u
         1970   621r, 706u
         1979   706u
age
         1897   7zc, 13zc, 19gc, 19z, 34g, 35d, 41d, 47d, 61d, 64d,
                    65gc, 151k, 152k, 380sy, 381sy, 394u
         1926   109gc, 111kgc, 113zvc, 127s, 128sy, 131sy, 147k,
                    151k, 152k, 164u, 166r, 168r, 169u, 171u, 173gml,
                    174y, 190s, 192s, 192sy, 193s, 204k, 206k, 207k,
                    217u, 219u, 220u, 244gc, 254s, 268k, 288u, 376s,
                    377sy, 378mlc, 379b, 380sy, 381sy, 392y, 393c,
                    394u, 397y, 401ml, 402ml
ages 9-49 (one age group)
         1897   528r, 529r, 621r, 706u
         1926   528r, 529r, 621r, 706u
         1939   528r, 529r, 529o, 621r, 706u
         1959   528r, 529r, 529o, 621r, 706u
         1970   621r, 706u
         1979   706u
language
         1897   18zc, 19gc, 19z, 46d, 47d
         1926   105gc, 106gc, 111kgc, 119s, 120s, 138k, 139k, 140k,
                    158u, 159u
marital status
         1926   173gml, 190s, 204k, 217u
nationality
         1926   105gc, 106gc, 109gc, 111kgc, 113zvc, 119s, 120s,
                    132sgml, 138k, 140k, 147k, 158u, 159u, 169u, 171u,
                    382s, 383sg, 384b, 395u, 396g
occupation, position in
         1926   173gml, 175y, 190s, 191s, 192s, 193s, 204k, 205k,
                    207k, 217u, 218u, 220u, 401ml, 402ml
occupations
         1897   61d, 64d, 65gc
         1926   174y, 175y, 190s, 191s, 192s, 192sy, 193s, 204k,
                    205k, 206k, 207k, 217u, 218u, 219u, 402ml
religion
         1897   18zc, 46d
sex
         1897   7zc, 13zc, 18zc, 19gc, 19z, 34g, 35d, 41d, 46d,
                    47d, 61d, 64d, 65gc, 151k, 152k, 380sy, 381sy,
                    394u, 528r, 529r, 621r
         1926   105gc, 106gc, 109gc, 111kgc, 113zvc, 119s, 120s,
                    127s, 128sy, 131sy, 132szml, 132sgml, 138k, 139k,
                    140k, 147k, 151k, 152k, 158u, 159u, 164u, 166r,
                    168r, 169u, 171u, 173gml, 174y, 175y, 190s, 191s,
                    192s, 192sy, 193s, 204k, 205k, 206k, 207k, 217u,
                    218u, 219u, 220u, 244gc, 254s, 268k, 288u, 376s,
                    377sy, 378mlc, 379b, 380sy, 381sy, 382s, 383sgml,
                    384b, 385bg, 392y, 393c, 394u, 395u, 396g, 397y,
                    401ml, 402ml, 528r, 529r, 621r
         1939   528r, 529r, 529o, 621r
         1959   528r, 529r, 529o, 621r
         1970   621r
social group
         1897   13zc, 41d
urban-rural
         1897   2zc, 7zc, 13zc, 18zc, 19gc, 34g, 41d, 46d, 47d,
                    151k, 152k, 528r, 529r, 621r, 706u
         1926   105gc, 106gc, 109gc, 111kgc, 113zvc, 119s, 120s,
                    127s, 128sy, 131sy, 132sgml, 132szml, 138k, 140k,

Keyword Index

             147k, 151k, 152k, 158u, 159u, 164u, 166r, 168r,
             173gml, 190s, 193s, 204k, 207k, 217u, 220u, 244gc,
             254s, 268k, 288u, 376s, 377sy, 379b, 383sgml,
             385bg, 392y, 396g, 528r, 529r, 621r, 706u
    1939   528r, 529r, 529o, 621r, 706u
    1959   528r, 529r, 529o, 621r, 706u
    1970   621r, 706u
    1979   706u

LIVING STRUCTURES (see BUILDINGS)
LODGING (see BUILDINGS)
LONE INDIVIDUALS (see PERSONS LIVING ALONE)
MARITAL STATUS
   all entries
    1897   9zc, 14gc, 20gc, 21zc, 37d, 42g, 48d, 49d, 60gc, 63d
    1926   173gml, 190s, 204k, 217u, 228gc, 229y, 230c, 234y,
             234gm, 263k, 235c, 235ml, 246s, 246sy, 247s, 254s,
             258k, 259k, 270u, 270r, 271u, 272u, 288u, 292uml,
             293y, 359m
    1939   521r
    1959   520r, 521r, 522o, 568r, 613r, 630u, 631r
    1970   613r, 630u, 631r
    1979   722r, 738r
   age
    1897   9zc, 21zc, 37d, 49d, 60gc, 63d
    1926   228gc, 229y, 230c, 234y, 235c, 235ml, 246s, 246sy,
             247s, 254s, 258k, 259k, 263k, 270u, 270r, 271u,
             272u, 288u, 359m
    1939   521r
    1959   520r, 521r, 568r, 613r, 630u, 631r
    1970   613r, 630u, 631r
   language
    1897   20gc, 48d
   literacy
    1926   173gml, 190s, 204k, 217u
   marriage, length of
    1926   348ml, 349ml, 350ml
   nationality
    1926   228gc, 234y, 234gm, 235c, 235ml, 258k, 263k, 271u
    1959   568r, 630u, 631r
    1970   630u, 631r
   occupation, position in
    1926   173gml, 190s, 204k, 217u, 229y, 230c, 234y, 234gm,
             235c, 235ml, 247s, 259k, 263k, 272u, 292uml, 293y
   occupations
    1897   60gc, 63d
    1926   190s, 204k, 217u, 292uml
   sex
    1897   9zc, 14gc, 20gc, 21zc, 35d, 42g, 48d, 49d, 60gc, 63d
    1926   173gml, 190s, 204k, 217u, 228gc, 229y, 230c, 234y,
             234gm, 235c, 235ml, 246s, 246sy, 247s, 254s, 258k,
             259k, 263k, 270u, 270r, 271u, 272u, 288u, 292uml,
             293y, 359m
    1939   521r
    1959   520r, 521r, 522o, 568r, 613r, 630u, 631r
    1970   613r, 630u, 631r
    1979   722r
   social group
    1897   14gc, 42g
   urban-rural
    1897   9zc, 14gc, 20gc, 21zc, 37d, 42g, 48d, 49d
    1926   190s, 204k, 228gc, 234y, 234gm, 246s, 246sy, 247s,
             254s, 258k, 259k, 263k, 270u, 270r, 272u, 288u, 292uml
    1959   520r, 520o, 613r

```
              1970  613r
              1979  722r
MARRIED (see MARITAL STATUS)
MEANS OF LIVELIHOOD
    all entries
        1926  245y, 245gc, 255s, 269k, 289u, 399ml
        1939  535r
        1959  534r, 535r, 536o, 537r, 580u, 646r
        1970  645r, 646r, 647r, 679r, 715u, 726r
        1979  715u, 725r, 726r, 742r, 743r, 751r, 752r
    able-bodied ages
        1959  536o, 537r
    mothers
        1970  679r
    sex
        1926  245y, 245gc, 255s, 269k, 289u, 399ml
        1939  535r
        1959  534r, 535r, 536o, 580u, 646r
        1970  645r, 646r, 647r
        1979  742r, 743r, 751r, 752r
    social group
        1970  647r
    urban-rural
        1926  245gc, 255s, 269k, 289u
        1959  534r, 536o, 537r, 580u, 646r
        1970  645r, 646r, 647r, 679r, 726r
        1979  725r, 726r, 751r, 752r
MENTAL ILLNESS (see PHYSICALLY HANDICAPPED; all 1926 entries
              listed there also contain data on mental illness)
MENTAL LABOR (see LABOR)
MIGRATION (see also BIRTH, PLACE OF; RESIDENCE, LENGTH OF)
    all entries
        1970  658r, 659re, 660o, 661o, 662re, 663re, 664u
    able-bodied ages
        1970  663re
    city and settlement size
        1970  662re
    nationality
        1970  664u
    sex
        1970  659re, 660o, 664u
    urban-rural
        1970  659re, 660o, 662re, 663re, 664u
MORTALITY
    1959  581u
MOSCOW (tables with geographic code "m")
    1897 census
              72m, 73m
    1926 census
              121syml, 123sgml, 124sgml, 125sgml, 126sgml,
              132szml, 132sgml, 172gml, 173gml, 173gml, 179ml,
              180gml, 182m, 231gml, 233gml, 234gm, 235ml, 236m,
              237mlc, 238gml, 239gml, 240gml, 242gml, 252gml,
              281gml, 292uml, 294uml, 304uml, 305uml, 306uml,
              307uml, 308uml, 309uml, 310uml, 311uml, 331yml,
              332yml, 335ml, 336ml, 337ml, 338ml, 339ml, 340ml,
              341ml, 342ml, 343ml, 344ml, 345ml, 346ml, 347ml,
              348ml, 349ml, 350ml, 351ml, 353skbgml, 354skbyml,
              355skbyml, 356skbyml, 357skbgml, 358skbyml, 359m,
              360m, 378mlc, 383sgml, 398ml, 399ml, 400ml, 401ml,
              402ml, 403ml
MOTHERS
    all entries
        1926  345ml, 348ml
```

Keyword Index 293

```
          1970   675r, 678r, 679r, 680r
          1979   737r, 738r, 739r, 740u
     age
          1970   675r
     children (see also MOTHERS, children ever born)
          1926   345ml, 348ml
          1970   675r, 678r, 679r, 680r
     children ever born
          1979   737r, 738r, 739r, 740u
     education
          1970   680r
          1979   739r
     marriage, age at
          1926   348ml, 351ml
     means of livelihood
          1970   679r
     nationality
          1979   740u
     social group
          1926   348ml
          1970   678r
     urban-rural
          1970   675r, 678r, 679r, 680r
NATIONALITY
     all entries
          1897   no nationality data (see LANGUAGE, NATIVE)
          1926   105gc, 109gc, 110gc, 111kgc, 112zvc, 113zvc, 119s,
                 120s, 123sgml, 124sgml, 132sgml, 138k, 140k, 144kg,
                 147k, 148k, 149k, 150k, 158u, 159u, 162r, 160u,
                 170u, 171u, 172gml, 178g, 179ml, 201k, 210k, 228gc,
                 231y, 231gml, 234y, 234gm, 235c, 235ml, 240gml,
                 253s, 258k, 260k, 263k, 264k, 271u, 287u, 367d,
                 368d, 369r, 371g, 372u, 373y, 375g, 382s, 383sg,
                 384b, 395u, 396g
          1939   569r
          1959   562r, 563ran, 564o, 565r, 566u, 566s, 568r, 569r,
                 570u, 570s, 579u, 622u, 623r, 624a, 630u, 631r,
                 632ran, 635r, 758u
          1970   622u, 623r, 624a, 625r, 625o, 626o, 630u, 631r,
                 632ran, 633u, 634r, 635r, 636r, 664u, 673r, 674an,
                 713u, 756u, 757u, 758u
          1979   713u, 714r, 720o, 721r, 735u, 740u, 756u, 757u, 758u
     age
          1926   109gc, 110gc, 111kgc, 113zvc, 147k, 148k, 149k,
                 150k, 159k, 169u, 170u, 171u, 228gc, 231y, 234y,
                 235ml, 258k, 260k, 271u
          1959   566u, 566s, 568r, 570u, 570s, 630u, 631r
          1970   630u, 631r, 633u, 634r
     education
          1939   569r
          1959   569r, 570u, 570s, 632ran, 635r, 758u
          1970   632ran, 633u, 634r, 635r, 636r, 758u
          1979   758u
     family size
          1959   579u
          1970   673r, 674an
          1979   735u, 748r
     language, native
          1926   105gc, 109gc, 111kgc, 119s, 120s, 138k, 140k, 149k,
                 150k, 158u, 159u
          1959   562r, 564o, 566u, 566s, 622u
          1970   622u, 625r, 625o
          1979   713u, 720o
```

294   *Index and Guide*

    language, second
        1970 622u, 625r, 625o, 713u, 757u
        1979 713u, 720o, 757u
    literacy
        1926 105gc, 106gc, 109gc, 111kgc, 113zvc, 119s, 120s, 132sgml, 138k, 140k, 147k, 158u, 159u, 169u, 171u, 382s, 383sg, 384b, 395u, 396g
    marital status
        1926 228gc, 234y, 234gm, 235c, 235ml, 258k, 263k, 271u
        1959 568r, 630u, 631r
        1970 630u, 631r
    mothers
        1979 740u
    occupation, position in
        1926 172gml, 178g, 179ml, 201k, 210k, 234y, 234gm, 263k
    occupations
        1926 178g, 179ml, 210k
    sex
        1926 105gc, 106gc, 109gc, 110gc, 111kgc, 112zvc, 113zvc, 119s, 120s, 123sgml, 132sgml, 138k, 140k, 143kg, 147k, 148k, 149k, 150k, 158u, 159u, 169u, 170u, 171u, 172gml, 178g, 179ml, 201k, 210k, 228gc, 231y, 231gml, 234y, 234gm, 235c, 235ml, 240gml, 253s, 258k, 260k, 263k, 264k, 271u, 287u, 369r, 371g, 372u, 373y, 375g, 382s, 383sg, 384b, 395u, 396g
        1939 569r
        1959 562r, 564o, 566u, 566s, 568r, 569r, 630u, 631r, 632ran, 635r
        1970 625r, 630u, 631r, 632ran, 635r, 636r, 664u, 757u
        1979 757u
    urban-rural
        1926 105gc, 106gc, 109gc, 110gc, 111kgc, 113zvc, 119s, 120s, 123sgml, 124sgml, 132sgml, 138k, 140k, 143kg, 144kg, 147k, 148k, 149k, 150k, 158u, 159u, 162r, 201k, 210k, 228gc, 231y, 231gml, 234y, 234gm, 235c, 235ml, 240gml, 258k, 260k, 263k, 369r, 371g, 372u, 373y, 396g
        1939 569r
        1959 562r, 564o, 566u, 566s, 569r, 570u, 570s, 579u, 632ran, 635r
        1970 625r, 625o, 632ran, 633u, 634r, 635r, 636r, 664u, 673r, 674an, 757u
        1979 735u, 748r, 756u, 757u
    working population
        1959 569r, 635r
        1970 635r, 636r
NON-GAINFULLY EMPLOYED (nearly all 1926 census entries under GAINFULLY EMPLOYED also contain data on non-gainfully employed, except for the numbers below; see also DEPENDENTS; MEANS OF LIVELIHOOD)
    all entries
        1926 236m, 413k
OCCUPATION, POSITION IN
    all entries
        1926 172gc, 172gml, 173gml, 174y, 175y, 177gc, 178y, 178gc, 178g, 179ml, 180gml, 182m, 182y, 183y, 184y, 185gc, 186z, 187s, 188sy, 189sgc, 189sz, 190s, 191s, 192s, 193s, 195s, 196s, 198s, 199s, 200s, 201k, 202ky, 203kgc, 204k, 205k, 206k, 207k, 209k, 210k, 212k, 213k, 214k, 215u, 216r, 217u, 218u, 219u, 220u, 222u, 223u, 225u, 226u, 227u, 229y, 230c, 231y, 231gml, 232y, 233y, 233gml, 277u, 234y, 234gm, 235c, 235ml, 236m, 237m1c, 238gml, 239c, 239gml, 247s, 248s, 248sy, 249s, 250s, 251s, 251sy,

Keyword Index 295

259k, 260k, 261k, 262k, 263k, 272u, 274r, 275u,
276u, 279r, 280u, 281gml, 284r, 285y, 292uml, 292u,
293y, 294uml, 330u, 331yml, 332yml, 333u, 333y,
347ml, 360m, 398ml, 399ml, 400ml, 401ml, 402ml,
403ml, 406y, 407c, 408g, 409y, 409r, 412r, 413y,
414u

age
1926   173gml, 174y, 175y, 179ml, 182m, 182y, 190s, 191s,
        192s, 204k, 205k, 206k, 207k, 217u, 218u, 219u,
        220u, 229y, 230c, 231y, 233y, 234y, 235ml, 236m,
        247s, 250s, 251s, 259k, 260k, 262k, 272u, 276u,
        277u, 280u, 292u, 293y, 347ml, 401ml, 402ml

agriculture (see also the all entries list above)
1926   174y, 178y, 184y, 192s, 200s, 206k, 214k, 219u,
        227u, 229y, 330u, 414u

children
1926   347ml

literacy
1926   173gml, 175y, 190s, 191s, 192s, 193s, 204k, 205k,
        207k, 217u, 218u, 220u, 401ml, 402ml

marital status
1926   173gml, 190s, 204k, 217u, 229y, 230c, 234y, 234gm,
        235c, 235ml, 247s, 259k, 263k, 272u, 292uml, 293y

nationality
1926   172gml, 173g, 179ml, 201k, 210k, 234y, 234gm, 263k

part-time occupations
1926   178y, 178gc, 179ml, 180ml, 183y, 184y, 195s, 196s,
        198s, 199s, 200s, 209k, 210k, 212k, 213k, 214k,
        222u, 223u, 225u, 226u, 227u, 414u

persons living alone
1926   330u

sex
1926   172gc, 172gml, 173gml, 174y, 175y, 177gc, 178y,
        178gc, 178g, 179ml, 180gml, 182m, 182y, 185gc,
        186z, 187s, 190s, 191s, 192s, 193s, 195s, 196s,
        198s, 201k, 204k, 205k, 206k, 207k, 209k, 210k,
        212k, 215u, 217u, 218u, 219u, 220u, 222u, 223u,
        225u, 229y, 230c, 231y, 231gml, 232y, 234y, 234gm,
        235c, 235ml, 236m, 237mlc, 238gml, 239c, 239gml,
        247s, 248s, 248sy, 249s, 251s, 251sy, 259k, 260k,
        261k, 263k, 272u, 274r, 275u, 276u, 279r, 280u,
        292uml, 292u, 293y, 294uml, 330u, 347ml, 360m,
        398ml, 399ml, 400ml, 401ml, 402ml, 403ml, 406y,
        407c, 408g, 412r, 413y

urban-rural
1926   172gc, 173gml, 177gc, 178y, 178gc, 185gc, 186z,
        187s, 189sgc, 190s, 193s, 195s, 196s, 198s, 201k,
        204k, 207k, 209k, 210k, 212k, 215u, 217u, 220u,
        222u, 223u, 225u, 232y, 233y, 233gml, 234y, 234gm,
        235c, 235ml, 237mlc, 247s, 248s, 248sy, 249s, 250s,
        251s, 251sy, 259k, 261k, 262k, 263k, 272u, 274r,
        275u, 276u, 277u, 279r, 280u, 292uml, 294uml, 406y,
        409r, 412r

OCCUPATIONS
all entries
1897   24g, 25zc, 26zc, 27z, 52u, 52d, 53g, 53d, 54u, 55d,
        55g, 58y, 58gc, 58z, 59gc, 60gc, 61d, 62gc, 63d,
        64d, 65gc, 83d, 84g
1926   174y, 175y, 177gc, 178y, 178gc, 178g, 179ml,
        180gml, 181gc, 182m, 182y, 183y, 184y, 190s, 191s
        192sy, 192s, 193s, 194s, 196s, 197s, 198s, 199s,
        200s, 204k, 205k, 206k, 207k, 208k, 210k, 211kyc,
        212k, 213k, 214k, 217u, 218u, 219u, 220u, 221u,
        223u, 224u, 225u, 226u, 227u, 237mlc, 292u, 292uml,

               330u, 360m, 399m1, 400m1, 402m1, 403m1, 411sky,
               414u, 557r
       1939   555r, 556r, 561r
       1959   550r, 551r, 552r, 553r, 554r, 555r, 556r, 557r,
               561r, 651r, 652r, 657r
       1970   651r, 652r, 653r, 654r, 657r, 733u, 753r, 754r
       1979   733u, 753r, 754r
    age
       1897   24g, 52u, 58y, 60gc, 61d, 63d, 64d, 65gc
       1926   174y, 175y, 179m1, 182m, 182y, 190s, 191s, 192sy,
               193s, 194s, 204k, 205k, 206k, 207k, 208k, 217u,
               218u, 219u, 220u, 221u, 247s, 292u, 402m1
       1959   550r, 551r
       1970   654r
    agriculture (see also the all entries list above)
       1897   27z, 55d, 55g, 62gc, 63d, 64d
       1926   174y, 178y, 181gc, 184y, 192s, 192sy, 194s, 197s,
               200s, 206k, 208k, 211kyc, 214k, 219u, 221u, 227u,
               330u, 414u
       1959   553r, 554r
    education
       1939   561r
       1959   561r, 657r
       1970   657r, 733u, 753r, 754r
       1979   733u, 753r, 754r
    language, native
       1897   26zc, 54u
    literacy
       1897   61d, 64d, 65gc
       1926   174y, 175y, 190s, 191s, 192s, 192sy, 193s, 204k,
               205k, 206k, 207k, 217u, 218u, 219u, 402m1
    marital status
       1897   60gc, 63d
       1926   190s, 204k, 217u, 292um1
    nationality
       1926   178g, 179m1, 210k
    part-time
       1897   27z, 55d, 55g
       1926   178y, 178gc, 179m1, 180gm1, 183y, 184k, 196s, 198s,
               199s, 200s, 210k, 212k, 213k, 214k, 223u, 225u,
               226u, 227u, 414u
    persons living alone
       1926   330u
    sex
       1897   24g, 25zc, 26zc, 27z, 52u, 52d, 53g, 54u, 55d, 58y,
               58gc, 60gc, 61d, 62gc, 63d, 64d, 65gc
       1926   174y, 175y, 177gc, 178y, 178g, 178gc, 179m1,
               180gm1, 181gc, 182m, 182y, 190s, 191s, 192s, 192sy,
               193s, 194s, 196s, 197s, 198s, 204k, 205k, 206k,
               207k, 208k, 210k, 211kyc, 212k, 217u, 218u, 219u,
               220u, 221u, 223u, 224u, 225u, 237m1c, 292u, 292um1,
               330u, 360m, 399m1, 400m1, 402m1, 403m1, 411sky
       1939   555r, 556r
       1959   550r, 551r, 553r, 554r, 555r, 556r, 652r
    urban-rural
       1897   25zc, 26zc, 52d, 53d, 58y, 58gc, 83d, 84g
       1926   177gc, 178y, 178gc, 181gc, 190s, 193s, 194s, 196s,
               197s, 198s, 204k, 207k, 208k, 210k, 211kyc, 212k,
               217u, 220u, 221u, 223u, 224u, 225u, 237m1c, 292um1,
               411sky
    women (see also OCCUPATIONS, sex)
       1939   556r
       1959   551r, 554r, 556r, 652r
       1970   652r

Keyword Index 297

PART-TIME OCCUPATIONS (see OCCUPATIONS, part-time; see also
                OCCUPATION, POSITION IN, part-time)
PERSONS LIVING ALONE
    all entries
        1897 5zc, 33g
        1926 304r, 304um1, 305r, 305um1, 306r, 306um1, 307r,
              307um1, 312yc, 313yc, 314yc, 315yc, 321gc, 323yc,
              324yc, 325yc, 326yc, 330u, 331ym1, 332ym1, 334r
        1939 573r
        1959 571o, 573r, 576r, 577r, 667r
        1970 665r, 666o, 667r, 677r
    age
        1959 576r
        1970 677r
    agriculture
        1926 330u, 331ym1, 332ym1
    occupation, position in
        1926 330u
    occupations
        1926 330u
    sex
        1897 5zc, 33g
        1926 330u, 331ym1, 332ym1
        1939 573r
        1959 571o, 573r, 577r, 667r
        1970 665r, 667r, 677r
    social group
        1926 304r, 304um1, 305r, 305um1, 306r, 306um1, 307r,
              307um1, 312yc, 313yc, 314yc, 315yc, 334r
        1959 577r
    urban-rural
        1897 5zc, 33g
        1939 573r
        1959 571o, 573r, 576r, 577r, 667r
        1970 665r, 666o, 667r, 677r
PHYSICAL LABOR (see LABOR)
PHYSICALLY HANDICAPPED (all 1926 entries also contain data on
                mental illness)
    all entries
        1897 21zc, 22zc, 23zc, 49d, 50d, 51g
        1926 240zc, 240gm1, 241gc, 242gm1, 242y, 243y, 244gc,
              245y, 245gc, 252sgm1, 253s, 254s, 255s, 256s, 257s,
              264k, 265k, 266k, 267k, 268k, 269k, 286r, 287u,
              288u, 289u, 290u, 291u
    age
        1897 21zc, 49d
        1926 243y, 244gc, 254s, 267k, 268k, 288u
    birth, place of/ residence, place of
        1926 242gm1, 242y, 257s, 266k, 291u
    cause of disability
        1926 241gc, 256s, 265k, 290u
    foreigners
        1897 23zc, 51g
    gainfully employed/ non-gainfully employed
        1926 245y, 255s, 269k, 289u
    language, native
        1897 22zc, 50d
    literacy
        1926 244gc, 254s, 268k, 288u
    marital status
        1897 21zc, 49d
        1926 254s, 288u
    means of livelihood
        1926 245y, 255s, 269k, 289u

Index and Guide

nationality
    1926   240gm1, 253s, 264k, 287u

sex
    1897   21zc, 22zc, 23zc, 49d, 50d, 51g
    1926   240zc, 240gm1, 241gc, 242gm1, 242y, 243y, 244gc, 245y, 252sgm1, 253s, 254s, 255s, 256s, 257s, 264k, 265k, 266k, 267k, 268k, 269k, 286r, 287u, 288u, 289u, 290u, 291u

social group
    1897   23zc, 51g

urban-rural
    1897   21zc, 22zc, 23zc, 49d, 50d, 51g
    1926   240gm1, 242y, 244gc, 254s, 255s, 257s, 264k, 266k, 268k, 269k, 288u, 289u, 291u

POPULATED PLACES (see SETTLEMENTS)

POPULATION (entries here contain population by age, sex, or urban and rural only; data for these factors for urban and rural population also found under CITIES and SETTLEMENTS; entries that contain any other factors are found under those subject headings)

age
    1897   6zc
    1926   130sy, 167r
    1939   515r
    1959   515r, 518o, 610r
    1970   610r

rural (see also POPULATION, urban-rural)
    1897   1gc, 88g
    1926   101z 102v, 103z, 116sg, 117sy, 135ky, 136ky, 155r, 156r
    1959   510r, 511u, 512r, 514o
    1970   606o, 607o

sex
    1897   1gc, 2zc, 4zc, 6zc, 30g, 31g, 32g, 66z, 67g, 68gc, 69g, 70l, 72m, 74c, 76c, 77z, 78g, 79gc, 80g, 86gc
    1926   104gc, 118sgc, 130sy, 137ky, 157r, 167r, 364g, 365g, 366c
    1939   505r, 608r, 609r, 704u
    1959   503o, 505r, 518o, 608r, 609r, 610r, 704u, 755r
    1970   608r, 609r, 610r, 637r, 704u, 755r
    1979   704u, 755r, 760r

urban (see also POPULATION, urban-rural)
    1897   1gc, 31g, 66z, 67g, 69g, 79gc, 80g, 87g, 89gc, 90gc
    1926   100g, 103zc, 104gc, 115sg, 117sy, 118sgc, 134ky, 136ky, 154r, 156r, 157r, 356g, 508r
    1939   507c, 508r
    1959   507c, 508r, 509o, 602oc, 603r
    1970   602oc, 603r, 604o

urban-rural (see also POPULATION, urban and rural)
    1897   2zc, 4zc, 6zc, 32g, 77z, 78g, 81z, 82g, 82z, 700u
    1926   114sz, 130sy, 133kg, 153y, 167r, 361y, 362z, 364g, 500u, 500r, 501u, 501r, 700u
    1939   500u, 500r, 501u, 501r, 505r, 505o, 506o, 600r, 608r, 609r, 700u, 701r, 704u
    1959   500u, 500r, 501u, 501r, 503o, 505r, 505o, 506o, 518o, 600r, 601oc, 608r, 609r,. 610r, 700u, 701r, 704u, 755r
    1970   600r, 601oc, 608r, 609r, 610r, 637r, 700u, 700r, 701r, 755r
    1979   700u, 701r, 702o, 704u, 755r, 759r

POPULATION DENSITY
    1897   2z, 30g
    1926   114sz, 133kg, 153y, 361y, 362z
    1959   502o, 504rc

RAYONS (minor administrative divisions)
    1926   100g, 115sg, 134ky, 154r
    1959   513o
    1970   605o
RELIGION
    all entries
        1897   3zc, 16zc, 18zc, 29zc, 44g, 46d, 57d, 81z, 86gc
    age
        1897   29zc, 57d
    language, native
        1897   18zc, 46d
    literacy
        1897   18zc, 46d
    settlements of 500 or more population
        1897   86gc
    sex
        1897   16zc, 18zc, 29zc, 44g, 46d, 57d
    urban-rural
        1897   3zc, 16zc, 18zc, 29zc, 44g, 46d, 57d, 81z
RENT (see BUILDINGS)
RESIDENCE, LENGTH OF (see also BIRTH, PLACE OF; MIGRATION)
    all entries
        1926   234y, 234gm, 235c, 235ml, 236m, 237mlc, 251s,
                   251sy, 263k, 278u, 279r, 280u, 294um1, 295y
        1979   741r
    age
        1926   234y, 235c, 235ml, 236m, 251s, 263k, 278u, 280u
    sex
        1926   all entries
    urban-rural
        1926   234y, 234gm, 251s, 251sy, 263k, 278u, 279r, 280u,
                   294um1, 295y
        1979   741r
RURAL SETTLEMENTS (see SETTLEMENTS)
SELF-SUPPORTING (see GAINFULLY EMPLOYED; MEANS OF LIVELIHOOD;
                NON-GAINFULLY EMPLOYED)
SETTLEMENTS (see also CITIES)
    all entries
        1897   1gc, 85gc, 86gc, 88gc, 90gc
        1926   102v, 103z, 104gc, 113zvc, 114sz, 117sy, 118sgc,
                   133kg, 136ky, 137ky, 153y, 156r, 157r, 304um1,
                   305um1, 306um1, 307um1, 308um1, 309um1, 310um1,
                   311um1, 352skb, 352skby, 353skby, 353skbgm1, 361y,
                   362z, 363y, 508r
        1939   507c, 508r, 603r
        1959   507c, 508r, 509o, 510r, 511u, 512r, 602oc, 603r
        1970   602oc, 603r, 604o, 607o, 662re
    rural (see also SETTLEMENTS, all entries)
        1897   1gc, 88g
        1926   102v, 103z, 113zvc, 114sz, 117sy, 133kg, 136ky,
                 153y, 156r, 361y, 362z, 363y
        1959   510r, 511u, 512r
        1970   607o
    urban (see also SETTLEMENTS, all entries)
        1897   1gc, 90gc
        1926   103z, 104gc, 113zvc, 114sz, 118sgc, 133kg, 136ky,
                 137ky, 153y, 156r, 157r, 304um1, 306um1, 307um1,
                 308um1, 309um1, 310um1, 311um1, 352skb, 352skby,
                 353skby, 353skbgm1, 361y, 362z, 363y, 508r
        1939   507c, 508r, 603r
        1959   507c, 508r, 509o, 602oc, 603r
        1970   602oc, 603r, 604r, 662re

SOCIAL GROUPS (for 1926 see mainly OCCUPATION, POSITION IN)
  all entries
    1897 3zc, 10zc, 12zc, 13zc, 14gc, 23zc, 28zc, 38g, 40g,
          41d, 42g, 51g, 56d, 711, 73m, 75c
    1926 284r, 285y, 304r, 304um1, 305r, 305um1, 306r,
          306um1, 307r, 307um1, 308r, 308um1, 309r, 309um1,
          310r, 310um1, 311r, 311um1, 312yc, 313yc, 314yc,
          315yc, 316yc, 317yc, 318yc, 319yc, 322yc, 331ym1,
          332ym1, 333u, 333y, 334r, 334gc, 335m1, 336m1,
          337m1, 338m1, 339m1, 340m1, 341m1, 342m1, 343m1,
          344m1, 345m1, 346m1, 347m1, 348m1, 349m1, 350m1,
          351m1
    1939 531r, 543r, 544r
    1959 530r, 531r, 532o, 533r, 538r, 540r, 541u, 542r,
          543r, 544r, 544o, 553r, 554r, 577r, 578r, 638r,
          639o, 640r, 641o, 642r, 643r, 644o, 649r
    1970 638r, 639o, 640r, 641o, 642r, 643r, 644o, 647r,
          648r, 649r, 672r, 678r, 729r
    1979 727r, 728r, 729r, 736u, 749r
  age
    1897 13zc, 41d
    1926 335m1, 340m1, 341m1, 342m1, 343m1, 344m1, 346m1,
          347m1, 348m1, 351m1
    1959 541u
  education
    1897 13zc, 41d
    1939 543r, 544r
    1959 540r, 541u, 542r, 543r, 544r, 544o, 642r, 643r, 644o
    1970 642r, 643r, 644o, 729r
    1979 729r
  family
    1926 304r, 304um1, 305r, 305um1, 306r, 306um1, 307r,
          307um1, 308r, 308um1, 312yc, 313yc, 314yc, 315yc,
          316yc, 317yc, 331ym1, 332ym1, 333u, 333y, 334r,
          335m1, 336m1, 337m1, 338m1, 339m1, 340m1, 341m1,
          342m1, 343m1, 344m1, 345m1, 346m1, 347m1, 348m1,
          349m1, 350m1, 351m1
    1959 577r, 578r
    1970 672r
    1979 736u, 749r
  labor
    1959 553r, 554r
  language, native
    1897 28zc, 56d
  literacy
    1897 13zc, 41d
  marital status
    1897 14gc, 42g
  means of livelihood
    1970 647r
  mothers
    1926 348m1
    1970 678r
  persons living alone
    1926 304r, 304um1, 305r, 305um1, 306r, 306um1, 307r,
          307um1, 312yc, 313yc, 314yc, 315yc, 334r
    1959 577r
  sex
    1897 10zc, 12zc, 13zc, 14gc, 23zc, 28zc, 38g, 40g, 41d,
          42g, 51g, 56d, 711, 73m, 75c, 76c
    1926 331ym1, 332ym1, 335m1, 336m1, 337m1, 338m1, 339m1,
          340m1, 341m1, 342m1, 343m1, 344m1, 346m1, 347m1
    1939 543r

Keyword Index 301

```
            1959    530r, 532o, 538r, 540r, 541u, 542r, 543r, 544o,
                    553r, 554r, 577r, 578r, 638r, 640r, 642r, 643r, 644o
            1970    638r, 640r, 642r, 643r, 644o, 647r, 648r, 729r
            1979    729r
    urban-rural
            1897    3zc, 10zc, 12zc, 13zc, 14gc, 23zc, 28zc, 38g, 40g,
                    41d, 42g, 51g, 56d, 81z
            1939    543r
            1959    530r, 538r, 540r, 542r, 543r, 544o, 577r, 578r,
                    638r, 640r, 642r, 643r, 644o
            1970    638r, 640r, 642r, 643r, 644o, 647r, 648r, 672r,
                    678r, 729r
            1979    727r, 728r, 729r, 736u, 749r
    working population
            1939    543r, 544r
            1959    533r, 538r, 542r, 543r, 544r, 640r, 641o, 643r,
                    644o, 649r
            1970    640r, 641o, 643r, 644o, 648r, 649r, 729r
            1979    711u, 728r, 729r
SOURCE OF INCOME (see MEANS OF LIVELIHOOD)
SOVIETS (Councils)
    rural
            1926    101z, 102v, 116sg, 135ky, 155r, 361y, 362z
            1959    514o
            1970    606o
    urban
            1926    100g, 115sg, 134ky, 154r, 361y, 362z
UNEMPLOYMENT (see also OCCUPATION, POSITION IN)
    all entries
            1926    180gml, 185gc, 195s, 196s, 198s, 209k, 210k, 212k,
                    222u, 223u, 225u, 292u, 292uml, 293y, 294uml, 295y,
                    334gc, 336ml, 340ml, 344ml, 345ml, 346ml, 359m,
                    360m, 404y, 405c, 410y, 411sky, 414u
    age
            1926    292u, 293y, 340ml, 344ml, 346ml, 359m
    city type and size
            1926    292uml, 294uml
    family type
            1926    336ml, 340ml, 344ml, 345ml, 346ml
    length of
            1926    292u, 292uml, 293y, 294uml, 360m
    marital status
            1926    292uml, 293y, 359m
    occupation, previous
            1926    180gml, 196s, 198s, 210k, 212k, 223u, 225u, 292u,
                    292uml, 360m, 414u
    sex
            1926    180gml, 195s, 196s, 198s, 209k, 210k, 212k, 222u,
                    223u, 225u, 292u, 292uml, 293y, 294uml, 295y,
                    340ml, 344ml, 346ml, 359m, 360m, 404y, 405c, 411sky
    social group
            1926    336ml, 340ml, 344ml, 345ml, 346ml
    type of
            1926    185gc, 292uml, 293y
    urban-rural
            1926    185gc, 195s, 196s, 198s, 209k, 210k, 212k, 222u,
                    223u, 225u, 292uml, 294uml, 404y, 410y, 411sky
URBAN SETTLEMENTS (see SETTLEMENTS)
VOLOST (geographic code "v" for volost-level data)
            1926    102v, 112zvc, 113zvc
VOLOST (number of; population-size groups)
            1926    100g, 101z, 102v, 115sg, 116sg, 154r
WATER SUPPLY (see BUILDINGS, water supply)
```

302   *Index and Guide*

WOMEN (see also MOTHERS and the subcategory sex)
    all entries
        1926   233gm1, 233y, 250s, 262k, 277u
        1939   556r
        1959   551r, 554r, 556r, 652r
        1970   652r
        1979   737r, 738r, 739r, 740u
    occupations
        1939   556r
        1959   551r, 554r, 556r, 652r
        1970   652r
WORKERS (see also OCCUPATION, POSITION IN; OCCUPATIONS; SOCIAL
           GROUPS; WORKING POPULATION)
    all entries
        1897   59gc, 60gc, 61d, 62gc, 63d, 64d, 65gc
        1926   174y, 176y1, 180gm1, 194s, 198s, 206k, 208k, 212k,
                  219u, 221u, 225u, 233y, 233gm1, 250s, 262k, 277u,
                  323yc, 324yc, 325yc, 326yc, 327yc, 328yc, 329yc,
                  332ym1
    agriculture
        1897   62gc, 63d, 64d
        1926   174y, 176y1, 194s, 206k, 208k, 219u, 221u
    factory-and-works industries, living conditions of
        1926   323yc, 324yc, 325yc, 326yc, 327yc, 328yc, 329yc
WORKING POPULATION
    all entries
        1939   539r, 543r, 544r, 620ra, 709u, 710u, 711u, 761u
        1959   533r, 538r, 539r, 542r, 543r, 544r, 545r, 546r,
                  547u, 569r, 619o, 620ra, 635r, 640r, 641o, 643r,
                  644o, 649r, 709u, 710u, 711u, 712ra, 761u
        1970   619o, 620ra, 635r, 636r, 640r, 641o, 643r, 644o,
                  648r, 649r, 676r, 708u, 709u, 710u, 711u, 712ra,
                  729r, 732r, 750r, 753r, 754r, 761u
        1979   708u, 709u, 710u, 711u, 712ra, 719o, 728r, 729r,
                  730r, 732r, 750r, 753r, 754r, 761u
    age
        1959   545r
    economy, sectors of
        1939   539r
        1959   538r, 539r, 545r, 546r, 547u, 649r
        1970   648r, 649r
        1979   730r
    education
        1939   543r, 544r, 620ra, 709u, 710u, 711u, 761u
        1959   542r, 543r, 544r, 546r, 547u, 569r, 619o, 620ra,
                  635r, 643r, 644o, 709u, 710u, 711u, 712ra, 761u
        1970   619o, 620ra, 635r, 636r, 643r, 644o, 708u, 709u,
                  710u, 711u, 712ra, 729r, 732r, 750r, 753r, 754r,
                  761u
        1979   708u, 709u, 710u, 711u, 712ra, 719o, 729r, 730r,
                  732r, 750r, 753r, 754r, 761u
    nationality
        1959   569r, 635r
        1970   635r, 636r
    sex
        1939   539r, 543r, 620ra, 710u
        1959   538r, 539r, 542r, 543r, 545r, 546r, 547u, 569r,
                  619o, 620ra, 635r, 640r, 643r, 644o, 710u
        1970   619o, 620ra, 635r, 636r, 640r, 643r, 644o, 648r,
                  710u, 729r, 750r
        1979   710u, 729r, 750r
    social group
        1939   543r, 544r

    1959   533r, 538r, 542r, 543r, 544r, 640r, 641o, 643r,
           644o, 649r
    1970   640r, 641o, 643r, 644o, 648r, 649r, 729r
    1979   728r, 729r
urban-rural
    1939   543r, 620ra, 711u
    1959   538r, 542r, 543r, 569r, 619o, 620ra, 635r, 640r,
           643r, 644o, 711u
    1970   619o, 620ra, 635r, 636r, 640r, 643r, 644o, 648r,
           676r, 711u, 729r, 750r
    1979   711u, 728r, 729r, 750r

ALL TABLES WITH 1939 DATA
    1959 census
        500u, 500r, 501r, 501u, 505r, 505o, 506o, 507c, 508r,
        515r, 521r, 524r, 526o, 528r, 529r, 529o, 531r, 535r,
        539r, 543r, 544r, 548r, 549r, 555r, 556r, 560r, 561r,
        569r, 573r, 575r
    1970 census
        600r, 603r, 608r, 609r, 617r, 618o, 620ra, 621r
    1979 census
        700u, 701r, 704u, 706u, 709u, 710u, 711u, 761u

Geographic Units of the Russian and Soviet Censuses

Each entry in the list of Census Tables includes information on the geographic units that are represented by individual tables. The purpose of this section is to explain the meanings of those units, to describe how the units change from one census to another, and then to provide a list of all of the major geographic units used in these censuses.

Transliteration of place-names. All of the units listed in this section are direct transliterations of the Russian place-names, with two exceptions: USSR and Moscow are used instead of SSSR and Moskva because they are universally accepted English equivalents of those words. The adjectival endings of all place-names have been retained, since there is no single method of anglicizing these words which is unambiguous in all cases. Although many of the users of this guide are probably accustomed to the Library of Congress system for Cyrillic-English transliteration, the transliterations used here are based on the system of the U.S. Board on Geographic Names because it is the most authoritative system and the one most widely recognized in other English-speaking countries. The only modification of that system here was the dropping of the soft sign at the end of the word "oblast."

Abbreviations of regional units. The standard abbreviations of Soviet administrative units which were used in these lists or in the table entries are the following: SSR (Soviet Socialist Republic or Union Republic), RSFSR (Russian Soviet Federated Socialist Republic or simply Russian Republic), ASSR (Autonomous Soviet Socialist Republic), AO (Autonomous Oblast or Autonomous Okrug), NO (National Okrug), and g. (gorod or city).

Comparing units among censuses. Many of the units retain their place-names or even their positions in the administrative structure from one census to another. For example, the 1926 census contains a number of ASSRs (Bashkirskaya, Yakutskaya, Dagestanskaya) which are also found in the unit lists of all subsequent censuses. The presence of a unit of the same name in two or more censuses, however, does not necessarily mean that the territories of those units are also the same. The administrative structure of the Soviet Union has been reorganized and unit boundaries have been changed so many times that there is in fact little comparability between units in the 1926 census and those in 1959, 1970, or 1979. Therefore, it is not possible to compare these unit lists alone to see if a unit is the same from one census to another. However, by comparing the area of a particular administrative unit in 1959 (entry No. 502o) with its area in 1970 or 1979 (from Narodnoye khozyaystvo SSSR of various years), one can estimate the extent of territorial change and thus the degree of unit comparability among the three most recent censuses.

Compilation of the unit lists. These lists were taken directly from the various censuses, with only minor modifications. The order of units in each list and the spelling are the same as the original. The order of units presented in the census table from which this list was taken, however, is not necessarily the same as that in all other tables of the same census. Explanations of regional units ("Rayons under republic authority") which appear in the censuses, as opposed to actual place-names, were translated. In a few cases, units that were clearly part of the census but did not appear in the main list of census units were added.

1897 Census

The highest order units of the 1897 census are referred to in this guide as "main divisions of the Russian Empire." They are given below as the section titles. Eighty-nine guberniyas and oblasts, each of which has its own census volume, make up the main census units. In addition, four of the volumes are actually two volumes each, one for a guberniya and one for a large city within its borders. These cities (Moscow, S.-Peterburg, Odessa, and Varshava) are included as separate units whenever the census gives data by guberniya. Guberniyas and oblasts are divided into uezds, which are too numerous to list here. Many of the 1897 census tables also give data for one or more individual urban settlements or cities in each uezd.

In addition to these 89 guberniyas and oblasts, some census tables also give data for other parts of the empire. These include the population of individual principalities of Finland, the Russian population of Bukhara, and the Russian population of Khiva. Tables that include these units are noted in the table list.

Evropeyskaya Rossiya

1. Arkhangel'skaya guberniya (3)
2. Astrakhanskaya guberniya (2)
3. Bessarabskaya guberniya
4. Vilenskaya guberniya (3)
5. Vitebskaya guberniya (3)
6. Vladimirskaya guberniya (2)
7. Vologodskaya guberniya (2)
8. Volynskaya guberniya
9. Voronezhskaya guberniya (2)
10. Vyatskaya guberniya
11. Grodnenskaya guberniya
12. Donskogo voyska oblast
13. Yekaterinoslavskaya guberniya
14. Kazanskaya guberniya
15. Kaluzhskaya guberniya (2)
16. Kievskaya guberniya
17. Kovenskaya guberniya
18. Kostromskaya guberniya
19. Kurlyandskaya guberniya
20. Kurskaya guberniya
21. Liflyandskaya guberniya
22. Minskaya guberniya
23. Mogilevskaya guberniya
24. Gorod Moskva (2)
    Moskovskaya guberniya
25. Nizhegorodskaya guberniya (2)
26. Novgorodskaya guberniya (2)
27. Olonetskaya guberniya (3)
28. Orenburgskaya guberniya
29. Orlovskaya guberniya
30. Penzenskaya guberniya
31. Permskaya guberniya
32. Podol'skaya guberniya
33. Poltavskaya guberniya
34. Pskovskaya guberniya (2)
35. Ryazanskaya guberniya
36. Samarskaya guberniya
37. Gorod S.-Peterburg (2)
    S.-Peterburgskaya guberniya
38. Saratovskaya guberniya
39. Simbirskaya guberniya
40. Smolenskaya guberniya
41. Tavricheskaya guberniya
42. Tambovskaya guberniya
43. Tverskaya guberniya

44. Tul'skaya guberniya
45. Ufimskaya guberniya (2)
46. Khar'kovskaya guberniya
47. Gorod Odessa
    Khersonskaya guberniya
48. Chernigovskaya guberniya
49. Estlyandskaya guberniya
50. Yaroslavskaya oblast

Privislyanskiye gubernii

51. Gorod Varshava
    Varshavskaya guberniya
52. Kalishskaya guberniya
53. Keletskaya guberniya
54. Lomzhinskaya guberniya
55. Lyublinskaya guberniya
56. Petrokovskaya guberniya
57. Plotskaya guberniya
58. Radomskaya guberniya
59. Suvalkskaya guberniya
60. Sedletskaya guberniya

Kavkaz

61. Bakinskaya guberniya
62. Dagestanskaya oblast
63. Yelisavetpol'skaya guberniya
64. Karskaya oblast (2)
65. Kubanskaya oblast
66. Kutaisskaya guberniya
67. Stavropol'skaya guberniya
68. Terskaya oblast
69. Tiflisskaya guberniya
70. Chernomorskaya guberniya (3)
71. Erivanskaya guberniya

Sibir'

72. Amurskaya oblast (2)
73. Yeniseyskaya guberniya
74. Zabaykal'skaya oblast
75. Irkutskaya guberniya
76. Primorskaya oblast (3)
77. Ostrov Sakhalin (2)
78. Tobol'skaya guberniya
79. Tomskaya guberniya
80. Yakutskaya oblast

Srednyaya Aziya

81. Akmolinskaya oblast
82. Zakaspiyskaya oblast
83. Samarkandskaya oblast
84. Semipalatinskaya oblast
85. Semirechenskaya oblast
86. Syr'-Dar'inskaya oblast
87. Turgayskaya oblast
88. Ural'skaya oblast
89. Ferganskaya oblast

The census volumes for guberniyas that are marked with a (2) were published in two separate parts or <u>tetrady</u>; those marked with a (3) were published in three separate <u>tetrady</u>.

1926 Census

The administrative divisions of the 1926 census are considerably more complex than those of 1897. Not only is there a set of units for normal administrative purposes, there is also a set of ethnic units. The country is divided into six union republics: RSFSR, Belorusskaya SSR, Ukrainskaya SSR, Zakavkazskaya SFSR, Uzbekskaya SSR, and Turkmenskaya SSR. These are the highest level census units. Although the three units in the Zakavkazskaya SFSR are also SSRs, they are not included in this list of union republics. Therefore, data for these units are not given in those cases where the census gives data by union republic.

Below the union republics, the census gives data by a set of rayons, which are indented in the first subheading under each union republic. These second-order units include SSRs, ASSRs, rayons, podrayons (subregions), krays, and oblasts. Note that "SSR" is a term also applied to first-order units. Units at the third level also include ASSRs and podrayons. Therefore, there is no consistent pattern by which units are classified as second-order units as opposed to third-order units other than, presumably, by size or importance. Union republics and rayons each have a separate volume or part of a volume for each of the first three otdely of the 1926 census. The third and lower order units, which appear in the list below as the first or second subheading under each rayon, are included in those rayon volumes. The three numbers given in the list after each union republic and rayon are the respective volume numbers for the first three otdely of the census.

The third-order units are referred to in the table entries and in the geographic codes in the index as guberniyas. Most of the European RSFSR is divided into these units. Outside of this area, however, most of the third-order units, which are equivalent to guberniyas, are called okrugs. Other third-order units are the ethnic divisions ASSR and autonomous oblast (avtonomnaya oblast).

Fourth-order units are referred to in the table entries and in the geographic codes in the index as uezds. These units are too numerous too list here. Most of the guberniyas are divided into uezds, and most of the other third-order units are divided into equivalent units, which have a wide variety of names. Many okrugs, including those in Ukrainskaya SSR, Belorusskaya SSR, Turkmenskaya SSR, and Uzbekistan (in Uzbekskaya SSR), are divided into "rayony"; some Moslem ethnic units are divided into "kantony"; other ethnic units are divided into "dayra" or "vidayet"; and many guberniya-level units, especially those which are sparsely populated, have no fourth-order divisions. Administrative divisions below the uezd level are referred to as volosts, although there is a also a wide variety of names for these fifth-order units.

The source of the following unit list is the table represented by entry No. 364.

```
USSR    (17, 34, 51)
RSFSR   (9, 16, 43)
   Severo-Vostochnyy rayon (or Severnyy rayon)   (1, 18, 35)
      Arkhangel'skaya guberniya
      Vologodskaya guberniya
      Komi (Zyryanskaya) avtonomnaya oblast
      Severo-Dvinskaya guberniya
   Leningradskaya oblast i Avtonomnaya Karel'skaya respublika
         (or Leningradsko-Karel'skiy rayon)   (1, 18, 35)
      Karel'skaya ASSR
      Leningradskaya guberniya
```

        Murmanskaya guberniya
        Novgorodskaya guberniya
        Pskovskaya guberniya
        Cherepovetskaya guberniya
Zapadnyy rayon   (2, 19, 36)
        Bryanskaya guberniya
        Smolenskaya guberniya
Tsentral'no-Promyshlennyy rayon   (2, 19, 36)
        Mosk.-Promyshlennyy podrayon
                Vladimirskaya guberniya
                Ivanovo-Voznesenskaya guberniya
                Kaluzhskaya guberniya
                Kostromskaya guberniya
                Moskovskaya guberniya
                Nizhegorodskaya guberniya
                Tverskaya guberniya
                Yaroslavskaya guberniya
        Ryazano-Tul'skiy podrayon
                Ryazanskaya guberniya
                Tul'skaya guberniya
Tsentral'no-Chernozemnyy rayon   (3, 20, 37)
        Voronezhskaya guberniya
        Kurskaya guberniya
        Orlovskaya guberniya
        Tambovskaya guberniya
Vyatskiy rayon   (4, 21, 38)
        Votskaya avtonomnaya oblast
        Vyatskaya guberniya
        Mariyskaya avtonomnaya oblast
Ural'skaya oblast   (4, 21, 38)
        Predural'ye
                Komi-Permyatskiy okrug
                Kungurskiy okrug
                Permskiy okrug
                Sarapul'skiy okrug
        Gorno-Zavodskiy Ural
                Verkhne-Kamskiy okrug
                Zlatoustovskiy okrug
                Sverdlovskiy okrug
                Tagil'skiy okrug
        Zaural'ye
                Irbitskiy okrug
                Ishimskiy okrug
                Kurganskiy okrug
                Troitskiy okrug
                Tyumenskiy okrug
                Chelyabinskiy okrug
                Shadrinskiy okrug
        Tobol'skiy Sever
                Tobol'skiy okrug
Bashkirskaya ASSR   (4, 21, 38)
Sredne-Volzhskiy rayon   (3, 20, 37)
        Orenburgskaya guberniya
        Penzenskaya guberniya
        Samarskaya guberniya
        Tatarskaya ASSR
        Ul'yanovskaya guberniya
        Chuvashskaya ASSR
Nizhne-Volzhskiy rayon   (3, 20, 37)
        Astrakhanskaya guberniya
        Kalmytskaya avtonomnaya oblast
        Nemtsev-Povolzh'ya ASSR
        Saratovskaya guberniya
        Stalingradskaya guberniya

Krymskaya ASSR (5, 22, 39)
Severnyy Kavkaz (or Severo-Kavkazskiy kray) (5, 22, 39)
   Stepnoy Prikazovskiy podrayon
      Donskoy okrug
      Taganrogskiy okrug
   Stepnoy Vostochnyy podrayon
      Donetskiy okrug
      Sal'skiy okrug
      Stavropol'skiy okrug
      Sunzhenskiy okrug
      Terskiy okrug
      Shakhtinskiy okrug
   Stepnoy Prikubansko-Chernomorskiy podrayon
      Adygeysko-Cherkesskaya avtonomnaya oblast
      Armavirskiy okrug
      Kubanskiy okrug
      Maykopskiy okrug
      Chernomorskiy okrug
   Gorniy podrayon
      Vladikavkaz avtonomnyy gorod
      Grozniy avtonomnyy gorod
      Ingushskaya avtonomnaya oblast
      Kabardino-Balkarskaya avtonomnaya oblast
      Karachaevskaya avtonomnaya oblast
      Severo-Osetinskaya avtonomnaya oblast
      Cherkesskaya avtonomnaya oblast
      Chechenskaya avtonomnaya oblast
Dagestanskaya ASSR (5, 22, 39)
Kazakhskaya ASSR (8, 25, 42)
   Zapadnyy podrayon
      Adaevskiy uezd
      Aktyubinskaya guberniya
      Kustanayskiy okrug
      Ural'skaya guberniya
   Vostochnyy podrayon
      Akmolinskaya guberniya
      Semipalatinskaya guberniya
   Yuzhnyy podrayon
      Dzhetysuyskaya guberniya
      Kara-Kalpakskaya avtonomnaya oblast
      Syr-Dar'inskaya guberniya
Kirgizskaya ASSR (8, 25, 42)
Sibirskiy Kray (6, 23, 40)
   Yugo-Zapadnaya Sibir'
      Barabinskiy okrug
      Barnaul'skiy okrug
      Biyskiy okrug
      Kamenskiy okrug
      Novosibirskiy okrug
      Omskiy okrug
      Rubtsovskiy okrug
      Slavgorodskiy okrug
      Tarskiy okrug
      Oyratskaya avtonomnaya oblast
   Severo-Vostochnaya Sibir'
      Achinskiy okrug
      Irkutskiy okrug
      Kanskiy okrug
      Kirenskiy okrug
      Krasnoyarskiy s Turukhanskim rayonom
      Kuznetskiy okrug
      Minusinskiy okrug
      Tomskiy okrug
      Tulunovskiy okrug

            Khakasskiy okrug
    Buryato-Mongol'skaya ASSR (6, 23, 40)
    Yakutskaya ASSR (7, 24, 41)
    Dal'ne-Vostochnyy Kray (7, 24, 41)
        Zabaykal'ye
            Sretenskiy okrug
            Chitinskiy okrug
        Amurskiy podrayon
            Amurskiy okrug
            Zeyskiy okrug
        Primorskiy podrayon
            Vladivostokskiy okrug
            Nikolaevskiy okrug
            Khabarobskiy okrug
        Sakhalin
        Kamchatka
Belorusskaya SSR (10, 27, 44)
    Bobruyskiy okrug
    Borisovskiy okrug
    Vitebskiy okrug
    Gomel'skiy okrug
    Kalininskiy okrug
    Minskiy okrug
    Mogilevskiy okrug
    Mozyrskiy okrug
    Orshanskiy okrug
    Polotskiy okrug
    Rechitskiy okrug
    Slutskiy okrug
Ukrainskaya SSR (11, 28, 45)
    Poles'ye (11, 28, 45)
        Zhitomirskiy okrug
        Glukhovskiy okrug
        Konotopskiy okrug
        Korostenskiy okrug
        Chernigovskiy okrug
    Pravoberezhnaya Lesostep' (12, 29, 46)
        Belotserkovskiy okrug
        Berdichevskiy okrug
        Vinnitskiy okrug
        Kamenetskiy okrug
        Kievskiy okrug
        Mogilevskiy okrug
        Proskurovskiy okrug
        Tul'chinskiy okrug
        Umanskiy okrug
        Cherkasskiy okrug
        Shepetovskiy okrug
    Levoberezhnaya Lesostep' (12, 29, 46)
        Izyumskiy okrug
        Kremenchugskiy okrug
        Kupyanskiy okrug
        Lubenskiy okrug
        Nezhinskiy okrug
        Poltavskiy okrug
        Prilukskiy okrug
        Romenskiy okrug
        Sumskiy okrug
        Khar'kovskiy okrug
    Step' (13, 30, 47)
        Zinov'yevskiy okrug
        Mariupol'skiy okrug
        Melitopol'skiy okrug
        Nikolaevskiy okrug

                Odesskiy okrug
                Pervomayskiy okrug
                Starobel'skiy okrug
                Khersonskiy okrug
                Moldavskaya ASSR
            Dnepropetrovskiy promyshlennyy rayon   (13, 30, 47)
                Dnepropetrovskiy okrug
                Zaporozhskiy okrug
                Krivorozhskiy okrug
            Gorno-promyshlennyy rayon   (13, 30, 47)
                Artemovskiy okrug
                Luganskiy okrug
                Stalinskiy okrug
    Zakavkazskaya SFSR   (14, 31, 48)
        Azerbaydzhanskaya SSR   (14, 31, 48)
            Nagornogo Kapabakha avtonomnaya oblast
            Nakhichevanskaya ASSR
        Armyanskaya SSR   (14, 31, 48)
        Gruzinskaya SSR   (14, 31, 48)
            Abkhazskaya DSSR
            Adzharskaya ASSR
            Yugo-Osetinskaya avtonomnaya oblast
    Uzbekskaya SSR   (15, 32, 49)
        Uzbekistan
            Andizhanskiy okrug
            Bukharskiy okrug
            Zeravshanskiy okrug
            Kashka-Dar'inskiy okrug
            Samarkandskiy okrug
            Surkhan-Dar'inskiy okrug
            Tashkentskiy okrug
            Ferganskiy okrug
            Khodzhentskiy okrug
            Khorezmskiy okrug
            Kenimekhskiy rayon
            Isfaneyskiy rayon
        Tadzhikskaya ASSR
    Turkmenskaya SSR   (16, 33, 50)

1959 Census

The hierarchy of administrative units in the 1959 census is very clearly defined in comparison with 1926. Only two levels of geographic divisions are commonly used: (1) fifteen union republics, which are the first-order divisions; and 2) ASSRs, AOs, NOs, oblasts, and krays, which make up the second-order divisions. These lower level units are referred to in the entries (and in the geographic codes of the index) as oblasts, unless there is a particular reason for distinguishing different kinds of second-order divisions (as in some tables on nationality). Although the administrative levels of these secondary units are not the same, they are treated as if they were the same level for most census purposes. That is, whenever data in a table are given below the republic level, they are usually given for all of these secondary units. Table titles most commonly refer to data that are given down to the oblast level as data "by Republics, Krays, and Oblasts."

In addition to these oblast-level data, tables that give secondary units usually include data for all union republic capital cities and Leningrad. Cases where not all of these cities are included are noted in the particular entries. The cities that are sometimes omitted are Tallin, Riga, Vil'nyus, Yerevan, and Kishinev.

The source of the following unit list is the table represented by entry No. 506.

```
USSR
RSFSR
   Severo-Zapadnyy rayon
      Arkhangel'skaya oblast
         Nenetskiy natsional'nyy okrug
      Vologodskaya oblast
      Kaliningradskaya oblast
      Leningrad and urban settlements under the authority of the
         city soviet
         g. Leningrad
      Leningradskaya oblast
      Murmanskaya oblast
      Novgorodskaya oblast
      Pskovskaya oblast
      Karel'skaya ASSR
      Komi ASSR
   Tsentral'nyy rayon
      Bryanskaya oblast
      Vladimirskaya oblast
      Ivanovskaya oblast
      Kalininskaya oblast
      Kaluzhskaya oblast
      Kostromskaya oblast
      Moscow and urban settlements under the authority of the
         city soviet
         Moscow
      Moskovskaya oblast
      Ryazanskaya oblast
      Smolenskaya oblast
      Tul'skaya oblast
      Yaroslavskaya oblast
   Volgo-Vyatskiy rayon
      Gor'kovskaya oblast
      Kirovskaya oblast
      Mariyskaya ASSR
      Mordovskaya ASSR
      Chuvashskaya ASSR
```

Tsentral'no-Chernozemnyy rayon
   Belgorodskaya oblast
   Voronezhskaya oblast
   Kurskaya oblast
   Lipetskaya oblast
   Orlovskaya oblast
   Tambovskaya oblast
Povolzhskiy rayon
   Astrakhanskaya oblast
   Volgogradskaya oblast
   Kuybyshevskaya oblast
   Penzenskaya oblast
   Saratovskaya oblast
   Ul'yanovskaya oblast
   Tatarskaya ASSR
Severo-Kavkazskiy rayon
   Krasnodarskiy kray
      Adygeyskaya avtonomnaya oblast
   Stavropol'skiy kray
      Karachaevo-Cherkesskaya avtonomnaya oblast
   Rostovskaya oblast
   Dagestanskaya ASSR
   Kabardino-Balkarskaya ASSR
   Kalmytskaya ASSR
   Severo-Osetinskaya ASSR
   Checheno-Ingushskaya ASSR
Ural'skiy rayon
   Kurganskaya oblast
   Orenburgskaya oblast
   Permskaya oblast
      Komi-Permyatskiy natsional'nyy okrug
   Sverdlovskaya oblast
   Tyumenskaya oblast
      Khanti-Mansiyskiy natsional'nyy okrug
      Yamalo-Nenetskiy natsional'nyy okrug
   Chelyabinskaya oblast
   Bashkirskaya ASSR
   Udmurtskaya ASSR
Zapadno-Sibirskiy rayon
   Altayskiy kray
      Gorno-Altayskaya avtonomnaya oblast
   Kemerovskaya oblast
   Novosibirskaya oblast
   Omskaya oblast
   Tomskaya oblast
Vostochno-Sibirskiy rayon
   Krasnoyarskiy kray
      Khakasskaya avtonomnaya oblast
      Taymyrskiy (Dolgano-Nenetskiy) natsional'nyy okrug
      Evenkiyskiy natsional'nyy okrug
   Irkutskaya oblast
      Ust'-Ordynskiy Buryatskiy natsional'nyy okrug
   Chitinskaya oblast
      Aginskiy Buryatskiy natsional'nyy okrug
   Buryatskaya ASSR
   Tuvinskaya ASSR
   Yakutskaya ASSR
Dal'nevostochnyy rayon
   Primorskiy kray
   Khabarovskiy kray
      Evreyskaya avtonomnaya oblast
   Amurskaya oblast
   Kamchatskaya oblast
      Koryakskiy natsional'nyy okrug

        Magadanskaya oblast
            Chukotskiy natsional'nyy okrug
        Sakhalinskaya oblast
Ukrainskaya SSR
    Donetsko-Pridneprovskiy rayon
        Dnepropetrovskaya oblast
        Donetskaya oblast
        Zaporozhskaya oblast
        Luganskaya oblast
        Poltavskaya oblast
        Sumskaya oblast
        Khar'kovskaya oblast
    Yugo-Zapadnyy rayon
        Vinnitskaya oblast
        Volynskaya oblast
        Zhitomirskaya oblast
        Zakarpatskaya oblast
        Ivano-Frankovskaya oblast
        Kiev
        Kievskaya oblast
        Kirovogradskaya oblast
        L'vovskaya oblast
        Rovenskaya oblast
        Ternopol'skaya oblast
        Khmel'nitskaya oblast
        Cherkasskaya oblast
        Chernigovskaya oblast
        Chernovitskaya oblast
    Yuzhnyy rayon
        Krymskaya oblast
            g. Sevastopol
        Nikolaevskaya oblast
        Odesskaya oblast
        Khersonskaya oblast
Zapadnyy rayon
Litovskaya SSR
    g. Vil'nyus
Latviyskaya SSR
    g. Riga
Estonskaya SSR
    g. Tallin
Zakavkazskiy rayon
Gruzinskaya SSR
    Tbilisi and urban-type settlements and rural localities under
        the authority of the city soviet
        g. Tbilisi
    Rayons under republic authority
    Abkhazskaya ASSR
    Adzharskaya ASSR
    Yugo-Osetinskaya avtonomnaya oblast
Azerbaydzhanskaya SSR
    Baku and urban settlements and rural localities under the
        authority of the city soviet
        g. Baku
    Rayons under republic authority
    Nakhichevanskaya ASSR
    Nagorno-Karabakhskaya avtonomnaya oblast
Armyanskaya SSR
        Yerevan and rural localities under the authority of the
            city soviet
            g. Erevan
Sredneaziatskiy rayon
Uzbekskaya SSR
    Andizhanskaya oblast

        Bukharskaya oblast
        Samarkandskaya oblast
        Surkhandar'inskaya oblast
        Tashkent
        Taskentskaya oblast
        Ferganskaya oblast
        Khorezmskaya oblast
        Kara-Kalpakskaya ASSR
Kirgizskaya SSR
    Frunze
    Rayons under republic authority
    Oshskaya oblast
    Tyan'-Shan'skaya oblast
Tadzhikskaya SSR
    Dushanbe and urban-type settlements under the authority of the
        city soviet
        g. Dushanbe
    Rayons under republic authority
    Gorno-Badakhshanskaya avtonomnaya oblast
Turkmenskaya SSR
    Ashkhabad
    Rayons under republic authority
    Maryyskaya oblast
    Tashauzskaya oblast
    Chardzhouskaya oblast
Kazakhstanskiy rayon
Kazakhskaya SSR
    Zapadno-Kazakhstanskiy kray
        Aktyubinskaya oblast
        Gur'yevskaya oblast
        Ural'skaya oblast
    Tselinnyy kray
        Kokchetavskaya oblast
        Kustanayskaya oblast
        Pavlodarskaya oblast
        Severo-Kazakhstanskaya oblast
        Tselinogradskaya oblast
    Yuzhno-Kazakhstanskiy kray
        Dzhambulskaya oblast
        Kyzl-Ordinskaya oblast
        Chimkentskaya oblast
    Alma-Ata
    Alma-Atinskaya oblast
    Vostochno-Kazakhstanskaya oblast
    Karagandinskaya oblast
    Semipalatinskaya oblast
Belorusskaya SSR
    Brestskaya oblast
    Vitebskaya oblast
    Gomel'skaya oblast
    Grodnenskaya oblast
    Minsk
    Minskaya oblast
    Mogilevskaya oblast
Moldavskaya SSR
    g. Kishinev

1970 Census

The administrative structure of the Soviet Union which was used in the 1970 census was virtually identical to that which was employed in the 1959 census. Most important, the same two levels of units were used to represent the census data: (1) the fifteen union republics and (2) all lower units, including ASSRs, AOs, NOs, oblasts, and krays. In addition to the oblast-level units, the second-order units also include the capital cities of all union republics and Leningrad. Some of these capital cities are not listed as main entries in the census table from which this unit list was derived; they are, however, listed as units in most tables that give oblast-level data, so they were added to the list. As with the 1959 census, the use of the phrase "by Republics, Krays, and Oblasts" in the table titles or descriptors means that all of these second-order units are given.

The tables on migration in the 1970 census also use economic regions as units. These regions consist of each of the sections in the RSFSR and Ukrainskaya SSR which is called a "rayon," plus each of the other union republics (the three Baltic republics are one unit, as are the three republics in the Transcaucasus and the four republics in Central Asia).

Entry No. 601 is the source of the unit list below.

USSR
RSFSR
   Severo-Zapadnyy rayon
      Arkhangel'skaya oblast
         Nenetskiy natsional'nyy okrug
      Vologodskaya oblast
      Leningrad and urban settlements under the authority of the city soviet
      Leningradskaya oblast
      Murmanskaya oblast
      Novgorodskaya oblast
      Pskovskaya oblast
      Karel'skaya ASSR
      Komi ASSR
   Tsentral'nyy rayon
      Bryanskaya oblast
      Vladimirskaya oblast
      Ivanovskaya oblast
      Kalininskaya oblast
      Kaluzhskaya oblast
      Kostromskaya oblast
      Moscow and urban settlements under the authority of the city soviet
      Moskovskaya oblast
      Orlovskaya oblast
      Ryazanskaya oblast
      Smolenskaya oblast
      Tul'skaya oblast
      Yaroslavskaya oblast
   Volgo-Vyatskiy rayon
      Gor'kovskaya oblast
      Kirovskaya oblast
      Mariyskaya ASSR
      Mordovskaya ASSR
      Chuvashskaya ASSR
   Tsentral'no-Chernozemnyy rayon
      Belgorodskaya oblast
      Voronezhskaya oblast
      Kurskaya oblast
      Lipetskaya oblast

            Tambovskaya oblast
      Povolzhskiy rayon
            Astrakhanskaya oblast
            Volgogradskaya oblast
            Kuybyshevskaya oblast
            Penzenskaya oblast
            Saratovskaya oblast
            Ul'yanovskaya oblast
            Bashkirskaya ASSR
            Kalmytskaya ASSR
            Tatarskaya ASSR
      Severo-Kavkazskiy rayon
            Krasnodarskiy kray
                  Adygeyskaya avtonomnaya oblast
            Stavropol'skiy kray
                  Karachaevo-Cherkesskaya avtonomnaya oblast
            Rostovskaya oblast
            Dagestanskaya ASSR
            Kabardino-Balkarskaya ASSR
            Severo-Osetinskaya ASSR
            Checheno-Ingushskaya ASSR
      Ural'skiy rayon
            Kurganskaya oblast
            Orenburgskaya oblast
            Permskaya oblast
                  Komi-Permyatskiy natsional'nyy okrug
            Sverdlovskaya oblast
            Chelyabinskaya oblast
            Udmurtskaya ASSR
      Zapadno-Sibirskiy rayon
            Altayskiy kray
                  Gorno-Altayskaya avtonomnaya oblast
            Kemerovskaya oblast
            Novosibirskaya oblast
            Omskaya oblast
            Tomskaya oblast
            Tyumenskaya oblast
                  Khanti-Mansiyskiy natsional'nyy okrug
                  Yamalo-Nenetskiy natsional'nyy okrug
      Vostochno-Sibirskiy rayon
            Krasnoyarskiy kray
                  Khakasskaya avtonomnaya oblast
                  Taymyrskiy (Dolgano-Nenetskiy) natsional'nyy okrug
                  Evenkiyskiy natsional'nyy okrug
            Irkutskaya oblast
                  Ust'-Ordynskiy Buryatskiy natsional'nyy okrug
            Chitinskaya oblast
                  Aginskiy Buryatskiy natsional'nyy okrug
            Buryatskaya ASSR
            Tuvinskaya ASSR
      Dal'nevostochyy rayon
            Primorskiy kray
            Khabarovskiy kray
                  Evreyskaya avtonomnaya oblast
            Amurskaya oblast
            Kamchatskaya oblast
                  Koryakskiy natsional'nyy okrug
            Magadanskaya oblast
                  Chukotskiy natsional'nyy okrug
            Sakhalinskaya oblast
            Yakutskaya ASSR
Ukrainskaya SSR
      Donetsko-Pridneprovskiy rayon
            Voroshilovgradskaya oblast

```
        Dnepropetrovskaya oblast
        Donetskaya oblast
        Zaporozhskaya oblast
        Kirovogradskaya oblast
        Poltavskaya oblast
        Sumskaya oblast
        Khar'kovskaya oblast
    Yugo-Zapadnyy rayon
        Vinnitskaya oblast
        Volynskaya oblast
        Zhitomirskaya oblast
        Zakarpatskaya oblast
        Ivano-Frankovskaya oblast
        Kiev
        Kievskaya oblast
        L'vovskaya oblast
        Rovenskaya oblast
        Ternopol'skaya oblast
        Khmel'nitskaya oblast
        Cherkasskaya oblast
        Chernigovskaya oblast
        Chernovitskaya oblast
    Yuzhnyy rayon
        Krymskaya oblast
        Nikolaevskaya oblast
        Odesskaya oblast
        Khersonskaya oblast
Pribaltiyskiy rayon
Litovskaya SSR
    Vil'nyus
Latviyskaya SSR
    Riga
Estonskaya SSR
    Tallin
Kaliningradskaya oblast
Zakavkazskiy rayon
Gruzinskaya SSR
    Tbilisi and the urban-type settlement Tskhneti under the
        authority of the city soviet
    Rayons under republic authority
    Abkhazskaya ASSR
    Adzharskaya ASSR
    Yugo-Osetinskaya avtonomnaya oblast
Azerbaydzhanskaya SSR
    Baku and urban settlements under the authority of the city
        soviet
    Rayons under republic authority
    Nakhichevanskaya ASSR
    Nagorno-Karabakhskaya avtonomnaya oblast
Armyanskaya SSR
        Yerevan
Sredneaziatskiy rayon
Uzbekskaya SSR
    Andizhanskaya oblast
    Bukharskaya oblast
    Kashkadar'inskaya oblast
    Namanganskaya oblast
    Samarkandskaya oblast
    Surkhandar'inskaya oblast
    Syrdar'inskaya oblast
    Tashkent
    Tashkentskaya oblast
    Ferganskaya oblast
    Khorezmskaya oblast
```

    Karakalpakskaya ASSR
Kirgizskaya SSR
    Frunze
    Rayons under republic authority
    Issyk-Kul'skaya oblast
    Narynskaya oblast
    Oshskaya oblast
Tadzhikskaya SSR
    Dushanbe and the urban-type settlement Takob under the
        authority of the city soviet
    Rayons under republic authority
    Leninabadskaya oblast
    Gorno-Badakhshanskaya avtonomnaya oblast
Turkmenskaya SSR
    Ashkhabad and the urban-type settlement Firyuza under the
        authority of the city soviet
    Rayons under republic authority
    Maryyskaya oblast
    Tashauzskaya oblast
    Chardzhouskaya oblast
Kazakhstanskiy rayon
Kazakhskaya SSR
    Aktyubinskaya oblast
    Alma-Ata
    Alma-Atinskaya oblast
    Vostochno-Kazakhstanskaya oblast
    Gur'yevskaya oblast
    Dzhambul'skaya oblast
    Karagandinskaya oblast
    Kzyl-Ordinskaya oblast
    Kokchetavskaya oblast
    Kustanayskaya oblast
    Pavlodarskaya oblast
    Severo-Kazakhstanskaya oblast
    Semipalatinskaya oblast
    Taldy-Kurganskaya oblast
    Turgayskaya oblast
    Ural'skaya oblast
    Tselinogradskaya oblast
    Chimkentskaya oblast
Belorusskiy rayon
Belorusskaya SSR
    Brestskaya oblast
    Vitebskaya oblast
    Gomel'skaya oblast
    Grodnenskaya oblast
    Minsk and the urban-type settlement Vostochnyy under the
        authority of the city soviet
    Minskaya oblast
    Mogilevskaya oblast
Moldavskaya SSR
    Kishinev

1979 Census

The administrative divisions used for the 1979 census are the same as those used in the two previous censuses with only minor exceptions. Although the arrangement of the units in the list here is quite different, mostly because the units in the RSFSR and Ukrainskaya SSR are presented alphabetically by type of unit and not by economic region, the actual units are basically the same. A few new oblasts, however, were formed between 1970 and 1979.

This list as published in the census (table entry No. 702) differs from those of the other two censuses in that economic regions are not listed and fewer capital cities of union republics are included. The remaining capital cities were added to the list here in parentheses, because most of the small number of tables that give data down to the oblast level include them. Table titles that specify that data are given for republics, krays, and oblasts include all of these second-order units. National okrugs (<u>natsional'nyye okrugy</u>) were renamed by the 1977 Soviet constitution; they appear below under the new name "<u>avtonomnyy okrug</u>," but they represent the same units as in earlier censuses.

USSR
RSFSR
    Altayskiy kray
        Gorno-Altayskaya avtonomnaya oblast
    Krasnodarskiy kray
        Adygeyskaya avtonomnaya oblast
    Krasnoyarskiy kray
        Khakasskaya avtonomnaya oblast
        Taymyrskiy (Dolgano-Nenetskiy) avtonomnyy okrug
        Evenkiyskiy avtonomnyy okrug
    Primorskiy kray
    Stavropol'skiy kray
        Karachaevo-Cherkesskaya avtonomnaya oblast
    Khabarovskiy kray
        Evreyskaya avtonomnaya oblast
    Amurskaya oblast
    Arkhangel'skaya oblast
        Nenetskiy avtonomnyy okrug
    Astrakhanskaya oblast
    Belgorodskaya oblast
    Bryanskaya oblast
    Vladimirskaya oblast
    Volgogradskaya oblast
    Vologodskaya oblast
    Voronezhskaya oblast
    Gor'kovskaya oblast
    Ivanovskaya oblast
    Irkutskaya oblast
        Ust'-Ordynskiy Buryatskiy avtonomnyy okrug
    Kaliningradskaya oblast
    Kalininskaya oblast
    Kaluzhskaya oblast
    Kamchatskaya oblast
        Koryakskiy avtonomnyy okrug
    Kemerovskaya oblast
    Kirovskaya oblast
    Kostromskaya oblast
    Kuybyshevskaya oblast
    Kurganskaya oblast
    Kurskaya oblast
    g. Leningrad

Leningradskaya oblast
Lipetskaya oblast
Magadanskaya oblast
    Chukotskiy avtonomnyy okrug
Moscow
Moskovskaya oblast
Murmanskaya oblast
Novgorodskaya oblast
Novosibirskaya oblast
Omskaya oblast
Orenburgskaya oblast
Orlovskaya oblast
Penzenskaya oblast
Permskaya oblast
    Komi-Permyatskiy avtonomnyy okrug
Pskovskaya oblast
Rostovskaya oblast
Ryazanskaya oblast
Saratovskaya oblast
Sakhalinskaya oblast
Sverdlovskaya oblast
Smolenskaya oblast
Tambovskaya oblast
Tomskaya oblast
Tul'skaya oblast
Tyumenskaya oblast
    Khanty-Mansiyskiy avtonomnyy okrug
    Yamalo-Nenetskiy avtonomnyy okrug
Ul'yanovskaya oblast
Chelyabinskaya oblast
Chitinskaya oblast
    Aginskiy Buryatskiy avtonomnyy okrug
Yaroslavskaya oblast
Bashkirskaya ASSR
Buryatskaya ASSR
Dagestanskaya ASSR
Kabardino-Balkarskaya ASSR
Kalmytskaya ASSR
Karel'skaya ASSR
Komi ASSR
Mariyskaya ASSR
Mordovskaya ASSR
Severo-Osetinskaya ASSR
Tatarskaya ASSR
Tuvinskaya ASSR
Udmurtskaya ASSR
Checheno-Ingushskaya ASSR
Chuvashskaya ASSR
Yakutskaya ASSR
Ukrainskaya SSR
    Vinnitskaya oblast
    Volynskaya oblast
    Voroshilovgradskaya oblast
    Dnepropetrovskaya oblast
    Donetskaya oblast
    Zhitomirskaya oblast
    Zakarpatskaya oblast
    Zaporozhskaya oblast
    Ivano-Frankovskaya oblast
    g. Kiev
    Kievskaya oblast
    Kirovogradskaya oblast
    Krymskaya oblast
    L'vovskaya oblast

　　　　Nikolaevskaya oblast
　　　　Odesskaya oblast
　　　　Poltavskaya oblast
　　　　Rovenskaya oblast
　　　　Sumskaya oblast
　　　　Ternopol'skaya oblast
　　　　Khar'kovskaya oblast
　　　　Khersonskaya oblast
　　　　Khmel'nitskaya oblast
　　　　Cherkasskaya oblast
　　　　Chernigovskaya oblast
　　　　Chernovitskaya oblast
　　Belorusskaya SSR
　　　　Brestskaya oblast
　　　　Vitebskaya oblast
　　　　Gomel'skaya oblast
　　　　Grodnenskaya oblast
　　　　g. Minsk
　　　　Minskaya oblast
　　　　Mogilevskaya oblast
　　Uzbekskaya SSR
　　　　Andizhanskaya oblast
　　　　Bukharskaya oblast
　　　　Dzhizakskaya oblast
　　　　Kashkadar'inskaya oblast
　　　　Namanganskaya oblast
　　　　Samarkandskaya oblast
　　　　Surkhandar'inskaya oblast
　　　　Syrdar'inskaya oblast
　　　　g. Tashkent
　　　　Tashkentskaya oblast
　　　　Ferganskaya oblast
　　　　Khorezmskaya oblast
　　　　Karakalpakskaya ASSR
　　Kazakhskaya SSR
　　　　Aktyubinskaya oblast
　　　　g. Alma-Ata
　　　　Alma-Atinskaya oblast
　　　　Vostochno-Kazakhstanskaya oblast
　　　　Gur'yevskaya oblast
　　　　Dzhambulskaya oblast
　　　　Dzhezkazganskaya oblast
　　　　Karagandinskaya oblast
　　　　Kzyl-Ordinskaya oblast
　　　　Kokchetavskaya oblast
　　　　Kustanayskaya oblast
　　　　Mangyshlakskaya oblast
　　　　Pavlodarskaya oblast
　　　　Severo-Kazakhstanskaya oblast
　　　　Semipalatinskaya oblast
　　　　Taldy-Kurganskaya oblast
　　　　Turgayskaya oblast
　　　　Ural'skaya oblast
　　　　Tselinogradskaya oblast
　　　　Chimkentskaya oblast
　　Gruzinskaya SSR
　　　　Abkhazskaya ASSR
　　　　Adzharskaya ASSR
　　　　(Tbilisi)
　　　　Yugo-Osetinskaya avtonomnaya oblast
　　Azerbaydzhanskaya SSR
　　　　(Baku)
　　　　Nakhichevanskaya ASSR
　　　　Nagorno-Karabakhskaya avtonomnaya oblast

Litovskaya SSR
   (Vil'nyus)
Moldavskaya SSR
   (Kishinev)
Latviyskaya SSR
   (Riga)
Kirgizskaya SSR
   (Frunze)
   Issyk-Kul'skaya oblast
   Narynskaya oblast
   Oshskaya oblast
Tadzhikskaya SSR
   (Dushanbe)
   Kulyabskaya oblast
   Kurgan-Tyubinskaya oblast
   Leninabadskaya oblast
   Gorno-Badakhshanskaya avtonomnaya oblast
Armyanskaya SSR
   (Yerevan)
Turkmenskaya SSR
   g. Ashkhabad
   Ashkhabadskaya oblast
   Krasnovodskaya oblast
   Maryyskaya oblast
   Tashauzskaya oblast
   Chardzhouskaya oblast
Estonskaya SSR
   (Tallin)

Library of Congress Cataloging-in-Publication Data

Research guide to the Russian and Soviet censuses.
  Includes index.
  1. Soviet Union—Population—Study and teaching. 2. Soviet Union—Census—History—Study and teaching. I. Clem, Ralph S.
  HB3607.R43   1986   304.6′0947   86-47638
  ISBN 0-8014-1838-0 (alk. paper)

www.ingramcontent.com/pod-product-compliance
Lightning Source LLC
Chambersburg PA
CBHW020324170426
43200CB00006B/265